400 LANDMARKS of AMERICA

Channel Islands National Monument (see California—4)

where to go and what to see

Rainbow Bridge National Monument (see Utah—12)

400 LANDMARKS of AMERICA

where to go and what to see

By the Editors of Country Beautiful

COUNTRY BEAUTIFUL
Waukesha, Wisconsin

White House, Washington Monument, Jefferson Memorial and Potomac River (see District of Columbia—4, 8 and West Virginia—4)

How To Use This Book

The entries in this volume fall into nine geographic areas of the United States, beginning in the northeast and generally moving south and west. Within each region, states are listed in alphabetical order. Within each state, landmarks are also listed in alphabetical order. On small state maps, numbers corresponding to the alphabetical ordering in the text indicate the location of each landmark within the state.

Some natural landmarks extend many miles into more than one state. Those landmarks are to be found in whatever state appears first in the book. A cross-reference is found as a separate numbered entry in the other state, except for rivers and trails.

Major rivers that flow through more than one state are treated in the state of their source or the state in which they predominate. Trails appear in the state where they begin, or, in the case of the Appalachian and Pacific Crest trails, the northernmost point. Rivers and trails are not indicated on individual state maps but on U.S. map on page 292.

Often the landmarks featured in this volume include or are near to other significant sites. Those sites which are important enough to be treated in some detail are indicated in boldface type throughout the text.

Generally, cross-references in the text have been held to a minimum. Complete references on a subject or category can be found in the Index.

COUNTRY BEAUTIFUL: *Publisher and Editorial Director:* Michael P. Dineen; *Vice President, Editorial:* Robert L. Polley; *Vice President, Operations:* Donna Griesemer; *Vice President, Finance:* Duane C. Buerth; *Art Director:* Buford Nixon; *Senior Editors:* Kenneth L. Schmitz, James H. Robb, Stewart L. Udall; *Managing Editor:* John M. Nuhn; *House Editor:* Kay Kundinger; *Contributing Editor:* Barbara Foye; *Editorial Assistants:* Jeanie Holzwart, Leslie B. McDonald; *Promotion and Sales Director:* Sally K. Repa; *Production Manager:* Fran Gregg; *Accounting Manager:* Bruce L. Schneider.

Country Beautiful Corporation is a wholly owned subsidiary of Flick-Reedy Corporation: *President:* Frank Flick; *Vice President and General Manager:* Michael P. Dineen; *Treasurer and Secretary:* August Caamano.

ACKNOWLEDGEMENTS

The Editors wish to thank the many people who contributed to the production of this book, and in particular, John Bacone, Turkey Run State Park, Indiana; Lloyd C. Hulbert, Kansas State University; Richard H. Maeder, Fort Laramie, Wyoming; L. H. Tumlin, Jr., Etowah Mounds Archeological Area, Georgia; Richard Guy Walton, Virginia City, Nevada; William Weimhoff, Auditorium Theatre Council, Chicago; Waukesha, Wisconsin, Public Library staff; Walker Art Museum and Guthrie Theater, Minneapolis, Minnesota; Charleston, South Carolina, Chamber of Commerce; Columbus, Indiana, Visitor Center; West Virginia Department of Commerce, and the Texas Highway Department.

Photo Credits

Gene Ahrens, 199, 212; Frank Aleksandrowicz, 20; Thomas H. Algire, 143; William Aliff, 93; Shirley Althoff and Dick Weddle, 117; *America's Historic Houses*, 97, 120; Don C. Arns, 229; Art Institute of Chicago, 114; John Bacone, 122 (bottom); William A. Bake, Jr. 98, 197; Sandor Balatoni, 276-7; Bellingrath Gardens, 80; Les Blacklock, 135; Edith Brockway, 235; Burco Cards, San Antonio, 190; Bureau of Sport Fisheries and Wildlife, by J. Malcolm Greany, 17; Busch Gardens, 83; Cal. Dept. of Parks and Recreation, 272; Camerique, 65; Kit Carson Memorial Foundation, 233 (center); Bud Carter, 284, 287; Church of Jesus Christ of Latter-Day Saints, 239, 243; Circus World Museum, 144-5; Clemson University, 103; Colonial Williamsburg, 68 (all); Columbus Visitors Center, 123; Community Photo Studio, 60; Ed Cooper, 186-7, 196, 226-7, 265, 271, 274, 280, 293; Country Beautiful, 95 (right), 115; Creative Photographers, 19; Cypress Gardens, 82; Cyr Agency by John Allen, 203; Harris Edward Dark, 166-7; Charles Davis, 151; Dementi Studio, 66-7; Denver Art Museum, Rush J. McCoy photo, 225; Ken Dequaine, 133; Des Moines Art Center, 157; Devaney, 61; Ingvard Eide, 260-1; Dwight D. Eisenhower Library, 160; Herman D. Ellis, 125; *Executive Mansions and Capitols*, 11, 36-7, 40-1, 46, 48-9, 71, 81, 101 (bottom), 158, 233 (top); Henry Ford Museum, Dearborn, Mich., 128; Freelance Photographers Guild, 64, 267; FPG by Bob Glander, 87; FPG by Arthur Griffin, 23; FPG by J. Linton Houser, 13; FPG by Ellis Sawyer, 59, 180; FPG by Joan Sydlow, 51 (top); FPG by H. Wendler, 26 (bottom), 27; FPG by Jack Zehrt, 63; Louis H. Frohman, 12; Georgia State Dept., 90; Thomas Gilcrease Institute of American History and Art, Tulsa, 173; Arthur Griffin, 148; Shelly Grossman, 251; Dan Guravich, 131; Hancock Shaker Village, 21; Havcoc Photoramic, 69; Helmsley Spear, Inc., 52; Historic Charleston Foundation, 105; Historical Pictures Service, Chicago, 108; Houston Sports Association, Inc., 181; Lloyd C. Hulbert, 159; Arnout Hyde, Jr., 141, 245; Jefferson Memorial Foundation, 35; Jerome State Historical Park, 216; Ky. Dept. of Public Information, 91; Doyle Kline, 233 (bottom); Gary Ladd, 218-9; Lincoln Center for the Performing Arts, Inc., Morris Warman photo, 57; Longfellow House, Cambridge, Mass., 22; Los Angeles County Museum of Art, 268; Dorothy C. Mahoney, 24; George and Judy Manna, 32; Phil McCafferty, 217; Steve and Dolores McCutcheon, 248 (top), 249; Mrs. E. N. McKinnon, 88; Don Carlos Miller, 240; Robert S. Miller, 147; Wilford L. Miller, 171; Milwaukee Public Museum, 150; Minn. Theater Company Foundation, 132; Mo. Highway Dept., 165; Mount Vernon Ladies Association, 70; David Muench, 38, 73, 206-7, 210-1, 215, 221, 228, 241, 246-7, 255, 257, 259, 263 (top), 283; Museum of African Art, 39; Music Center Operating Company, Los Angeles, 273; National Aeronautics and Space Administration, 184 (all); National Baseball Hall of Fame and Museum, 58; National Gallery of Art, 43; National Geographic Society, c. by White House Historical Association, 45; National Park Service, 1, 53, 55, 110, 154, 155, 175, 176, 183, 193, 244, 286; NPS by Bob Bergman, 47; NPS by Jack Boucher, 126-7; NPS by William S. Keller, 248 (bottom); NPS by Ray Littler, 209; NPS by Abbie Rowe, 4-5; NPS by M. Woodbridge Williams, 89, 109, 111; Neb. Game and Parks Commission, 152-3, 169; New York City Dept. of Parks, 51 (bottom); Richard Nickel, 116; Charles P. Noyes, 54, 56; John M. Nuhn, 9 (bottom), 14-5, 95 (left), 279; David S. Ochsner, 100; Old Sturbridge Village, 25; Old Sturbridge Village, Bruce Lasting photo, 26 (top); Robert L. Polley, 201; Preservation Society of Newport County, 31; Pro Football Hall of Fame, 137; Publix Pictorial Service, Donahue photo, 112-3, 163, 252-3; Publix Pictorial Service, Kabel Art photo, 106-7; Rapho-Guillumette by Laurence Lowry, 139; H. Armstrong Roberts, 195; Sage Advertising, 204 (left); Shelburne Museum, Shelburne, Vt., *Vermont Life* Photos, 33 (all); John G. Shedd Aquarium, 118; Ken Short, 121, 129, 224; Ed Simonek, 9 (top); Clyde H. Smith, 28; Dick Smith, 79; Smithsonian Institution from *American Folk Art* by Peter Welsh, 42; Howard Sochurek, 62; S. Dak. Division of Tourism, 177; Bob and Ira Spring, 263 (bottom); Ezra Stoller Associates, 122 (top); Stryker's Western Fotocolor, 191; David Sumner, 194; Helga Teiwes-French, 223; Tex. Highway Dept., 189; Tryon Palace Commission, 101 (top); U. S. Air Force Academy, 231; U. S. Air Force Museum, 140; U. S. Dept. of the Interior, Bureau of Reclamation, 213, 288; U. S. Dept. of the Interior, Indian Arts and Crafts Board, Museum of the Plains Indian, 202; U. S. Forest Service, 77, 200, 280; Utah Highway Dept., 2-3, 236-7; Van Cleve Photography, David Muench photo, 179; Walker Art Center, 136; Richard Guy Walton, 290-1; William J. Weber, 85; W. Vir. Dept. of Natural Resources, Arnout Hyde, Jr. photo, 75; Henry Francis du Pont Winterthur Museum, 37; Wis. Conservation Dept., M. Thayer photo, 149; Wis. Dept. of Natural Resources, 146; Gus Wolfe, 204 (right); Wyoming Recreation Commission, 208.

Copyright ©MCMLXXIV by Country Beautiful Corporation. Library of Congress Catalogue Card Number 74-76835. ISBN 0-87294-056-X. All rights reserved. This book, or parts thereof, must not be reproduced in any form without permission from the publisher. Book designed by Gerald Beyersdorff. Manufactured in the United States of America.

CONTENTS

I. NEW ENGLAND
Connecticut 10
Maine 14
Massachusetts 18
New Hampshire 27
Rhode Island 30
Vermont 32

II. MIDDLE ATLANTIC
Delaware 36
District of Columbia 38
Maryland 46
New Jersey 48
New York 50
Pennsylvania 63
Virginia 66
West Virginia 75

III. SOUTH to the CARIBBEAN
Alabama 80
Florida 82
Georgia 88
Kentucky 91
Louisiana 94
Mississippi 96
North Carolina 98
South Carolina 102
Tennessee 106
Virgin Islands 109

IV. UPPER GREAT LAKES
Illinois 114
Indiana 121
Michigan 124
Minnesota 130
Ohio 137
Wisconsin 142

V. PLAINS and the PRAIRIES
Arkansas 154
Iowa 156
Kansas 158
Missouri 162
Nebraska 168
North Dakota 170
Oklahoma 172
South Dakota 174
Texas 180

VI. NORTHERN ROCKIES
Idaho 194
Montana 198
Wyoming 204

VII. SOUTHERN ROCKIES
Arizona 212
Colorado 224
New Mexico 232
Utah 236

VIII. PACIFIC NORTHWEST and ALASKA
Alaska 248
Oregon 254
Washington 258

IX. CALIFORNIA, NEVADA and HAWAII
California 266
Hawaii 284
Nevada 288

Map 292
Index 293

**Connecticut   Maine   Massachusetts
New Hampshire   Rhode Island   Vermont**

NEW ENGLAND

It was not a particularly ingenious name John Smith supplied for the region he mapped in 1614 for England, but the people who settled in his "New England" proved to be ingenious—and hardy and inventive—enough to survive there. They were able to wrest a livelihood from sea and rocky land.

Seasons provide great variety, and day-to-day weather is so mercurial it is a subject of conversation and local pride. How spring is relished after a long, cold winter! The lengthy, dry fall, though, is the most appealing time of year. Hillsides of beech, birch and maple are drenched in amber, orange, red and gold.

Almost the entire countryside seems to consist of stony hummocks and depressions. On many of these various hamlets, towns and cities are sprinkled, poured, heaped or, like too-fluid frosting, piled up at the base. Craggy hills sprinkled with tiny valleys lead to the White and Green mountains in New Hampshire, Maine, Vermont, Connecticut and Massachusetts. Thousands of lake-spattered forested acres show few touches of man in parks, wildlife refuges and national seashores. Then there is the incomparable coast—dunes and long crescents of smooth beckoning beaches, as well as rockbound barrierlike stretches.

The well-peopled spots boast of centuries-old traditions and display artifacts from the past to illustrate them. Villages of all sizes have white-painted homes and churches. The degree of homogeneity in architecture found nowhere else in the country speaks appealingly of an orderliness on a human scale.

It is easy to catch the flavor of all eras of America—colonial days, Revolution years, whaling and lobstering ages and artistic renaissances, which were usually centered in New England. Visiting here, one meets natives who look back level-eyed with typical Yankee reserve. And one leaves with a sense of what is proper and venerable.

Above: Minute Man *statue by Daniel Chester French stands at one end of North Bridge, Concord, Massachusetts, the site of the battle between the colonials and British soldiers on April 19, 1775. Today this is part of Minute Man National Historical Park. Below:* Mystic Seaport, Connecticut, *a reconstruction of a coastal village during the whaling era.*

Connecticut

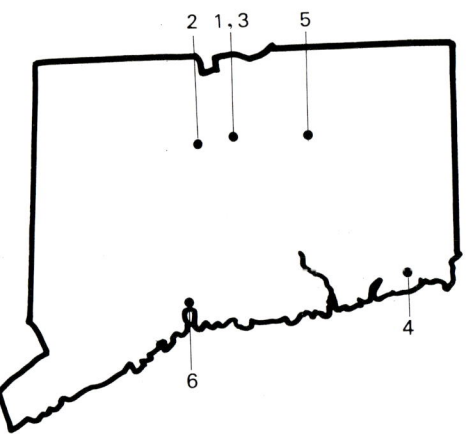

1) CAPITOL, Hartford

Connecticut's State Capitol in Hartford, a Gothic-type structure capped by a golden dome and located adjacent to the beautiful forty-one acre Bushnell Park, became the official seat of the state government in 1879. The building's exterior is of marble from the old quarries at East Canaan, Connecticut, and granite from Westerly, Rhode Island. The interior columns are also of marble and granite, and the floor designs are famous for their beauty. The woodwork finish is oak, black walnut and ash.

Particularly eye-catching in the House of Representatives chambers are the beautiful, multihued, stained-glass windows and the blue carpet colorfully emblazoned with the armorial bearings of the state. In contrast to the blue of the House, the carpeting in the Senate is a deep red, which harmonizes with the wall paneling and desks.

The ornately carved chair on the rostrum from which the lieutenant governor presides over the Senate was made from the celebrated "Charter Oak," the giant tree which once concealed the Charter of Connecticut from the British.

A bronze statue of Nathan Hale stands in the first floor corridor of the Capitol facing the east entrance. Its marble base carries the immortal words uttered by the patriot when he was about to be hanged. (See 5, below.)

2) FIRST CHURCH OF CHRIST

Continuously occupied since its construction in 1771, the First Church of Christ, Farmington, has a spire considered by many to be the most beautiful in New England. Captain Judah Woodruff, a Farmington resident who studied Boston's Old North Church before building this, built it with a touch for lightness and proportion. Although not a professional architect, he fashioned a steeple that sharply contrasts with the angular Yankee meetinghouse it complements. The tower is topped by an octagonal, columned belfry, and above this is another octagonal design from which rises the spire. The delicate columns, arched openings and the upward sweep of line from cornice to vane make the tower memorable.

The church itself fits the pattern of many colonial New England meetinghouses: a gallery, pews with doors and a raised pulpit. What is a credit to the builders and the Congregational congregation is its intact condition. No major restoration has been necessary in its two centuries of service.

3) MARK TWAIN HOUSE

To a passerby pausing at 351 Farmington Avenue in Hartford in 1874, the new three-storied residence of Samuel L. Clemens, more renowned as Mark Twain, and his wife Olivia, was "one of the oddest buildings in the state ever designed for a dwelling, if not in the whole country." A year after Clemens' marriage to Olivia Langdon of Elmira, New York, the couple decided to settle among friends such as Isabella Beecher Stowe, half-sister of Harriet Beecher Stowe, in Nook Farm Colony, a section of Hartford favored by artists and writers. Edward Tuckerman Potter of New York, who had

Statues of Connecticut's colonial leaders and men of letters adorn all four exterior walls of the elaborate statehouse in Hartford. The building is the only Gothic-style capitol in the United States.

designed the Church of the Heavenly Rest, was hired to draw plans for the house which took more than a year to complete for a most impatient and changeable client.

This unique house was "part steamboat, part medieval stronghold, and part cuckoo clock," nineteen rooms and five baths inside a brick house patterned in black and scarlet, festooned with balconies, turrets and porches, and trimmed with fern-bearing flower boxes every angle of the way. The interior, decorated in 1881 mainly by Louis Comfort Tiffany, lived up to the promise of the exterior. One could safely say Tiffany caught the spirit of the architect and spared nothing—not a stenciled wall, not a stained-glass window, not a glass tile.

It was in the billiard room of his Hartford house in the winter and Quarry Farm, Elmira, in the summer that Clemens wrote *The Adventures of Huckleberry Finn, The Adventures of Tom Sawyer, The Prince and the Pauper* and *A Connecticut Yankee at King Arthur's Court.* He was described by his friend William Dean Howells, "at the crest of the prosperity which enabled him to humor every whim or extravagance."

In 1929, the Mark Twain Library and Memorial Commission bought the home, renting out portions to the public library. The house stands today as a remarkable memorial to the man Mark Twain and to the gilded age in which he lived. The rooms have been furnished appropriately for the period and the family's taste. Particular care has been given to the restoration of the interior decor. Not far away in this illustrious neighborhood, the Harriet Beecher Stowe House can be seen. (See **Mark Twain Home**, Missouri—5.)

4) MYSTIC SEAPORT

Mystic was never the largest or most lucrative or famous of New England seaports; Salem, New Bedford and Nantucket surpassed it on all counts. But this town near Long Island Sound is a popular place today because of Mystic Seaport, an accurate reconstruction of a typical maritime town.

Within thirty-seven acres on the Mystic River, visitors can relive nineteenth-century New England. Here along cobblestoned waterfront streets are shops where skilled craftsmen still practice such rare arts as figurehead carving, shipsmithing and sailmaking. The seaport includes a captain's house, a one-room schoolhouse, an apothecary shop, a tavern and an old-fashioned New England church. The Stillman Whaling Museum houses a fine collection of nautical relics.

But Mystic Seaport's primary feature is a variety of sea vessels. The most famous, the full-rigged whaler *Charles W. Morgan*, was built in 1841 in New Bedford, Massachusetts, and is the only remaining whaler of its kind. Another ship, the *Joseph W. Conrad*, has an international history, having sailed under three flags. There are also more than one hundred smaller crafts on display at various times. Most are accurate reconstructions of nineteenth-century vessels.

5) NATHAN HALE HOUSE

In 1776, Nathan Hale, the schoolmaster turned revolutionary soldier and spy, was hanged by the British and his famous last words indelibly recorded in history, "I only regret that I have but one life to give for my country." One

Left: *The Nathan Hale Home in Coventry is classically Early American architecture.* Opposite, above: *In Hartford, the Mark Twain House combines steamboat-style balconies with brick patterns.*

month and nine days after his death, Nathan's family moved into a new house on South Street in Coventry, which is now an official memorial to the valiant young schoolmaster and, in a larger sense, to the Puritan family that produced him. Shortly after their move, the smaller adjacent structure, where Hale had been born, was pulled down.

The clapboard house is a classic example of Early American architecture, simple and severe—with an austere beauty nevertheless. Two and a half stories tall, with gable roofs, it has two chimneys over the main section and one over the ell. There are no overhangs or architectural ornamentation, but the clapboards are graduated, narrow above the baseboard, increasing in width above. Part of the ell was built at the same time as the main portion, and the north wall of the old house, Hale's birthplace, was grafted to the south side of the ell. Several years were required to finish the interiors, and the fine paneling and woodwork reflect changes of taste and the work of various craftsmen.

The fabrics on display in the house are unusual. Most of them are original materials, some of which were found in trunks in the attic. In the chamber over the schoolroom the curtains and bed hangings of eighteenth-century rose-red furniture check are original fabrics and contrast with the blue and white resist coverlet on the bed and with the white walls.

The simplicity of the homestead, which also displays a considerable degree of refinement and craftsmanship for its time and place, reflects the character of the Hale family and of the son and brother who died a hero.

6) YALE UNIVERSITY ART GALLERY

Yale University Art Gallery, the first university art museum in the United States and one of the finest art museums in the country, stands on the Yale campus in New Haven at 1111 Chapel Street. Begun in 1832 as the Trumbull Gallery, the original museum was built to house the works of John Trumbull, a Revolutionary War colonel who designed the small, classical structure and made the donation "to be exhibited forever for the benefit of poor students" in return for a $1000 lifetime annuity.

Today the museum and the Yale Art School are housed in a modern building, completed in 1953 as an addition to a 1927 building adorned with fascinating gargoyles. Yale's outstanding collections include extensive examples of Early American paintings, furniture and silver, as well as the *Société Anonyme Collection* of modern art, the Near and Far Eastern art and textiles, the Linton Collection of African sculpture, the Stoddard Collection of Greek and Roman vases and the James Jackson Jarvis Collection of Italian Renaissance paintings.

Maine

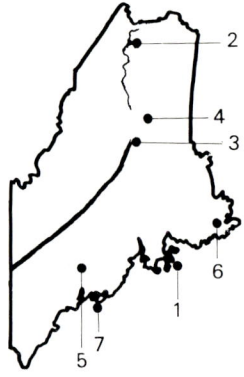

1) ACADIA NATIONAL PARK

There is an air of aristocracy about Acadia National Park, though the Bar Harbor "cottager," whose cottage required a dozen household servants to maintain, is no longer the chief visitor. It is the new aristocrat, the American family vacationer, who now appreciates the beauty of these 41,642 acres, preserved as a national park since 1919.

Here is the pink granite of Cadillac Mountain (highest point on the Eastern Seaboard); here is the wild crashing sea surging into Thunder Hole; here are the still waters of Somes Sound.

The name "Acadia" was first used in ancient Greece (in the form of "Arcadia") to mean a place of rest and delight-in-nature. Early French colonists found the name appropriate for the lands they settled in southeastern Canada, and when the area around Bar Harbor, Maine, became the first national park east of the Mississippi, it was appropriate that eventually it would be called Acadia National Park.

Most of the park is on Mount Desert Island which was discovered by Champlain in 1604. He named it *L'Isle de Monts-deserts,* that is, "The Island of the Solitary Mountains."

In 1820 Maine became a state and what is now Acadia National Park supported a thinly settled fishing economy. But during the nineteenth century artists rediscovered the beauty of the area and summer boats from Boston brought it out of the wilderness and within reach of the affluent, who responded to its loveliness.

East of Mount Desert Island, across Frenchman Bay, there is another portion of the park on Schoodic Peninsula, and southwest of Mount Desert is the park's truly isolated wilderness of Isle au Haut ("High Island") which can be reached only by boat.

But to most of the visitors, who arrive in great numbers only to be swallowed by the winding trails and sheltered glens and surf-tossed

Variations of traditional New England architecture characterize these houses near Northeast Harbor, just outside Acadia National Park.

beaches, Acadia National Park lies along the loop of Ocean Drive, a major park road curving along the Atlantic, gliding in and out of spruce forests, dipping beside quiet inland ponds.

2) ALLAGASH NATIONAL WILD AND SCENIC RIVER

One of the rivers included in the system of national wild and scenic rivers is the Allagash in northern Maine, called the Allagash Wilderness Waterway. The Allagash flows almost ninety miles in many changing moods through the Northeast's last great wilderness, from Telos Lake, west of Baxter State Park nearly to the St. John River, a land of forest, mountains, lakes and abundant wildlife. Here the pine, spruce, cedar, balsam fir, birch and beech tower over the smaller plant life, giving protection to moose, deer, black bear, grouse, bobcat, beaver, fox and mink, as well as the rare fisher. It is a region of great beauty, and at the same time a land of excellent recreational opportunities— superb trout fishing and unmatched canoeing. Administered by the State of Maine, it is wilderness in every sense of the word: its waters deep, clear and cold and its air scented with evergreens.

3) APPALACHIAN TRAIL

To these quiet forests come the seekers of peace, to these aged mountains come the searchers after tranquility. The rocky ancients, worn smooth through eons of sunrises and snowfalls and crowned by wisps of fog, remain a sanctuary to visitors. Walking is the best way of enjoying the pleasures of the Appalachian Trail that stretches from Mount Katahdin in Maine to Springer Mountain in Georgia. Particularly enchanting are the Smokies, the Blue Ridge Mountains and the Shenandoah Valley at any season of the year.

The Appalachian Trail is the longest marked path in the world, covering 2,021 miles along the crest of Appalachia from northern New England into the Deep South. It traverses fourteen states. Virginia has the longest section, 500 miles; West Virginia, the shortest, 10 miles. The trail embraces 507 miles in eight national forests (White Mountain, New Hampshire; Green Mountain, Vermont; George Washington and Jefferson, Virginia; Pisgah and Cherokee, North Carolina and Tennessee; Nantahala, North Carolina; and Chattahoochee, Georgia, where it reaches its southern terminus), as well as 172 miles through two national parks, 452 miles through state lands and the remainder of the trail through private lands. The National Trails Act of 1968 established the Appalachian Trail as a national scenic trail.

The "AT" is more than a footway; it is a concept of recreation brought to reality almost entirely though the voluntary efforts of patriotic people who felt the need to stir the pioneer spirit and to provide new generations of Americans with the lure of exploration.

The idea of the Appalachian Trail was proposed in 1921 by the eminent Benton MacKay, forester and regional planner. He formulated the project for the mountain footpath from his wanderings in his native New England forests. In 1922 the first part of the trail was constructed by hiking clubs of New York and New Jersey. New England had much to add with the trail systems of the Appalachian Mountain Club, Green Mountain Club and the Dartmouth Outing Club.

The walker who sets out to cover the entire Appalachian Trail and averages seventeen miles a day will complete his journey in 123 days and nights. He will be within 150 miles of half a dozen of the country's largest cities — Boston, New York, Philadelphia, Baltimore, Washington, Atlanta — and cross an occasional motorway, but essentially he would be far removed from the works of man. His lodgings would be campsites, shelters and cabins. He would know what makes a mountain trail a supreme adventure is the combination of natural diversity, the touch of intimacy at hand, and the fullness of distant vistas. The AT has all of these elements. (See map, p. 292.)

4) BAXTER STATE PARK

Located in north-central Maine, Baxter is one of the largest state parks in the country.

Highest point in Maine and main attraction in Baxter is Mount Katahdin, the northern terminus of the well-known Appalachian Trail. In the hundred million years since a mass of granite rock was thrust up, the mountain's countenance has been carved and rearranged by erosion and glacial action. Today the park's over 200,000 acres are honeycombed with more than 130 miles of trails that wind through the rocks and forests. Although visitors have passed through the area for more than one hundred years, and loggers once enthusiastically began transforming virgin timber into ships' masts, the charm of the Katahdin region prevails.

In Baxter two distinct vegetation zones are found. The forest zone features hardwoods and conifers. The low matted forest known as *Krummholz,* found in the alpine zone along the steep upper slopes and tableland of Mount Katahdin, features short spruce and fir trees that have grown stunted and gnarled in retaliation from the strong winds.

A prime ingredient in the mysterious attraction of Baxter State Park is its variety and abundance of wildlife. The lordly moose is free to crash through the bushes and then hunt with his broad muzzle for succulent aquatic plants in the park's clear waters. White-tailed deer often visit the campsites of quiet and patient campers. Although the black bear accepts handouts, he is normally timid and grows cantankerous when his food supply is not as easily available. Smaller animals include mink, weasels, the snowshoe hare and two species of marten.

5) CAPITOL, Augusta

Maine's distinguished State House is located on a beautifully landscaped thirty-four-acre site on the Kennebec River at State and Capitol streets. Completed in 1831, the original structure was designed by the eminent architect, Charles Bulfinch, and built of granite from nearby Hallowell, Maine.

In 1909-10, the Capitol was redesigned by G. Henri Desmond in Greek Renaissance style and almost completely rebuilt. Little more than the Bulfinch front was retained. A 185-foot dome, crowned by W. Clark Noble's copper figure of Wisdom, covered with gold, gives the building imposing height.

Along the Capitol's corridors hang portraits of distinguished sons of Maine, and battle flags are exhibited in the rotunda. In the state museum, live, land-locked salmon and brook trout swim in a stream, across which stretches a replica of an old-fashioned covered bridge.

6) MOOSEHORN NATIONAL WILDLIFE REFUGE

Moosehorn National Wildlife Refuge is the essence of Maine. Rocky shores take the shapes of little inlets, bays and secret coves, with evergreens marching right to the sea's edge. The offshore islands are covered with pine, and the ocean waters are crowded with buoys marking the locations of lobster pots. Inland the air is sweet with the smell of balsam fir, hemlock and pine growing on the rolling landscape.

Located on the extreme eastern tip of Maine, Moosehorn is mostly uplands. The refuge is divided into two units: the Baring Unit on the north near the town of Calais, and the Edmunds Unit twenty miles south near Whiting.

In spite of its name, Moosehorn was established primarily for the protection of the woodcock, a small brown nocturnal bird which blends in beautifully with the dead leaves and sticks on the ground. Moosehorn is the center of its northeastern nesting grounds, and it winters mostly in the southern Atlantic states.

Two hundred other species of birds have been identified on the refuge, many of them nesting here. Ring-necked ducks, which do not nest on many of the wildlife refuges, are abundant here, along with a great variety of other ducks, teals, grebes, mergansers, loons, hawks, ospreys, warblers, sparrows and the handsome snowy owl, rare in the East and seen only in winter.

Of course, the refuge does have moose, for Maine is one of the few states where one still sees "moose crossing" signs on the main highways. Largest of the deer family and tallest mammal of the Americas, it stands six or seven feet at the withers and weighs up to 1,200 pounds. As the largest antlered animal in the world, their horns are immense, spreading up to sixty inches tip to tip. The sighting of an adult moose in the wilds of these Maine forests, with its horns sparkling white after ridding itself of

It is still possible to catch sight of the broad-antlered moose in Maine's forests. Tallest mammal in the Americas, this member of the deer family is seldom found away from water.

their moss, is a memorable experience for any outdoorsman.

7) PEMAQUID LIGHTHOUSE

Gone forever are the romantic days when sailing ships plied the waters along the Eastern Seaboard. Intriguing reminders of this era are the picturesque lighthouses which guided and still guide vessels through heavy seas and fog, sometimes shining down on scenes of great tragedy and heroism.

One of the most beautiful of these landmarks along the coast of Maine is Pemaquid Lighthouse on ruggedly beautiful Pemaquid Point. Built in 1827, Pemaquid Lighthouse was originally lit by kerosene. A white pyramidal tower, thirty-four feet high, its 11,000 candlepower light can be seen for fourteen miles in clear weather.

The lighthouse keeper's house and surrounding area, no longer needed after the light was automated in 1934, were sold to the the Town of Bristol to be used as a park. The Fisherman's Museum, with exhibits depicting the life and work of area fishermen, has been set up in the keeper's house. The tower itself remains under the jurisdiction of the United States Coast Guard and is not open to the public.

Massachusetts

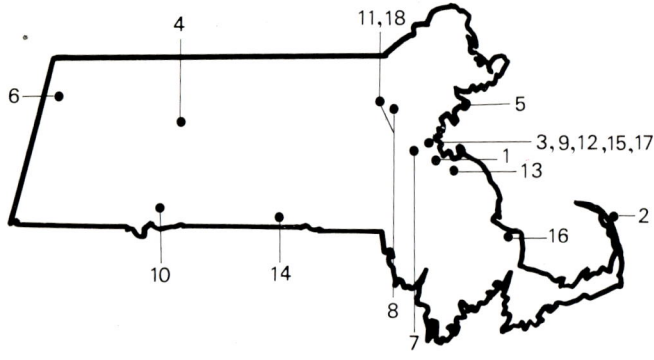

1) ADAMS "OLD HOUSE"

Throughout their years in public life, Quincy was an oasis to both Abigail Adams and her husband John. Quincy to the Adams meant a pleasant, isolated, colonial-style house eight miles from Boston with a gabled mansard roof, gray clapboard siding and green shutters. John Adams purchased this house, now at 135 Adams Street, in 1787 from a descendant of the original builder, Major Leonard Vassall, who had begun its construction in 1731.

With two bedrooms on the second floor and three small rooms in the attic, the house grew, over years of necessary additions, to twenty rooms. It acquired an ell, a study, a mahogany-lined sitting room, and a number of names that did not stick for very long. "Mr. Jefferson lives at Monticello, the lofty mountain. I live at Montezillo, a little hill," said Adams. His Montezillo was also referred to as a "wren's house," the Old House, Peacefield and Stony Field.

John Adams lived on at Quincy for twenty-six years after his Presidential term. It was later used as a summer home by his son and grandson, John Quincy and Charles Francis Adams.

In 1947 Abigail Adams' cherished Quincy, filled with family furnishings and paintings, its nearly five acres including the library, garden and stables, was given to the Federal Government by the Adams Memorial Society. Now the public may visit the home of this astonishing family who served their country and their fellow men as diplomats, writers and ambassadors, apparently with tireless dedication.

2) CAPE COD NATIONAL SEASHORE

Cape Cod is a slender rampart jutting more than seventy miles from the Massachusetts coast into the wind and waves of the turbulent Atlantic Ocean. A large section of it became part of the national park system as a result of the interest and leadership of former President John F. Kennedy. The storm-lashed seas surge over the shoals and dash against marine scarps and, miles away, these same seas gently lap the slopes of barrier beaches. The Cape, one of the nation's most dramatic headlands, is the northernmost of our national seashores. Its high, shifting dunes, great ponds and historic places make a fascinating outdoor playground in summer or winter.

Cape Cod is shaped much like a man flexing his arm muscles. It was named by explorer Bartholomew Gosnold in 1601 for the "grate stoare" of codfish in the vicinity. The Cape, aided by the lengthening of a sandspit called Monomoy Island which extends south from the "elbow" of the Cape, is responsible for the relatively quieter waters of Cape Cod Bay and Nantucket Sound. Sandbars and shoals surrounding the Cape have been a burying ground for ships from the time of the Pilgrims, who first touched New World soil at what is now Provincetown on the northern tip of the Cape.

Rooted strongly in sand dunes and silts, the cattails, marsh grass, bearberry, heath and pitch-pine woods stand against the rasping waters, collecting new sand from each windstorm. Glacial movement in the area resulted in an overlapping of northern and southern plant life growing on the Cape.

Ornithologists describe Monomoy Island as an unparalleled area in which to observe shorebirds. Since its establishment as a 3,300-acre wildlife refuge in 1944, more than 300 bird species have been identified here. During seasonal migrations millions of shore, sea and marsh birds stop over at the island regularly.

In the Adams "Old House" in Quincy, the second floor study is dominated by a Louis XVI secrétaire à abbatant *from France.*

Cape Cod National Seashore, established in 1961, consists of almost 27,000 acres along the outermost one-third of the Cape, primarily facing east and north directly onto the Atlantic.

3) CAPITOL, Boston

At the summit of Boston's Beacon Hill stands the Massachusetts State House. On the Fourth of July, 1795, the cornerstone was carried to the site by fifteen white horses, representing the number of states in the Union at that time, and was laid by Governor Samuel Adams, assisted by Paul Revere. Completed in 1798, the building replaced a smaller State House which had been the seat of Massachusetts' colonial government for more than sixty years before the American Revolution.

Facing south, on a sunlit day the State House is a colorful sight with the sun bringing out the warmth of the red brick walls, the gleam of the white pillars and trim, and the brilliant reflection of the gold-leaf dome. Extensive improvements have been made since the original construction, including five additions.

The impressive dome, originally shingled and painted a lead color, was covered with copper by Paul Revere and Sons in 1802. Since 1874, it has been covered with gold leaf. World War II brought a temporary transformation to battleship gray. The dome itself has been rebuilt twice in an effort to reproduce the lines and proportions of the original.

4) EMILY DICKINSON HOUSE

Emily Dickinson's House at 280 Main Street in Amherst was known to contemporaries as "the Mansion." It was here that America's greatest woman poet was born in 1830; here she lived the life of a recluse, writing some of the greatest poems of all time.

Built in 1813 by Emily Dickinson's grandfather and a founder of Amherst College, "the Mansion" was the first brick house in Amherst. Today it serves as a faculty residence for Amherst College and is open by appointment.

The poet's second-floor bedroom has been restored with original pieces including a writing table and chair. One can imagine her, seated at this table which was situated to provide a view of the bustle of life on Main Street below:

Sweet hours have perished here,
  This is a timid room—
Within its precincts hopes have played
  Now fallow in the tomb.
                    Emily Dickinson

5) ESSEX INSTITUTE

The Essex Institute, founded in 1848 when two older local historical societies merged, is one of the oldest and largest historical societies in the country. Its museum contains outstanding collections of books, manuscripts and furnishings from the colonial and Federal periods in Essex County and Salem. A number of fine Old Salem homes, some moved within the Institute grounds and some directly adjacent, complete this marvelous passport into the past. The museum structure itself was built in 1857 as a library for the Salem Athenaeum.

Here, Old Salem seems very much alive. The Lye-Tapley Shoe Shop revives the memory of this handicraft industry which thrived from 1750 to 1850. The Elizabeth Vough collection of dolls and toys is housed in what is thought to be Salem's first Quaker Meeting House.

The ground floor rooms of the John Ward House, built in 1684, provide a realistic glimpse of the seventeenth-century life-style. The Crownshield-Bentley House, built in 1727, brings to life the lovely interior designs produced by the eighteenth century. The Peirce-Nichols House of 1782 and the Gardner-Pinagree House of 1804 are outstanding products of Samuel McIntire, a master builder of the early Federal period. The Assembly Hall, originally built in 1782, was remodeled as a residence by McIntire in 1796. The exquisite architecture and elegant, imported furniture found in these homes reflect Salem's prosperous seafaring era.

6) HANCOCK SHAKER VILLAGE

Hancock Shaker Village, first settled in 1780, has been a museum since 1960. This restoration of the early community provides a fascinating glimpse into the life and work of the members of

Cape Cod Light, one of the Cape's several lighthouses, stands in Truro, near Provincetown.

Near Pittsfield at Hancock Shaker Village, religious dissenters once formed a farming community that has since been restored to the plain and functional lines shown in this 1841 woodcut.

an intensely religious sect who made a success of communal living here and in seventeen other settlements throughout the Northeast and Midwest. Excellent examples of Shaker handicraft and progressively functional architecture are found in a neat, quiet setting reminiscent of another more peaceful era.

The village reached its zenith in the 1830's when some 300 people lived and worked in complete self-sufficiency. Six "families" were organized around the basic tenets of the Shaker faith: separation from the world, common property, confession of sin and celibacy. Men and women worked diligently and led separate but equal lives within their "families". After the mid-1800's the community's population declined and the last two members of the sect left the site of the present restoration in 1960.

Today's village includes nineteen buildings which housed the "Church Family." Of the restored structures the most intriguing is the unique and functional Round Stone House, built in 1826. A cylinder ninety-five feet in diameter, the barn can be entered on three levels, each designed for a specialized and labor-saving purpose. Hay wagons could enter the top level balcony from which the hay could easily be dumped into the center of the second level where the cattle were housed. One person could easily feed the animals. The lower level was the manure pit and could be served by hay wagons.

Also restored are a variety of dwellings and service buildings, including the Tan House, Sisters Shop, Brethrens Shop and Ice House. A Garden House has been built on the site of the original, surrounded by an herb garden based on the design of the Shaker garden at Mount Lebanon, New York. Such herbs form the basis of Hancock's herb and extract industry. Planted along the white fencing are the red roses used by the Shakers to make rosewater.

7) LONGFELLOW HOUSE

In 1837 Henry Wadsworth Longfellow, poet and professor of modern languages at Harvard University, moved into "two large and beautiful rooms" in the Craigie house at 105 Brattle Street in Cambridge. He thought his residence in the old house "a paradise" and felt that it looked like "an Italian villa." What Longfellow could not possibly have envisioned then was that he had moved into that home for the remaining forty-five years of his life, to live there with his wife and five children and to write some of his most memorable poems.

Longfellow married Fanny Appleton in July 1843, and was given the house by his father-in-law that autumn, a much appreciated present. The Longfellows lived in this handsome Georgian-style house with flair and affluence, and among myriad private mementos—paintings (by Stuart and David among others), pictures, drawings, busts and bronzes. Books were, and are, everywhere, even in the dining room.

Today, sitting atop a double terrace facing south, the imposing two-storied frame house displays an expansive hip roof containing four outstanding elements: a massive yellow chimney at either end, a white balustraded widow's walk, a white-trimmed pediment with delicate fanlight in the center of the front and, flanking the pediment, two large dormers.

The Longfellow House has a history dating back to the American Revolution. The house served as a hospital after the Battle of Bunker Hill and, later, it housed Colonel John Glover's "amphibious regiment" of Marblehead fishermen, an event that has caused some people to consider the house as the "first headquarters of the American navy." Most memorable of all, General George Washington made the house his headquarters when he arrived in Cambridge to take command of the continental forces in July 1775, remaining until March 1776.

In 1973 the Longfellow House Trust, which had administrated the house and grounds since 1913, turned the property over to the National Park Service. The first floor, which has the most historical rooms, is open to the public.

Another of Longfellow's homes remains extant, administrated in Portland by the Maine Historical Society. It is the house where he lived from childhood until moving to Cambridge.

8) MINUTE MAN NATIONAL HISTORICAL PARK

In the midst of Boston's suburban area, Minute Man National Historical Park is seeking to preserve some of the historic landmarks associated with the beginning of the American Revolution. The 750 acres to be included in the Park will consist of three units: Battle Road Unit, a four-mile corridor along the historic battle road where local militia and minutemen fought the redcoats from behind bushes and fenceposts; North Bridge Unit, around the Old North Bridge in Concord which separated the British from the American patriots; and the Wayside Unit, the Concord homes of the Alcotts, Nathaniel Hawthorne and Margaret Sidney. The Battle Road Unit and the North Bridge Unit are now open to the public.

Between Lexington and Concord along the old Battle Road, interpretive markers will highlight the route taken by the British soldiers marching to teach rebellious colonists a lesson and by riders carrying the alarm to the countryside. Within Lexington and Concord considerable restoration is planned so that the park area will

Longfellow lived in Cambridge for forty-five years. Many poems were written at this standing desk in his study.

again look as it did that fateful day in April 1775, when "the shot heard round the world" was fired on the Lexington Green.

9) MUSEUM OF FINE ARTS

The visual world presented at Boston's Museum of Fine Arts is as old as objects from Egypt's Great Pyramids of Giza and as new as the eternal questions of Gauguin's painting *Where do we come from? What are we? Whither are we going?* The museum, however, did not acquire the impressive reputation as the second most comprehensive museum in the Western hemisphere by asking moot questions, but by moving ahead, acquiring, exploring India and Egypt and Europe, innovating such improvements as the appointment of scholar-specialists as curators and in providing docents for the public.

The Huntington Avenue attraction was first set up on Copley Square and, when the expanding museum needed new quarters only several decades after its founding in 1870, the most carefully planned museum building in the country was designed and finally completed on its present site in 1909. Scrupulous attention was given to lighting and wall color and texture. Superlatives do not only apply to the technical qualities of the building; superlatives also fit the collections at the fingertips of Bostonians.

Here is the most important collection of Asiatic art in the Western world. The classical collection shares honors with New York's Metropolitan Museum of Art. The Karolik Collection of American furniture of the colonial and early Federal periods, and watercolors and paintings from 1800-75 is the most complete of its type in the nation. Priceless silver pieces worked by Paul Revere and portraits of patriots and politicians by Stuart and Copley highlight the history of the United States which is so richly relived through the many galleries.

10) NAISMITH MEMORIAL BASKETBALL HALL OF FAME

The entire spectrum of basketball is covered at the Naismith Memorial Basketball Hall of Fame in Springfield. Unique among the sports halls of fame, the museum includes significant representation from all phases of the game, professional, college, Olympic and high school.

Here on the campus of Springfield College, then the International Y.M.C.A. Training School, this all-American game was born in 1891, the product of Dr. James Naismith's desire to develop an interesting form of indoor exercise in the winter. Today, in a replica of the original gym, the game's first thirteen rules are displayed under the peach basket first used. An extensive collection of memorabilia traces the history of the game to its present widespread popularity and sophistication.

In the Honors Court the greats of basketball are enshrined in a magnificent setting, a hand-painted, floor-to-ceiling stained-glass window devoted to each.

11) OLD MANSE

From this home in Concord on April 19, 1775, Ralph Waldo Emerson's grandfather, the Reverend William Emerson, watched the firing of the famous "shot heard round the world" which his grandson was later to immortalize. The sage of New England Transcendentalism spent part of his boyhood in the house on Monument Street. The most famous occupant of the house, however, was Nathaniel Hawthorne who brought his bride to the Old Manse in 1842 for a four-year stay.

It is a two-and-a-half-story clapboard structure with a gambrel roof and two pedimented doorways. For its day it was a large house. There are four rooms and a central hall downstairs, in addition to the usual sheds in the rear. On the second floor there are four bedrooms and the third floor has several small chambers for visitors, including one room on the third floor known as the "saints chamber," kept for the use of visiting clergymen.

In the course of their family life, the Hawthornes left their mark on the house. On a windowpane one can still see, scratched with Mrs. Hawthorne's diamond, a note about her daughter: "Una Hawthorne stood on this window sill January 22, 1845, while the trees were all glass chandeliers, a goodly show, which she liked much tho' only ten months old."

The Old Manse, built in 1769 and remaining today essentially the same as when the Reverend William Emerson moved into it, was turned over to the state-controlled Trustees of Reservations in 1939.

12) OLD NORTH CHURCH

The role played by Boston's Old North Church in the American Revolution has guaranteed its place in history. In its steeple on April 18, 1775, two lanterns were hung to tell Paul Revere and William Dawes that the British were approach-

Famous as a silversmith as well as a patriot, Paul Revere is honored in historic Boston. Behind him rises the steeple of Old North Church which figured in his immortal ride. He was closely associated with the church throughout his life.

ing Boston by sea. The restored steeple, including the original window from which the original lanterns shone, still stands out majestically when viewed from the Charlestown shore.

Known officially as Christ Church, the historic edifice at 193 Salem Street is the oldest existing church building in Boston. Begun in 1723 to house the city's second Church of England Parish, the elegant, gracefully proportioned structure was modeled after the best in English architecture of the day. Construction spanned a twenty-year period.

The famous Old North Church steeple was added seventeen years after the building was begun, in part through the donations of English merchants from the Bay of Honduras, in Central America, who desired a landmark to guide them into Boston Harbor. In 1745 the first peal of bells brought to America was placed in the steeple. As a boy of fifteen Paul Revere organized a guild to ring the bells. Revere was closely associated with Christ Church throughout his lifetime.

13) OLD SHIP CHURCH

Still functioning as a Unitarian Church, Old Ship Church at 107 Main Street, Hingham, is the oldest structure in the United States continually used as a place of worship and the oldest wooden church building in America.

Taking its name from its unusual roof structure which resembles an inverted ship's hull, the church was erected by the Hingham townspeople in 1681. Its magnificent curved oak frames were hand-hewn and no two are exactly alike. After many interior changes over the years, the large rafters and ceiling joists were rediscovered in 1930 and restored to their original appearance. The building is a registered national historic landmark.

Ebenezer Gay, minister of Old Ship Church from 1718 until 1787, is listed by John Adams as one of the three founders of American Unitarianism. His achievements were part of the church's distinguished liberal tradition.

14) OLD STURBRIDGE VILLAGE

A page out of New England's history has been beautifully recreated at Old Sturbridge Village. A resident of an early nineteenth-century New England rural community who found himself transplanted to Old Sturbridge Village would feel completely at home. Some forty authentic period structures from throughout the region have been moved to this idyllic 200-acre site and furnished with period materials.

Unitarian Old Ship Church in Hingham is the oldest wooden church building in the country. Its curved oak frames were hand-hewn in 1681.

At the center of the village is a green or common, dominated by the Baptist Meetinghouse, built in Sturbridge in 1832. Homes and shops cluster around the green. The evolution of home design can be seen in the houses which range from the early Colonial salt-box to the spacious and luxurious Federal home.

In Miner Grant's unpainted General Store penny candy is still sold. Craftsmen practice their trades in such buildings as the pottery shop, the printing shop and Moses Wilder's solid granite blacksmith shop. The daily chores of farmers of a century and a half ago are performed on the Pliny Freeman Farm.

Founded in 1946 by Albert B. and J. Cheney Wells, brothers and accomplished collectors of American antiques, Old Sturbridge Village is continuing to expand.

15) PAUL REVERE HOUSE

The Paul Revere House, located at 19 North Square (which is actually a triangle) in Boston, was nearly 100 years old when the famed colonial patriot purchased it in 1770. It is believed to be the oldest wood-frame house in urban America and is the point from which the celebrated "midnight ride" began in 1775.

As far as is known, during Revere's occupancy it was always a three-story frame dwelling with an ell at the rear, and a medieval-looking overhang at the first level. After Revere left the house in 1800, it underwent a series of changes, including the installation of a store-front on the first floor. During the seventeenth century the house had two stories and it was given its original configuration at the time of its restoration in the twentieth century.

16) PLYMOUTH

In 1620, after first stopping at the present site of Provincetown on Cape Cod, the 102 passengers on board the *Mayflower* sailed into Plymouth Harbor. On December 11 (21st by new-style calendar), an exploring party went ashore. Thus the English Separatists we call the Pilgrims established the first permanent settlement in America north of Virginia. By spring, severe weather and disease had reduced their numbers by nearly half.

Among the places at Plymouth today are: Plymouth Rock, legendary spot of the first landing; Plimoth Plantation, a hundred acres of replicas of Pilgrim dwellings; *Mayflower II*, a reproduction, built in England, of the original ship; and Pilgrim Hall, containing artifacts such as Governor William Bradford's Bible and the cradle of Peregrine White, first white child born in Massachusetts.

17) U.S.S. CONSTITUTION

The *Constitution* was one of the first three ships launched in 1797 to form the nucleus of the United States Navy. Combining the best features of French and English ships, she was built longer, broader and higher out of the water than any frigate of the day.

Because of her length and stability, the *Constitution* could carry a vast spread of sail and attain great speed. The live oak that formed the backbone of the ship has held her together so well that it has been possible over the years to effectively restore and rebuild her. Only about fifteen percent of the original *Constitution* remains today.

In the Fitch House at Old Sturbridge Village, a highboy and simple slat-back chairs add to the mellow mahogany cast of a cozy room.

The *Constitution* earned her famous nickname, "Old Ironsides," when she defeated the British man-of-war H.M.S. *Guerrière* during the War of 1812. Shot fired from the *Guerrière* glanced ineffectually off the *Constitution*. As a result of the fierce battle which lasted only thirty minutes, the United States became recognized as a strong naval power.

Today this proud old ship is moored at the Boston Navy Yard, the oldest commissioned United States warship afloat. She was saved from destruction in large part because of Oliver Wendell Holmes' famous poem "Old Ironsides."

18) WALDEN POND STATE RESERVATION

In 1845 Henry David Thoreau built a cabin near a pond outside Concord on the land of a good friend, Ralph Waldo Emerson. He stayed there, he wrote later, because "I wished to live deliberately, to front only the essential facts of life, and see if I could learn what it had to teach." What he learned is set down in *Walden*, the only writing of this great naturalist and social critic that sold well during his lifetime. He created not only a tremendous testimonial to his own integrity, but left a lasting testament to any reader.

In 1922 the Emerson family willed Walden Pond to the State of Massachusetts under the jurisdiction of the Middlesex County Commissioner, stipulating that no "improvements"—campsites, concessions, etc.—be allowed.

The 300 acres of Walden Pond State Reservation remain wooded as they were in Thoreau's day. There is a stone marker where the cabin once stood, the only sign of his presence.

At Old Sturbridge Village, a painted tin document box and tea caddies bear variations of floral and fruit designs.

Oldest commissioned warship afloat, the Constitution *was launched in 1797 and now rests at Boston Navy Yard.*

New Hampshire

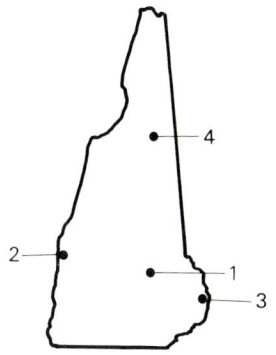

1) CAPITOL, Concord

New Hampshire's classic State House in Concord, built in 1819, is the oldest in the nation with the legislature still occupying its original chambers.

The Granite State's granite Capitol was originally a two-story parallelogram surmounted by a silolike dome upon which a hand-carved, seventy-eight-inch wooden "war" eagle was perched peering eastward toward possible European hostiles.

The State House now has a handsome Doric-colonnaded frontage. It also boasts an enlarged dome and a "peace" eagle of metal composition, erected in 1955 when its predecessor's tail feathers had "molted" beyond repair. On the lawn around the State House repose statues of such famous sons of New Hampshire as Daniel Webster and President Franklin Pierce.

Granite for the original building was hewn from giant boulders on nearby Rattlesnake Hill, said to have rolled into Concord twenty thousand years earlier during a glacial period. Blocks for the two enlargements were blasted from the bowels of the same hill, said by geologists to be some twenty million years in age. A marked difference in texture is plainly visible to this day.

2) CORNISH-WINDSOR BRIDGE

The Cornish-Windsor Bridge is the longest covered bridge in the nation, spanning the Connecticut River for 460 feet from New Hampshire to Vermont several miles upriver

Controversial naval figure John Paul Jones roomed here at two different times in one of Portsmouth's most patrician houses.

Opposite: Among the most nostalgic of sights is the old-fashioned covered bridge. While most bridges are no longer covered, there are still five crossing the Connecticut River, including the Cornish-Windsor Bridge. It still has the roof that increases its life tenfold.

from Windsor. This picturesque structure, along with the other covered bridges on the Vermont-New Hampshire border, is owned by New Hampshire. When the independent-minded residents of Vermont decided to become the fourteenth state rather than a part of New York or New Hampshire, New Hampshire insisted that the border between them be the west bank of the river, making the Connecticut River part of its domain.

By the mid-1800's towns and trade flourished along the river and covered bridges had established themselves as a distinctive part of the riverscape. The bridges were covered, as one farmer put it, "for the same reason women wear long skirts: to protect their underpinnings." In other words, the covering shielded the large supporting timbers from the rotting effects of sun and rain. A covered bridge has a life of about eighty years, about ten times longer than that of an uncovered bridge. Built in 1866 and the fourth bridge on the site, the Cornish-Windsor is one of five covered bridges that still cross the Connecticut.

3) JOHN PAUL JONES HOUSE

The most romantic and controversial American naval figure, John Paul Jones was born in Scotland, served in Russia, died in France and is reburied at Annapolis. But he is remembered in the sea town of Portsmouth by having the house where he boarded renamed in his honor. It was at Mrs. Purcell's on Middle and State streets, now called the John Paul Jones House, where he lived in the best front bedchamber during the year 1777 while the sloop of war *Ranger* was being built at Langdon's Island and where he returned on August 13, 1781, while he supervised the construction of the seventy-four-gun ship *America*.

The John Paul Jones House holds its own nobly in this town of distinguished dwellings. It is one of the finest examples of frame houses built by many leading citizens during the eighteenth century. Standing two and a half stories with pedimented lintels over the first-floor windows and the third-floor end dormers, the house has been expanded a number of times over the years, which is also typical of many Portsmouth houses. In 1973 it was designated a national historic landmark.

Today the house is furnished with many interesting pieces of period furniture and collections of objects brought back from the Orient by New England sailors. Filling a large part of the space in the bedroom which Jones occupied are models of ships built in Portsmouth, a copy of the flag John Paul Jones flew and a letter written by him. Here also is a model of the *Ranger*, the ship that originally caused the dashing hero to come to Portsmouth where today much of the flavor of a prosperous eighteenth-century seaport has been recaptured.

4) MOUNT WASHINGTON

New Hampshire's White Mountains present a grand appearance because, though not nearly as high as the Rockies, the contrast between these mountaintops and the surrounding countryside is far greater. Mount Washington in the Presidential Range, the most prominent peak at an altitude of 6,288 feet, towers a mile above the picturesque valley. On a clear day the view from its summit extends one hundred miles in any direction. Occasionally the mountain is visible from the Atlantic Coast seventy-five miles away.

Mount Washington can be scaled on foot by many routes, ranging from relatively simple to extremely challenging. The Mount Washington Automobile Road is a challenging eight-mile gravel road which ascends steeply from the base entrance at Glen House. Views from the many turnouts along the way are magnificent and varied. A gradual evolution from verdant valley to sparse alpinelike summit contributes to an awesome sense of the mountain's immensity. The Mount Washington Cog Railway also makes the scenic trip to the summit.

Rhode Island

1) CAPITOL, Providence

Although Rhode Island was the first colony to declare its independence from Great Britain, it was the last to decide on a single city to serve as its state capital. It was not until 1900 that the seat of government was permanently fixed at Providence and the present impressive State House was occupied.

The Capitol's marble dome, illuminated at night by a battery of floodlights, was the first in the United States and one of only four in the world (Minnesota's Capitol in St. Paul, the Taj Mahal in India and St. Peter's in Rome, the only one larger than this). A symbolic bronze statue of the "Independent Man" watches over the state from atop the dome at a height of 235 feet.

A quotation from the Royal Charter of 1663 is carved in marble above the portico. Inscribed on the building's north side are the milestones of Rhode Island history: founding, incorporation, chartering and independence. At the entrance are bronze statues of two great Rhode Island military leaders, General Nathanael Greene of Revolutionary fame and Commodore Oliver Hazard Perry, hero of the War of 1812.

The original parchment charter granted by King Charles II, July 8, 1663, which continued in force (except for 1686-89) until the present constitution of the state became operative on May 2, 1843, is housed in the State House.

2) MARBLE HOUSE

Combining both Greek and French designs, Marble House, the sumptuous mansion of Mr. and Mrs. William K. Vanderbilt, was named for the wide variety of marble used in its construction. Located on Bellevue Avenue in Newport, the house was completed in 1892. During the American Renaissance of architecture, it was considered among the finest homes in the country.

Richard Morris Hunt—who had designed The Breakers for Mr. Vanderbilt's brother Cornelius, the famous financier—designed Marble House in the fashion of Louis XIV, who was greatly admired by both Mr. and Mrs. Vanderbilt. Some say that the White House played a part in Hunt's inspiration, while others mention the Petit Trianon at Versailles. In any case it is lavish throughout, in a summer resort noted for its lavish homes, many of which were built after Marble House. The home is now maintained by the Preservation Society of Newport County.

The entrance hall to the mansion is twenty feet high and is lined and paved with yellow marble from the *Monte Arenti* quarry near Montagnola, Italy. The ceiling has stucco relief in the form of masks and elaborate arabesques, i.e., ornamental fruit, foliage and animals.

The richest of the rooms in the mansion is the Gold Room, which served as a ballroom at some of the extravagant receptions and dances held by the Vanderbilts. The outstanding ornamentation in the room is found in the gilt-wood panels in carved relief, believed to be the work of Karl Bitter, a protégé of architect Hunt. All the panels are done in red, green and yellow-gold.

3) TOURO SYNAGOGUE

Touro Synagogue, located at 72 Touro Street in Newport, is worthy of its designation as a national historic site both as a lovely Georgian style building modified to Sephardic Jewish tradition and as a symbol of the American religious freedom which made its construction possible.

This, the oldest synagogue in America, was dedicated in 1763. It was built by an active and prosperous community over a century after the first Jewish colonists arrived, inspired by the guidelines of religious freedom set down by Rhode Island's founder, Roger Williams. Not far away is the cemetery which was the first project of the Newport Jewish community in 1677.

Noted architect Peter Harrison was commissioned to design the synagogue and it is often called his masterpiece. The stark brick exterior contrasts sharply with the rich and airy synagogue chamber. A gallery where, according to Orthodox tradition, women must sit is supported by twelve Ionic columns representing the twelve tribes of Israel. Above, twelve Corinthian columns brace the domed ceiling. Hanging from the ceiling are five massive brass chandeliers dating from the eighteenth century.

Closed after the Revolutionary War because the decline of the once bustling port city of Newport caused a dwindling of the Jewish population, Touro Synagogue was among the first unoccupied historic structures to be preserved through the generosity of private philanthropists. Two bequests by the sons of the congregation's first spiritual leader, Rev. Isaac Touro, made possible the restoration. In 1883 the synagogue was permanently reopened.

Newport is notable for the number of pre-Revolutionary War buildings. It is also home of Marble House, the Vanderbilt mansion raised during the American Renaissance of architecture. Bronze furniture commands attention against dark pink marble walls.

Vermont

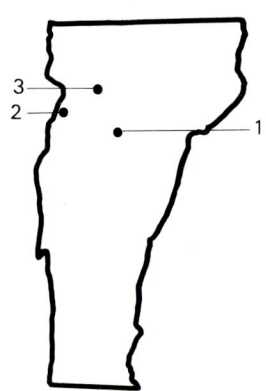

1) CAPITOL, Montpelier

Vermont's majestic State Capitol, dedicated in 1859, includes a central building with a Doric Greek Revival portico plus two wings that form a Greek cross. Appropriately, the exterior material is Vermont granite. The apex of the Doric portico rises sixty feet, and behind it, a gold-leaf dome and cupola add another fifty-six feet, nine inches. Topping this is a statue of Ceres, the goddess of agriculture, modeled after the work of Vermonter Larkin G. Mead.

Entered from the portico, the first story presents a striking appearance, with a black and white tessellated marble floor, deep double-sunk ceiling panels, and ornamented iron stairs. The columns in the lobby are Ionic.

Mead's bust of Lincoln faces the main entrance; his marble statue of Ethan Allen stands in the portico. Portraits of famous sons of Vermont line the walls.

The Grecian motif is carried on throughout the interior, with fluted columns and a handsome ornamented ceiling in the Senate Chamber and, in the House of Representatives, fluted pilasters, Corinthian capitals, enriched entablature and a paneled cove.

2) SHELBURNE MUSEUM

Those with a taste for the unusual in early Americana call Shelburne near Lake Champlain the champagne of American villages. Shelburne's forty-five acres do not encompass an authentic village but rather a collection of collections: hat boxes, dolls and doll houses, cigar-store Indians, patterns for brass and bronze castings and quilts.

Snow-covered trees bordering the Vermont countryside help create inviting scenes of serenity.

Over a thousand decoys can be seen at Shelburne Museum. The hollow swan (above) was carved in Maryland, and while the Eskimo curlew (right) was factory-made, the yellowlegs to its right was handmade.

Mrs. Electra Havemeyer Webb had collected folk art sculpture since her childhood and, when in her sixties, founded the Shelburne in 1947 as a display for her assortment of 200 carriages as well as the other 125,000 items she had acquired.

Most of the buildings have been moved to their location—sometimes brick by brick—after being earmarked for destruction elsewhere. The unique entrance to the grounds is a two-laned covered bridge—Vermont's last—that Mrs. Webb transported from Cambridge thirty-five miles away after it was to be replaced by a steel bridge. The water it spans is a specially constructed lily pond. From two miles away at Lake Champlain the S.S. *Ticonderoga* needed a respectable dry dock. The short overland journey for the plush Victorian sidewheeler took two months. The *Ticonderoga* is the last vertical beam passenger and freight steamer intact in the country and was declared a national historic landmark in 1963.

Along with a sawmill and a private railroad station are other period buildings: the Vergennes School with drawings from the early 1800's; the Charlotte Meeting House awaiting Sunday worshipers; the Dorset House with over a thousand decoys.

Shelburne is a credit to an independent woman who was also blessed with good taste. Had young Electra listened to her mother, Shelburne, an exuberant expression of the American spirit, would not be ours. For Mrs. Webb's mother disapproved of Electra's collection of "American trash" and wanted her to concentrate on Rembrandts and Manets.

3) STOWE AREA

Famed for its abundant snow and called the "Ski Capital of the East," Stowe is a beautiful place throughout the year. Mount Mansfield, the area's most prominent attraction and Vermont's highest mountain at 4,393 feet, was first sighted by Samuel de Champlain in 1609 as he sailed down the lake which bears his name. Since that time it has provided pleasure for countless numbers. The imposing peak resembles an upturned face and the view from its summit is breathtaking. Ralph Waldo Emerson, visiting in 1868 when a hotel built just below the "Nose" was patronized by those attracted by Stowe's quiet charm, described the view as "a perpetual illusion."

Today, Stowe's outstanding ski facilities include a high-speed gondola ride to the Mount Mansfield "Chin" area near the mountain's highest point. Sunny Spruce Peak also provides attractive and open ski runs. Ski instructions and a variety of accommodations are available.

Delaware   District of Columbia   Maryland
New Jersey   New York   Pennsylvania
Virginia   West Virginia

MIDDLE ATLANTIC

Moving up the Atlantic Coast that had been first sighted by an Italian (or most likely, even before that, a Viking), then settled by the English in Virginia, the Swedes in Delaware and the Dutch in New York, William Penn fashioned a colony in Pennsylvania in the 1680's. He invited everyone to come and live in harmony in Philadelphia, the city of brotherly love. Ever since, the Middle Atlantic has been home to people from as many parts of the world as the ships docked in its great ports.

Topographically the Middle Atlantic region is also a montage. Between the coast that is scratched and rebuilt by a devilish ocean on the east and the graceful Appalachian Mountains to the west is a broad coastal plain. From the other side of the mountains to the Great Lakes and the St. Lawrence River valley stretch flat, fertile lowlands of Pennsylvania and New York.

Wild places, mountain retreats, quiet pastoral scenes, venerable historic sites and mildly bustling cities characterize much of the region. In this area where much of the early history of the country was written, a great deal of tomorrow's history is being forged. On a beautiful location bordering the Potomac River is the national seat of government, Washington, in the District of Columbia. The hub of the Middle Atlantic is New York City, North America's cultural and financial center and the focus of a megalopolis spreading up and down the Atlantic Ocean and inland for hundreds of miles.

In the industrial complexes and rich farmlands that comprise the Middle Atlantic live the progeny of staunch forefathers—colonists, patriots, Civil War soldiers, and inventors, bankers and mechanical geniuses who revolutionized manufacturing techniques and created the age of technology.

Opposite: Jefferson's designs, such as that of Monticello, have had a great influence on American architecture. He spent his whole life designing and redesigning his home.

Delaware

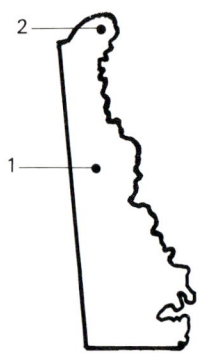

1) CAPITOL, Dover

Known as Legislative Hall, Delaware's Capitol was completed in 1933, replacing the Old State House, which had served as the seat of government since 1792. The building, constructed of handmade brick and following the style of the old Capitol, emphasizes Georgian colonial architecture. Subsequent additions have carefully preserved the colonial atmosphere appropriate to the nation's first state.

Legislative Hall is located east of The Green in Dover and is easily recognized by its formal beauty, highlighted with gables, chimneys and a three-tiered tower.

The interior of the building is reminiscent of the eighteenth century with woodwork and other appointments following the theme of that era. This is particularly noticeable in the governor's office suite, which is furnished in eighteenth-century decor. Two paintings by Thomas Sully hang in the governor's office. Both are portraits of Delaware-born heroes of the War of 1812, Commodore Thomas MacDonough and Commodore Jacob Jones. Hallways of Legislative Hall are lined with portraits of distinguished Delawarians, including many World War II heroes.

2) WINTERTHUR MUSEUM

Henry Francis du Pont spent more than half a century collecting American decorative arts and displaying them in period rooms of his country home, Winterthur, northwest of Wilmington. Winterthur honors the early American artisans who fashioned pewter, textiles, ceramics, silver, etc., for the home. Du Pont ingeniously installed interior woodwork from early houses along the Eastern Seaboard in his mansion and then added antiques from the same date.

Legislative Hall, Delaware's Capitol, has a formal colonial atmosphere.

The thousands of examples of interior architecture, furniture and accessories, dating from the seventeenth to nineteenth centuries, were first made available for public viewing when the Du Ponts moved to a nearby new residence. Since then sections of their new estate have been open to the public.

Surrounding the museum named for the Swiss home of the original owner are sixty acres of gardens that, due to Du Pont's horticultural skill, appear as natural growth among the native foliage. The harmony in hue of flowers, shrubs and trees that has made the gardens world famous is especially delightful in spring and fall.

A spice chest made in 1679, Winterthur Museum.

District of Columbia

1) CORCORAN ART GALLERY

The oldest art gallery in the nation's Capital and one of the oldest in the nation, the Corcoran Gallery of Art was founded in 1859 by William Wilson Corcoran to "promote and encourage the American genius." Today the gallery houses an outstanding and comprehensive collection of American art and one of the largest collections of Corot and Monticelli paintings in America. Schools of art from the Hudson River period to modern times are represented in chronologically arranged displays. Almost no recognized American artist is neglected.

Corcoran carries out the mandate of its founder through biennial exhibitions of contemporary American oil painting, begun in 1907.

The Corcoran School of Art, founded in 1890, is the only professional studio school of art in Washington.

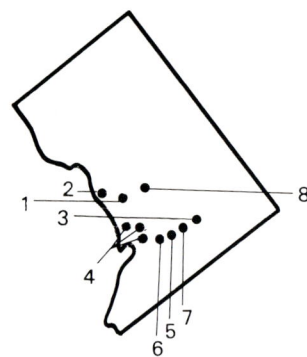

2) JOHN F. KENNEDY CENTER FOR THE PERFORMING ARTS

Truly a complex worthy of the nation's Capital, the John F. Kennedy Center for the Performing Arts is the culmination of a project begun in 1958 when President Eisenhower signed an authorization for a national cultural center. It is the natural outgrowth of a young nation whose first leaders struggled to develop the foundations of a truly civilized society. It is the only official memorial in Washington to John F. Kennedy, the late President who was a dedicated patron of the arts.

Since Kennedy Center's opening with Leonard Bernstein's *Mass* in 1971, the finest in music, dance and theater companies from America and abroad have performed. Outstanding works have been created in and for the center. Included in the complex are the 1,150-seat Eisenhower Theater, devoted primarily to drama; the Opera House seating 2,300, which also hosts musical comedy, ballet and modern dance; the Concert Hall with a capacity of 2,750; and the American Film Institute Theater, which seats 224 people. A 500-seat experimental theater is to be completed.

Designated by Congress as the nation's cultural center, Kennedy Center is a separately administered bureau of the Smithsonian Institution.

The Lincoln Memorial was designed to symbolize the union of the country. The nineteen-foot statue of our sixteenth President is of white Georgia marble.

The Museum of African Art was the residence of Frederick Douglass, the "Father of the Civil Rights Movement."

3) MUSEUM OF AFRICAN ART

Africa's culture and history are rich and varied, but largely unknown to Americans. The Museum of African Art, the first of its kind in the country, provides a glimpse into this world.

Housed appropriately in the Capitol Hill townhouse which was the first Washington residence of Frederick Douglass, a former slave who is considered the "Father of the Civil Rights Movement," the museum was opened in 1964. One gallery has been designated the Frederick Douglass Memorial Room and displays original furniture and memorabilia.

The Museum of African Art features materials depicting the distinctive African contributions to European and American culture. Within the twelve galleries are more than 400 examples of traditional sculpture, textiles, jewelry and utensils. Special exhibits include "The Impact of African Sculpture on Modern Art" and "2,000 years of Nigerian Art."

Largely through the efforts of his wife, Douglass' last home has also been preserved. Cedar Hill is a handsome two-story brick colonial house overlooking the city near the Anacostia River. For thirteen years before he died, Douglass lived in the spacious and comfortable twenty-room house.

4) NATIONAL CAPITAL PARKS

The majestic Capital of the United States, planned in 1791 by Frenchman Pierre Charles L'Enfant as a city in a park, rises from the flatlands of the Potomac River. In the center of the city are five structures that form a cross, three of which honor presidents. The Capitol building itself is at the east end of the Grand Mall, L'Enfant's "crown jewel," envisioned as a park with fountains and a canal. At the intersection site south of the White House and west of the Capitol stands the Washington Monument. Directly south across the Tidal Basin is the Jefferson Memorial. At the west end of the Grand Mall, between a reflecting pool and the river, is the Lincoln Memorial.

Washington Monument, the great obelisk honoring the first President and military leader of the United States, George Washington, is almost in the center of the cross. From an engineering point of view, the white marble 555-foot shaft is remarkable masonry. The shape is that of ancient Egyptian obelisks and tapers one-fourth inch to the vertical foot. The walls, covered with white Maryland marble, are fifteen feet thick at the bottom and eighteen inches at the top.

Inside the memorial are 190 carved memorial stones presented by various groups, individuals, states and countries to the government. The view from the top of this needle is breathtaking. The top can be reached by elevator or stairs.

The actual construction of the monument is laced with controversy, shortage of funds and, initially, ground too soft to support the structure. The cornerstone was laid in 1833, but it was only in 1888 that the dedication took place.

The Capitol of the United States represents the achievements and aspirations of the nation through its dignity and grandeur.

Of all the monuments to the third President of the country, the most impressive is the **Jefferson Memorial,** the white Vermont marble memorial on the south bank of the Tidal Basin. John Russell Pope designed the circular colonnaded building in the Pantheon style. The structure is 165 feet in diameter and 103 feet high.

Sculptor Rudolph Evans prepared the nineteen-foot-high statue of Jefferson standing that dominates the interior of the domed memorial hall. On the white Georgia marble walls four panels, carved in bronze, contain excerpts from his works avowing principles Jefferson held

high, such as freedom of the mind and the necessity for educating all of the people.

The memorial was dedicated in 1943 on the bicentennial of Jefferson's birth. Early April is undoubtedly the best time to visit here. Then the hundreds of cherry trees given to the city of Washington by the city of Tokyo in 1912 are in magnificent bloom.

Honoring the sixteenth President of the United States, the **Abraham Lincoln Memorial** is an outstanding Greek-temple-style structure. Henry Brown, the New York architect who also designed the Lincoln Monument in Lincoln, Nebraska, planned the memorial to symbolize the union of the country. Built on a grand scale, it is 257 by 187 feet. Thirty-six Greek Doric columns, one for each of the states at the time of Lincoln's death, surround the hall. Above the colonnade of white Colorado-Yule marble is a frieze with a border inscribed with the names of the forty-eight states in existence when the memorial was completed in 1922.

Dominating the interior is a nineteen-foot statue executed in white Georgia marble by Daniel Chester French. Seated, Lincoln is contemplative. In the two side chambers are carved the texts of the Gettysburg Address and his sec-

ond inaugural address. On murals above the tablets Jules Guerin has depicted in allegorical fashion principles derived from the Illinois rail-splitter's life.

These three structures are a central feature of the National Capital Parks, which includes more than 300 park units in the immediate area of the District of Columbia.

5) NATIONAL GALLERY OF ART

Belonging to all citizens of the United States, the National Gallery of Art was established by joint resolution of Congress and is operated and maintained by public appropriation. Though technically a bureau of the Smithsonian Institution, the gallery is an autonomous organization with high public officials as ex officio members of its board.

Andrew W. Mellon contributed the funds for the construction of the gallery and its collections are continually being expanded through private donation. The collections encompass every major West European and American school of art from the thirteenth century to the present day. Included are the Mellon, Kress and Widener collections of painting and sculpture, the Widener collection of decorative arts, the Rosenwald collection of prints and drawings, the Dale collection of nineteenth and twentieth century French paintings and a painting by Leonardo da Vinci.

6) SMITHSONIAN INSTITUTION

Once known as "Uncle Sam's Attic," the immense Smithsonian Institution was established in 1864 through the bequest of James Smithson, an Englishman who never visited America, to create "an establishment for the increase and diffusion of knowledge among men." The Smithsonian fulfills its mandate. It serves as the major repository of the cultural, historical and scientific history of the United States. Its inclusive complex of museums, educational and research facilities include some of Washington's most venerable institutions. The United States National Museum consisting of the Museum of Natural History and the Museum of History and Technology, the National Zoological Park, the National Air and Space Museum, the Radiation Biology Laboratory, the Science Information Exchange, the International Exchange Service, the National Collection of Fine Arts, the National Portrait Gallery and the Freer Gallery of Art are all bureaus of the Smithsonian. Also part of its vast network are the Astrophysical Observatory in Cambridge, Massachusetts, and the Tropical Research Institute in the Panama Canal Zone.

The **United States National Museum** contains more than fifty-nine million items. This continent's physical evolution is traced in the biological and mineralogical collections in its component **Museum of Natural History.** Such historical treasures as the inaugural gowns worn by every First Lady are displayed in the **Museum of History and Technology.**

Located on a beautifully wooded, 168-acre site in northwestern Washington's Rock Creek Valley, the **National Zoological Park** was founded in 1889. Today 600 animal species are represented by a population of several thousand. Many of the residents are not to be found anywhere else in the country. Among the rarest are Ling-Ling and Hsing-Hsing, the giant pandas from China; the Komodo dragon of Indonesia; the kiwis, flightless birds from New Zealand.

Neptune, the trident-bearing god of the seas, is depicted in this nineteenth-century steamboat housing on display in the Smithsonian Institution.

Built for the citizens of the United States, the National Gallery of Art includes collections of all major West European and American schools of art since the thirteenth century.

7) UNITED STATES CAPITOL

Nothing in America attests more vividly to the strength of the nation and the foresight of its founders than the Capitol building of the United States. At the time the site was chosen in the new Federal City of Washington in 1791, it was planned that the building should be both serviceable and monumental.

Construction of the building in five sections covered a period of seventy years, from the laying of the cornerstone by President Washington in 1793 to the placement of the Statue of Freedom atop the present dome in 1863. To further complement the monumental majesty of the structure, the terraces were added in 1884, and the east-central portion was extended, enlarged and reconstructed in 1957-62.

The Capitol now has 540 rooms on five floors and covers four acres of land. The Capitol grounds total 131 acres, including the nearby legislative office buildings. The landscaping was largely the work of Frederick Law Olmsted, who planned New York's Central Park in the mid-1870's.

The interior of the Capitol is a treasure house of beautiful paintings, sculpture, and assorted Americana, with over 500 artistic items displayed on or within the halls, chambers, rotunda and offices. The most notable artistic display is in the rotunda. Entered from the east front, under pediment figures of America flanked by Justice and Hope (President John Quincy Adams' suggestion), past statues of War and Peace, through the massive ten-ton bronze doors telling the story of Columbus, the rotunda is nearly 100 feet in diameter and more than 180 feet high.

The rotunda walls display eight huge paintings, each about fourteen by twenty feet, of early American history. The ceiling of the dome presents Constantino Brumidi's gigantic allegory, *Apotheosis of Washington*. In the 4,464 square feet of fresco, the first President, in general's uniform, sits between Liberty and Victory, with thirteen other figures for the original states completing an inner chain. Below Washington, in the outer circle, is Freedom, with other groupings of Greek deities and American heroes symbolizing arts and sciences, maritime progress, commerce, mechanics and agriculture. Beneath the dome is the rotunda frieze, a panorama in fresco of the nation's history.

South of the rotunda is Statuary Hall, which was the House Chamber from 1807 to 1857. A few feet west of the rotunda is the small and simple nondenominational Prayer Room. There, members of both houses can go for individual meditation and prayer, reminded of the words from the Sixteenth Psalm on the stained-glass window: "Preserve me, O God, for in thee do I put my trust."

The House Chamber itself, a rectangular area 139 by 93 feet, is paneled in walnut, with gray marble behind the rostrum on which is inscribed the national motto: "In God We Trust." State seals border the ceiling, and portraits of Washington and Lafayette flank the dais. An encircling gallery looks down on the 435 Congressmen, seated where they wish, but with Democrats to the right of the Speaker and Republicans to his left.

Outside the House Chamber, to the sides beyond the cloak rooms, are the magnificent Grand Staircase East and Grand Staircase West. The Senate also has two great stairways.

In the Senate Chamber, special desks are assigned to the one hundred Senators, with Republicans and Democrats to the vice president's left and right, respectively. On the gallery are marble busts of twenty former vice presidents.

Less known and visited are the many other areas in the Capitol which serve every possible need of the building and its occupants: from post office to restaurants, from carpenter shop to barber shop, these make the Capitol a virtual city within a city.

More than all this, however, more than the grandeur of its art and architecture, the Capitol of the United States stands for the nation's past achievements and its future aspirations, truly a "temple dedicated to the sovereignty of the people."

8) WHITE HOUSE

In the more than a century and a half that it has been the official residence of the presidents of the United States, the White House has undergone many changes; some necessitated by fire, some to meet expanding needs, some to meet changing conventions and, during President Truman's administration, to save the building from collapse.

The main part of the house is essentially the same as was designed by the Irish-born architect James Hoban, who was given the commission in 1792. It is magnificent without being flamboyant; dignified, yet it has found room for the romping of children through its halls, as well as the more sedate pace of distinguished worldwide guests.

By 1800, when John Adams and his wife, Abigail, moved in, they found the house far from finished. "The house is made habitable," Abigail recounted in a letter to her daughter, "but there is not a single apartment finished. . . . We do not have the least fence, yard or other convenience, without, and the great unfinished audience room [the East Room] I make a drying room of to hang up the clothes in."

When Thomas Jefferson moved into the Executive Mansion in 1801, he found the house "big enough for two emperors, one Pope and the Grand Lama." Jefferson introduced a French and continental motif which was carried on by President James Madison and his wife, Dolley, until they were forced to flee in the summer of 1814 in the face of the British assault on Washington. Sadly, the mansion was burned and looted. The Gilbert Stuart portrait of George Washington was ordered removed from the building by Mrs. Madison and is the only object from the time of President Madison known to have survived. Hoban was recalled to direct the reconstruction of the burned-out mansion and it was eventually ready for occupancy by President Monroe.

In 1902 during the administration of Theodore Roosevelt, there was a major restoration and expansion. The main building was left

The interior of the White House has a quiet dignity. The Red Room depicts an early nineteenth-century Empire parlor.

intact, but the Victorian interior was changed to a restrained classic style. It was at this time that the separation of house and office functions was finally achieved with the building on the west side of a new Executive Wing connected to the house by a colonnade.

In 1948 it was found that the interior of the White House was unsound and the floors were in danger of collapsing. President Truman and his family moved out and the entire interior of the mansion was removed. Wall paneling and other decorative details were carefully removed, numbered and stored. A new basement and foundation were built under the exterior walls and a steel framework was erected in the interior before these historic materials were brought back and reinstated.

Mrs. Jacqueline Kennedy, wife of the late President John F. Kennedy, refurbished much of the interior during their occupancy, in several instances drawing from furniture and paintings which had been relegated to storage.

The interior of the White House has always been impressive, but in recent years it seems to have taken on an air of quiet dignity in keeping with the nation's role in the world.

There have been times, particularly in 1948, when suggestions were made to raze the building but these have been rejected. The White House is one of the most cherished parts of the nation's heritage.

Maryland

1) ASSATEAGUE ISLAND NATIONAL SEASHORE

A vast expanse of sand and sea makes up Assateague Island National Seashore. Thirty-seven miles long and generally a mile to a mile and a half wide, this barrier island has many moods—from a quiet summer evening with the soothing wash of waves and the crying of terns the only sounds, to a winter storm raging over the sand, the surf thundering onto the shore.

The island was born of the sea and will die of the sea, as it is rapidly pushed toward the Delmarva Peninsula where three states (Delaware, Maryland and Virginia) share the Atlantic coastline. The continuing change in topography is phenomenal. Before 1933 Assateague was actually a peninsula, but a storm that year cut an inlet separating it from the barrier island

A statue of Roger Brooke Taney (1777-1864), fourth Chief Justice of the United States, stands in front of the Maryland State House.

to the north which has nearly completed its cycle of being pushed into the mainland.

The sand dunes, built up of grains carried and deposited by ocean currents and surf and then blown above the tide marks by winds, protect the inland portions of the island. The dunes are fragile and unstable, anchored only by grasses that are tolerant of salt spray but vulnerable to feet.

Beyond the dunes, loblolly pines and thickets of wax myrtle, bayberry, sumac, rose and greenbrier have a hold in the packed sand; and deer, foxes, raccoons and forest birds dwell here. Marshes and many small islands make up the bay shoreline, and in Chincoteague Bay itself, named for a vanished tribe of Indians who lived in this region, are found oysters, clams and crabs which are the source of a substantial fishing industry.

One of the most interesting aspects of Assateague Island is its herd of wild ponies. Legend says they are the descendants of ponies that swam ashore from a shipwrecked Spanish galleon, but no one really knows their origin.

But it is the Assateague beach that draws the most attention. Thirty-seven miles long, it has a gently sloping bottom, fine surf and lack of strong undertow, making it attractive to bathers.

About two-thirds of the national seashore is in Maryland; the Virginia third (the southern third), is comprised of the **Chincoteague National Wildlife Refuge.** There is a marked difference between the upper and lower portions of Assateague Island—the lower is greater in vegetation and its marshes are larger, providing excellent cover for more than 225 species of birds.

Assateague Island National Seashore almost failed to become a reality. Although the National Park Service had recommended the is-

Assateague Island is famous for wild herds of ponies that roam its vast expanse of sand and marsh.

land for seashore status in the 1930's, this seemed doomed when a private developer bought a large section of the island and chopped it into over eight thousand homesites and sold them to gullible buyers. But in March 1962, a powerful northeastern storm struck Assateague, destroying most of the man-made structures. This gave conservationists a second chance, and in 1965 President Lyndon B. Johnson signed a bill to make Assateague the largest public seashore on the mid-Atlantic Coast.

2) CAPITOL, Annapolis

The Maryland State House in Annapolis, an imposing edifice with a prominent place in American history, is the oldest State Capitol still fulfilling its original purpose. Construction on this building, the third to occupy its commanding site of the town's highest point, was begun in 1772 at a cost of 7,500 pounds sterling. The large, unique wooden dome, made without nails and held together with wooden pegs, was added after the War of Independence.

Early in the twentieth century the State House was redesigned in such a way as to preserve all of its original colonial features, while adding a $600,000 annex to the west. The original colonial building can be recognized by its beautiful architecture, using plaster walls and wooden columns.

In the room now on display as the Old Senate Chamber, George Washington appeared before Congress and resigned his commission as Commander in Chief of the Continental Army. Thomas Jefferson, author of the Declaration of Independence, was there; so were signers Richard Lee, who had offered the resolution that the Declaration be adopted; Samuel Chase, future Justice of the United States Supreme Court; and James Monroe, future President.

Three weeks later in the same room the Treaty of Paris was approved by Congress, thus officially ending the American Revolution. And here, in 1786, the Annapolis Convention issued its call for the gathering which met in Philadelphia the following year to write the American Constitution.

3) U.S.S. CONSTELLATION

The U.S.S. *Constellation*, one of the oldest United States warships, was launched in 1797, under the command of Captain Thomas Truxtun, a former Revolutionary War privateer. Her stirring victories over two French frigates, *L'Insurgente* in 1799 and *La Vengeance* in 1800, earned her the respect of her nation and established her place in history. The *Constellation* also saw action in the War of 1812 and the Civil War. During World War II she was the symbolic relief flagship of the Atlantic Fleet.

Considerably modernized and rebuilt, the *Constellation* now lives in quiet retirement from active duty at the Pratt Street Pier in Baltimore, the city of her origin. She now contains a maritime museum. The restoration process continues.

New Jersey

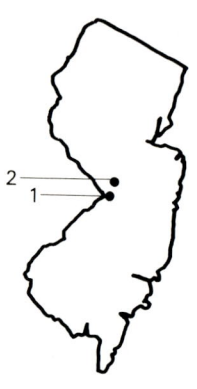

Morven, New Jersey's most historic mansion, has survived the great events of both pre-Revolutionary and post-Revolutionary America.

1) CAPITOL, Trenton

Located on an eight-acre site on State Street in Trenton on the Delaware River, the original portion of the massive New Jersey State Capitol, a plain, bare, rough-cast building, has evolved into a complex structure through numerous additions.

After the front section of the 1792 structure was destroyed by fire in 1885, a new rectangular, Renaissance-style building was finished in 1889.

The Capitol walls are constructed of solid, fireproof, brick masonry, faced with a light-colored stone from Indiana, known as Salem oolitic, with foundations trimmings of New Jersey freestone from the Prallsville quarries in Hunterdon County. The portico, doorhead and trimmings about the door are of the same material. The portico, with balcony, is supported by massive pillars of polished granite and surmounted by the coat of arms of the State.

2) MORVEN MANSION

The story of Morven, New Jersey's historic governor's mansion in Princeton, covers more than two and a half centuries and involves some of the great events of both pre-Revolutionary and post-Revolutionary America.

The earliest section of the house was built in 1701 by Richard Stockton on a tract purchased from William Penn. As the Stockton family grew in wealth and prominence, Morven was enlarged and by the time the American Revolution began, its appearance was much the same as it is today, although the house has burned twice—once by the British during the Revolution and again in 1821.

The owner in residence during the War for Independence was another Richard Stockton, grandson of the builder. It was his wife, Annis Boudinot Stockton, who gave Morven its name, after the home of a legendary Celtic king. Stockton gave up his position as a member of the supreme court of the colony to support the Revolutionary movement and became one of the signers of the Declaration of Independence. During the celebrated Princeton campaign the Stockton family was forced to flee in the face of the British and General Cornwallis seized Morven for use as his personal headquarters.

The house is early Georgian in style, reflecting the influence of Italian Renaissance architecture which became popular in England in the seventeenth century, but it was still radically different from American colonial dwellings, particularly those in a frontierlike settlement.

Although there is some question as to whether present-day Morven resembles the early eighteenth-century dwelling, it would appear that the rooms of the central section of the house have not changed to any appreciable degree. Today's decorations and furniture follow, as closely as possible, those of an eighteenth-century country home.

Down through the years the Stocktons played a prominent role in both state and national affairs and maintained ownership of Morven until it was acquired by Governor Walter E. Edge in 1945, who left it to the state. In 1955 it became designated as the offical executive residence, with tours available at the discretion of the governor.

New York

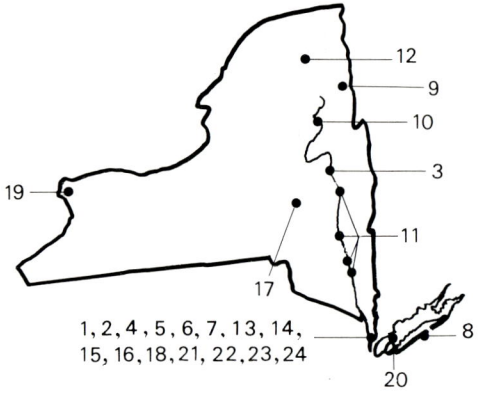

1) AMERICAN MUSEUM OF NATURAL HISTORY

New York City's American Museum of Natural History, founded in 1869, is a fascinating place. Exhibits depicting the origins of man and the wonders of nature run the gamut from the world's largest whale to an amoeba, dinosaur eggs to shrunken heads and coral reefs. Over 200 life-size dioramas showing animals from every continent in their natural surroundings and thousands of other displays are housed in its thirty-five exhibit halls. The entire museum collection includes twenty-three million specimens and artifacts used in the extensive educational and research programs, as well as for the displays prepared for the public.

Of special interest is the recently opened Alexander M. White Natural Science Center, the museum's "urban ecology center." Here, in an exhibit especially designed for city children, the natural and man-made environmental structures of New York City are dramatically and realistically recreated.

The museum complex, including the Hayden Planetarium where realistic "skyshows" are presented, is located on a twenty-three-acre quadrangle known as Roosevelt Square. Although the complex as a whole is an architectural mixture, three of the nineteen interconnected buildings have been declared "New York Landmarks" in a study done by the Municipal Art Society of New York.

2) BRIDGES OF NEW YORK CITY

Manhattan Island, the center of New York City, has been faced throughout its history with the formidable task of maintaining communications with and convenient access to the adjacent boroughs and suburbs on Long Island, Staten Island and the mainland. This need has inspired a number of creative feats of bridge engineering.

In 1868, the need for a bridge across the East River joining downtown Manhattan with Brooklyn on Long Island, meant that a way had to be found to construct a bridge with a far longer span than any yet built. John A. Roebling, a civil engineer who had emigrated from Germany, developed the technique which made the crossing possible, weaving the suspension cables in their final position. Construction of the **Brooklyn Bridge,** once under way, took thirteen years and was marked by much tragedy. One tragedy injured Roebling's foot and he died the following year from the effects. The four cables, each containing 5,700 wires and weighing 900 tons, took twenty-one months to spin. The 6,775-foot-long Brooklyn Bridge held the record as the longest suspension bridge for twenty years.

Construction of a bridge across the much wider Hudson River joining Manhattan with New Jersey presented another great challenge which was finally met in 1931. Masterminded by O. H. Ammann, the **George Washington Bridge,** with a main span of 3,500 feet, more than doubled the previous record for span

Above: *Ocean-going vessels enter New York Harbor beneath the Verrazano-Narrows Bridge, the world's longest suspension span.* Below: *Central Park, a natural recreation area within the crowded city.*

length. Its total length is 4,660 feet. Its four cables are thirty-six inches in diameter and are made up of 26,474 parallel wires. A lower level was opened in 1962 to handle the growing volume of traffic. Eight lanes of traffic can cross on the upper level; six on the lower level.

Across the entrance to New York Harbor, connecting Brooklyn to Staten Island, is the

Verrazano-Narrows Bridge. This monumental structure has a main span of 4,260 feet, the longest suspension span in the world, exceeding that of the Golden Gate by sixty feet. Its total length is 6,690 feet. Another product of Ammann's genius, it is designed to permit the largest ocean-going vessels to enter the port. This bridge, built to be bigger, stronger and

The Empire State Building, the "Queen of the Skyscrapers," was the world's tallest building for forty years.

longer than any other, also was the product of a need, the ever-growing pressures brought on by the age of the automobile in the largest city in the United States. Instead of connecting Manhattan with its close neighbors, the Verrazano-Narrows Bridge makes it possible for motorists to avoid congested New York traffic while traveling along the Atlantic Coast.

3) CAPITOL, Albany

Started shortly after the Civil War, New York's Renaissance and Romanesque State Capitol took thirty years to build and today still ranks as one of the nation's most unusual public buildings. Five stories atop Albany's Capitol Hill, it commands a sweeping view of downtown Albany and the beautiful Hudson River Valley.

Chief among its distinctive features are the superbly finished executive and legislative chambers, swirling staircases and elaborate, carved stonework recreating dramatic moments in the state's history. Busts of famous Americans are sculpted into the Corsehill freestone. This work alone took many years to complete. Curiously included are some unrecognized heads, believed to be friends and relatives of the sculptors.

The building itself is a massive rectangle with the base reminiscent of a medieval fortress. One of the largest staircases in the world, 100 feet wide at the bottom, extends 166 feet eastward from the main building and rises to the main entrance on the second floor.

4) CATHEDRAL OF ST. JOHN THE DIVINE

"The world's largest cathedral," the Cathedral of St. John the Divine is the mother church of the Protestant Episcopal Church's New York Diocese. This magnificent edifice on Amsterdam Avenue near Columbia University can accommodate about 8,600 worshipers at the present time. It is an awesome, inspiring place although nearly one-third of the construction remains to be completed.

The cathedral was incorporated under the Rev. Mr. Horatio Potter, the sixth Bishop of New York, in 1873. Construction of the all-stone structure was finally begun in 1892. When finished the cathedral will be the largest Gothic structure in the world. Cruciform in shape, it is now 601 feet long and will cover an area of 121,000 square feet, stretching 330 feet wide across the transepts. No major work has been done since 1941.

The original design for the cathedral was Transitional Byzantine with overtones of the Romanesque. The awe-inspiring choir and sanctuary were begun along these lines. Beginning in 1911, a second group of architects developed a French Gothic plan, a definitely American adaptation with some features suggesting older European cathedrals. The baptistry, with its vaulted dome and octagonal lantern, is considered the most beautiful in the New World. The font is a copy of the one found in the baptistry of St. John in Siena.

5) CENTRAL PARK

In the mid-nineteenth century, such renowned figures of the day as journalist and poet William Cullen Bryant and authors Washington Irving and George Bancroft spearheaded an effort to preserve and beautify an open space within the growing city of New York. Thanks to their foresight, the nation's largest city possesses a lovely pastoral retreat from the urban press. Central Park is a world within itself, with pleasant paths, wooded and manicured grounds, picturesque lakes and marvelous recreational facilities.

Fire Island is the largest remaining barrier beach off the south coast of Long Island.

The park, covering 840 acres, was officially opened in 1876. The designers, Frederick Law Olmsted and Calvert de Vaux, inspired by the nineteenth-century conception of the landscaped garden, attempted to recapture nature, adding to it and smoothing its contours. Olmsted eloquently expressed this idea:

> A park is a single work of art, and as such subject to the primary law of every work of art, namely, that it shall be framed upon a single, noble motive, to which the design of all its parts, in some more or less subtle way, shall be confluent and helpful.

Central Park today is an outstanding monument to its visionary creators.

6) CLOISTERS

The Cloisters, located in Fort Tryon Park at the northern tip of Manhattan Island, is a branch of the Metropolitan Museum of Art devoted to European medieval art which goes beyond the usual conception of a museum. The building, designed to resemble a medieval fortified monastery, and its natural setting on a hillside overlooking the Hudson River, furnish an eerie sensation of having stepped into the past. The exhibits, lighting and recorded medieval music add to the effect.

The Cloisters takes its name from the fact that the original plans were derived from elements of the cloisters of five French monasteries. Portions of several medieval structures were transplanted here from Europe and rebuilt stone by stone. Yet the museum provides a functional and unobtrusive setting for the museum's outstanding collections. Significant among these are the Unicorn tapestries, a series of nine beautiful Flemish tapestries depicting a unicorn hunt, and the Chalice of Antioch, an intricately wrought cup which supposedly inspired the legend of the Holy Grail.

7) EMPIRE STATE BUILDING

New York City's Empire State Building, its tower soaring regally to a height of 1,472 feet, is located in the heart of Manhattan's business district. For nearly forty years this 102-story "Queen of the Skyscrapers" was the tallest building in the world and she is still a study in superlatives.

From the 102nd-floor observatory, 1,250 feet above the city, the view is magnificent. On clear days the surrounding countryside is visible for a distance of eighty miles in any direction. Ships can be spotted forty miles out to sea.

Some of the vital statistics of the building known as "The World's Most Distinguished Address" present an awesome picture. Slender and graceful in design, the building weighs 360,000 pounds. Sixty thousand tons of steel were used in the structure. Seventy-three high speed elevators are enclosed in seven miles of elevator shaft. For the courageous, 1,860 steps lead from street level to the 102nd floor. Thirty-five hundred miles of telephone and telegraph cables and 18,000 phones meet the communication needs of the 16,000 people who use this business address.

Approximately 35,000 visitors come daily, paying tribute to this historic landmark completed in 1931.

8) FIRE ISLAND NATIONAL SEASHORE

One by one over the thousands of years since their glacial creation, most of the barrier beaches off the south coast of Long Island have been joined with the mainland. The largest remaining beach, Fire Island, is a narrow divider island between land and the stormy Atlantic.

Scenic mansions line the banks of the historic Hudson River.

Here are thirty-two miles of white sandy beaches, wind-twisted pines, grassy wetlands, salt marshes, forests and sand dunes located almost within sight of the man-made towers of Manhattan.

In order to preserve this last isolated, largely unspoiled shoreline in this densely populated region, most of the barrier island, from one-half mile to less than 200 yards wide, became Fire Island National Seashore in 1964. It is an island with a delicately balanced ecology, and the few hundred people who live on it know this and are helping to preserve its appeal.

The sand on Fire Island, composed of fine quartz mixed with red garnet and black magnetite, stretches over the horizon on Great South Beach and extends hundreds of feet towards the island's interior. Holding the sand dunes in place are plant communities essential to the island's life, including beach grass, wild rose and beach plum.

Toward the west end of the seashore is the unusual Sunken Forest, a virgin woods located a little below sea level. Here may be found unusually large serviceberry, birch, blackgum and gnarled American holly trees, some of which are several hundred years old, with ferns and azalea growing beneath them.

On the Atlantic side of the seashore, surf fishermen catch mackerel, weakfish and striped bass, and bluefish, winter flounder and fluke can be found on the bay side. Clams and scallops lie in the waters of the bay.

9) FORT TICONDEROGA

Fort Ticonderoga has been called the "Key to a Continent." Located on a rocky promontory above Lake Champlain, it controlled the all-important water route between colonial New York and Canada. Built by the French in 1755 and named Fort Carillon, it acquired its present name when it was captured and rebuilt by the English in 1759. In 1775 Ethan Allen and his Green Mountain Boys took the fort in a bloodless surprise attack. The following year Benedict Arnold gathered the first American fleet here. The British regained the fort in 1777, burning it to the ground when they retreated the same year. After the Revolution, Ticonderoga was no longer of military importance. It became a stone quarry for returning settlers.

Restored entirely on its original foundation, Fort Ticonderoga today recreates its fascinating past for the visitor. In some places on the outer walls the original masonry is still visible. Fort Ticonderoga contains an outstanding military museum, with collections including interesting memorabilia from the fort and the American colonial period.

Today's authentic restoration is due to the vision and perseverance of several generations of one family. William Ferris Pell purchased the ruins in 1820 and began the process of preservation. His beautiful, low-slung, Doric-columned Greek Revival mansion, the Pavilion, was built on the sweep of land that dips down to Lake Champlain below the fort.

In 1908, his great-grandson Stephen Pell began the restoration and the fort was opened to the public the next year. The Pell mansion has also been beautifully refurbished. A member of the Pell family still heads the Fort Ticonderoga Association.

10) HUDSON RIVER

"We found a pleasant place below steep little hills, in the midst of which flowed into the sea a very big river, which was deep within the mouth." This note sent to Francis I by Giovanni da Verrazano, who had been commissioned by the French king to explore the New World in 1524, marked the beginning of the recorded history of one of the most historic and storied and, unfortunately, most abused rivers of America—the Hudson. (See map, p. 292.)

Hyde Park, overlooking the Hudson River, was the lifetime home of President Franklin Roosevelt.

Starting as a little trout stream on the highest peak in the Adirondacks, the river flows southwest for 100 miles, gathering water from other streams until, at Great Bend in Saratoga County, it turns eastward into its great north-south channel. The Mohawk River, largest of the Hudson's tributaries, makes its contribution south of Great Bend. Three miles below Great Bend the river becomes navigable for the last 150 miles of its journey.

The basalt cliffs of the Palisades, a great stone wall 350 to 550 feet high, lines the western bank of the lower river for twelve miles. From the river's mouth at New York Bay, an immense undersea gorge, with walls two miles high in some places, extends out into the Atlantic for over 150 miles.

The lower half of the Hudson is virtually a huge arm of the sea. Much of it lies below sea level and there are four-and-one-half-foot tides at Albany, 150 miles inland. Salt water extends well upriver, but it lies at the bottom of the river with the lighter fresh water flowing above it.

The history of the Hudson's settlement is a story of romance. The seventeenth-century Dutch patroons, who received large grants of land along the river from the Dutch West India Company, built great fortunes at the expense of those whom they encouraged to emigrate to the region. The Dutch period and the lovely countryside provided the material for the picturesque tales by Washington Irving. During the nineteenth century he was one of many artists to reside along the Hudson. Here the only recognized American "school" of painting developed, the Hudson River School.

During the American Revolution the Hudson was of great strategical importance because the British hoped by capturing it to separate New England from the South. This was the scene of Benedict Arnold's near disastrous treachery. Following the Revolution the Hudson entered an age of prosperity when trade flourished. Robert Fulton's refinements of the steamboat allowed its profitable introduction to the scene.

11) HUDSON RIVER MANSIONS

The Hudson River Valley is one of the most scenic regions of the nation and, since the days when the Dutch first settled the area, it has been the location of many famous homes.

Olana, a Moorish castle near the town of Hudson, was built and furnished by Frederick Edwin Church, landscape artist of the Hudson River School. All of his ability is evident in this thirty-seven room attraction, for the materials used in its construction utilize light in all ways to reflect or silhouette. The house ranks as one of the most sophisticated Victorian creations still extant in three ways—historically, artistically and architecturally. In addition to the artifacts on display from Church's worldwide journeys are many of his realistic landscapes.

The castle with its lavish yet functional furnishings is administered by the State of New York and has been declared a national historical landmark.

Hyde Park, north of Poughkeepsie, was the home of Franklin Delano Roosevelt from the day he was born. The house at the edge of a gently rolling plateau overlooking the Hudson has undergone many alterations since Roosevelt's father purchased it in 1867. The original clapboards were removed and the walls recovered with stucco. The front of the house was completely changed to include a sweeping balustrade and a colonnaded portico. The in-

Olana, the colorful and fanciful home of artist Frederick Church, Hudson River School painter, is near Hudson, New York.

terior remains furnished in a solid, comfortable, old-fashioned way.

The Hyde Park portico is well known to all Americans and to many from foreign lands. It was here that F.D.R. was cheered by his Dutchess County friends on four triumphant election nights. Here he met the King and Queen of England, and later Prime Minister Winston Churchill.

Adjacent to the Roosevelt home is a library and museum which contains many public and private papers of Franklin and Eleanor Roosevelt. Their graves, marked by a plain white marble monument, are on the grounds.

Boscobel is located across from West Point on thirty-six acres of beautiful landscaped grounds. Only a man of extravagant fancy, of well-honed architectural sensibility and a full appreciation for the latest fashions in the decorative arts would have chosen to build such a splendid mansion. States Morris Dyckman was exactly that sort of man.

Boscobel at Garrison is a Neoclassic house built in the Adamesque style, unrivalled in its grace and delicate detailing. States Dyckman never lived to see completed his pedimented mansion with its delicately carved swags surmounting the columned portico, a balustrade framing the roof, tall windows and superbly worked interiors. He died in 1806. But Boscobel, from the Italian *bosco bello* ("beautiful woods"), was destined to wait for more than 150 years before its interiors would be furnished as exquisitely as Dyckman might have wished. The house was moved fifteen miles north to its present location in the mid-1950's through the efforts of Boscobel Restoration Incorporated. Restoration was completed in 1961 and the residence opened to the public.

Van Cortlandt Manor at Croton-on-Hudson is the country seat of a Dutch dynasty. In 1749 Van Cortlandt Manor was transformed from a rudimentary dwelling into a bustling farmhouse home. The lower walls of this house were the frame of a hunting lodge or Indian trading post before 1697.

The restoration of the once sprawling estate has turned back the clock to the era when the household chores and farmwork were carried out by six or seven slaves, by tenants and hired hands. There were apple orchards and a dairy farm to tend, saw and grist mills to oversee, a carpenter's shop, smithy and the ferry operations to maintain.

An early eighteenth-century appearance has been achieved by Sleepy Hollow Restoration, Inc. The task of peeling off the layers of age and decoration applied by Van Cortlandt heirs who lived here through 1941—a remarkably long continuous occupancy of almost 250 years for one family—was eased somewhat by the careful records of changes in interior architecture and the furnishings kept by many family members.

Washington Irving's unique nineteenth-century home **Sunnyside,** now a national historic site, is located at Tarrytown. The house stands on a high bank of the river, but bears little resemblance to the seventeenth-century Dutch cottage which the famed American author purchased in 1835. Looking at it himself after he had made a series of changes, he described it as "a little old-fashioned stone mansion, all made up of gable ends, and as full of angles and corners as an old cocked hat."

Despite his rather facetious description, Sunnyside has a charm all its own. Quiet glens and sheltering groves surround the house. There is also a duck pond, which Irving called his "Little Mediterranean," and a waterfall. Nearby are the service buildings: the woodshed, root cellar and a steepled ice house. Inside the house is much of Irving's furniture and personal library.

The Lincoln Center for the Performing Arts houses the best theater, dance and music. It was completed in 1969.

12) LAKE PLACID SKI AREA

Nestled in the Adirondacks beneath Whiteface Mountain and between Mirror Lake and Lake Placid, picturesque Lake Placid resort area is probably the East's most famous winter sports center. Over twenty miles of cross-country and touring ski trails are to be found in the area. Slalom courses, downhill trails and open slopes are readily available. For big mountain skiing, nearby Whiteface Mountain with the greatest vertical drop in the Eastern United States, offers miles of challenging trails.

Lake Placid has hosted numerous national and international sporting events, including the Kennedy Games, the World University Games and the Winter Olympics. Mount Van Hoevenberg to the southeast is the home of the famous Olympic Bobsled Run. The Olympic Arena in the village offers year-round indoor ice skating.

With the lovely lakes and magnificent mountain scenery, the Lake Placid region is truly a place which provides *re*-creation in every season. Beaches, 150 miles of bridle paths and hiking trails are attractive ways to experience this restful beauty in the warmer months.

13) LINCOLN CENTER FOR THE PERFORMING ARTS

The Lincoln Center for the Performing Arts is a distinctive culture center which provides a home for prominent institutions devoted to theater, music and dance. It is located off Broadway on New York City's west side.

Here on Lincoln Square's fourteen acres, classically inspired buildings surround attractive plazas and parks, developed under an area urban renewal project and administered by the New York City Parks Department. Ground was broken for the center in 1959. The last structure was completed in 1969.

Covered with Italian travertine marble, the buildings which comprise Lincoln Center are functional and modern within, yet each transmits a sense of ancient splendor. Architecturally harmonious, they have in common rectangular floorplans peristyle and flat or terraced roofs. A total of 11,000 spectators can be accommodated in the complex.

Philharmonic Hall, now known as Avery Fisher Hall, the first structure finished in 1962, has a peristyle of forty-four columns, seven stories high. Its concert hall is the home for the New York Philharmonic Orchestra, the oldest orchestra of its kind in America.

Across a central Plaza from Philharmonic Hall is the New York State Theater, used by the

This depiction of baseball in the early days is in the National Baseball Hall of Fame which displays the history of the sport and honors its immortal players.

New York City ballet and opera. The ten-story marble colonnade of the Metropolitan Opera House forms the background of this attractive plaza with its interesting black marble fountains. Replacing the celebrated "Met," the Opera House has a beautifully designed concert hall where the Metropolitan Opera performs.

The renowned Juilliard School of Music and a unique branch of the New York Public Library, the Library and Museum of the Performing Arts, added an outstanding educational dimension to the Lincoln Center complex. Completing this fascinating world of the arts are Vivian Beaumont Theater, home of the New York Shakespeare Festival at Lincoln Center, and Alice Tully Hall, home of the Chamber Music Society of Lincoln Center.

14) METROPOLITAN MUSEUM OF ART

The Metropolitan Museum of Art in New York City provides an awe-inspiring microcosm of the world of art. Art covering 5,000 years, from prehistory to the twentieth century, has been gathered in magnificent collections which include over 2,000 European paintings, 2,500 European drawings, 250,000 prints, 4,000 objects of medieval art, 3,000 American paintings and statues and 4,000 musical instruments. Approximately one-fourth of the collection is displayed in the museum's 234 galleries at a time.

Thoroughly exploring the "great gray lady of upper Fifth Avenue" in Central Park is not a one-day adventure, but selective viewing can provide a fascinating glimpse of man's limitless creativity. The Egyptian collection spans forty centuries with the reconstructed tomb of Per-Neb, a Memphite of the fifth dynasty, and the striking Temple of Dendur, saved from the waters unleashed by the Aswan Dam and contributed by the Egyptian government. Other large collections include outstanding Greek and Roman art and extensive medieval holdings shared with the Cloisters (see New York —6). The painting collection is said to be one of the most comprehensive in the world.

The Metropolitan was founded in 1870 by a group of prominent New Yorkers. Its first permanent home, which still forms part of the present structure, was begun in 1879. The Renaissance facade of gray limestone was finished in 1902. Today's immense Metropolitan is the product of gradual and continuing expansion and renovation.

15) MUSEUM OF MODERN ART

Housed in a pleasant, functional geometric building on 53rd Street is New York City's Museum of Modern Art. The museum was begun in 1929 through the efforts of three New York women, Miss Lillie P. Bliss, Mrs. Cornelius J. Vanderbilt and Mrs. John D. Rockefeller, who were concerned about the attention given to great modern artists. The museum's first exhibit introduced the "Paris School," including such artists as Matisse, Braque and Picasso.

Today the Museum of Modern Art's extensive collections encompass all of the visual arts— painting, sculpture, engraving, architecture, industrial design, interior decoration, photography and the cinema. Some 20,000 art objects represent major trends in modern art since approximately 1875. The collections are drawn from throughout the world, but American art receives the greatest representation. A library of 15,000 books, a collection of 75,000 photographs and a film library complete the extensive resources of the magnificent repository of modern cultural achievement.

16) MUSEUM OF THE AMERICAN INDIAN

America's first citizens left an indelible mark on contemporary life and culture. New York City's Museum of the American Indian contains some of the most extensive collections of Indian artifacts from throughout the Americas and provides an invaluable source of information for laymen and scholars.

The Museum's rotating exhibits provide a visual overview of the cultures of over 250 tribes. Household goods, clothing, arms, magnificent jewelry and ceremonial direct the visitor's imagination to a world which now seems far removed from an urban museum.

Products of North American tribes of prehistoric and historic times are featured on the first two floors. The third floor is devoted to

Indians called Niagara Falls "Thundering Waters." It is a series of falls and rapids in the course of the Niagara River that drops 326 feet. The three major connected falls are American, Horseshoe and Bridal Veil.

Sagamore Hill, President Theodore Roosevelt's home, has been authentically restored. Its Victorian style is a striking contrast to the United Nations Headquarters (opposite).

the cultures of contemporary Central and South American Indians and West Indians, as well as artifacts from the pre-Columbian period.

Located on Broadway at 155th Street, the Museum of the American Indian was founded by Dr. George G. Heye in 1916. It shares an area known as Audubon Square with five other specialized institutes, the American Academy of Arts and Letters, the American Geographic Society, the American Numismatic Society, the Hispanic Society of America and the National Institute of Arts and Letters.

17) NATIONAL BASEBALL HALL OF FAME AND MUSEUM

Cooperstown in upstate New York is baseball's traditional point of origin. It is also the site of the National Baseball Hall of Fame and Museum, dedicated in 1939. Baseball's immortals are enshrined here in an impressive gallery where Vermont black marble columns support a towering twenty-five-foot ceiling. Bronze bas-relief plaques honor each of the Hall of Fame members, telling stories of their achievements.

Preserved in the National Baseball Museum is a vast collection of baseball memorabilia. As a visitor passes through this impressive shrine, the evolution of baseball gradually unfolds. Exhibits include a wide variety of objects, from uniforms, balls, bats and gloves to contracts, trophies, photographs, lockers and stadium seats. The National Baseball Library, completed in 1968, is an extensive repository of baseball history and folklore.

18) NEW YORK STOCK EXCHANGE

In the heart of the Wall Street financial district the Greek-columned New York Stock Exchange building at 20 Broad Street is the home of the nation's largest organized securities market. At the front entrance a tree commemorates the spot at Wall and William streets where twenty-four brokers met under a buttonwood tree to found the predecessor of the present exchange in 1792.

A gallery overlooking the exchange floor allows the visitor to observe firsthand the seemingly chaotic process by which shares in over 1,100 American businesses are bought and sold. The history of the New York Stock Exchange is depicted in the second floor Exhibit Hall, where three-dimensional exhibits recreate the industry at work.

19) NIAGARA FRONTIER STATE PARKS

The Niagara River, actually a strait, flows in a northerly direction for only thirty-four miles connecting Lake Erie to Lake Ontario. Erie, however, is 572 feet above sea level, and Ontario, 246 feet. Niagara Falls is the result of this great drop of 326 feet along the river's course, most of it occurring in a collected series of falls and rapids that has the high falls as the central attraction. Here, at the "Thundering Waters," as the Indians named the spot, fifteen million cubic feet of water a minute plunge down the escarpment. Nearly a mile wide at this point, the falls are divided into two main areas, the American and the Canadian or Horseshoe falls.

The Canadian Falls carries ninety-four percent of the water and has a crest line of 3,010 feet and a drop of 158 feet. The American Falls has a crest line of 1,060 feet, but a drop of 167 feet. While the foot of the American Falls is shallow and rocky, the pool below the Canadian Falls reaches a depth of 160 feet. Between them is Bridal Veil Falls, well known as the site favored by honeymooners.

The State Reservation at Niagara was established in 1885 and is called the first state park in New York. A dozen state parks have since been established in the area, sufficient to accommodate and offer recreational opportunities for the many visitors who come to see the falls, this legend of living water.

20) SAGAMORE HILL

Sagamore Hill in Oyster Bay, Long Island, is exactly the type of house one would associate with President Theodore Roosevelt. The rambling twenty-three-room Victorian dwelling,

even from the outside, is a projection of his personality. Inside, there could be no doubt as to the family who lived there.

Designed by Roosevelt himself and built in the 1880's, the house was named Sagamore Hill for the Indian chief who ceded the land to the first settlers.

The first floor of the house's exterior is brick, the second and third floors are clapboarded. Standing on a site exposed to the strong winds of Long Island Sound, the house is solidly built, with foundations twenty inches thick. Roosevelt's beloved and spacious piazza looks out from the south and west sides of the house over Oyster Bay Harbor.

Among the rooms on the first floor is the Trophy Room, or North Room, which was added in 1904-05 when Roosevelt felt the need to expand in order to accommodate the many visitors to the summer White House. It is a momentous room, thirty feet wide and forty feet long, both impressive and personal, ornamented with columns of Philippine mahogany and stuffed with treasures.

In 1950 the house and eighty-three acres of land were purchased by the Roosevelt Memorial Association and donated to the Federal Government by authority of Congress on July 12, 1962. The house is completely restored as authentically as possible, with the help of relatives' memory and actual documents, to its peak Victorian comfort. (See also **Theodore Roosevelt National Memorial Park,** North Dakota—2.)

21) ST. PATRICK'S CATHEDRAL

St. Patrick's, the monumental Roman Catholic cathedral of New York, is dedicated to the patron saint of the Irish, so heavily represented in New York City's population. The white marble and stone edifice, patterned after the Gothic cathedral at Cologne, seats some 2,200 people, making it one of the largest churches in the United States. Its twin spires rise over 330 feet.

Opening into the nave are three portals with beautifully sculptured bronze doors. The nave is lighted by Gothic-style, stained-glass windows, with unusually intense blue shades. The cross-ribbed Gothic arches which soar 110 feet above the nave are supported by thirty-foot pillars.

At the time St. Patrick's was begun in 1858 worshipers complained that its location on 5th Avenue at 50th Street was too far out of town. Today, because of the city's northward expansion, the cathedral is in the heart of midtown Manhattan.

Since 1886, the Statue of Liberty has been a symbol of new hope and freedom for millions of immigrants.

22) STATUE OF LIBERTY NATIONAL MONUMENT

Standing majestically at the entrance of New York Harbor, the Statue of Liberty with her famous torch has been a symbol of new hope and freedom for millions of immigrants. Presented to the United States by France to commemorate the alliance between the two countries during the American Revolution, the great lady was formally unveiled and dedicated in 1886. This was the culmination of a joint French and American project proposed by historian Edward de Laboulaye in 1865.

The statue was sculpted in France by Frederick Auguste Bartholdi and transported to the United States in its component parts to be reassembled on Bedloe's Island, now Liberty Island. Measuring 151 feet high, the Statue of Liberty stands on a 156-foot American-built pedestal. An observation platform in the crown provides a panoramic view of the harbor.

This inspiring international symbol was made a national monument in 1926. The American Museum of Immigration is located appropriately at the base. Nearby Ellis Island, for years the clearinghouse for immigrants to the United States, was added in 1965.

23) TRINITY CHURCH

Trinity Church on Broadway at the beginning of Wall Street was the highest building in New York City for nearly fifty years. Today, though this venerable Episcopal Church, the first parish in the city, is dwarfed by surrounding skyscrapers, its stately beauty remains undiminished.

The original structure, completed in 1697, resembled a country chapel with a spire and narrow, spear-shaped windows. King College occupied a schoolhouse behind the church in 1754. Fire destroyed the first church building in 1776.

The present Trinity Church structure was finished in 1846. At that time its 180-foot bell tower soared majestically above the surrounding houses.

In the cemetery behind Trinity Church are the graves of many famous New Yorkers, including Robert Fulton and Alexander Hamilton.

24) UNITED NATIONS HEADQUARTERS

United Nations Headquarters, situated in the heart of New York City, is a striking symbol of the ideals of world peace and human progress conceived by the founding nations in 1945. The imposing Secretariat Building, domed General Assembly Building, Conference Building and Hammarskjold Library were planned and decorated by leading architects and artists from around the world. Flags representing all 135 member nations are displayed in alphabetical order at precisely the same height to illustrate their equality.

This complex, the permanent home of the United Nations since 1950, forms a microcosm of the world. Delegates and staff members hail from every corner of the globe, each making a unique cultural contribution to this self-contained world. Five languages are used here — Chinese, English, French, Russian and Spanish — and simultaneous translations of all proceedings are available through earphones in the visitors' galleries.

Pennsylvania

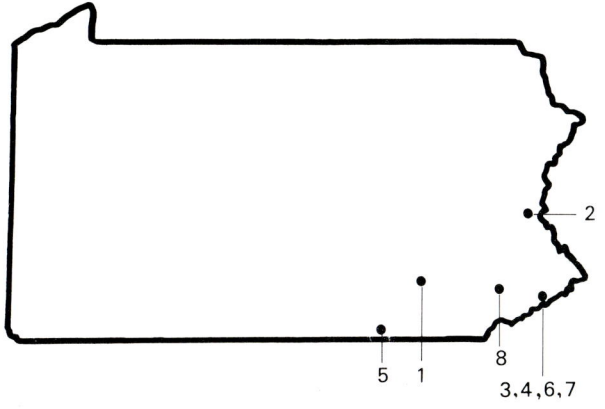

1) CAPITOL, Harrisburg

The dome of Pennsylvania's Italian Renaissance State Capitol is reminiscent of St. Peter's in Rome. The bronze statue at its peak represents the Commonwealth, but is nicknamed "Miss Penn" after William Penn's family.

Completed in 1906, the building's exterior is of Vermont granite. Flanking the main entrance are two statuary groups by Pennsylvania-born George Gray Barnard. One represents man's spiritual burden, while the other depicts humanity advancing through work and brotherhood.

Around the immense Rotunda are Penn's words:

There may be room for such a holy experiment. For the nations want a precedent. And my God will make it the seed of a nation. That an example may be set to the nations. That we may do the thing which is truly wise and just.

Paintings by noted native artists, illustrating significant influences on the state's history, decorate major areas of the Capitol. Carvings along the corridors represent some of the state's most outstanding persons of different national origins.

2) CENTRAL MORAVIAN CHURCH AND OLD MORAVIAN CHAPEL

Bethlehem, Pennsylvania, founded by a small group of Moravian immigrants from Bohemia and Saxony, was given its name on Christmas Eve, 1741.

In 1751 the community, then numbering over 200, constructed what is today called the Old Chapel as a unit in a row of buildings. Construction of this thick-walled, two-story addition took only three months and four days, an amazing achievement in that time.

Originally the Old Chapel had no door leading directly to the outside. Doorways connected the church auditorium with two older buildings which supplied parts of its walls, the Bell House and the *Gemeinhaus* (community house). The present north end of the chapel and vestibule were added in 1865.

Still used by the Moravian congregation for small services, its simple and dignified beauty keeps the Old Chapel in great demand as a site for weddings.

Bethlehem's Central Moravian Church was completed in 1806, replacing the Old Chapel as the site of community worship services. Built to seat 1,500 people at a time when the total population of Bethlehem was 580, it was probably the largest church building in Pennsylvania. This venerable church is still in use today and is considered the seat of the Moravian Church in America.

3) CHRIST CHURCH

Philadelphia's Christ Church on Second Street between Market and Arch streets, founded in 1695, played a memorable role in the birth of the nation. Of the members of the Continental Congress and the signers of the Declaration of Independence, two-thirds worshiped

Gettysburg was the site of one of the decisive battles of the Civil War. Today, the area is preserved in a national military park.

Celebrations complete with fireworks are held each Fourth of July at historic Independence Hall where the Declaration of Independence was signed July 4, 1776.

in this historic church and numerous messages of inspiration to the patriots were delivered from its pulpit.

Seven signers of the Declaration of Independence are buried in the churchyard and the nearby Christ Church Burial Grounds. Of these, by far the most famous is Benjamin Franklin, his grave marked, according to his wishes, by a plain marble slab.

The present church building, begun in 1727, is an early Georgian-style structure designed by vestryman Dr. John Kearsley, who was also one of the architects for nearby Independence Hall. This edifice has survived more than two centuries without significant alteration. The church tower and 200-foot-high steeple were financed in part by lotteries which Benjamin Franklin helped organize.

Old Christ Church is still an active Episcopalian parish. Although the church has been designated by Congress as a national historical shrine, it neither seeks nor accepts government support, relying on private contributions to preserve its historic structure.

4) FRANKLIN INSTITUTE

The Franklin Institute Science Museum and Planetarium in Philadelphia is an intriguing place. Young and old can explore familiar and unfamiliar aspects of the world around them in a realistic multidimensional setting. In the museum, such action exhibits as "Patterns—A New Look at Math" and "Energy" dramatically reproduce the processes of science and technology. Demonstration programs are given throughout the day from carts which are moved through the museum's halls.

The Planetarium provides fascinating, up-to-date tours of outer space. Its traditional Christmas show is a beautiful annual spectacle.

Benjamin Franklin National Memorial, the only privately maintained national memorial in the United States, is also found within the museum building. This shrine contains James Earle Fraser's great statue of the statesman and inventor for whom the Institute was named.

5) GETTYSBURG NATIONAL MILITARY PARK

On July 1, 2 and 3, 1863, the most decisive battle of the Civil War was fought at Gettysburg. Here, on twenty-five square miles of ground, 97,000 men of the Federal Army of the Potomac met 75,000 men of the Confederate Army of Northern Virginia under General Robert E. Lee. In one of the bloodiest battles in history, Lee's army was defeated.

On November 19, 1863, President Abraham Lincoln delivered his famous "Gettysburg Address" at the dedication of the Soldier's National Cemetery on the battlefield where a total of 51,000 soldiers lost their lives. The cemetery contains the graves of 3,706 Civil War casualties.

Gettysburg National Military Park encompasses 3,200 acres and the cemetery covers seventeen acres. Tours of the battlefield take the visitor past monuments and historical markers tell the story of the epic battle which turned the tide of the War between the States.

The Gettysburg Cyclorama in the Visitors' Center depicts Pickett's Charge, the "High Water Mark of the Confederacy," in a dramatic painting, 356 feet in circumference and twenty-six feet high.

6) INDEPENDENCE NATIONAL HISTORICAL PARK

Many of the great events which led to the birth of this nation took place in and around Philadelphia's Independence Square. The nucleus of Independence National Historic Site is a four-block area extending from Second Street to Sixth Street between Walnut and Chestnut streets. Such historic structures as Independence Hall, site of the signing of the Declaration

The house at Valley Forge where Washington headquartered during the winter of 1777–78 has been preserved with the reconstructed quarters of his Continental army.

of Independence and home of the Liberty Bell; Congress Hall, where the United States Congress met from 1790 to 1800; the First Bank of the United States; Old City Hall, used by the Supreme Court from 1791 to 1800; and Carpenters' Hall, meeting place of the First Continental Congress and longest continually operated guild hall in the nation, have been carefully restored to preserve the milieu in which so much of our history was written.

After the American Revolution, Congress met in various towns and cities, but Philadelphia remained the principal city of the nation under the Articles of Confederation. Thus, beginning on May 25, 1787, the Federal Constitutional Convention met in Independence Hall with George Washington as Convention President. Four months later the Founding Fathers (except for Thomas Jefferson who was minister to France and John Adams who was minister to England) produced the U.S. Constitution. On September 17 it was signed by 39 of the 55 delegates who had participated from twelve states (Rhode Island was not represented), and all but three then present. It was submitted to the Congress which was in session in New York. Congress voted to submit it to the conventions of the states for ratification.

7) PHILADELPHIA MUSEUM OF ART

One of the five largest art museums in the country, the Philadelphia Museum of Art is a massive building covering ten acres and echoing the style of a Greek temple. The Minnesota dolomite structure dominates one end of the Benjamin Franklin Parkway.

Half a million art objects are displayed in over 200 galleries in the two main floors of the building. From its beginnings as the 1876 Centennial Exposition's art gallery, to its next designation as the Pennsylvania Museum, dedicated to the development of "art industries" in the state, the museum broadened its emphasis on the industrial arts to include the fine and decorative.

The present building was completed in the 1920's under the directorship of Fiske Kimball. To him is credited the innovative method of display throughout the upper story. In order to "enable the visitor to retrace the great historic pageant of the evolution of art," Kimball arranged galleries in historic order, including in them paintings, sculpture, furniture, and other objects of the time.

The artifacts date from the Christian era to today. Extraordinary collections are numerous: remarkable paintings by Philadelphian Thomas Eakins; the Arensberg Collection of pre-Columbian sculpture and early twentieth-century artists, including Duchamp, Picasso and Klee; the Joseph Lees Williams Memorial Collection of Oriental carpets; the Stern collection of paintings and sculpture.

A few minutes walk down the parkway is the Rodin Museum which houses the largest collection of the French sculptor's work outside Paris.

8) VALLEY FORGE STATE PARK

One of the most famous shrines of American patriotism, Valley Forge State Park preserves on 2,000 acres the site of the quarters for Washington's Continental forces during the winter of 1777-78. Although a relatively mild winter, an estimated 3,000 men out of 10,000 died here or in hospitals to which they were taken. Despite this, it was here that the losers of earlier campaigns were transformed into the victors of Monmouth and Yorktown (see **Jamestown and Yorktown,** Virginia—10).

The reason for this transformation was the military reforms Washington brought about because Congress finally accepted his recommendations on military matters. He was able to strengthen the officer corps, obtain more recruits and improve army administration. As quartermaster, General Nathanael Greene straightened out the supply chaos, and "Baron" von Steuben, a Prussian drillmaster, gave the men the professional training they needed.

Reconstructed huts, the remains of forts and earthworks and the house that Washington used as his headquarters are preserved in the park today, along with Washington's field tent on display in the museum. An observation tower provides a view of the entire site.

Virginia

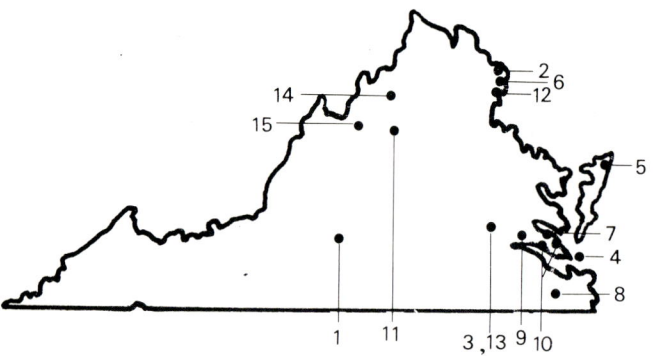

The Virginia State Capitol in Richmond, once the Capitol of the Confederacy, was designed by Thomas Jefferson.

1) APPOMATTOX COURT HOUSE NATIONAL HISTORICAL PARK

The end finally came to America's tragic Civil War in the small village of Appomattox Court House, three miles northeast of the town of Appomattox, when General Robert E. Lee agreed to surrender the remnants of the Confederate Army of Northern Virginia to Union General Ulysses S. Grant on April 9, 1865. Confederate soldiers entered the village on April 12 and laid down their arms, four years to the day after the firing of the first shots at Fort Sumter.

Today on a 970-acre park the village has been restored to appear much as it did in 1865. The McLean House where Lee and Grant met was dismantled in 1893 when speculators made an abortive attempt to move it to Washington, D.C. The present structure is a complete reconstruction. The reconstructed courthouse contains a museum and visitor center. Memorial markers indicate the locations of Lee's and Grant's headquarters, the site of the last shots fired by Confederate forces, and the place where their arms were finally surrendered.

2) ARLINGTON NATIONAL CEMETERY

Arlington National Cemetery is a solemnly beautiful and impressive place. Row upon row of simple white headstones contrast sharply with imposing monuments marking graves of officers.

The cemetery was established in 1864 when the estate of Confederate General Robert E. Lee was seized by the Federal Government. Since that time many famous persons from all walks of life have been interred in this most renowned of all national cemeteries. Here, directly across the Potomac from Washington, lie Oliver Wendell Holmes, William Jennings Bryan and John Foster Dulles along with General John J. Pershing, Rear Admiral Richard E. Byrd and General George C. Marshall.

President John F. Kennedy's grave is marked by an eternal flame and excerpts from his most memorable speeches are engraved on a horizontal slab. His brother Robert F. Kennedy lies a short distance away.

The starkly simple Tomb of the Unknown Soldier is a moving memorial to the nation's war dead. Created from one of the largest blocks of marble ever quarried, weighing seventy tons before carving, it contains the body of an unknown American brought from France after World War I. In 1958 the remains of unknown soldiers from World War II and the Korean War were placed in crypts at the head of the tomb.

The stately Custis-Lee Mansion, known as Arlington House, has been restored, with many original pieces belonging to members of the Custis and Lee families returned. The home's grand portico faces the Potomac and affords a marvelous view of Washington. It was here that young Robert E. Lee wooed and won Mary Ann Randolph Custis, granddaughter of Martha Washington. The Lee family resided at Arlington House for about thirty years.

3) CAPITOL, Richmond

The aristocratic Virginia State Capitol at Richmond, once the capital city of the Confederacy, was designed by Thomas Jefferson, with the aid of French architect Charles Clérisseau. Plans for the structure were based on the Maison Carrée at Nîmes, which Jefferson called "one of the most beautiful, if not the most beautiful morsel of architecture left us by antiquity." The cornerstone was laid in 1785.

The old hall of the House of Delegates was the scene of many historic events. Here, in 1807, Chief Justice John Marshall presided over the trial of Aaron Burr for treason. Various constitutional conventions were held here, and on April 23, 1861, Robert E. Lee was appointed commander of the armed forces of Virginia. Nine years later a spectacular disaster occurred when the floors of the Supreme Court of Appeals, located on the story above, collapsed. Hundreds of people had crowded into the courtroom to hear arguments as to who was the rightful mayor of Richmond, and the weight of the spectators caused the tragedy which killed 62 persons and injured 251 others.

Through the years additions and various modern improvements have been made. The old chamber of the House of Delegates has been restored and contains numerous statues and busts, including those of all eight Virginia-born presidents and Jefferson Davis.

4) CHESAPEAKE BAY BRIDGE-TUNNEL

The Chesapeake Bay Bridge-Tunnel, completed in 1964, formed the final link in the coastal highway system extending from Canada to Key West, Florida. The longest vehicular crossing in the world, the complex seventeen-and-a-half-mile route connects the Virginia Tidewater region (Norfolk) with the rural Delmarva Peninsula.

This structure represents a monumental achievement because it stands firmly in the rough waters of Chesapeake Bay which is affected by the fierce winds and powerful tides of the Atlantic Ocean. Four man-made islands were required to provide portals and bridge connections for the two mile-long tunnels which were built above ground, then sunk to allow traffic to pass beneath the major shipping lanes. A floating island (actually a 70-foot-by-150-foot barge) was created as a support from which to drive the piles used to support the twelve-mile trestle highway. Two high-level bridges are located near the north end of the system.

5) CHINCOTEAGUE NATIONAL WILDLIFE REFUGE

See **Assateague Island National Seashore,** Maryland—1.

6) CHRIST CHURCH

Christ Church, located at Columbus, Cameron and Washington streets in Alexandria, was built between 1767 and 1773. Constructed of native brick with stone trimmings from a quarry south of Alexandria, the Protestant Episcopal building was patterned after the traditional English country church. Designer James Wren, reputedly a relative of the famed Sir Christopher Wren, also lettered the beautiful tablets still in place on either side of the pulpit.

This venerable church building remains much as it was when George Washington purchased pew sixty for thirty-six pounds, ten shillings. Washington regularly attended services here and his family Bible is a treasured possession of the church.

Robert E. Lee also considered this his home church. Here he was confirmed in 1853. Following morning worship services on Sunday, April 21, 1861, Lee, who had just resigned his United States Army commission, was offered command of the Army of Virginia.

7) COLONIAL WILLIAMSBURG

Colonial Williamsburg is an outstanding restoration where a visitor may return in spirit to a time and place crucial in the growth of America. The theme of this well-documented project is "that the future may learn from the past."

From 1699 until 1780, Williamsburg was capital of the Virginia Colony and an influential political and cultural center. Here, Patrick Henry delivered his famous "Caesar-Brutus" speech and his fiery resolutions protesting the Stamp Act. The May 15, 1776, Resolution for Independence, the direct precursor of the fateful July 4 decision, was framed in Williamsburg.

Running a mile from the Capitol on the east to the Wren Building of the College of William and Mary (the second oldest institution of higher learning in America) on the west, the historic area covers 173 acres. Preserved in or near this area are more than eighty structures from the eighteenth and early nineteenth centuries. Others have been carefully rebuilt on their original sites. Lovely colonial gardens complete the setting.

In Colonial Williamsburg, Virginia's Governor's Palace (above) and Capitol (below) are well restored.

Shirley is the ancestral home of Robert E. Lee. The unique style of the house lends itself to an atmosphere of warmth and hospitality that was characteristic of the South.

In the thirty homes, shops and public buildings which are open to the public are some 211 authentic period rooms which provide insights into a variety of colonial life-styles, from the humble to the elegant. Informed hostesses are on hand to describe the history of the buildings and their inhabitants.

In twenty craft shops, costumed artisans skillfully practice their trades much as craftsmen did 200 years ago. Many of these trades are nearly extinct, making their practitioners rare, valuable people in this age of mass production.

Also of interest is nearby Carter's Grove, a mansion once described as "the most beautiful house in America." The plantation home was built by Carter Burwell in 1750-53 on the estate once owned by his grandfather, Robert "King" Carter. It remained in the Burwell family for nearly a century.

8) DISMAL SWAMP

A vast expanse of swampland, straddling the Virginia-North Carolina state line southwest of Norfolk, Dismal Swamp is the northernmost of America's great Southern swamps. Dismal once covered 1.4 million acres, but man, since 1763 when George Washington organized the "Ad-

Mount Vernon, the exquisite home of George Washington, stands today little changed from the way its owner-designer left it.

venturers for Draining the Great Dismal Swamp," has attacked the region with ditches and canals, reducing its size by two-thirds.

George Washington called this eerie world "a glorious paradise" for wildlife. Dismal still provides a home for the large black bear, deer and wildcat. A surprising variety of bird, fish and animal life has been cataloged, contradicting the assessment of early explorer Colonel William Byrd II, who characterized the swamp as a "horrible desert" where "nor indeed do any birds care to fly over it ... for fear of the noisome exhalations that rise from this vast body of dirt and nastiness."

Dismal is unique among swamps. Its land slopes gently outward from Lake Drummond, a shallow, nearly circular body of water. Thick peat beds slow the drainage of water from the lake and a clay floor holds water on the surface.

While other Southern swamp areas include forests, marshes and prairies, Dismal is totally forested. Yet this forest growth is anything but homogenous. In the wetter Dark Swamp, bald cypress, gum and red maple predominate. The drier Light Swamp supports juniper, pine and mixed hardwoods. Much of the region has been cut over and the second-growth forests have allowed more light to penetrate, thus permitting more ground vegetation.

Numerous legends have grown up around the eerie lights commonly seen at night. These strange lights are caused by foxfire (a light given off by the decaying of wood by certain fungi), burning methane gas escaping from decomposing vegetation, or slow-burning peat.

In 1973 the Union Camp Corporation, a major forest-products company, donated its entire 50,000-acre holdings in the Virginia section of Dismal Swamp, including Lake Drummond, to the Nature Conservancy. This nonprofit organization in turn gave the land to the U.S. Department of the Interior for preservation as a wildlife refuge. Thus this unique wilderness area which seemed destined for oblivion under private ownership has received a new lease on life.

9) JAMES RIVER MANSIONS

The mansions along Virginia's James River provide a glimpse into the life-style of the South's early plantation society. Many outstanding Americans trace their origins to this prosperous and romantic world. Just west of Charles City are three exemplary mansions.

Berkeley is a plantation that is by origin, incident and association as well as architecture, the stuff of history. The beautifully balanced brick mansion was built by Benjamin Harrison IV in 1726 on a slight elevation nearly a quarter of a mile back from the river. The house was made with three-foot-thick walls, hand-hewn heart pine floors and a full brick basement to serve as a wine cellar.

Two and a half stories high, Berkeley's pediment roof, said to be Virginia's first, was a significant utilitarian advance over the hip type because it provided useful end rooms in the attic without dormers (although Berkeley has three dormers on each of the fronts) and ventilation where it was needed.

Benjamin Harrison V, who signed the Declaration of Independence, had the honor of reading its preamble before Congress. His son William was the ninth President of the United States. William Henry Harrison wrote his inaugural address at Berkeley in the room where he was born. His grandson was Benjamin Harrison, the twenty-third President of the United States.

During the Civil War, Berkeley became a camping ground for General McClellan and over 100,000 Union troops, after they withdrew from Malvern Hill. It was during this period in 1862 that General Daniel Butterfield composed the world-famous bugle call, "Taps."

William Byrd II was one of the most literate and elegant characters in the history of the Virginia colony, and one of the most refreshing diary-keepers of any time. His home, **Westover,** is regarded as a great piece of Georgian architecture, a beautifully proportioned house that gives the onlooker the feeling of "its growing from its low meadow by the river." It sits on a large, level bluff behind a row of tulip poplars.

Built in the early 1700's, the facade of Westover facing the river is the most impressive one along the James. The dominant element is the central section's elaborate doorway at the top of gray stone pyramid steps. It is framed by detailed composite pilasters supporting a broken ogee pediment with pineapple finial.

The approach to the house from the land, or north, side is made through a pair of splendid wrought-iron gates beneath a scrolled overthrow with the initials of William Byrd interwoven in its intricate design and hung from ten-foot brick piers, each surmounted by a magnificent lead falcon perched on a ball. No such

The "White House" of the South, now a museum, was the home of Jefferson Davis while he was President of the Confederacy.

entrance gates are known to exist anywhere else in America.

Shirley, the ancestral home of General Robert E. Lee, is an impressive mansion close by the river, extraordinary even in comparison with other Virginia plantation houses. Here, Lee's mother, Anne Carter Hill, married the colorful "Light Horse Harry" Lee.

The house was completed by 1769 or 1770, although the date of the present two-story porches on the two fronts is 1831. Approaching the house from the drive on the east, the visitor passes through the forecourt with its four symmetrical dependencies. Beyond, partially hidden by the great ancient trees, is the mansion standing three stories high, its unusually steep roof containing four dormers along each side and five on each front and topped, quite appropriately, with a large pineapple finial symbolizing hospitality.

The mood of the house, both inside and outside, is one of warmth and conviviality. Shirley's record of friendships, entertainments and agricultural enterprise is a record in microcosm of the manners and mores of the affluent South. The home today remains the property of the ninth generation of the Carter family.

10) JAMESTOWN and YORKTOWN

Jamestown, founded on May 13, 1607, was the first permanent English settlement in North America. On that day, three small ships, the *Susan Constant,* the *Godspeed* and the *Discovery,* landed with over 100 settlers on an island in the James River.

The island was unsafe and unhealthy, located in mosquito-infested swamps with no reliable water supply. Because of disease, starvation and hostile Indians only forty colonists survived into December. New settlers then began to arrive, including, in the fall of 1608, the first two women and "eight Dutchmen and Poles" skilled in making pitch and tar, potash and soap ashes and glass, thus creating some of the first industries in the New World.

Initially there was dissension among the designated leaders, but then a real leader, Captain John Smith, came to the fore. He learned to speak Algonkian and was able to bargain with the Indians for their corn. Smith was injured, returned to England, and his departure was followed by the terrible winter of 1609-10, which only sixty of the 500 colonists survived. The remnant was starting for England in June when they met the new governor, Lord Delawarr (Delaware) at the mouth of the James. He had provisions so they returned to the settlement. For thirteen years, stockaded James Fort, built close on the river, was the lone English toehold on the Atlantic seaboard. It grew into "James City," for ninety-two years the capital of Virginia, until Williamsburg replaced it.

The cultivation of tobacco, begun by John Rolfe in 1612, gave the colony new economic life, and two years later in Jamestown Rolfe married Pocahontas, daughter of Chief Powhatan. In 1619 the first legislative assembly in America was held in the Epsicopal Church in Jamestown, and slavery was introduced when a few Africans were brought in. In 1640 the first brick house on the continent was erected.

Today Jamestown's site is part of **Colonial National Historical Park,** which also includes **Yorktown Battlefield,** where the Revolutionary War ended, and Cape Henry Memorial at the entrance to Chesapeake Bay. The only structure remaining in Jamestown from the seventeenth century is the ruined brick tower of the Episcopal Church, which probably dates from 1676-84. In the Jamestown Glasshouse, a conjectural reconstruction with thatched roof, craftsmen demonstrate colonial methods of blowing glass. A number of foundations has also been uncovered. Adjacent to the historical park is Jamestown Festival Park which contains, afloat in the river, full-scale copies of the three vessels that brought the first settlers to Jamestown.

On August 1, 1781, during the American Revolution, General Cornwallis and his British army of over 7,000 men arrived in Yorktown. For two months they had been chasing the smaller Continental force under General Lafayette. But after Lafayette was reinforced by Anthony Wayne and von Steuben in June, Cornwallis decided to establish a base at Yorktown so he could maintain communication by sea with other British forces. French Admiral de Grasse's fleet, however, blockaded the sea routes to Yorktown, and after a British attempt in September to break the blockade failed, de Grasse brought an American-French army under Washington and Rochambeau to nearby Williamsburg and the siege of Yorktown began. Since the Allied army now totaled well over 16,000 men, the fate of Cornwallis' army was sealed and he surrendered on October 18, thus ending the last great military engagement of the Revolution.

Today several of the earthworks from the siege have been expertly preserved, while others have been reconstructed. Along the twisting siege line points of interest are indicated and

A frontier cabin nestles in Shenandoah National Park.

old cannons are in place, some of them fired at Yorktown. On display are military tents used by Washington and a full-scale reconstruction of a section of the gun deck and captain's cabin of a British frigate sunk during the siege. Preserved also are Moore House, where the terms of surrender were drawn, and several historic structures in the old town.

11) MONTICELLO

Monticello is like no other home in America, so well does it express the character of its designer and builder. Thomas Jefferson was one of the first great American architects and he exercised a great influence on the designs for public and private buildings in the Classical Revival style. The great statesman candidly admitted "architecture is my delight, and putting up and pulling down, one of my favorite amusements." From early manhood until his death at eighty-three, Jefferson was engaged in building and improving Monticello.

Although a three-story building, Monticello was designed to appear as a one-story structure. There are thirty-five rooms including twelve in the basement. The dominating feature is the dome which commands the garden or west front. The dome was the first erected over an American house. The room under the dome, octagonal in shape, is often referred to as the ballroom; however, Jefferson always referred to it as the sky or dome room.

Though the house and grounds were sold for financial reasons shortly after Jefferson's death on July 4, 1826, Monticello can be seen today much as it was when Jefferson retired to enjoy the last years of his life there among his family and his gardens. In 1923 the house and about 683 acres were purchased by the Thomas Jefferson Memorial Foundation whose purpose is to preserve the house and restore the gardens as they were in Jefferson's day. The gardens on the east and west lawns of Monticello, neglected for many years, were restored in 1939-40.

Jefferson also designed the buildings at the University of Virginia in Charlottesville—often called the most beautiful campus in the country.

12) MOUNT VERNON

"No estate in United America is more pleasantly situated than this. It lies in a high, dry and healthy country 300 miles by water from the sea."

Thus George Washington described the estate of Mount Vernon in a letter to an English correspondent. Time and circumstance have done little to change the Mount Vernon he loved. It stands as a monument to the builder, "pleasantly situated" on a commanding eminence overlooking the Potomac and the low Maryland hills on the opposite shore.

Mount Vernon is an outstanding example of colonial architecture. It is unique in many ways and owes its charm more to harmony of composition than to the beauty of its component parts. Washington had access to eighteenth-century English books on the design of country houses; the Palladian window and other details of the house, interior and exterior, were copied or derived from one or more of these books.

The most striking architectural feature of the mansion is the high-columned piazza, extending the full length of the house. It seems to be a complete innovation, and would, in itself, entitle Washington to distinction among architects.

In Washington's day, the Mount Vernon estate of over 8,000 acres was divided into five farms, each a complete unit, with its overseer, workers, livestock, equipment and buildings. Washington was one of the most progressive farmers of his day, despite the major diversions created by his public service.

During the half century following Washington's death in 1799, Mount Vernon's owners were unable to maintain its buildings and grounds. Neither the State of Virginia nor the Federal Government expressed an interest in the property. But in 1853, just as it looked as if the estate might crumble into ruins, a woman from South Carolina, Ann Pamela Cunningham, became interested in its preservation and devoted the next twenty-one years of her life to the project. To her and the Mount Vernon Ladies' Association, which maintains it today, is due the credit for saving Washington's home.

This organization has refurnished the house with period pieces; but year after year, through bequest, purchase and donation, the furnishings that were at Mount Vernon in the time of Washington are being acquired.

13) MUSEUM OF THE CONFEDERACY

An angular white-stuccoed brick house at 12th and Clay streets in Richmond, now known as the Museum of the Confederacy, was the home of Jefferson Davis and his family during the years he served as President of the Confederacy and was the South's "White House."

The house, designed by Robert Mills, was begun by Dr. John Brockenbrough in 1818. At that time it was just two stories high; the front and rear porches were adorned with Ionic and Doric columns, respectively, and a parapet encompassed the extensive flat roof. During the mid-1850's, however, the building was "Victorianized." A third story was added, above which a small louvered cupola was installed, and the parapet around the front portion of the house was eliminated.

After the fall of Richmond, troops of the Union armies occupied the house for five years. Then for twenty years the mansion served as a schoolhouse before it was acquired by the Confederate Memorial Literary Society, which has restored several of the rooms so that they appear as they might have during the occupancy of the Davises. Among their personal possessions are a pair of Dresden vases, a glass wine cooler and some decanters, and a berry bowl and silver egg boiler. Since 1893 it has also been a museum of Civil War relics.

14) SHENANDOAH NATIONAL PARK

Shenandoah National Park, cradled against the breast of gentle mountains grown mellow with the age of the Eastern half of our continent, spreads in a generous north-south sweep down northwestern Virginia, encompassing great but not unconquerable mountains and brooks running in a grandfatherly way through the coolness of stately trees. Authorized in 1935, the park covers over 193,000 acres of prime Appalachian Mountain scenery.

Many who see Shenandoah travel Skyline Drive, a winding, 105-mile road on the crest of the Blue Ridge, offering seventy-five parking overlooks of the valleys and mountain slopes. Often visitors stop to walk some of the 200 miles of foot trails. Ninety miles of the long Appalachian Trail lies in Shenandoah.

Walking is the best way to enjoy the subtle pleasures of the park, such as seeing water shift its course to the other side of a rock, or feeling beneath one's feet the crunch of the brown, leaf-strewn floor of the forest.

The Shenandoah Valley was recognized as the Confederacy's "breadbasket" and the back door to the nation's capital during the Civil War. In Brown's Gap are earthworks believed to have been built by Confederate forces when they occupied the pass.

The **Blue Ridge Parkway,** separately administered but actually an extension of Shenandoah and Great Smoky Mountains national parks, winds slowly for 659 miles from its lowest elevation crossing the James River in Virginia upward to its highest point of more than 6,000 feet in the Balsam range south of Asheville, North Carolina. From it one can see the rolling hills of the Virginia Piedmont, across the fertile fields of the Great Valley, to the Alleghenies and then onward to the Black Mountains and the Great Smokies. (See also **Appalachian Trail,** Maine—3 and **Great Smoky Mountains National Park,** North Carolina—4.)

15) WOODROW WILSON HOME

Woodrow Wilson was born in 1856 in a stately white Presbyterian manse. The house in Staunton where his father, the Reverend Mr. Joseph Ruggles Wilson, prayed five times daily and led his family in hymns at night has been turned into a museum which reflects very specifically the main interests of the Wilsons.

The restoration of the house was begun in 1938 when the Woodrow Wilson Birthplace Foundation acquired it. The street front of this late Greek Revival brick house built in 1846 is a modest one with two small columns and two stories. As with a number of houses in this hilly section of Virginia, however, the slope allows the house an extra story on the garden front, and this has been designed with a stately four-column, two-story porch and garden-level kitchen and dining room.

The interior is perhaps what one would expect of a residence for an earnest Presbyterian minister and his family—honest and comfortable if somewhat austere. A wide central hall runs to the rear of the house and affords a splendid view of the garden.

When young "Tommy," as Woodrow Wilson was known, was about a year old, the family moved and lived in a number of parsonages during his childhood.

After leaving the Presidency, Wilson moved to a comfortable three-story brick house at 2340 S Street, N.W., in Washington with a view across the Potomac. Here, he lived out his life in pleasant comfort.

West Virginia

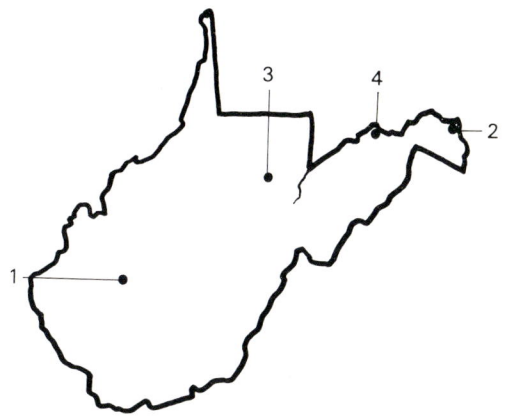

1) CAPITOL, Charleston

Both the West Virginia State Capitol and its setting in Charleston are among the most attractive in the United States. Many architects have, in fact, called the Capitol building one of the world's outstanding examples of Italian Renaissance architecture.

Completed in 1932, the main building and its two wings are on a sixteen-acre esplanade above the Kanawha River, with a fine view overlooking the river area. From Kanawha Boulevard below the Capitol, a majestic stone stairway leads down to the water.

The Capitol's steel skeleton is covered by buff-colored Indiana limestone. Of its eighty-six columns, those on the main portico are Roman Corinthian, the others are a modified Doric. The golden dome, 300 feet high, is lit at night.

Bronze doors open onto marble-columned foyers. Marble is used extensively inside: Imperial Danby for the walls, Italian travertine and white Vermont for the floors. From a fifty-four-foot gold chain suspended from the center of the dome's ceiling, a two-ton chandelier, 180 feet above the floor, lights the rotunda.

In the Capitol's showpiece, the governor's reception room, the standout attraction is the light turquoise rug which measures twenty-seven by seventy-two feet, is two feet thick and weighs one ton.

Harpers Ferry National Historical Park has preserved the engine house where John Brown was captured by Lieutenant James E. B. Stuart, October 16, 1859.

2) HARPERS FERRY NATIONAL HISTORICAL PARK

In 1859 Harpers Ferry was a comfortable, prosperous community, nestled under the picturesque Blue Ridge Mountains at the confluence of the Potomac and Shenandoah rivers. Today, the town, with much of its antebellum atmosphere restored, stands as a reminder of a crucial chapter of American history.

Harpers Ferry's pleasant life-style was suddenly and irrevocably changed on October 16, 1859, when fanatical abolitionist John Brown and eighteen of his men staged a bloody raid on the Federal Armory. They intended to incite slaves to insurrection, providing them with arms. But the slaves were not interested, and instead of fleeing, Brown stayed in the town until captured two days later by then U.S. Army Colonel Robert E. Lee. Brown was tried for treason and murder and hanged late that year. Tensions between the North and the South were strained almost to the breaking point by the incident and this country was pushed further on its inexorable course toward the Civil War.

Harpers Ferry National Historical Park is still under development. Four separate tracts of land—downtown Harpers Ferry, Bolivar Heights and Loudoun Heights, West Virginia, and Maryland Heights, Maryland—are included in the 1,450-acre park. John Brown's Fort, scene of the raiders' capture, and John Brown's Monument highlight the events of the famous raid. Evidence of the many Civil War battles fought in the area can also be seen in the park.

3) PHILIPPI COVERED BRIDGE

The two-way, 285-foot-long Philippi Covered Bridge spans the Tygarts River and still carries traffic after more than a century of continual use, thus linking the beauty of America's past with the demands of modern civilization. The picturesque bridge roof, which contributes much to the charm of the American scene, actually was intended to protect the wooden supports and trusses from the elements.

Built in 1852 by Lemuel Chenoweth, pioneer builder of many of West Virginia's covered bridges, the historic Philippi bridge was the site of the first land battle of the Civil War a month after war was declared. Here, in the upper central part of the state on June 3, 1861, a small band of Confederate soldiers, some billeted inside the bridge, were surprised by Northern forces and driven from Philippi.

4) POTOMAC RIVER

The Potomac River is a corridor of history and beauty, and an important part of our nation's heritage. Formed at Cumberland, Maryland, the river begins its flow northeasterly through Valley and Ridge Country, one of the four physiographic provinces through which the river passes before reaching Chesapeake Bay. Each of the regions—Valley and Ridge, Great Valley, Piedmont and Coastal Plain—gives the river a different character.

In a series of great loops, the river passes over a land having more deer and turkeys than people. Tumbling through the corrugated Valley and Ridge province and confined in the narrow canyons it has carved, the river runs over a washboard of rapids and troughs to spill out between Martinsburg, West Virginia, and Hagerstown, Maryland, into the wide and populated Great Valley. It and the lesser valleys to the east are formed by the low, parallel mountains running southwest to northeast that were uplifted after the Potomac had already established its course. However, because of the buzz-saw effect of the river's erosional forces, it still flows toward Chesapeake Bay by cutting across these mountains.

At the Great Valley's eastern edge, the Potomac receives its largest tributary, the historic Shenandoah River, at Harpers Ferry. Leaving Harpers Ferry and West Virginia, the river becomes the border between Virginia and Maryland and at Point of Rocks slices through its last barrier, the northern Blue Ridge Mountains, to enter the Piedmont region.

From Point of Rocks to Great Falls, fifteen miles above Washington, D.C., the Potomac is a typical Piedmont river. It flows through a valley lined with stone palisades often rising 100 to 200 feet above the river.

Now a strong, mature stream, the Potomac dashes over rocks of schist and granite at Great Falls. Twenty-five miles below Washington, D.C., its waters spread out, becoming two to seven miles wide. No longer a freshwater river, the Potomac at this point becomes an extension of the sea. For the last 117 miles of its 287-mile journey, it is increasingly brackish, its current almost imperceptible.

The outlet into Chesapeake Bay adds an important dimension to the river. The bay connects the Atlantic Ocean to the only river system on the mid-Atlantic seaboard penetrating the Appalachians. (See map, p. 292.)

Opposite: The scenic Potomac River winds through rugged landscape, heavily populated with deer and wild turkeys. Here, it flows past Eagle Rock in the Monongahela National Forest, West Virginia.

**Alabama   Florida   Georgia   Kentucky
Louisiana   Mississippi   North Carolina   South Carolina
Tennessee   Virgin Islands**

SOUTH to the CARIBBEAN

In history, climate, dialect and social attitudes, the South has been the most distinctive region of our nation. The Civil War—or War Between the States—establishes that fact. Far more than any other section it is a region of natives, being born and dying in their homeland. While other areas seem to exchange populations, that of the South is now quite stable. Florida and the Virgin Islands are exceptions. Florida's identity is somewhat altered because of her year-round influx of vacationers and settlements of retired people. The Virgin Islands off her coast in the Caribbean Sea share only geographic affinity with the South, having become part of the United States in 1917, many years after the Civil War.

Most unique to Southerners is an almost mystical attachment to the land. The geography is unlike any other in the country and is dominated by a humid, subtropical climate. The coast alternates between bright, extensive beaches and huge, mysterious, tangled swamps of mangrove and cypress. Inland, pine forests of loblolly, longleaf and shortleaf cover thousands of acres on a warm sandy plain arching from North Carolina to Louisiana. Further inland are several ranges of the Appalachians, the Great Smokies and Blue Ridge among them, where the weather is not so much subtropic as it is hushed and hazy. On both sides of the Mississippi River in Louisiana and Mississippi, a cobweb of bayous traces through the rich soil of the alluvial plain.

Romantic images that first come to mind when "the South" is mentioned are of hospitable and sumptuous plantations, presided over by owners preoccupied with agrarian concerns to whom the ideals of family honor and community fellowship are great traditions. Much of this remains and it has even been enhanced after a century of struggle toward continuing and progressive, although still incomplete, resolution of racial tensions. The tenor of the area today is still charming, though it is more highly tuned to industrialization, diversification and growth.

Opposite: The dark waters of the cypress swamp mirror one of the picturesque bridges found in Magnolia Gardens, South Carolina. The floral wonderland has twenty-five acres of flower gardens, three lakes and sixteen acres of oak-planted lawns.

Alabama

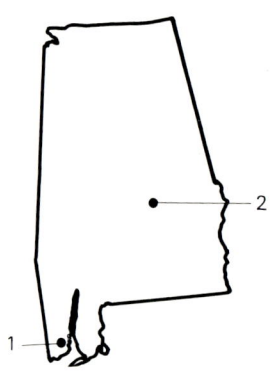

Oriental-American Garden at Bellingrath.

1) BELLINGRATH GARDENS

In a lush tropical setting between Mobile and the Gulf of Mexico, there is a surprising sixty-five-acre garden in Theodore where flowers bloom without interruption the year around. This is Bellingrath, the garden that began as a fishing camp. About fifty years ago Walter D. Bellingrath, who was destined to make a fortune from selling the then little-known drink Coca-Cola, brought his friends to hunt and fish here on the quiet banks of the Isle-aux-Oies River. Inspired by some of the famous European gardens, the Bellingraths then decided to landscape their beautiful estate.

The name Bellingrath has become a watchword for fine azaleas. Starting in the early spring (February in Alabama) to mid-April, a quarter of a million azaleas of 200 varieties begin their blooming season. Azaleas are found everywhere in the garden, their colors varying from pink and salmon to deep rose, lavender, magenta, ivory, white and yellow. Many are more than a hundred years old and range from fifteen to twenty feet high with a diameter of twenty to thirty feet.

Bellingrath is a haven for hundreds of varieties of birds and animals. The growing deer herd is carefully protected. At least 200 species of birds either stay here the year around or stop off during their migration.

The Bellingrath house, with its collection of priceless antiques and china, was opened to the public in 1956. This lovely home in the center of the gardens built of hand-pressed antebellum bricks and the magnificent garden on the Isle-aux-Oies River are willed to the public, the Bellingraths' only heirs. The Boehm Gallery contains one of the largest collections of porcelains by the internationally known artist, Edward Marshall Boehm. The proceeds of the garden go to certain churches and colleges.

2) CAPITOL, Montgomery

When, in 1846, the legislature selected Montgomery as the state capital, the city of Montgomery donated a tract of land for the Capitol at the head of Dexter Avenue, which had been set aside for that purpose by the foresighted founder of the city, Andrew Dexter. The city issued bonds and the Capitol, completed in late 1847, was built at no expense to the State of Alabama.

On December 14, 1849, the thirtieth anniversary of Alabama statehood, a fire burned the roof of the House of Representatives. Most of

Representatives of the seceding Southern states met in the State Capitol of Alabama to draft the constitution of the Confederacy. Jefferson Davis was inaugurated first President of the Confederacy on this famous front portico.

the contents of the Statehouse were rescued, but the building was gutted within three hours. The Capitol was rebuilt on the foundations of the old one, of brick and plaster, and with some alterations in the original design. Additions, including a classic dome and stately columns, were completed in 1851. Although additions were made in 1885, and again in 1905 and 1911, there has been no alteration of the 1851 structure.

At the invitation of the Alabama Secession Convention, representatives from the other seceding states met in the Senate Chamber of the State Capitol on February 4, 1861. In the Senate Chamber the provisional and permanent constitutions were drafted and approved and Jefferson Davis was elected president of the provisional government of the Confederate States. He was inaugurated first President of the Confederacy on the front portico of the Capitol. Over the dome of the Capitol the first Confederate flag, the Stars and Bars, was raised by Letitia Tyler, granddaughter of President John Tyler, on March 4, 1861.

Florida

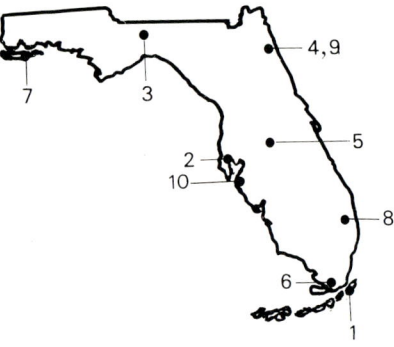

1) BISCAYNE NATIONAL MONUMENT

Wild bird calls and the splash of marine life are the only interruptions to the peaceful silence of the narrow, low-lying islands and barrier reefs of the upper Florida Keys. The higher ground of these keys, nine or ten feet above the tidal marshes, has rare Sargent palms, mahoganies and dense mangrove thickets.

Here in the northern limits of living coral reefs along United States coasts—protected at last by national park conservation practices—small numbers of the endangered North American crocodiles may still maintain haunts in the quiet waters. The rare manatee (sea cow) and bottle-nosed dolphin share the waters surrounding the keys with many colorful and varied fish.

A rainbow of color and life is everpresent along the miles of paths that meander through Cypress Gardens.

2,500 exotic birds inhabit the tall palms and lush tropical landscape of Busch Gardens. In addition to the wide lawns and lagoons, there are 300 acres based on an African theme, complete with wild animals and a veldt.

Located a few miles south of Miami, Biscayne National Monument contains about 4,200 acres of uplands and more than 92,000 acres of submerged reefs.

Elliott Key, Adams Key, Old Rhodes Key and Sands Key form an almost continuous island barrier bisecting the submerged areas of the monument. The submerged lands form two broad, divided habitats. On the Biscayne Bay side, the bottom is a deposit of marl mud and marine grass.

Underwater terrain on the Atlantic Ocean side of the islands is more variable with the bottom gradually deepening to the edge of the rubble reefs. The rocky limestone outcroppings, bottom shoals, coral, coralline algae and marine grasses support an extremely rich and varied tropical marine biota.

Although this area has been near a well-traveled sector of the Atlantic Coast since the beginning of European occupation, and in earlier times by Indians, it remains relatively undisturbed. Relics of the boisterous era of Spanish galleons loaded with gold bullion and English sea rovers searching the seas for the loot lie rotting in these reefs to this day.

2) BUSCH GARDENS

One of the country's most modern and ingenious garden installations is Busch Gardens, adjoining the Anheuser-Busch Brewery in Tampa. In 1959, as an experiment in community relations, fifteen acres of the sandy slopes next to the brewery were transformed into a lush tropical garden, replete with wide lawns, tall palm trees and three connecting lagoons.

The gardens' focal point is the heptagonal-roofed Hospitality House. The roof seems to float over this unusual structure overlooking one of the lagoons. There is a broad observation deck cantilevered out over the water where white swans swim in the sparkling blue waters. The flowers provide a brilliant accent for the lush green of the trees and shrubbery. Thousands of marigolds line the entranceway and red salvia, petunias, gardenias and camellias are beautifully displayed in massed plantings.

Rivaling the floral beauty at Busch Gardens is the shimmering color of 2,500 birds which comprise one of the largest avian displays in the world.

The experiment with the garden proved to be such a thorough success that almost 300 more acres were added with an African theme. Visitors can safari with cameras through a veldt— an African prairie—and capture more than 800 animals, such as an oryx, eland, Kuku antelope or a wildebeest. One section of the veldt has been set aside as a special breeding ground for species near the vanishing point. In addition to a petting zoo and elephant rides, the expanded gardens offer a nineteenth-century African train ride and a duplicate African village to explore called Stanleyville.

3) CAPITOL, Tallahassee

The offices of Florida's state government are located in a beautiful landscaped section of Tallahassee known as Capitol Center and the focal point is the Capitol building itself. A handsome, striking edifice, its architecture follows classic Greek styling, including six Doric columns. Also attractive is a high dome, with still another atop an arch-supported cupola.

Its cornerstone was laid in 1826, but because of financial difficulties the building was not completed until 1845, the year Florida was admitted to the Union.

The Capitol has been the scene of historic moments in both state and American history. Here, in 1861, the Secession Convention declared Florida's withdrawal from the Federal Union and established the independent Republic of Florida. Later, Florida became a member of the Confederate States of America.

4) CATHEDRAL OF ST. AUGUSTINE

The seat of the oldest Catholic parish in America, founded shortly after the Spanish first landed at St. Augustine in 1565, the original Cathedral of St. Augustine was begun in 1795 and completed in 1797. A coquina rock structure, it is rectangular in shape, 120 feet long and 42 feet wide. The walls of the church facade swoop up in graceful ogee curves to a picturesque Moorish belfry. The four historic tower bells combine with the window and clock below to form a complete cross.

The cathedral was seriously damaged in a fire in 1887, but its walls were left intact. Virtually all of the original church remains essentially as it was and forms the nave of the reconstructed and enlarged cathedral. The present facade looks much as it did at the beginning of the nineteenth century. The original bells, refurbished in 1965, now ring again in the tower. Still to be found within the venerable Cathedral of St. Augustine is the true atmosphere of Old Spain. The cathedral provides a beautiful link with the beginnings of Western civilization in this part of the world.

5) CYPRESS GARDENS

Cypress Gardens, located five miles southeast of Winter Haven in central Florida, is something of a miracle in more ways than one. It is first a miracle of color created by bright azaleas, green lawns, sparkling lagoons and tall palm trees. It is also a miracle of engineering. Nearly half the garden was dredged out of a Florida swamp by an amazing horticultural businessman, Dick Pope, whom local residents once scoffingly called the Swami of the Swamp.

Cypress Gardens opened in 1936. Two years later there were ten electric boats for scenic rides through the meandering waterways under the tall cypress trees which first attracted the attention of the garden's founder. Despite local skepticism, Cypress Gardens began to prosper, in part due to Pope's expert publicity.

One of the garden's outstanding features is, of course, the abundance of cypress trees. Only one species, the bald cypress, is found here. The trees range in age from 150 to 1,800 years and are native to the region. They grow only about an inch and a half at the base every forty-six years. Hanging eerily from the branches of the cypress are clouds of Spanish moss. With the stately cypress and the great variety of flowers and plants, Cypress Gardens seems to grow steadily in beauty each year.

6) EVERGLADES NATIONAL PARK

Quiet, calm, flat, mysterious—the Florida Everglades are a unique part of the American landscape, the largest subtropical wilderness in North America.

Lake Okeechobee, massively spilling over to the north, created this river of grass, broad, short and shallow, with multifarious water creatures thriving in and about its swampy lushness, characterizing the biological wealth of the area.

Leggy wading birds lift their fishy meals from the waters; alligators, turtles, otter and fish flutter, creep and splash in natural patterns through the willows, submerged roots, drenched grass and spatterdock.

All this lush, growing green can be seen best from the jungle spots on elevated islands which are called hammocks. Towering trees, dangling vines, carpets of ferns, West Indian in character, flourish here, where thrive the Liguus tree snails, so beautiful in aspect and so rarely seen elsewhere.

Here, where dark, tangled coastal forests drove Spanish horsemen to more maneuverable coasts, are ghostly clusters of mangrove trees, cypress heads, bayheads and stands of Caribbean pine. Many trees grow above tangles of crooked roots which sustain their trunks above the water. The roots interlock and are a hazard to the legs of men landing from pole-propelled flatboats. The pines are slender-tufted, fire-resistant and fire-perpetuated, and they have been used extensively in the building of termite and rot-resistant structures. Here, too, in the enormous brackish zone, is a natural, inaccessible nursery for numerous edible fish which eventually supply the needs of commercial and sport fishing operations amid the keys and along the Gulf Coast. Here, too, are rookeries of storks, increasing and multiplying, a continent removed from the storied stork-nest roofs of Denmark.

The dark memory of the plume hunters can be vividly recalled in this expanse, where ruthless exploiters once threatened to bring exquisite species of waterfowl to the point of extinction.

Established as a national park in 1947, this vast southern Florida wilderness with its wildlife population is now preserved for future generations. Dangerous and beguiling, the Everglades is now attainable in areas of minimal discomfort for the bird-watcher, the naturalist and the boater. The strange beauty of the Everglades is ours.

7) GULF ISLANDS NATIONAL SEASHORE

Wide, gently sloping beaches of unusually fine, white "sugar" sand, clear blue waters reminiscent of Caribbean bays, unique flora and fauna, and several historically important forts are the characteristics of Gulf Islands National Seashore. Consisting of about 13,600 acres of barrier and offshore islands stretching 150 miles from Florida to Mississippi, the seashore is a prime example of what dedicated citizens can do for the preservation of our natural resources.

Citizen interest in these islands was developed in the 1960's when it was learned that sea erosion was undermining Fort Massachusetts, of Civil War fame, on Mississippi's Ship Island, now included within the seashore. The area achieved national seashore status in 1971 but, while legislation was pending, local residents formed an organization which succeeded in erecting a protective wall around the old structure.

Saved from further commercial development are some of Mississippi's offshore islands, namely Horn, Petit Bois (meaning "little woods" and locally pronounced "pretty boy") and Ship Islands, and in Florida, parts of Santa Rosa Island (formerly the Santa Rosa National Monument which was deactivated in 1946), the eastern half of Perdido Key across the channel from Santa Rosa, and sections of Naval Live Oaks Reservation and the Pensacola Naval Air Station, both on the mainland. The two states are separated by Alabama's Gulf Coast.

Flora in the seashore is extremely varied. For example, Horn Island contains over 204 species of plants. Slim slash-pine trees fight to survive the salt and sand driven by stormy winds. Some of the sand dunes have been stabilized by species of magnolia dunes, palmetto and live oak, while the unstabilized dunes are mostly covered with beach grass and sea oats.

The monument provides many places for the Gulf's increasingly rare sea turtles to lay their eggs, and it is the only habitat for a species of beach mouse which has developed a very light coloration to blend into the white sand.

Now protected in the Loxahatchee National Wildlife Refuge, the common egret barely escaped extinction at the turn of the century when its elegant plumage was widely sought.

85

A great number of birds nest within the seashore, especially on Horn and Petit Bois islands. Here the interior ponds, lagoons and marshes serve as wintering grounds for blue and snow geese and several species of ducks. The beaches support laughing gulls and Sandwich and royal terns; redhead ducks are abundant on the shallow gulf waters.

8) LOXAHATCHEE NATIONAL WILDLIFE REFUGE

One of the largest remaining areas of the southern Florida Everglades is Loxahatchee National Wildlife Refuge, containing 220 square miles and located between Lake Okeechobee and Fort Lauderdale. Established in 1951, the refuge preserves the habitat of a fantastic number of birds and animals.

Loxahatchee is roughly pear-shaped, bounded by levees on all sides. Just inside are the canals which expedite the movement of water in or out of the region as called for by the rainfall, which averages sixty-two inches annually. It was originally the bottom of a great sea, but dying vegetation has built up a large body of organic soil rising up to fifteen feet above sea level.

Although crisscrossed with questionable drainage ditches, much of the unique beauty of this section of the Everglades remains. Dense stands of Tracy's beakrush flourish in shallow water flats, and sawgrass continues to cover large areas. Smartweeds, white water lilies and other wet-soil aquatic plants grow here, while the tree islands support mixed stands of redbay, wax-myrtle and holly.

Both wading birds and waterfowl come here by the thousands all year round. The rarest bird found in the refuge is the Everglade kite, of which there are only about one hundred in existence.

Alligators, though an endangered species nationally, seem to thrive in this refuge. These reptiles can be seen floating partially submerged or sunning on the edge of a canal.

9) "OLDEST HOUSE"

The "Oldest House," located in Saint Augustine, is thought to have risen from the ashes of a primitive, Spanish colonial structure which was burned during an English raid on that settlement in 1702. However, archeological dating of the site's first occupancy reveals the presence of some dwelling early in the 1600's. Saint Augustine itself was settled in 1565. It is the oldest permanent European settlement in the United States.

The "Oldest House," as it appears today, is a combination of both Spanish and English influences, compromising the exact period of the house to about the late eighteenth century.

After the Spanish regained possession of the city, an upper portico with a lean-to roof was added to one end of the house. The supporting timbers for this portico later served as the corner posts for a first-floor apartment, added to the house around 1900. A large tower, removed during the twentieth century restoration, was constructed in the late 1800's. At this time the interior of the house was refinished with intricate paneling from the neighboring Presbyterian church, razed in 1884.

In 1918 the house was purchased by the Saint Augustine Historical Society after their previous headquarters was destroyed by fire. The last owner had used the house as a museum for nearly a generation before this, so the society merely supplemented the collection it found there.

In 1959, an extensive restoration returned the masonry-and-wood building to its late eighteenth century appearance, preserving in its architecture the conflicting European ideals which gave rise to Florida's violent arrival as a territory of the United States.

10) RINGLING MUSEUMS

"Flamboyance" and "spectacle" are words that leap to mind in connection with the name John Ringling, linked as it is to the American circus, with all its expansive color and glamor. Yet when Ringling decided to create a museum he did not think of a museum of the circus; that was left for his heir, the State of Florida, to accomplish in recognition that an important part of American life might otherwise soon be lost. John and Mable Ringling envisioned an outstanding museum of art to complement their palatial Venetian-style residence on the shores of Sarasota Bay with a splendid building to house the Renaissance and Baroque paintings they most enjoyed.

Their home recalls the Palace of the Doges in the design of its bayside facade. The Italian Renaissance style of the structure that houses the works of art brought lasting dignity to the estate built on drained swampland. Ringling had built his mansion and the museum in the late 1920's, the John and Mable Ringling Museum of Art opening in 1930. The U-shaped museum building encloses a garden court in the Italian manner.

Ringling's death in 1936 cut short his plans for the museum. In 1946 the museum reopened

The "Oldest House" in St. Augustine began as a single-level, tabby-and-masonry structure in the early 1700's. Its final form reflects the conflicting Spanish and English influences in the area's history.

as a public institution, under the capable direction of A. Everett Austin, Jr. In 1947 he opened the Ringling residence to the public as a historic house documenting the opulence of the 1920's; he started the Circus Museum in 1948; and in 1949 he acquired the internal structure of the eighteenth-century theater, originally built for the great hall of a castle near Venice. The State of Florida paid for the purchase, and by 1957 it was permanently installed and in use near the art museum. It is equipped with eighteenth-century furniture, paintings and decorative objects and is unique in the Western Hemisphere.

The most impressive gallery in the museum is the one containing four of the eleven large paintings by Rubens (1577-1640), prepared as full-scale cartoons for tapestries that were to be woven by Brussels weavers. The number of paintings by Rubens, including the important *Departure of Lot and His Family from Sodom* and the portrait of *The Archduke Ferdinand*, make this the largest collection of major works by Rubens in the United States.

The Museum of the Circus is devoted primarily to that marvelous and unique art form, the American Circus. Specializing in the development of "The Greatest Show on Earth" and of John Ringling whose name became synonymous with the circus in this country, the museum collections also include memorabilia from other great circuses. An outstanding collection of woodcuts, engravings and printed bills immortalize the performers featured in the sixteenth and subsequent centuries.

Georgia

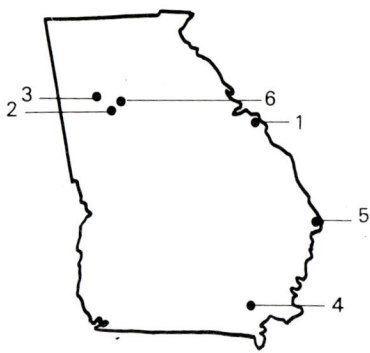

1) AUGUSTA NATIONAL GOLF CLUB

Every April the greatest golfers gather in Augusta to challenge the legendary Augusta National Golf Course and vie for the traditional green coat presented to the winner of the "Masters," a tournament held annually since 1934. Millions of Americans participate vicariously through television.

While the last four holes of the course, especially the water-guarded fifteenth and sixteenth, have become the most famous because of their national television coverage during the tournament, it is the eleventh, twelfth and thirteenth holes, referred to as the Amen Corner, which usually decide the tournament winner.

One of golf's early immortals, Bobby Jones, was instrumental in the course's development. Just after his retirement from competition in 1930, he and a group of his associates commissioned Scottish golf architect Dr. Alister McKenzie to design what McKenzie referred to as the "World's Wonder Inland Golf Course." This goal has clearly been achieved. The course was opened in 1932.

Augusta National is operated as a private club, with its distinguished members hailing from throughout the United States.

2) CAPITOL, Atlanta

The massive Georgia State Capitol at Atlanta was finished and occupied in 1889. Ironically, because of the General Assembly's strict limitation on expenditures, the Capitol was built not of Georgia marble, which was in abundant supply in the state, but of less expensive Indiana limestone. Georgia marble was used, however, for the interior finish of walls, floors and steps, as well as for the cornerstone.

The style of architecture of the Capitol is classical Renaissance. The Byzantine dome of the Capitol is seventy-five feet in diameter and is surmounted by a fifteen-foot statue. As part of a renovation which took place in 1957 and 1958, forty-three ounces of native Georgia gold were donated by the citizens of Dahlonega and of Lumpkin County and were applied in the form of gold leaf to the dome.

The Capitol is on a hill where Federal troops camped during Sherman's occupation of the city in 1864. In recent years a number of handsome new state office buildings have been built around the hill. From the Capitol dome the entire surrounding area may be viewed, including beautiful Kennesaw and Stone mountains.

3) ETOWAH MOUNDS ARCHEOLOGICAL AREA

The Etowah area near what is now Cartersville was the scene many centuries ago of well-cultured Indians. They left behind lasting memorials, three temple mounds built like flat-topped pyramids. The surrounding village was encircled by a thirty-foot-wide moat on three sides and the Etowah River on the other. The largest mound is over sixty feet high. The struc-

The Isaiah Davenport House is one of the most elegant Georgian-style homes in Savannah.

Okefenokee National Wildlife Refuge is one of the largest, most primitive swamps in the country. The dark waters, peat bogs and cypress trees are a haven for many wild birds and animals.

tures were used for worship ceremonies and burials were made at the base.

Artifacts unearthed in the only mound thus far excavated fill the museum on the grounds and retell a story of wealthy, highly civilized and well-traveled citizens.

The society that produced the mounds was Middle Mississippian. (See **Cahokia Mounds State Park**, Illinois—6.) The influx of this culture around 1350 into a people belonging to the Woodland culture led to a fusion of the two into a new culture, the Lamar, which lasted until 1650. Experts have been unable to ascertain why the Indians disappeared then.

The archeological site has long been known as an outstanding example of Indian earthworks. Part of a plantation belonging to the same family since 1838, the fifty-acre site was purchased by the State of Georgia in 1953 and designated a national historical landmark a year later.

4) OKEFENOKEE NATIONAL WILDLIFE REFUGE

Those who want to study an unimpaired swampland environment should come to Okefenokee. One of the largest, oldest and most primitive protected swamps in the United States, it covers 412,000 acres in extreme southeastern Georgia. Vegetation includes many huge cypress trees mixed with blackgum, redbay and pine.

Sometimes a large piece of peat will break away from the swamp bottom and float on the surface. Smaller plants take root until trees and large bushes grow on these floating islands. The islets frequently become anchored by the trees extending their roots down through the water to the bed of peat below, which may be as thick as twenty feet. The stamping of feet on one of these peat islands will cause the nearby trees to shake, thus the Choctaw name *owaquaphenogau* ("Land of the Trembling Earth"). Okefenokee is simply an anglicized version of this Indian word.

The most readily recognizable animal in the swamp is the American alligator, rare in almost every other part of the country, but abundant here.

Four-fifths of the swamp is under the protection of the Bureau of Sport Fisheries and Wildlife as the Okefenokee National Wildlife Refuge.

Trips into the interior of Okefenokee can be accomplished only by boat, and a guide is required in the closed areas. Stephen Foster State Park, in the interior of the refuge, can be reached via a paved road through the southwestern portion.

5) SAVANNAH HOUSES

Savannah is the site of many outstanding old mansions built during the early antebellum period when Savannah, Georgia's oldest city, was a great cotton trading center. The **Owens-Thomas House**, at 124 Abercorn Street, has been called by competent critics one of the finest American examples of the English Regency period, a Greco-Roman architectural phase of the Classic Revival. Designed by English

The temple mounds of the highly civilized Etowah Indians were used for religious ceremonies.

architect William Jay, it marked the beginning of his rise to prominence during this architectural period. The house, which was completed in 1819 and became the property of the Telfair Academy of Arts and Sciences, Inc., in 1951, was opened in 1954.

The English Regency style is best described as a "restrained Greco-Roman classicism." Its aim was to reveal beautiful classical lines. Walls were stripped of mass decoration where motif was obscured in an elaboration of detail. Decoration was used only to break the monotony or to change the effect of shape. This last use is exemplified in the ceiling of the salon of the Owens-Thomas House in which two Greek fret circles with fluted spandrels descend slightly, like drapery, to create an expansive room.

One of the most elegant houses in the time-hallowed city is the **Isaiah Davenport House**. Now a museum as well as headquarters of the Historic Savannah Foundation, Inc., it is widely acclaimed as the only Georgian-style residence of its period left in Savannah.

Completed in 1820, the comfortable four-story English brick residence at State and Habersham streets, opposite Columbia Square, has some exceptionally fine ornamental plaster moldings and hand-carved woodwork.

In designing his residence, Isaiah Davenport showed remarkable ability in the harmonious blending of various architectural styles both inside and out—styles as diverse as colonial Georgian, English Regency and Greek Revival.

Although comparatively small in scale, the Davenport residence makes up in dignity and appealing design what it lacks in size and spaciousness. The interior has been restored since 1954 and furnished with a variety of exquisite English and American antiques.

Built in 1818-21, the **Juliette Gordon Low House** is a lovely four-story English Regency townhouse with a picturesque brick courtyard and an attractive formal garden. Five generations of the Gordon family have lived in the home beginning with the grandfather of the woman who in 1912 founded the Girl Scouts in America. Victorian-style additions to the house were made in 1886.

The home and gardens have been carefully restored to their appearance in the 1860's and 70's when "Daisy" Gordon was growing up here. Many Gordon family furnishings help recall the early life of this noted woman and provide insight into the inception of Girl Scouting.

Juliette Gordon Low's birthplace in the historic city of Savannah has been owned by the Girl Scouts of the U.S.A. since 1953. The worldwide organization which Mrs. Low began in Savannah with eighteen girls and three adults has designated the home as well as adjacent buildings and grounds the Juliette Gordon Low Girl Scout National Center.

6) STONE MOUNTAIN

Rising to a height of 825 feet, Georgia's Stone Mountain just east of Atlanta is the largest piece of exposed granite in the world. On its north wall is an immense carving. Equestrian representations of Confederate President Jefferson Davis and generals Robert E. Lee and Stonewall Jackson carved in an area the size of a football field commemorate these great men and their roles in a critical period in American history. The Stone Mountain Memorial Carving is the product of three different sculptors, Gutzon Borglum, Augustus Lukeman and Walker Hancock, since it was begun in 1923.

Stone Mountain Park at the base of the mountain is a widely varied recreational facility. Almost every plant native to the Southeastern United States is represented. An attractive trail along the mountain's gentle western slope takes the hiker to the summit. A skylift passes close to the Memorial Carving on a breathtaking trip to the mountaintop.

Other attractions include the Scenic Railroad, Antique Auto and Music Museum, Game Ranch, a 732-bell carillon and the "War in Georgia" exhibit in which miniature soldiers recreate Sherman's historic "March to the Sea."

Kentucky

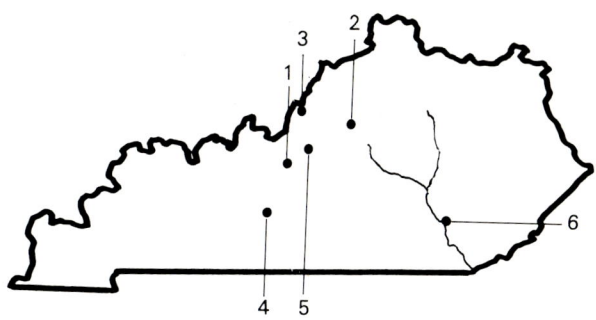

1) ABRAHAM LINCOLN BIRTHPLACE
See **Abraham Lincoln Home,** Illinois—1.

2) CAPITOL, Frankfort

Surrounded by a stone terrace, the present three-story Kentucky State Capitol at Frankfort has oolitic limestone facing above a base of Vermont granite. The outer walls are graced with seventy ornamental Ionic columns of Bedford stone. Completed in 1910, the building borders the Kentucky River.

Over the north entrance, the sculptured pediment shows Kentucky as a heroic woman, standing before the Chair of State and attended by the personified figures of Progress, History, Plenty, Law, Art and Labor.

Inside, thirty-six Vermont granite columns flank the long nave, adorned with oil paintings in lunettes and at each end with a mural scene from the life of Daniel Boone. Interior walls and stairway are of white Georgia marble, the floors of light Tennessee and dark Italian marble.

There is much French influence within. The rotunda, dome and lantern are copied after the Hôtel des Invalides, site of Napoleon's tomb in Paris. Stairways, balustrades and bannisters resemble those of the Paris Opera, while the State Reception Room was inspired by Marie Antoinette's drawing room in the Grand Trianon Palace at Versailles.

3) CHURCHILL DOWNS RACETRACK

Legendary Churchill Downs Racetrack near Louisville has been both the home of the Kentucky Derby and the pride of thoroughbred racing for nearly a century. It was in 1875 that

The famed Kentucky Derby attracts the attention of millions of Americans the first Saturday in May each year. The historic race has filled Churchill Downs with a special magic for 100 years.

10,000 people watched a striking red chestnut named Aristides defeat the illustrious Ten Broeck in the first Kentucky Derby. Since then more than 18,000 races have been run at Churchill Downs. Unique in the annals of racing history, the Kentucky Derby, Clark Handicap and Kentucky Oaks have been held every year without interruption.

Beautiful gardens and red brick courtyards present an enticing picture at any time, but the excitement of the first Saturday each May cannot be equaled. Well over 100,000 people gather to view the running of the Derby. As Kentucky journalist Irvin S. Cobb said, "Until you go to Kentucky and see a Derby, you ain't never been nowhere's and you ain't seen nothin."

The Kentucky Derby Museum houses memorabilia from "the jewel of races." Ten restored murals show the track and grounds in the 1890's.

4) MAMMOTH CAVE NATIONAL PARK

Kentucky's Mammoth Cave, which has been a lure to awestruck men since it was first trod by primitives, is still a place of mystery, a partially unexplored hollow of land beneath the surface. The ancients braved superstition and penetrated more than three miles of its vaulted passages, seeking gypsum. The dry, even-temperatured air has preserved for centuries their worn-out sandals and burnt torch ends, scattered here and there among sheer walls hacked with crude stone tools. Why they sought the soft mineral is not known.

Around 1800 white men came seeking saltpeter, or potassium nitrate, a prime ingredient of black gunpowder. The bored-out tree trunks used to carry the chemical solution to the vats are still here, along with other well-preserved artifacts of the operation.

The saltpeter industry died out after the War of 1812; then began Mammoth Cave's career as a tourist attraction, although much of it remained unexplored. Here Jenny Lind sang, her voice echoing through the rooms of stone, and Edwin Booth, the great Shakespearian actor, intoned the philosophy of Hamlet.

In 1837 a fifteen-year-old boy named Stephen Bishop, among the cave's first guides, crossed the Bottomless Pit on a slender pole, opening the way to extensive uncharted corridors and passages. At one time the cave housed an underground tuberculosis sanitarium. It became a national park in 1941, covering 51,354 acres in southwest-central Kentucky.

The cave is a maze of corridors connecting huge, domed chambers and deep pits. They were formed 340 million years ago when the limestone was the bed of an ancient sea. The land rose, and water inched into the rock, eroding the giant passages seen today. The formations have quaint, picturesque names—Fat Man's Misery, a narrow channel out into the floor of a large room; Frozen Niagara; the Snowball Room. The world's best-known underground stream, the Echo River, contains blindfish who have developed acute senses of touch and smell.

Above ground, two lovely rivers flow through the park, winding past deep green forests and a blaze of colorful wildflowers, a strange paradox to the weird, wonderful world spread out below.

5) "MY OLD KENTUCKY HOME"

This stately house at Bardstown survives today and is nationally renowned as "My Old Kentucky Home," because, according to tradition, it was in this place during a visit to his cousin, John Rowan, Jr., that Stephen Foster was inspired to write his best-known song. Aside from its association with Stephen Foster, Federal Hill stands as one of Kentucky's oldest and most historic residences. It was the seat of the Rowan family, members of which played vital roles in the state's early history. Today, the house is a museum and historic landmark in a park maintained by the State of Kentucky.

Most architectural historians agree that Federal Hill is one of the best examples in Kentucky of colonial Georgian architecture. It is three stories high, of brick and stone construction, and exceptionally well proportioned, both on its exterior and interior. All of the fireplace mantels are outstanding examples of the woodcarver's art. The main hall contains the most valuable piece in Federal Hill, the cherry and mahogany desk used by Foster when he visited the home. Throughout the home distinctive qualities of architecture, decor and human association make this a suitable memorial to the popular American composer who is best remembered for a song which pays tribute to the importance of these qualities.

6) WILDERNESS ROAD

In colonial days, the Appalachian Mountains provided a natural barrier to further settling. Thomas Walker, a doctor-turned-explorer, however, discovered a passage through the Allegheny ridges in 1750 and named the pass, the mountains and the river he found beyond, "Cumberland." He opened the way for settlement of the "Old West."

Gaps in the Cumberland Mountains provided passages through which pioneers could reach new Western territories.

Indians had fought many times on the land northwest of the gap which they called *Ken-ta-ke* ("dark and bloody ground"). Dr. Walker walked the same paths to explore what is now southeastern Kentucky. Subsequent travelers discovered the famed bluegrass region in central Kentucky where the grass is so green it appears blue.

Frontiersman Daniel Boone became an immortal hero during the years he explored and lived in the region. He and thirty axmen blazed the Wilderness Road through the Cumberland Gap in 1775—208 miles of trail through canes, reeds and trees in a single month. He led pioneers along the trail and built a fort on the Kentucky River, called Boonesborough, the second white settlement in Kentucky.

His Wilderness Road began at Long Island of the Holston River, now Kingsport, Tennessee, and ended at Boonesborough. Others branched to Harrodsburg, the first white settlement.

By the end of the American Revolution, most of Kentucky's 12,000 settlers had come by way of Boone's pack trail. A few years after Kentucky had become a state, the governor proposed making a real road out of the trail. Even though Boone volunteered his services in 1796, he did not receive the contract and two other men finished the road the same year. Thirty feet wide, it was capable of handling wagons hauling a ton of freight.

After 1800, when Kentucky's rivers replaced roads as main travel routes, the Wilderness Road faded in importance.

A two-mile stretch of Boone's original road is still visible in Cumberland Gap, a national historical park of about 20,000 acres in Virginia, Kentucky and Tennessee. The gap figured in many Civil War battles; remnants of fortifications are still visible.

The trail blazed by Boone is followed quite closely by sections of the Dixie Highway, U.S. 25, and U.S. 11.

Louisiana

1) CAPITOL, Baton Rouge

At the time of its construction in 1931-32, the Louisiana State Capitol in Baton Rouge was the tallest building in the South. Thirty-four stories, 450 feet in height, it was erected on the site of the old campus of Louisiana State University, which now is converted into twenty-seven acres of landscaped grounds.

The Capitol's elaborateness lies in intricate and costly artistic interpretations of the state itself. The story of Louisiana is the decorative theme of every detail and object that went into the edifice. Yet the building is efficiently designed and provides nearly six acres of floor space for governmental agencies.

The Capitol contains more than thirty varieties of marble and stone from every producing state and several foreign countries. The Memorial Hall is the most magnificent chamber of the building. Of huge proportions, the hall has a floor of polished lava from Mount Vesuvius. In the center of the floor is a huge bronze plaque on which is outlined in relief a map of Louisiana. The names of Louisiana's sixty-four parishes (counties) are carved around the border. Leading resources and products of each parish are also depicted.

From the observation tower it is possible on a clear day to see the surrounding country for a distance of twenty miles. The Mississippi River, winding out of the north, passes the Capitol near its base and disappears around a great bend into the south.

2) FRENCH QUARTER

New Orlean's French Quarter, or *le Vieux Carré*, exudes an atmosphere of charm and romance recaptured nowhere else. With its narrow streets and picturesque buildings framed by delicately featured, iron-trellised balconies, this was the New Orleans founded in 1718 by Jean Baptiste LeMoyne, the foremost French community in the New World. In 1742 the city was ceded to the Spanish and in 1803 it came to the United States as part of the Louisiana Purchase. Here are world-famous restaurants and delightful old shops. This is the section which comes alive each spring with the Mardi Gras celebration.

The focus of the French Quarter is **Jackson Square,** where early New Orleans greeted heroes and celebrated public occasions. Today, the square is a garden park, transformed in 1856 by Baroness de Pontalba. Each day artists create marvelous open-air shows around the perimeter of the square, painting and displaying their wares.

Flanking Jackson Square are the red-brick Pontalba buildings, erected by the baroness in 1849 and believed to be the oldest apartment buildings in the United States. They were intended to stem the exodus of businesses from *le Vieux Carré*. One of these, 1850 House, is now operated by the Louisiana State Museum and is furnished with authentic period pieces. Also near the square are the Presbytère and the Cabildo, historic structures that hold exhibits of the museum.

St. Louis Cathedral, facing Jackson Square, is one of the most beautiful and highly photographed churches in the world. Completed in 1794, it is the third edifice on the site. Within are paintings dating from 1796. In 1851 the cathedral was remodeled, altering its traditional Spanish architecture with steeples and a Greek Revival portico.

The city is a jazz center and each evening Bourbon Street comes alive with a variety of nightspots providing great entertainment. The New Orleans Jazz Museum relates the evolution of the art form from its origins in Afro-American rhythms and the European brass band to its contemporary styles. At Preservation Hall, Dixieland Jazz is performed nightly in its truest form by a rotating series of bands.

The French Market has a variety of quaint shops. Its coffee houses are traditional places to top off an evening.

Other attractions in the French Quarter include Old Absinthe House, a bar since 1826; Ursuline Convent, the first convent in Louisiana and now the oldest building in the Mississippi

The charm and romance of New Orleans's French Quarter is typified in the artistic, iron-trellised balconies.

Shadows-on-the-Teche, a Greek Revival mansion.

Valley, built in 1748; the U.S. Customs House, and the Musée Conti, a historical wax museum.

3) LONGFELLOW-EVANGELINE STATE PARK

The tale of two Acadian lovers who were tragically separated when their people were forced to leave Nova Scotia has been immortalized in Longfellow's epic poem, "Evangeline." Many Acadians eventually found a beautiful new homeland along the Bayou Teche in Louisiana, including the real-life prototypes for Evangeline and Gabriel.

Longfellow-Evangeline State Park is centered around an eighteenth-century Acadian house, said to have been the home of Louis Arceneaux, model for the storied Gabriel. This home, surrounded by live oaks and cypresses hung with Spanish moss, is a beautiful example of early Acadian architecture. Built of hand-hewn cypress held together by wooden pegs, its walls are made of moss mixed with abode and brick.

Now the Acadian House Museum, the house appears much as it did in the last half of the eighteenth century. An Acadian craft shop and a wood and mud reproduction of an Acadian cottage are also found in this 127-acre park which so beautifully recaptures the history of the area's early French settlers.

4) SHADOWS-ON-THE-TECHE

Moss hangs thick over the venerable oak trees that cluster around Shadows-on-the-Teche, shading its walks and loggias and casting lacy patterns on its tall Tuscan columns, its twin-chimney gabled roof and its trellised stairway. It is a cool vision in a sultry landscape, an image which the wealthy Louisiana planter David Weeks conceived when he set aside the land to build a town house for his growing family in 1825 and chose a plot on high ground in New Iberia.

Building of the Greek Revival mansion was begun in 1831 and completed in 1834. The neoclassic style then sweeping the country was adapted to the needs of the Louisiana climate. A generous overhang was planned so that the roof would shade the porches—galleries that echoed the Spanish building style common in the era to this part of the country.

Fallen into disrepair after the Civil War, the home was vitalized by Weeks Hall, great-grandson of the builder, when he returned from World War I. During the 1920's and 1930's it was as if the Civil War had never torn savagely through the very fabric of plantation life. The rooms echoed to the gaiety of his parties and sparkled with the care he lavished on their furnishings.

Following its bequest by Hall to the National Trust for Historic Preservation in 1958, the house was refurbished and opened to the public as a museum.

Mississippi

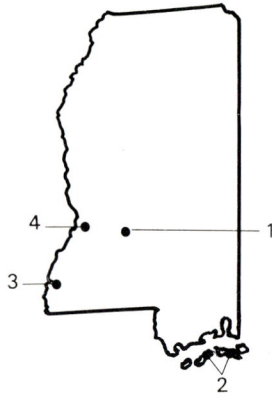

1) CAPITOL, Jackson

Mississippi actually has two State Capitol buildings in Jackson—the Old Capitol, built in 1839, which is now a historical museum, and the present Capitol, which was built in 1903 and has since served as the seat of government.

The present classical Renaissance Capitol is a symmetrical, four-story building, constructed of Bedford limestone with a base of Georgia granite. A high central dome and lantern which rises 180 feet above the entrance is topped by a copper eagle covered with genuine gold leaf.

2) GULF ISLANDS NATIONAL SEASHORE

See Florida—7.

3) NATCHEZ MANSIONS

Located on a high bluff on the eastern bank of the Mississippi River, Natchez is the oldest city on the great river. Natchez passed through British and Spanish hands before the American flag was first raised there in 1798.

Shortly after 1800, Natchez and the entire South began its half-century of wealth and splendor—the legendary golden age when cotton was king. The first steamboat came to Natchez in 1811, and within a decade the combination of cotton and steam had made it one of the wealthiest towns in America. The historic old town contains the largest collection of antebellum plantation houses of any city in America.

One of the most conspicuous of antebellum Natchez homes is **Cherokee,** named after a regional tribe of Indians. Built in 1794, this house is also among the oldest in the city. Its conspicuousness arises from its location on top of a small hill at Wall and High streets. In its long history, the house has had numerous owners who were prominent in early Natchez. Constructed of brick, the original dwelling now forms the mansion's rear section. During the era when cotton was king, the house was enlarged and a Greek Revival facade added by Frederick Stanton, who also built Stanton Hall.

Built in 1840, **D'Evereux** is an example of a pure classic type of Southern colonial architecture reminiscent of a Greek temple. The splendid white structure northeast of the downtown area has a spacious front gallery supported by six lofty, fluted Doric columns. The large, recessed doorway is overhung by a lacy wrought-iron balcony. Surmounting the whole is an observation tower or cupola with a bannistered widow's walk.

Inside, at the end of the wide, spacious hall, a doorway framed with fanshaped lights and sidelights of lacy design, offers a sharp contrast to the severe lines of the front door lights.

Among the most revered of the Natchez houses is **The Briars.** Situated a short distance south from the city and reached by a winding road canopied with magnolia trees, vines and briars and which crosses several dry bayous, The Briars was the scene of the 1845 marriage of Jefferson Davis, future President of the Confederacy. to Varina Howell.

The Briars is properly described as a typical prosperous Southern planter's house from the early nineteenth century rather than a mansion of the later, more extravagant era. It is a handsome, well-proportioned building, with many attractive architectural details. The white frame building is two stories high with a gable roof featuring lovely dormer windows.

Located near Cherokee is **Stanton Hall**. It is recognized as one of the most palatial and imposing antebellum houses in the South and was a fitting culmination to the period of lavish living in Natchez before the Civil War.

Frederick Stanton began building this "ornament for the town" in 1851 and chartered a ship to bring furnishings for it from Europe. He died a few months after the mansion was completed.

The house has large double galleries supported by towering Grecian columns. Part of a column was blasted away during a Civil War shell attack. Both upper and lower galleries are enclosed by beautifully designed wrought-iron grill rails of roses. Fluted columns frame the massive entrance door.

The building has a tremendous hall on its lower floor, seventy-four feet long, which runs between four large rooms. Suspended midway

D'Evereux was one of the many exquisite mansions built in Natchez during the golden era of King Cotton.

in the hall is a carved ceiling arch covered in Oriental design.

This most elaborate of all Natchez houses is probably more beautiful than ever because the live oaks that were saplings in Stanton's day are tall and majestic. Today, a city block forms the grounds for Stanton.

4) VICKSBURG

In early 1862 General U. S. Grant began his advance on the Confederate positions in the South's western sector. Having captured Forts Henry and Donelson in Tennessee, he pushed on toward Mississippi. On April 6 he was attacked at Pittsburg Landing, Tennessee, by Confederate General Albert Sidney Johnston. In one of the bloodiest battles of the entire war, Grant, with assistance from General Don Carlos Buell, managed to win a close victory at the Battle of Shiloh. Over 13,000 Union soldiers were killed, wounded, missing or captured, and one-fourth of the Confederate forces, over 10,000 men, were casualties, including Johnston who was killed while studying the emplacement of his forces. Today, **Shiloh National Military Park** commemorates this site.

Afterward, General Henry W. Halleck took command of the combined Union armies and tried to push to the strategic fortress city of Vicksburg, Mississippi, which overlooked the Mississippi River and was the key to the river's entire control. His advance soon bogged down and Grant was assigned to the task. Traveling downriver in December 1862, his troops at first made several unsuccessful attempts to capture the city from the difficult marshy terrain on the north. In the spring of 1863, however, Grant made a daring move. He bypassed the city through Louisiana and waited south of it for Admiral David Porter and his gunboats to run boldly the gauntlet of Vicksburg's artillery, which Porter did without losing a single man. Then Grant crossed the river, circled to the east and north, capturing forces at Jackson, and closed in on Vicksburg from the rear. After a forty-seven-day siege of nearly continuous shelling, the city surrendered on July 4, 1863.

Visitors to the 1,578-acre **Vicksburg National Military Park** today can take a sixteen-mile drive and see the elaborate system of Confederate and Union positions held during the siege.

In the city is the old courthouse from whose tower the Union troops finally raised the Stars and Stripes after the siege. Now a museum, the Greek Revival building houses one of the largest collections of Civil War memorabilia in the entire South.

The Mississippi River changed its course in 1876 and no longer runs beneath the bluffs of Vicksburg, but its tributary, the Yazoo, has taken over its old bed and visitors can still get an indication of how strategic this city was to both sides over 100 years ago.

Known as the cradle of Eastern American vegetation, plants and animals retreated to the inhabitable climates of the Great Smoky Mountains until the glaciers receded. Today, this area is a national park.

North Carolina

1) BILTMORE HOUSE AND GARDENS

Biltmore mansion, the magnificent country home of Commodore Cornelius Vanderbilt's grandson, George, contains one of the largest and most opulent collections of art treasures in the United States, selected personally by George on his travels around the world and shipped to Biltmore. Within the house, completed in 1895, paintings and prints by Durer, Renoir, John Singer Sargent, Giovanni Pellegrini, James McNeill Whistler and other artists complement the Wedgwood furniture, soft Persian carpets and rare *objets d'art*.

To equal and complement the magnificence of the mansion George Vanderbilt hired Frederick Law Olmsted, America's leading landscape architect, to design the gardens. Olmsted, best known for his design of Central Park in New York City, created gardens at Biltmore to include thirty-five acres of formal planting, as well as many acres of more informal plantings and woodlands. From the Lodge Gate at Biltmore Village, the approach road winds three miles through woods and massed naturalistic plantings of rhododendron, azaleas and other flowering shrubs and trees, until at the final turn, one views the entrance to Biltmore flanked by twin marble lions.

The opulence of the plantings is continued inside the mansion as well. Near the main entrance, under the high ceiling of the sunken Palm Court paved with marble, are the graceful green fronds of palms and banks of colorful flowers which are changed each season. In the center of the court is a fountain and sculpture of a boy with swans done by Karl Bitter, the Viennese artist who created the statues of Sculpture, Painting, Architecture and Music in front of the Metropolitan Museum of Art in New York City. Bitter also created other designs especially for the Biltmore mansion.

After Vanderbilt's death in 1914, his wife Edith deeded some 120,000 acres of land in the Mount Pisgah area to the United States Government. This was the nucleus for the Pisgah National Forest which now includes part of the famous Blue Ridge Parkway. Opened to the public in 1930 and declared a national historic site in 1963, Biltmore, with its remaining 12,000 acres, is now owned and operated by the Biltmore Company.

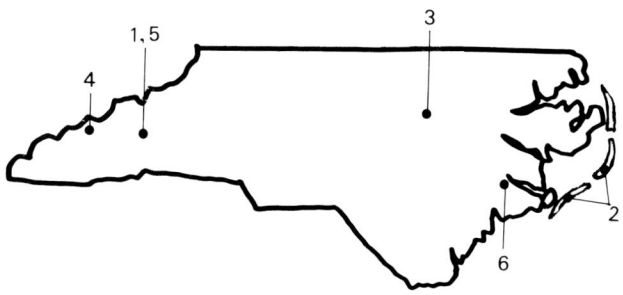

2) CAPES HATTERAS AND LOOKOUT NATIONAL SEASHORES

A northeaster storm on **Cape Hatteras** has to be experienced to be believed. The storms of the cape are so feared that seamen call North Carolina's Outer Banks the Graveyard of the Atlantic. The clash of warm Gulf Stream and cold Arctic waters, over twelve offshore miles of underwater shifting sandbars, plus enemy submarines in wartime, have combined to send more than 700 ships to the bottom from Cape Henry at the entrance of Chesapeake Bay to Cape Fear in southern North Carolina.

The history of the Outer Banks, which extend some thirty miles from the mainland at their farthest point at the tip of Cape Hatteras, is nearly a history of the United States. Roanoke Island at the northern point of Pamlico Sound which separates the cape from the mainland was the site of Sir Walter Raleigh's famous "Lost Colony," birthplace of Virginia Dare, first child of English parentage born in America.

During the eighteenth century, colonials from Virginia and Maryland moved onto the cape, becoming fishermen, navigators and sailors. They were called "bankers" and they founded the various towns along the cape.

On December 17, 1903, on a sandy plain called Kitty Hawk, about ten miles north of the national seashore, Wilbur and Orville Wright flew the world's first successful airplane.

Cape Hatteras National Seashore was established in 1953. It covers forty-five square miles stretched along seventy miles of shores of three barrier islands, each separated by an inlet.

Ocracoke, Hatteras and Bodie islands are barrier islands believed to have been formed by ocean currents and wave action on what were originally shoals to the east of the present shoreline. The islands are not more than three miles in width and are covered with sand dunes not yet stabilized and still moving.

Although animal life is limited to a few deer and some marsh rabbits, birdlife is abundant. Over 300 species can be found here. Pea Island National Wildlife Refuge—named after the upper island which existed when New Inlet split Hatteras Island—is renowned for being the wintering grounds of great numbers of Canada and snow geese. This 6,700-acre reserve, established in 1938, has the only large concentration of gadwall nesting on the Atlantic Seaboard.

Dawn on **Cape Lookout** may be much the same as dawn on other Atlantic barrier beaches with one exception—here man is no longer an intruder. Unlike Cape Hatteras National Seashore to the north, Cape Lookout National Seashore has no roads, no campgrounds and no thriving towns. Only the lighthouse, the extremely small town of Portsmouth on the north end (with a few summer residents only), and a number of shacks scattered along the shores give evidence of civilization.

Geographically, Cape Lookout differs from Cape Hatteras in that there are many small islands, mostly tidal marshes. Most of the lands here were bought and preserved by the State of North Carolina until Congress enacted a law in 1966 making the entire area a national seashore. The fifty-eight mile seashore contains about 15,800 acres, although actual acreage fluctuates with each large storm.

3) CAPITOL, Raleigh

The dominant feature of the heart of Raleigh is the North Carolina State Capitol which is centered in Union Square, a delightful parklike area of over six acres.

When Raleigh was planned as a city, this portion was set aside as the site of the Capitol. The first such structure was finished in 1794 in Union Square and was destroyed by fire in 1831. Construction on the current building was started two years later and it was finished in 1840.

Greek Revival was set as the architectural style and granite from a state-owned quarry near Raleigh was the main material used in construction. It is a cruciform shape and three stories high with a copper dome that has attained a rich green gloss through years of weathering.

The east and west facades have deep porticos. The Doric columns, five feet in diameter, and entablature are copied from the Parthenon.

Around the rotunda are various historical tablets and busts of famous native sons. The circular, stone second-floor balcony is cantilevered over the rotunda's first floor by nine feet. Massive stone stairways with wrought-iron railings lead to the second floor from the vestibules.

4) GREAT SMOKY MOUNTAINS NATIONAL PARK

Rising high between the states of North Carolina and Tennessee are the Great Smoky Mountains, the highest range of the Appalachian Chain which extends from Gaspe, Canada, to northern Georgia. The lofty range of the Smokies is the climax of the Appalachians and is the backbone of Great Smoky Mountains National Park. The park, established in 1930, covers 516,626 acres.

Known as the cradle of Eastern American vegetation, this area supplied plants and animals to the land exposed for the first time in thousands of years as the glacial ice sheet retreated northward. Primeval and timeworn as they are, vegetation densely covers the Smokies with a sea of green from base to summits, some rising more than 6,000 feet.

Cape Hatteras seashore.

The Royal Coat of Arms of King George III (above) appears in front of Tryon Palace (below). The home of William Tryon, North Carolina's colonial governor, it served as the state's first colonial capitol.

The mountains are steep, but not nearly unconquerable, faced with high rock, but not having the sheer face of the Tetons. Nature has mellowed the Great Smokies with time, gently filling deep valleys and rounding sharp peaks so that they have a graceful, undulating rhythm.

All this took time, 880 million years of it, before the Ice Age's glacial sheet covered the central United States down to the Ohio River, destroying all that lay before them. The Great Smoky Mountains escaped the earth-gnawing glaciers since they were beyond their reach and their climate an anathema to the masses of ice.

As life began to spread outward from what is now part of the park, the rivers came and cut channels through the land mass, creating valleys in a haphazard pattern. The ages have done the rest, wearing away mountain peaks, brushing away harsh corners and filling too-deep valleys with rock and silt so that vegetation might live and bring still more beauty to this ancient geological structure.

This country attracted settlers who were hardy, self-sufficient people, mostly from Scotland and England. Today, within the park, visitors can see the cabins and churches and the mill grinding cornmeal which remain behind commemorating these hardy mountain people.

5) THOMAS WOLFE HOUSE

In the short span of thirty-eight years beginning at the turn of the century, Thomas Wolfe made an indelible mark on American literary history. His home at 48 Spruce Street in Asheville served as the model for Dixieland, the boardinghouse which Wolfe described so movingly in *Look Homeward, Angel*. Asheville was the "Altamont" of his first published novel.

Preserved in this Victorian-style home is that romantic era when vacationers enjoyed leisurely stays here when it served as a boardinghouse. Authentic Wolfe family furnishings make the pages of *Look Homeward, Angel* come to life and provide insight into the man who created such entrancing prose. It is a fitting memorial to the genius who lived there from 1906 to 1916.

Wolfe is buried in Asheville's Riverside Cemetery, not far from another great American author, O. Henry.

6) TRYON PALACE

North Carolina's colonial governor had grandiose visions for his province-house built in New Bern. Governor William Tryon was charged with "gratifying his vanity," with building an "elegant monument of his taste and political influence at the expense of the interest of the province, and of his personal honor." The architecture of Tryon Palace, described as "the most beautiful building in the colonial Americas," was unique in the New World in that it was designed as a London vicinity house, and served not only as the colonial capitol but also as the governor's residence. Construction of the original large edifice and its two wings was begun in 1767 and finished in 1770 under the supervision of John Hawks, English master builder and "the first professional architect to remain in America."

The main building was destroyed by fire in 1798. Through trusts and bequests of the late Mrs. James Edwin Latham, a native of New Bern, the restoration of the palace on Pollock Street was begun in 1952 and completed in 1959. Extensive research has been put into the accurate redecoration of the palace. Furnished throughout with genuine eighteenth-century antiques, mostly predating 1770, the restored palace is almost a shrine for connoisseurs of early furniture, housewares, paintings, printed material, textiles, carpets and the accessories of twenty-seven large fireplaces.

South Carolina

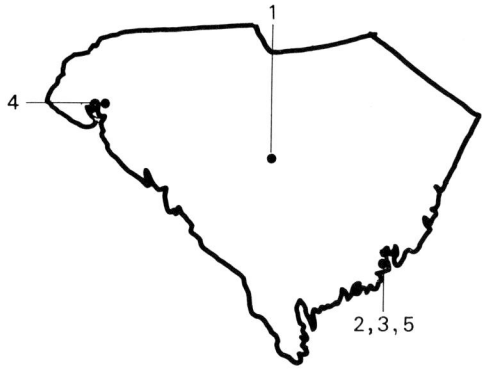

1) CAPITOL, Columbia

Just as Washington, D.C., was planned and built to serve as the nation's capital, Columbia was established specifically to function as the capital of South Carolina, and the Carolina city even has claim to primacy because it was founded well ahead of the District of Columbia, becoming the seat of government in 1790.

Construction of the present handsome Roman-Corinthian-style Statehouse in Columbia got underway in 1855. However, with the start of the Civil War, work came to a virtual standstill.

After the war, it was decided to complete the building, but the advent of the Reconstruction period caused further delay, and not until 1869 was the roof installed and the unfinished building occupied. Finally, by the end of the century, the north and south porticos, with immense monolithic granite columns, and the copper-covered dome, a substitute for the originally designed soaring tower, were erected. Still later the great flights of steps were built.

The main lobby, its lofty embossed ceiling going up into the dome, features a bronzed statue of John C. Calhoun.

2) CHARLESTON HISTORIC DISTRICT

Charleston is a city of history and a city with the foresight to preserve the landmarks of its illustrious past. Much of its delightful eighteenth-century atmosphere remains. The older section of the city, on the southern end of a peninsula, is still a preferred residential district. Many of the finest old homes are still lived in and some are still in the possession of the families which built them. A number of public buildings in daily use predate the Revolution.

The waterfront, one of the most important in the colonies, known as the Battery, is a fashionable place to visit.

The first permanent settlement at what was to become Charleston was established in 1670 by a small group of English settlers. By 1773 the city had a population of 12,000 and was called the "most eminent and by far the richest city in the Southern District of North America." These were certainly prosperous times for this venerable city. Her sea trade was described as "far surpassing even Boston."

Today, within the Charleston Historic District adjacent to the waterfront, many important and romantic episodes in American history can be recalled. Within a half-mile radius are such landmarks as the Dock Street Theater, the oldest playhouse in the United States, which opened in 1736. In the basement of the **Old Exchange Building** the "gentleman pirate" Stede Bonnet was imprisoned in 1718. His hanging ended pirates' threats on the Atlantic Ocean. The Exchange Building was completed as a customs house in 1771. Within its walls the Provincial Congress established the first independent government in America in July 1774.

Charleston's oldest church is the venerable St. Michael's Episcopal, dating from 1751. The bells in its soaring steeple have crossed the ocean five times.

Among other churches of note are the First Scots Presbyterian Church built in 1814, which for many years refused to associate with any presbytery outside Scotland; the only remaining French Huguenot church in America, where for 150 years services were conducted in French; and the second oldest Jewish Temple in the United States, Beth Elohim Reform Temple.

But perhaps it is for its homes that historic Charleston is noted. Along Church Street are a number of them made into house museums including the **Heyward-Washington**, Built in 1770 and owned by Thomas Heyward, Jr., a signer of the Declaration of Independence, it is an adaptation of the English Adam style with a central hall dividing the house. The back garden is geometrically patterned. George Washington stayed here while visiting the city.

The **Edmondston-Alston House**, built in 1828, has a lovely, unimpeded view across Charleston harbor. In 1838 the home changed owners and was redecorated in the Greek

Fort Hill, now a part of Clemson University, was the plantation home of John C. Calhoun, the historic "Voice of the South." Most of the furnishings in the home are original Calhoun heirlooms.

Revival style then in vogue. It has remained in the same family for over 135 years and is a treasure chest of priceless period furnishings.

The **Nathaniel Russell House** on Meeting Street is an outstanding example of delicately proportioned Adam-style architecture, built before 1809. Crossing the threshold, one is immediately astonished by a remarkable sight in the entrance hall—a free-flying staircase that, apparently unsupported, swings upward in sweeping curves to the third floor. Since 1955 this residence has been both a public museum and the headquarters of the Historic Charleston Foundation. Each spring when the city and her famous gardens are most beautiful, more than sixty historic dwellings are open on a series of tours for the benefit of the foundation's fund for preservation.

3) CHARLESTON VICINITY GARDENS

Charleston, one of the most prosperous of the early American port towns, sits on a fertile peninsula between two broad rivers, the Ashley and the Cooper. From its very beginning, this has been a focal point of American gardening. To the residents of Charleston the garden has always been a place to live in, to be married in and to enjoy the year around. The Carolina springtime brings thousands of visitors to see a trio of famous gardens: Cypress Gardens, Magnolia-on-the-Ashley and Middleton Place.

Cypress Gardens, found twenty-four miles north of Charleston on the Cooper River, was created on a typical cypress swamp. It covers 250 acres of lake and woodland. The great beauty of Cypress Gardens comes from the juxtaposition of the dark cypress to the flaming colors of azalea and other flowers on the shore of the lake and the islands. The stars of the floral show are camellias, which open the blossoming season at Thanksgiving and carry it on as, one after another, more than 300 varieties come into spectacular bloom. One of the best ways to see Cypress is by water in the small craft paddled by stoic Low Country boatmen.

The garden at Cypress was built in 1927; but the lake, a major part of the garden, was the reservoir of Dean Hall, a rice plantation, where, before the Civil War, there were more than 500 slaves and workmen. At the time the garden was created, a crew of some 200 men worked for several years simply to clear the tangled underbrush and debris from the lake and surrounding woodland.

In 1963 Cypress Gardens was given to the city of Charleston and is now operated by the city council and an independent board of advisors.

Magnolia-on-the-Ashley, southwest of Cypress, is the most famous of the trio of gardens and it is also considered by many to be the loveliest. It takes its name from the row of evergreen magnolia trees that once lined the walk from the Ashley River to the plantation manor house. The last of these magnificent trees along the avenue died in 1957, but fortunately many other large magnolias with broad wax-polished leaves and fragrant cuplike blossoms survive throughout the gardens along Highway 61. The fame of Magnolia-on-the-Ashley, however, is based on the beauty and great variety of azaleas and other flowers planted by the Reverend Mr. John Grimke-Drayton in the mid-nineteenth century.

Though it has only been planted in its present style since shortly before the Civil War, Magnolia—with its twenty-five acres of flower gardens, three beautiful lakes, and sixteen acres of oak-planted lawns—has received the accolades of many established garden connoisseurs down through the years and has been in the Drayton family since 1671.

Today the visitor at Magnolia still finds the long row of towering live oaks bordering the road to Magnolia Manor. The dark waters of the cypress swamp reflect the color, echoing the already dramatic image of white azalea, green cypress and rustic bridges. The general shape of this garden is fanlike with azalea-lined walks radiating outward from the house.

Middleton Place, upriver on the Ashley from Magnolia, is the oldest landscaped garden in the United States, planted in the 1700's by Henry Middleton, president of the First Continental Congress. The garden wears its age like a regal mantle. This, perhaps, is inevitable for so much of its beauty derives from the continuity of its being in the same family for two centuries.

The original design for Middleton had many similarities to the gardens of Le Nôtre at Versailles. It took the labor of one hundred slaves working daily for about nine years to complete the formal garden stretching out to the north and east of the manor house to include a flower garden and a long narrow reflecting pool or canal. Here in the formal garden stands the giant oak tree, now called the Middleton Oak, which even before the colony's settlement had been used by the Indians as a trail marker and which now towers over the garden with a limb spread of some 145 feet. This noble tree is estimated to be 900 years old.

The slope in front of the house is carved into a number of grassy terraces leading down to two lakes which were once part of an intricate system that irrigated nearby rice fields. These are the famous "butterfly lakes" ingeniously shaped to form wings while the grassy lawn between the two lakes takes the shape of a butterfly's body.

At the Plantation Stableyards, a recently developed attraction, visitors can view the work-a-day world of Middleton's agricultural economy through artifacts and demonstrations.

4) FORT HILL

Fort Hill, the spacious plantation house where John C. Calhoun lived, the man known in American history as "The Voice of the South," is now open to the public as a period museum and is maintained by the South Carolina Division of the United Daughters of the Confederacy. It was in 1825 that John C. Calhoun became owner of Fort Hill and its surrounding plantation. He proceeded to enlarge the house and to add to it the white-columned porticos and other architectural details that are so attractive today. It undoubtedly would have pleased him, had he lived long enough, to see that his plantation house, standing on its original site, is now part of the campus of Clemson

University, a leading institution of higher learning begun by his son-in-law, Thomas Clemson.

Designed in Southern colonial style, the Calhoun house is an attractive white, two-story dwelling of frame construction, with a gable roof, end chimneys, and a large, central entrance portico of Greek Doric design.

There are fourteen rooms in the house, nearly all of them furnished with original Calhoun and Clemson family heirlooms. Calhoun's desk, pier table and banjo clock are in the central hall. To the left of the entrance door is the large state dining room, perhaps the mansion's most gracious room. Furnished with a Duncan Phyfe African mahogany table with twelve matching chairs, Calhoun silver in a fiddle-thread colonial pattern and a steel engraving of Calhoun himself over the mantel, the dining room has gold velveteen drapes, complemented by the russet-brown figured wallpaper. The staunch sideboard was a present from Clay to Calhoun after Calhoun had spoken in defense of the Constitution of the United States.

Historic Charleston has preserved many interesting architectural landmarks. The Nathaniel Russell House, built before 1809, is an excellent example of Adam-style architecture.

5) FORT SUMTER NATIONAL MONUMENT

On April 12, 1861, the first shots of the Civil War were fired on Fort Sumter, a fort located on a small man-made island at the entrance of Charleston harbor. Eighty-five Federal soldiers under the command of Major Robert Anderson held the fort, one of the few which had remained in Federal hands after the Southern secession. They were forced to abandon the fort on April 14, having valiantly defended it for thirty-four hours. The next day President Lincoln called out 75,000 militia and the war had begun. Fort Sumter was to remain in Southern control throughout the conflict despite continued Union efforts to retake it.

Many changes have been made in the five-sided structure since 1865. For example, Spanish-American War gun emplacements predominate. An excellent museum provides information on the fort's significant role in American history. Fort Sumter can be reached by boat.

Also included in the national monument is nearby Fort Moultrie, scene of the first decisive victory of Americans over the British in the Revolutionary War.

The "Battle Above the Clouds" was fought on the slopes of Lookout Mountain near Chattanooga during the Civil War. The area has been preserved as a national military park.

Tennessee

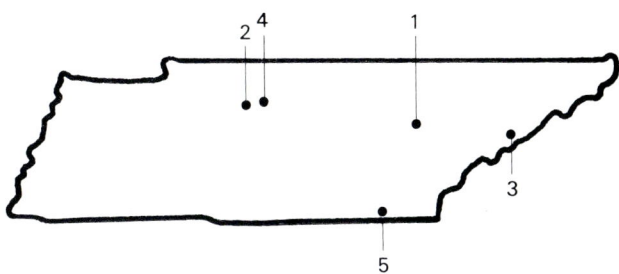

1) AMERICAN MUSEUM OF ATOMIC ENERGY

The city of Oak Ridge began during World War II as the site of early and highly secret nuclear research. Today, this community, set in the beautiful Appalachian foothills and surrounded by Tennessee Valley Authority (TVA) lakes, is a world-renowned center for nuclear research and education, dedicated to insuring an adequate supply of electrical energy.

Featured in the American Museum of Atomic Energy at Oak Ridge are exhibits and demonstrations describing present and future uses of nuclear energy in agriculture, industry and research. Mechanical hands used to handle radioactive materials and animals used in laboratory research may be seen. The many properties and uses of nuclear materials are depicted.

The museum is operated by Oak Ridge Associated Universities for the U.S. Atomic Energy Commission. An enlarged new museum building is now under construction to replace the converted World War II cafeteria. Also open to public view are the Oak Ridge Gaseous Diffusion Plant and the Graphite Reactor at the Oak Ridge National Laboratory.

2) CAPITOL, Nashville

Tennessee's State Capitol, overlooking downtown Nashville's Memorial Square, is truly a Grecian edifice. It has a Doric base; four Ionic porticos, modeled after the Erectheum in Athens; and Corinthian pillars in the lantern of the tower which resemble the Choragic monument of Lysicrates, sometimes called the Lantern of Demosthenes.

Despite the Grecian styling, the crystalline, fossilated limestone gives it a true Tennessee atmosphere, as this material was quarried near Nashville, then hewn into six- to ten-ton blocks for construction. Tennessee marble is also used extensively in the interior.

The building, completed in 1859, is surrounded by a terrace seventeen feet wide. Inside, a double flight of stairs leads to the House

Hermitage, home of President Andrew Jackson, is the only national shrine completely furnished with original pieces. Many of the trees planted on the estate are from sites of his military campaigns.

and Senate chambers on the main floor. The Hall of Representatives has a ceiling supported by sixteen fluted Ionic columns. In the smaller Senate Chamber, twelve Tennessee marble columns support a twelve-foot-wide gallery on three sides.

3) GREAT SMOKY MOUNTAINS NATIONAL PARK

See North Carolina—4.

4) HERMITAGE

Andrew Jackson, seventh President of the United States and hero of the Battle of New Orleans, purchased in 1804 a tract of 650 acres of fertile and rolling land approximately twelve miles from Nashville. A two-story block house, one of a number of cabins, was Old Hickory's first home on Hermitage Farm.

The original Hermitage mansion was built in 1819 and was a brick structure, probably designed by Jackson himself. In this simple, dignified home Jackson and his wife lived for nine years until Rachel's death. In 1831, while Jackson was President, the Hermitage was extensively remodeled and improved, but in 1834, the roof caught fire and much of the building was lost. Although a financial blow to him, Jackson had the home rebuilt in more spacious proportions.

Outstanding about the Hermitage, aside from its stately appearance and manicured, British-designed garden, is that it is the only national shrine furnished completely with original pieces. From the skeletal frame of Jackson's Phaeton Carriage, on display in the carriage house, to a Parisian marble vase in the front parlor, every piece of furniture, china and tapestry throughout the twelve-room house was witness to the passing career of the Tennessee-bred general and President.

5) LOOKOUT MOUNTAIN

The "Battle Above the Clouds" was fought on the slopes of Lookout Mountain near Chattanooga during the Civil War. Today, the 2,225-foot mountain is a significant part of the Chickamauga and Chattanooga National Military Park, the oldest and largest of the national military parks, which spans the Georgia-Tennessee state line. The 8,113-acre park commemorates several Civil War battles fought for control of Chattanooga in 1863. It was in this area that Sherman began his "March to the Sea."

Point Park, a Federal reservation, is located at the summit of Lookout Mountain, overlooking the city of Chattanooga and Moccasin Bend of the Tennessee River. The Lookout Mountain Incline Railway, one of the steepest in the world, makes its way to the top.

Worthy of note are the Rock City Gardens, a natural city of rocks encompassing ten acres of intriguing, lichen-covered sandstone formations atop the mountain. Ruby Falls, dropping 145 feet, is a spectacular subterranean phenomenon 1,120 feet beneath the earth in the enchanting Lookout Mountain Caves.

Virgin Islands

1) BUCK ISLAND REEF NATIONAL MONUMENT

A coral city in a turquoise world of tropical sunlight and quiet shadows populated by colorful, incredibly varied forms of marine life is one description of the horseshoe-shaped barrier reef called Buck Island. The living coral, just beneath the ocean surface only a few yards offshore, forms a lagoon of quiet waters.

Sea water, washing softly across the reef, freshens the lagoon constantly and maintains its salinity and crystal clearness. The uninhabited island maintains the lushness of tropical isles and has been kept free from the pollution of mankind. This minute piece of land, one and one-half miles northeast of St. Croix, was declared a national monument in 1961.

The lagoon, walled by glistening coral through which are seen twisting alleys paved with shimmering white sand, provides a near perfect backdrop for viewing both plant and animal life near the bottom. The water has such pristine clarity that coral masses, plants and fish may be seen through glass-bottom boxes towed behind rowboats or by skin divers and

Eerie coral fingers stretch toward the tropical Buck Island, off the tip of St. Croix. A colorful array of fish and plant life inhabits the barrier reef around the island.

swimmers equipped with snorkels in water depths ranging from ten to fifteen feet generally and from thirty-five to fifty feet at deeper points in the monument area.

2) VIRGIN ISLANDS NATIONAL PARK

The essence of the Caribbean's soft, luxuriant, provocative moods is nowhere better captured than at Trunk Bay of Virgin Islands National Park. The green waters are rich with multihued varieties of colorful coral, sponges and exotic tropical fish. The shimmering white beaches are fringed with palms. Off shore stands an occasional islet. Above, a royal blue sky. Inland, the dominant terrain is composed of rugged tropical forests and Bordeaux Mountain, 1,277 feet high.

The 15,150-acre park established in 1956 constitutes two-thirds of the Island of St. John, which is nine miles in length. The islands form a geological unit with Puerto Rico and the Greater Antilles, being of volcanic origin. St. John Island is a typical offspring of subsurface volcanic eruptions, dating back millions of years. Steep mountains, deep valleys, gleaming white beaches and extensive coral reefs growing on an underwater shelf of rock are characteristic of this unique national preserve. These are the islands that were discovered by

Trunk Bay in the Virgin Islands National Park typifies the spell-casting mood of the Caribbean. The park encompasses two-thirds of St. John Island.

An abundance of tropical fish live in the waters surrounding the islands. Snorkeling in organized groups or individually is a popular pastime.

Christopher Columbus on his second voyage, in 1493. He named them in honor of St. Ursula and her 11,000 virgins.

The relatively moist interior highlands of St. John, including steep-walled valleys, are dominated by a jungle forest of evergreen hardwoods. Drier slopes contain broad-leaved trees. Mangroves, turpentines, maho, cinnamon-bay kapok and soursop are the characteristic trees. Flowering shrubs and trees bloom in season, with a charm for the tourists increased by the knowledge that hibiscus, flamboyant, frangipani and bougainvillea are expensive commercial items back in the floral hothouses of the States.

About 100 species of birds abound in the islands with land birds more dominant. Herons, egrets, pelicans, gulls, frigate birds and terns can, however, be spotted along the shores. The pearly-eyed thrasher, smooth-billed ani, the mocking and humming birds are discernible in the forest and hills.

Snorkeling is a major activity in the park. Visitors have a chance to snorkel along the underwater trail at Trunk Bay, participate in a naturalist-led snorkel trip at Turtle or Cinnamon bays or explore on their own in a number of other good snorkeling areas (Hawksnest, Leinster, Francis and Lameshur bays). The water here is warm and clear.

The northeast trade winds temper the intense heat of the tropical sun, yielding pleasantly warm days and cool nights. The average annual temperature is seventy-nine degrees with only about six degrees difference between the winter and summer seasons.

**Illinois   Indiana   Michigan   Minnesota
Ohio   Wisconsin**

A scenic view of the island-studded Mississippi as seen from Pikes Peak Overlook, Iowa. On the west bank are McGregor and Effigy Mounds monument, with Prairie du Chien and Wisconsin to the east.

UPPER GREAT LAKES

Legendary men like Paul Bunyan and Hiawatha and real-life Johnny Appleseed once walked the forests and fields here. Their spirits still shadow this region, the heartland of the country.

The land is vivid and memorable, boasting such a catalog of vegetation that every hue of green is represented. Dense forests of pine, fir and birch in the northern sections of Michigan, Wisconsin and Minnesota mingle with hardwood stands of oak and maple toward the south of the region. Highlighting these forests is a spectacular network of clear streams and lakes that, like the Great Lakes and Mississippi and Ohio rivers that define the region, are sources of wealth in beauty and recreation opportunities. The miles of rockbound shores, shifting dunes and sculpted bluffs are spellbinding. South of the forests and lakes, grains, fruits and vegetables are harvested in such abundance from a rich and generous earth once covered with lush prairie grasses that it is one of the world's most productive areas.

The region is the water, land and air transportation hub around which the nation turns. The Mississippi and Ohio rivers (via the Gulf of Mexico) and the Great Lakes (via the St. Lawrence Seaway) provide easy access to the Atlantic Ocean. Easily traveled terrain has led to the development of impressive rail and vehicular systems. Industrial muscle is concentrated in cities strung along the lakeshores for a thousand miles, from Duluth, Minnesota, to Cleveland, Ohio, including Chicago, Illinois, and Detroit, Michigan.

Perhaps to compensate for a quite uniform geography of almost flat land leveled by ancient ice sheets, weather alters drastically, season to season and within each season. The Midwesterner is more than invigorated; he is trained to a beneficial patience.

In the eighteenth and nineteenth centuries immigrants from the Eastern and Southern United States and northwestern Europe settled along the rivers and lakes the French had explored in the seventeenth century. Even today, international influences—the late Senator Everett Dirksen called them a "cosmopolitan chemistry"—add flavor to the inhabitants who are known for their neighborliness and unquenchable spirit.

Illinois

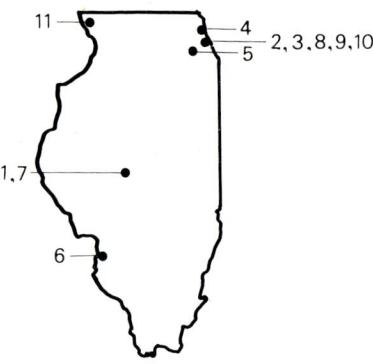

Grant Wood's classic depiction of middle America, American Gothic, is on display in the Art Institute of Chicago. Noted for its outstanding art collections dating from the fourteenth century, the building also houses Goodman Theater, Chicago's only resident professional theater company.

1) ABRAHAM LINCOLN HOME

In 1844, Abraham Lincoln bought a one-and-a-half story cottage which, except for one year (1847) during his term in the United States Congress, he was to occupy until he left Springfield as President-elect in 1861. Built in 1839, the frame house, which has been preserved on the original Eighth and Jackson streets site, achieved its final form when Mary Todd Lincoln added an extra half story in 1856. Reflected in its delicate trim and cornices, the house was designed in the Greek Revival style as it appeared on the frontier, framed in oak and sided and floored with black walnut.

Today, the Springfield house, designated a national historic site in 1971, contains some of the original furnishings: Lincoln's hatrack in the downstairs hallway, his favorite horsehair-covered rocker in the sitting room, his secretary in the back parlor, and his shaving mirror and chest of drawers in his bedroom.

Lincoln was born on February 12, 1809, in a log cabin on his father's 300-acre Sinking Spring farm, a few miles south of Hodgenville, Kentucky. What is assumed to be the original cabin is now on display in a memorial building completed near Sinking Spring in 1911. The **Abraham Lincoln Birthplace National Historic Site**, designated in 1959, includes 110 acres that were part of the Lincoln farm.

In 1816, the family moved to Indiana, and Lincoln spent his formative years, from ages 7 to 21, in a typical log cabin in Spencer County. This cabin and farmyard have been restored as the **Lincoln Boyhood National Memorial**. Here, the visitor finds a glimpse of the rugged pioneer life-style which shaped this revered President.

Lincoln moved to central Illinois in 1830 and settled in the small village of New Salem. It was here that he first ran for office, an unsuccessful bid for a seat in the Illinois House of Representatives in 1832. He tried again two years later and won, and in 1837 was admitted to the bar and moved to Springfield to begin law practice. The village of New Salem has been restored as it was when Lincoln lived there. Called **New Salem State Park**, the restoration includes twenty-three log cabins and buildings, including the store where Lincoln once served as postmaster.

2) ART INSTITUTE OF CHICAGO

Chicago's magnificent Art Institute on Michigan Avenue is noted for its outstanding

Many of Lincoln's original possessions are on display in his restored Springfield home. This piano was played at his 1842 wedding.

collections of paintings and watercolors ranging from the fourteenth century to the present. Among these are such works as El Greco's *Assumption of the Virgin* and the popular *American Gothic* by Grant Wood. Some of the greatest Impressionist and post-Impressionist works of art are effectively displayed. The museum contains the largest collection of nineteenth- and twentieth-century French paintings in the world.

Other facets of the institute's treasures include Japanese prints, Chinese sculptures and bronzes, and a varied collection of prints and drawings. Unique and intriguing are the Thorne Rooms, miniature rooms accurate to the most minute detail, which trace the history of English and American interior design from the sixteenth century to the present.

Also part of the institute, Goodman Theater, one block east, is the home of Chicago's only resident professional theater company and the oldest children's theater company in the country. The School of the Art Institute is one of the few fully accredited art colleges.

The building was constructed in 1892 in the Italianate Renaissance style for the World's Columbian Exposition, housing the Congress of Religions. The Art Institute opened in 1893.

3) AUDITORIUM THEATRE

Frank Lloyd Wright once called the Auditorium Theatre "the greatest room for music and opera in the world—bar none." Designed by noted architects of the Chicago School, Dankmar Adler and Louis Sullivan, it is one of the few remaining examples of that boldly creative period in the city from 1880 to 1893.

Thanks to the design genius of Sullivan and the brilliant acoustical engineering of Adler, the Auditorium is still one of the world's greatest theaters. A person standing on the stage and speaking in a normal tone can be heard and seen in any part of the hall, which seats 4,000 people.

For too many years the Auditorium lay dormant. Several times it narrowly escaped destruction and would probably not have survived were it not for its massivity and the fact that Roosevelt University now occupies the sections of the building complex which surround the theater. These were designed by Sullivan and Adler for hotel and office space.

The Auditorium was reopened in 1967. Since then, the stage of this venerable and functional landmark has seen many outstanding performances. Restoration and modernization have not affected its grand atmosphere.

4) BAHA'I TEMPLE

The Baha'i faith, which traces its origins to Persia, is an independent world religion. Basic Baha'i beliefs stress a sense of the oneness of God and all mankind and the essential unity of the world's religions. The American center of the religion is the Baha'i Temple in Wilmette. On each of its nine sides are doorways through which members pass into a united brotherhood.

The temple, completed in 1953, is surmounted by a magnificent lacelike dome of reinforced concrete which rises to a height of 162 feet. The two-story base, 153 feet in diameter, is geometrically ornamented with symbols of all the world's religions.

Architecturally similar to Moslem structures in Persia and India, the Baha'i Temple near the beautiful shores of Lake Michigan is unique and mysteriously beautiful. Grace and harmony are achieved, expressing the tenets of the faith which strives for simplicity and unity.

5) BROOKFIELD ZOO

Visiting a zoo can be a fascinating step into the animal kingdom. Individual animals—a mongoose, peccary or white Bengal tiger—can serve as meaningful ambassadors for their

Frank Lloyd Wright once described Chicago's Auditorium Theatre as "the greatest room for music and opera in the world—bar none."

species and for the preservation of a balanced ecological system. At the Brookfield Zoo, west of downtown Chicago, people of all ages can both learn and enjoy.

Extensive collections of 600 species of animals, birds and reptiles including a number of rare and endangered species, are housed in quarters designed to be as close to their natural habitats as possible. Moats are used instead of bars and cages, except for the "athletes"— jaguars, pumas and leopards. There are more than twenty separate exhibition areas covering almost 200 acres. Most of the buildings and landscaping follow the formal fifteenth-century Italianate style.

6) CAHOKIA MOUNDS STATE PARK

Preserved in the 760-acre Cahokia Mounds State Park near East St. Louis are remnants of the highest known order of prehistoric Indian civilization north of Mexico. The Cahokia site was first inhabited about A.D. 700. Approximately 850 to 900 the Mississippian culture emerged, so named because it was first discovered along the Mississippi River. (See **Etowah Mounds Archeological Area**, Georgia—3.) The city at Cahokia became the regional center for a highly developed agricultural society. Cahokia began to decline about 1300, and about 1550 its existence ended suddenly for reasons not known today.

The city of Cahokia covered six square miles and had a population numbering in the tens of thousands. About 1150 a twelve- to fifteen-foot-high stockade was erected around 400 acres of the center city. At least three more walls were subsequently built. The second wall comprising some 20,000 logs was built about 1200 and has been partially reconstructed.

At one time there were over 100 mounds in the area, but many have not survived the encroachment of progress. About forty of these earthen structures are now preserved in the park. Nearly fifty million cubic feet of earth were probably moved by the Indians for mounds' construction. Large depressions left by their digging, called borrow pits, can still be seen. A museum at Cahokia Mounds displays artifacts uncovered in archeological excavations of the area.

Most mounds were used for ceremonial purposes; only a few were burial mounds. They were built in a variety of shapes, but the most common type at Cahokia is the platform. Square or rectangular in shape with sloping sides, the flat tops were used as bases for ceremonial buildings or residences for rulers.

Monk's Mound, the largest platform mound at Cahokia, is also the largest prehistoric earthen construction in the world. It rises 100 feet in three terraces and has a base covering fourteen acres.

Sites of four circular sun calendars, which were probably used to record season changes and ceremonial occasions, have been uncovered. Because of their similarity to Stonehenge in England they are called woodhenges.

The cooperage where Lincoln often studied has been restored with twenty-three other log cabins and buildings in New Salem State Park.

Octavia Octopus welcomes visitors to Chicago's John G. Shedd Aquarium, the world's largest aquarium, containing over 7,500 living specimens.

7) CAPITOL, Springfield

Occupying nine acres of land in Springfield, the Illinois State Capitol is in the shape of a Latin cross. Construction of the building began in 1868 but was not completed until 1888.

The focal point of the Capitol is a vast dome which rises to a height of 361 feet, with still another forty-one feet to the tip of its flagstaff. The foundation, ninety-two feet in diameter, sits on solid rock. Farther below this stratum is a rich vein of coal.

The rotunda walls and arches are solid stone, faced with Missouri red granite. Various kinds of marble are used extensively throughout the interior, including the grand stairway. The interior is very impressive with marble mosaics, historical murals, oil paintings and statuary.

8) FIELD MUSEUM OF NATURAL HISTORY

Founded in 1893, an outgrowth of the natural science exhibits at the World's Columbian Exposition in Chicago that same year, the Field Museum has become one of the greatest institutions of its kind in the world. Housed in an immense building bordering Grant Park on Lake Michigan, it is a microcosm of the world in terms of the four great natural sciences—anthropology, botany, geology and zoology.

Of special note are the meteorite collection which includes nearly sixty percent of all known meteorites, the bronze and stone sculptures of the "Race of Man," and the fascinating Hall of Primitive Art.

The museum, a bequest to Chicago from Marshall Field, was a pioneer in the use of life-size dioramas. A series of dioramas tells the story of man's evolution. Outstanding specimens of wildlife from throughout the world are presented in three-dimensional likenesses of their natural habitats.

9) MUSEUM OF SCIENCE AND INDUSTRY

Unlike most museums which are primarily interested in collecting and preserving the past, Chicago's Museum of Science and Industry specializes in mankind's advances in scientific knowledge and applied technology. Most exhibits are three-dimensional and involve active participation by visitors.

Most famous of the more than 2,000 exhibits scattered over some fourteen acres in Jackson Park on Lake Michigan are the full-sized working coal mine, the German submarine U-505 which was captured during World War II, the hatching of baby chicks, and movie star Colleen Moore's elaborate dollhouse, the "Fairy Castle." Also displayed here are the Apollo 8 spacecraft which first orbited the moon, a sixteen-foot walk-through heart and a full-size model of a first-class cabin in a Boeing 747 jet. Exhibits tell the story of agriculture, electricity, petroleum, computers, nuclear engineering, medicine and many other applied fields. The fascinating Space Age Communications exhibit includes a working model of the Early Bird satellite.

The Museum of Science and Industry was opened in 1933, largely through the efforts of Chicago businessman Julius Rosenwald. It is housed in the restored Fine Arts Building of the 1893 World's Columbian Exposition.

10) SHEDD AQUARIUM

Chicago's John G. Shedd Aquarium provides a fascinating glimpse of the underwater world, a chance to see its residents set against the background of their natural habitats. Over 7,500 living specimens represent some 350 species in the world's largest aquarium.

Shedd Aquarium was opened in 1930 for the purpose of furthering man's knowledge of his aquatic environment. Of special interest is the coral reef, where over seventy-five species of colorful Caribbean fish swim against a beautiful coral backdrop. Here, the delicate interrelationships of the residents of a reef can be dramatically seen.

11) ULYSSES S. GRANT HOUSE

Ulysses S. Grant arrived in Galena in the spring of 1860 by steamboat to clerk in the

In 1865, the citizens of Galena, Illinois, paid tribute to their victorious general, Ulysses S. Grant, by presenting him with this handsome Victorian residence.

family leather goods store, and five years later the town was to present the victorious Union general with one of the finest Victorian homes in the city during a grand victory celebration.

The house on Bouthillier Street, not far from the Galena River, was built in 1859. Designed in the Italianate bracketed style, the two-story brick residence with wide, overhanging eaves, represented the best mid-Victorian architecture of the period.

Although Grant always considered the Galena home his legal residence, the period after the war until his death in 1885, including his terms as President from 1869–77, allowed him little time there. The mansion remained in the family until 1904 when it was deeded to Galena.

In 1932 the house passed to the State of Illinois and, in 1955, a complete restoration was undertaken. Use of the original plans and specifications, drawn by the builder in 1859, permitted authentic structural restoration and many of the original Grant furnishings were available for the interior. Among these, an old horsehair-covered parlor set is displayed on a new loop Brussels carpet, containing the same colors and exact pattern as the original. The Haviland china displayed in the dining room was bought for Grant's daughter in 1874.

Indiana

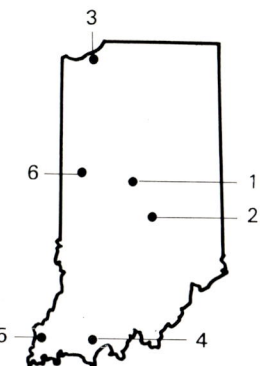

1) CAPITOL, Indianapolis

The Indiana State House in Indianapolis is a classic Corinthian-design four-story building of Indiana limestone. The distinguishing feature of the Capitol is the massive dome, 72 feet in diameter and rising from the center to a height of 234 feet. The dome is constructed of stone and rests on eight columns of Maine granite. Eight Italian Carrara marble statues of heroic size placed within the rotunda at the third floor level represent Law, Oratory, Agriculture, Commerce, Justice, Liberty, History and Art. On each floor a corridor sixty-eight feet wide extends the entire length of the building and is illuminated from attic to basement by skylights. A double row of marble columns, piers and pilasters support the upper structure.

2) COLUMBUS ARCHITECTURE

Some of the most exciting contemporary architecture in the United States can be found in the small, industrial city of Columbus in south-central Indiana.

It began when the **First Christian Church** commissioned the renowned Eliel Saarinen to create a new building, expressing the simple Biblical faith of its members with an uncluttered, geometric design. Constructed primarily of buff brick and limestone, the massive house of worship with its 166-foot bell tower was completed in 1942. The airy and light sanctuary is painted white and furnished in bleached oak. On the east wall hangs a tapestry designed in muted colors by Saarinen and his wife.

Continuing this tradition of excellence in design, Saarinen's son, Eero, was the architect for the Irwin Union Bank and Trust Company's main building in 1953. This structure's glass walls eliminated the stuffiness then common to many financial institutions.

Not long after the bank's completion, the Cummins Engine Foundation made a unique proposition to the local school board: It would pay the architect's fees for new school buildings

At the Indiana Dunes, new dunes up to 200 feet high are constantly formed, covering trees and vegetation that have immobilized the growth of older dunes.

provided the nation's best architects received the commissions. This offer was eventually expanded to include all public buildings. Besides the some seventeen structures already subsidized by the foundation, other buildings have been financed through a variety of sources.

One of the primary showpieces is the Cleo Rogers Memorial Library, designed by I.M. Pei. On the Library Plaza is a sculpture entitled *Large Arch* by Henry Moore. Other attractive buildings include the Lincoln Elementary

School by Gunnar Birkerts, which harmonizes rather than blends with the downtown scene, the W.D. Richards Elementary School by Edward Larrabee Barnes, and the Post Office by Kevin Roche, John Dinkeloo and Associates.

Just before his death in 1964, Eero Saarinen completed the drawings for Columbus' hexagonal **North Christian Church**. Its slender, 192-foot spire rises from a sloping roof and is topped by a gold-leaf cross. Through an oculus at the base of the spire, direct natural light reaches the sanctuary. Diffused light enters from under the edge of the roof line. The "in the round" sanctuary with the communion table at center is intended to stimulate participation by worshipers.

3) INDIANA DUNES NATIONAL LAKESHORE

The Indiana Dunes, a natural area in northern Indiana squeezed between urbanization and steel mills, became a national seashore in 1960. Through the pines and hardwoods at the top of the dunes you can see the setting sun silhouetting the impressive skyline of Chicago, thirty-five miles away across Lake Michigan. In the same gaze, you can see the dark, satanic steel mills in East Chicago and Gary with smoke billowing from their tall stacks. Indiana Dunes National Lakeshore contains about 8,200 acres in isolated areas along the shore and inland.

These dunes, which reach astonishing heights of up to two hundred feet, were once the sandy shores of a monstrous lake formed by retreating glaciers. As the lake receded, winds whipped the exposed sand into dunes which "moved" over the area. Through the centuries vegetation gradually covered and immobilized them. New dunes are constantly being formed, however, and sometimes they have gradually covered forests which had established themselves on the older dunes. Occasionally stiff winds blow a niche in a sand ridge, which gradually enlarges to form a "blowout." Five large "blowouts" can be seen in Indiana Dunes State Park, within the lakeshore's boundaries, and the largest one has exposed remnants of a dead forest, killed by the once-advancing sands.

Northern plants forced to move south because of the glaciers have somehow managed to survive here, mixing with plants from the south which migrated north during the post-glacier warming period. Thus, the prickly-pear cactus of the desert mingles with Arctic barberry. Jack and white pine grow on the dunes and tamarack and birch in the bogs, separated from their normal range to the north by about a hundred

The Roofless Church (above) reflects New Harmony's intellectually progressive spirit, while the Log Cabin Museum (below) at Turkey Run represents the hardy pioneer spirit.

miles, while the tulip tree, black gum and sassafras are at their northwestern limits.

4) LINCOLN BOYHOOD NATIONAL MEMORIAL
See **Abraham Lincoln Home**, Illinois—1.

5) NEW HARMONY

Founded in 1814 by Harmonists, members of a German religious sect, New Harmony was the scene of two historic experiments in communal living. Many reminders of these products of man's highest aspirations remain to intrigue the modern visitor.

The Harmonists, or Rappists, came to Indiana from Pennsylvania and in ten years had created a prosperous town. Members of the sect believed in community ownership of goods, celibacy and the imminent second coming of Christ. An individual Harmonist dwelling and a dormitory have been restored. Other unrestored Harmonist houses are still in use as private homes.

In 1824, the Harmonists returned to Pennsylvania, selling the town site to Welsh-Scottish industrialist Robert Owen. Owen also had an idea

A 192-foot spire topped by a gold-leaf cross rises majestically from the unique hexagonal North Christian Church, designed by Eero Saarinen in 1964.

for a utopian community, though not a religious one. With his precept "universal happiness through universal education," he attracted intellectuals and scientists from Europe and the Eastern United States. Though the grand experiment was short-lived, failing from want of skilled laborers for its everyday enterprises, the Owenists are credited with a number of achievements. The first kindergarten and the first free school system in America were begun in New Harmony, and the first free library.

The Roofless Church, its dome rising like an inverted rosebud, is New Harmony's most recent outgrowth of mankind's higher nature.

6) TURKEY RUN STATE PARK

Turkey Run State Park provides a rare opportunity to venture into the past and see the land as the pioneers first saw it. Stands of virgin timber cover 285 acres. These magnificent trees—beech, sassafras, tulip, walnut, black cherry, maple, hickory, sycamore and oak—grace the land once owned by Salmon Lusk, who came to this beautiful wilderness in west-central Indiana in the early 1800's. His son, John, stubbornly refused to yield his primeval paradise to the lumberman's axe. In 1916, the state acquired the land and formed the nucleus of Turkey Run State Park. Its name is derived from the flocks of wild turkeys that once gathered beneath the overhanging bluffs along the streams or runs.

The park now protects over 2,000 acres of exquisite beauty. The deep, rock-walled canyons and winding gorges here were cut into sandstone by glacial streams. Sugar Creek, one of the primary tributaries of the Wabash River, still cuts its way through a deep, narrow valley.

One of the unique features of the park are the relic stands of Eastern hemlock, normally found much further north and east, which were pushed into the area by glaciers.

Parke County, in which Turkey Run park is located, is famous for its concentration of scenic covered bridges. One of the county's thirty-five such bridges can be found in Turkey Run.

Michigan

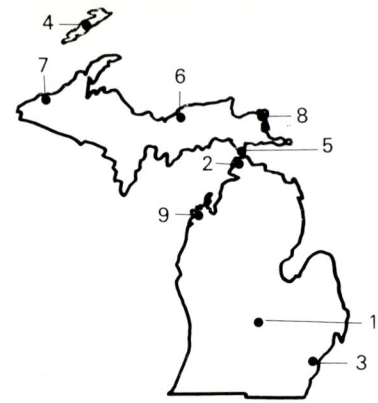

1) CAPITOL, Lansing

On a spacious landscaped site across from the Lansing City Hall stands Michigan's four-story Capitol, topped by a dome and spire rising sharply to 276 feet. Above a limestone foundation, its walls are faced with white Ohio sandstone.

The classical Renaissance Capitol's granite cornerstone was laid in 1873 and the building was dedicated in 1879. An allegorical bas-relief, symbolic of Michigan's development, decorates the pediment high above the east entrance.

On either side of the rotunda, a grand staircase rises from the ground floor to the fourth. Balconies look down upon the rotunda's display of battle flags and its floor of glass blocks set in iron. At the dome's base are murals of Michigan Science, Astronomy, Justice, Industry, Navigation, Education, Art and Agriculture.

2) FORT MICHILIMACKINAC

French trappers, traders and missionaries had been operating along the Straits of Mackinac for over half a century when Fort Michilimackinac was built about 1715. For the next sixty-five years the fortification at the top of lower Michigan carefully guarded this gateway to the West. Here, Indians came to trade and fur traders had their headquarters.

In 1761, after the French and Indian War, Fort Michilimackinac became a British enclave. Nearly all of the British at the fort were massacred in a Chippewa Indian uprising two years later. Soldiers regained control of the fort within a few months and the British maintained the outpost until 1780-81 when Fort Mackinac was constructed on Mackinac Island a short distance away. The move to the island was made because the mainland site was felt to be too vulnerable to American attack during the Revolution.

The abandoned fort was buried by blowing sand. Fortunately the site was not disturbed by modern construction. It was set aside as a local park as early as 1857, and in 1933-34 the stockade and several cabins were rebuilt.

In 1959, major archeological excavations and a full-scale reconstruction of the fort as it was in British hands were initiated by the Mackinac Island Commission and Michigan State University. The soldiers' barracks, the first structure completed, houses the Museum of Fort Michilimackinac. It contains a large collection of documents, pictures and artifacts as well as graphic displays telling the story of the fort. The massacre of 1763 is depicted in two life-size dioramas. The King's storehouse, rebuilt on its original site, is furnished with the supplies it might have held in 1775. Its original cobblestone floor dates from the French structures erected on the site in 1730.

At Fort Michilimackinac, as well as at Old Ford Mackinac which still dominates Mackinac Island, Michigan's history returns to life.

3) GREENFIELD VILLAGE AND HENRY FORD MUSEUM

"I am collecting the history of our people as written into things their hands made and used." So commented Henry Ford. His creations, the Henry Ford Museum and Greenfield Village, more than fulfill this aspiration.

Greenfield Village covers 260 acres at Dearborn. Included here are one hundred historic buildings, most carefully moved from their original sites, which are either representative of some aspect of American development since colonial times or are closely associated with the lives of famous citizens.

The village, designed to resemble a rural or early urban town, is centered around the Village Green. Surrounding it are a courthouse where Abraham Lincoln practiced law; the Clinton Inn, once a stagecoach stop; a general store of the last century; a one-room school; a chapel, and the Town Hall. Nearby are the birthplaces of George Washington Carver, Luther Burbank and Henry Ford. The Classical Revival mansion where Noah Webster completed his famous dictionary has also been transplanted here, along with Edison's Menlo Park Laboratory and Wilbur and Orville Wright's Cycle Shop. A number of mills,

Area residents yearly reenact the 1763 Chippewa massacre of the British at reconstructed Fort Michilimackinac. In the background is the Mackinac Bridge which connects Michigan's Upper and Lower peninsulas.

workshops, early factories and shops depict the evolution of American industry and commerce.

The Henry Ford Museum shares the grounds, but brings American history to life from another perspective. The monumental museum building covers fourteen acres, with a replica of Philadelphia's Independence Hall forming its entrance. Adjacent are copies of Congress Hall and the Old City Hall of Philadelphia.

The museum's extensive collections are divided into three categories: the American Decorative Arts Galleries which trace the development of American furniture and decoration; the Street of Early American Shops where late-eighteenth- and early-nineteenth-century shops filled with period tools and handicrafts line five blocks, and the eight-acre Mechanical Arts Hall with exhibits of early American agriculture, transportation, communications, lighting, industrial machinery and steam and electric power.

4) ISLE ROYALE NATIONAL PARK

Isle Royale, now a north woods wilderness held in a lake's solitude, is visibly haunted by the grace and majesty of its geologic past. This handsomely endowed protectorate of vast Lake Superior is enveloped by the greatest of the Great Lakes, the lake which marks the site of the southern end of an ancient and possibly one of the highest mountain ranges that ever ex-

Isle Royale is a retreat into untouched wilderness splendor. The forty-five-mile-long uninhabited island is the perfect escape from tedious everyday living.

isted on our continent. Only twenty-two miles from the Minnesota shore, yet a part of Michigan, Isle Royale National Park was established in 1940 and covers nearly 540,000 acres of north woods majesty.

Indian copper miners reportedly worked on forty-five-mile-long Isle Royale 4,000 years ago. The island's fjordlike harbors, sheltered bays and interior parallel ridges attaining a height of seven hundred feet were first looked upon by white men in 1699. These heroic French explorers named the island for Louis XIV.

Two hundred tiny islands and countless rocks, inviting water exploration, surround the main island; thus the entire park area can be called an archipelago. A coniferous sweep of trees covers the northeast and perimeter of the island, and maple-birch hardwoods dominate the

There are no roads on the island. The hiker and canoeist, however, can maneuver here with more than 120 miles of trails to be negotiated amid the wild splendor. Many small boats are handy to the seeker of water worlds at Rock Harbor and Windigo. Fishermen call the island "the pike capital of the nation" because of the abundance of pike in the 200 lakes and ponds. Isle Royale is the North Woods in autonomous compactness, with fascination for all.

5) MACKINAC BRIDGE

A monument to tenacity and ingenuity, the Mackinac Bridge is built to stand nobly and permanently in Michigan's beautiful north country. Although its main span is only 3,800 feet, shorter than either the Verrazano-Narrows or the Golden Gate bridges, it is the longest suspension bridge, stretching 26,444 feet across the Straits of Mackinac, connecting lower Michigan with its Upper Peninsula.

The bridge, completed in 1957, is extraordinarily strong, built to withstand the fierce winds and huge ice masses which are part of northern Michigan's winters. "Big Mack's" pier foundations weigh nearly one million tons. The designer, outstanding bridge engineer David B. Steinman, also added a number of unique features to insure safety and stability. Between the 48-foot-wide roadway and the sturdily anchored trusses Steinman allowed a ten-foot open space on either side. In addition, the two inner lanes of traffic and the central mall are constructed as an open grid.

6) PICTURED ROCKS NATIONAL LAKESHORE

From the waters of Lake Superior, the largest freshwater lake in the world, the late afternoon sun brings out the deep colors of the rocky cliffs—the reds, greens, browns and purples—and the various shapes of the rocks are accentuated by long shadows. Inland, the sun sparkles on the lakes and cascading streams, and the maples and birches ruffle in the breeze. The scent of pine drifts down the hillsides and, far away, a coyote howls. It is not hard to imagine a young Indian brave named Hiawatha paddling his birchbark canoe on these lake waters, for this is the land of the Gitche-Gumee, the shining Big-Sea-Water.

Although Longfellow's epic poem is fiction, much of his setting was based upon the Pictured Rocks area of Michigan's Upper Peninsula. The Chippewa Indians resided here for many years, and French explorers and missionaries, includ-

higher interior. Bald ridges, bogs, and spruce and cedar swamps dot the landscape, offering additional havens for water birds.

Approximately 600 moose constitute Isle Royale's relatively large population. Beavers, red foxes, snowshoe hares and red squirrels find refuge and sustenance here. The lonely cry of the loon, the din of the herring gull, the scream of the bald eagle are heard on the island reaches.

ing Pierre Radisson and Father Marquette, knew the area well.

The main attraction is the Pictured Rocks themselves, fifteen miles of sandstone cliffs rising abruptly from the lake as much as 200 feet. In the never-ending struggle against erosion, these rocks are fighting a losing battle, for the waves, rain and frost have carved arches, columns, promontories and thunder caves out of the cliffs. Groundwater, seeping to various sandstone levels and collecting minerals and chemicals on the way, drips down the sides of the eroded sculptures, depositing the staining chemicals. The names describe the formations: Miners Castle, Chapel Rock, Lovers Leap, Rainbow Cave and the Battleships. In the early 1900's Grand Portal, a magnificent series of several honeycombed arches jutting 600 feet into the lake, collapsed, leaving lesser arches, amphitheaters and debris.

Pictured Rocks National Lakeshore, approved by Congress in 1966, protects thirty-five miles of Lake Superior shoreline from Grand Marais to Munising. It also includes many thousands of acres of forested slopes and inland waters. The best way to see the Pictured Rocks is from the lake, and boat tours are available in Munising during the summer.

7) PORCUPINE MOUNTAINS STATE PARK

Over a century ago avaricious copper miners were drawn to the Porcupine Mountains, but neither the copper mines nor the silver mines operated later proved profitable. Since that time this remote area has changed little. Virgin forests of mixed hardwoods and conifers are preserved in the 58,000-acre state park established in 1945.

The highest range of hills between the Black Hills of South Dakota and the East's Alleghenies, the Porcupine Mountains roughly parallel the Lake Superior shoreline in a section of Michigan's Upper Peninsula. Here are beautiful, secluded lakes and many miles of wild rivers and streams. The most spectacular, the beautiful Presque Isle River, forms the southwestern boundary.

The "Porkies" are a rugged wilderness where a hiker must truly be a woodsman, but the exquisite beauty of the mountains is his reward.

A nineteenth-century soldier carved from pine is only one of the antique pieces that bring American history to life in the Henry Ford Museum.

8) SAULT STE. MARIE

At the northeastern tip of Michigan's Upper Peninsula, Sault Ste. Marie, the oldest town in the state and the third oldest surviving community in the United States, faces its Canadian twin city across the St. Mary's River. Though the French had visited the isolated region earlier, Father Marquette established the first permanent settlement in 1688. Preserved in this historic city are the Indian agency built in 1828 by Henry Schoolcraft, and the John Johnston Home, built in 1796, where Schoolcraft wrote the Indian legends which Longfellow used for *Hiawatha*.

The beautiful St. Mary's River is the connecting link between Lake Huron and Lake Superior. Through St. Mary's Rapids the higher waters of Lake Superior cascade down some eighteen feet in less than a mile. Ships can pass only by means of the famous Sault Ste. Marie Locks. The first lock was built in 1797-98 for the canoes of fur traders, but it was destroyed during the War of 1812. The first ship canal in the United States was completed here in 1855. Today, a 1,200-foot lock enables more than 100 million tons of freight annually to come through the busy St. Mary's Falls Ship Canal. The much diminished but still dramatic beauty of the *sault* or falls can be viewed from almost any point along the canal.

9) SLEEPING BEAR DUNES NATIONAL LAKESHORE

According to ancient Chippewa and Ottawa Indian legends, a black bear and her two cubs attempted to swim across Lake Michigan from the Wisconsin side. Nearing the shore the cubs became tired and lagged behind their mother, who climbed atop a bluff to watch and wait for her offspring. She is still there, the Sleeping Bear, a solitary dune covered with dark vegetation. The cubs still lag a few miles offshore, the forested North and South Manitou islands.

In fact, these massive sand dunes, glistening beaches, green forests, blue lakes and gently flowing streams are the result of glacial action. When the last stage of the Pleistocene Ice Age ended, the land was left in a jumble of glacial features. The basis of the Sleeping Bear region is the 300-foot-high Manistee Moraine, which snakes along a few miles inland. Other moraines, called interlobate moraines, extend out from Manistee and are responsible for the various points jutting out into the lake.

However, at Sleeping Bear Point erosion carved steep bluffs some 400 feet high. Continual battering of the eroded material by wind and waves formed sand particles which were blown up over the tops of the cliffs. At this point a decrease in wind caused them to drop and gradually cover the bluffs. Thus, Sleeping Bear Dunes differ from the Indiana Dunes 300 miles south because they are not pure dunes, but covered cliffs.

Blowouts, breaks in the sand ridges where the sand has been blown away, are also present here. Many of the older dunes have been stabilized with vegetation, but the younger dunes, particularly the Sleeping Bear Dune which towers 450 feet over Lake Michigan, are continuing to move inland, encroaching on the forests and glacial lakes.

Many clear blue lakes, notably Crystal, Platt and Glen lakes, are surrounded by forests of beech and sugar maple. The more sandy areas support pine, oak and aspen. Excellent stands of white cedar exist on the Manitou Islands, and beach grass and cottonwoods grow on the younger dunes of the mainland.

Sleeping Bear Dunes National Lakeshore was authorized in 1970 and contains 71,000 acres, including sixty-four miles of mainland shoreline and the two offshore islands.

The Sleeping Bear Dunes in Michigan are not pure dunes, but merely sand covered cliffs constantly shifting and reshaping.

Minnesota

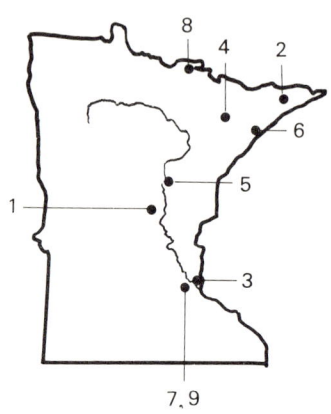

1) ABBEY AND UNIVERSITY CHURCH OF ST. JOHN THE BAPTIST

On the campus of St. John's University in Collegeville, the Abbey and University Church of Saint John the Baptist is symbolic of the movement within the Catholic Church to reexamine the faith and return to its basics. The structure's design, by the internationally famous architect Marcel Breuer, is modern, but it emphasizes the oldest ideals of church architecture.

A majestic bell banner stands at the church entrance, boldly introducing the building and creating a triumphal gateway into the house of worship. The bells and the cross which it supports proclaim a renewed hope and vitality. The church is entered through the baptistry.

Within, the concrete and steel materials develop a unifying statement of liturgical beliefs while creating a totally functional structure. The church is organized around the giving of the sacraments—the bapistry, altar and Abbot's throne constituting its central focus. The sanctuary is designed to bring the lay congregation close to the altar.

2) BOUNDARY WATERS CANOE AREA, SUPERIOR NATIONAL FOREST

Lost in a blue world of clear water below and an endless sky above, drawn back to earth only by the banks of whispering birch and pine on the horizon, canoeists slicing their way through the 2,000 portage-linked lakes and streams of Superior National Forest know wordless appreciation of the peaceful solitude a wilderness experience can bring. Located in northeastern Minnesota, the national forest offers three million acres of forested wilderness.

The backdrop seen by travelers of deep green north woods and sparkling waters has not changed significantly for centuries, since white men first began portaging the area in search of fur-bearing animals. Sometime during the seventeenth century fur trappers and traders, rough and independent men of French origin, known as *coureurs de bois* or "woods runners," plied the network of lakes west and south of Lake Superior. In their wake came the colorful and romantic *voyageurs*. (See **Voyageurs National Park**, Minnesota—8.)

Probably the most famous section of the Superior National Forest is the Boundary Waters Canoe area, the largest water-based wild area in the country. Stretching 185 miles along the Canadian border, the area abuts Ontario's Quetico Provincial Park. So popular is the Boundary Waters region that twenty-five percent of all the recreational activity throughout the national wilderness system is concentrated here. While many locations are becoming rather well-used, others not accessible by roads remain for the plucky explorer to discover. Regulations regarding the use of mechanized vehicles and the maintenance of an unpolluted environment are aimed at keeping the Boundary Waters as clear and charming as when the Indians were the only inhabitants.

In addition to the canoeing available, many trails, some of which were formerly old logging roads, lead to top fishing spots where bass and panfish await the patient fisherman, or to glens of blueberries, strawberries or chokecherries.

3) CAPITOL, St. Paul

The Minnesota Capitol in St. Paul, sitting atop a hill, can be seen for many miles in most directions and is well worth viewing. One of its many outstanding features is its huge dome, said to be the world's largest unsupported marble dome. It is 223 feet high and is topped by a columned lantern with a gold ball. The remainder of the building is of Georgia marble, except the foundation and steps of native gray

From its clear headwaters in Itasca, Minnesota, the Mississippi River is an ever-changing snake, winding toward the Gulf of Mexico.

granite. A large, eight-pointed glass star, set into the floor in the rotunda, symbolizes the North Star State.

Ground was broken for the Capitol in 1896 and the cornerstone was laid in 1898.

The virtues of Wisdom, Courage, Bounty, Truth, Integrity and Prudence are represented by six statues above the main entrance. These are the work of Daniel Chester French, who collaborated with Edward C. Potter on the gilded quadriga, "The Progress of the State," which stands at the base of the dome. The figure of Prosperity rides the chariot, while two young women guide the horses. The sculpture is of copper-clad sheet metal over steel framing, overlaid with gold leaf.

Minneapolis' Guthrie Theater was opened in 1963 to produce quality theater beyond New York City.

4) ICE HOCKEY HALL OF FAME

The North Star State of Minnesota has contributed many greats to the exciting and fast-growing sport of ice hockey, and the town of Eveleth, north of Duluth, has made the greatest contribution, sending eleven players to the National Hockey League. Thus, it was highly appropriate when the Ice Hockey Hall of Fame was opened in Eveleth in 1973. Twenty-five hockey immortals were enshrined the first year.

The main floor of this hall, which seems to glow with the fast-paced excitement of hockey, is devoted to these greats. The story of the origin and development of ice hockey is told by vivid sight and sound displays in a tunnel-like structure on the second floor. Many artifacts and a vast amount of information on the game, its players and its equipment are presented with audio-visual aids.

5) MISSISSIPPI RIVER

The Mississippi is born in northern Minnesota in the quiet beauty of Itasca State Park, a land of coniferous forests sprinkled with birch and clear glacial lakes and ponds.

By the time the Mississippi reaches Minneapolis it is a good-sized river. Its average fall is only about seven inches per mile, but in 500 miles the upper river falls 700 feet, including a 65-foot drop in three-quarters of a mile at St. Anthony Falls in Minneapolis, below which it is fully navigable.

Of the four basic flyways for migratory birds in the United States—the Atlantic, Mississippi, Central and Pacific—the Mississippi Flyway is the most important. Millions of geese, ducks, swans and other birds spend the winter somewhere along it or move through it to winter further south. One of the most important areas along the flyway is the 194,000-acre Upper Mississippi River Wildlife and Fish Refuge, which has the most extensive boundaries of any inland refuge for waterfowl. Established in 1924, it extends from Wabasha, Minnesota, approximately 280 miles along both sides of the Mississippi to Rock Island, Illinois, where it borders Mark Twain National Wildlife Refuge.

Because of its length, covering a number of life zones and differing climatic conditions, the refuge contains an extraordinary number of birds, mammals and fish. The extensive marshlands, river-bottom forests, damp slough-grass and sedge meadows and elevated sand prairies provide habitats for 270 species of birds, 50 species of mammals and 113 species of fish. Also in the refuge, steep wooded slopes of hardwoods with occasional red cedars and precipitous limestone cliffs, some as high as 600 feet above the valley floor, present some of the most attractive scenery in mid-America.

Farther downstream, the Mississippi becomes a truly great river when it picks up from the Missouri River much of the silt that eventually forms its immense delta at the Gulf. Each spring, waters of the Missouri push aside the Mississippi. Even when the Missouri is not flooding, it is impossible to overlook the effect that this long river has on the Mississippi. For the Missouri is not only the Mississippi's longest tributary, but its dirtiest as well. For many miles, the blue waters of the upper Mississippi resist merging with the muddy discharge of the Missouri, or Big Muddy, as it is nicknamed. The Mississippi appears to be two different rivers flowing in the same bed. Along one bank, its water is still clear; on the other bank, it is red-brown. Eventually, the entire river becomes

Opposite: Built on a 178-foot cliff, the tallest lighthouse in America, Split Rock Lighthouse, has been preserved in a state park.

opaque with the silt its tributary has robbed from Missouri, Iowa, Nebraska, Kansas, Montana, and North and South Dakota. Not even the clear water of the next major tributary, the Ohio River, which carries a much larger volume of water than the Missouri (one-fourth of all the water emptying into the Gulf), can remove the indelible stain that the Big Muddy has given to the Mississippi.

Below the mouth of the Ohio, where it is known as the lower Mississippi, the river passes the swampy mouth of the Arkansas River and then collects water from the Red River. In great bends, it winds its way through wide, fertile lands where cotton is king. After passing Baton Rouge, Louisana, it enters a rich bottomland that is marked by French names where cotton, rice and sugar cane are grown. After passing the levees of New Orleans, the river branches out into a land where salt and hovering gulls are in the air and hundreds of thousands of geese, ducks and other waterfowl winter in the 48,000-acre Delta Wildlife Refuge. Like a great artery that has been shattered into innumerable capillaries, the great river has finally completed its 2,552-mile journey. (See map, p. 292.)

The Mississippi is a wanderer, constantly decreasing or increasing its length by adding bends or carving out shortcuts. Because of this, its length cannot be measured in a direct line from Lake Itasca to the Gulf of Mexico. In *Life on the Mississippi*, Mark Twain noted:

It [the Mississippi] is ... the crookedest river in the world, since in one part of its journey it used up one-thousand-three-hundred miles to cover the same ground that the crow would fly over in six-hundred and seventy-five.

6) SPLIT ROCK LIGHTHOUSE STATE PARK

From 1910 until it became obsolete in 1969, the beacon of Split Rock Lighthouse shone for twenty-two miles across Lake Superior as a guide to ships passing in and out of the Duluth-Superior harbor. Today this picturesque landmark on Minnesota's north shore, perched on a rock jutting out into the lake which appears to be split when approached from the lake, is preserved in Split Rock Lighthouse State Park, opened in 1971.

The octagonal brick tower was built from materials brought in by water and hauled up the cliffs. The fifty-four-foot tower on top of the rock sent out a light 168 feet above the level of the lake. The original incandescent oil-vapor lamp was converted to electricity in 1941, but the original French-made revolving lens was still used to focus the light rays and magnify the beam that flashed every ten seconds. Compressed-air-operated diaphone fog signals pierced the air every twenty seconds when the fog rolled in from Lake Superior.

7) TYRONE GUTHRIE THEATER

Minneapolis' Guthrie Theater, opened in 1963, is the home of an outstanding professional repertory company, developed when a number of well-known theatrical people became concerned with the absence of first-rate professional theater outside of New York. Instrumental in the project were New York theater managers Peter Zeisler and Oliver Rea, as well as the world-renowned director, Sir Tyrone Guthrie. For many years Guthrie served as the company's director.

The theater facilities are worthy of the excellent acting company. Its excitingly modern structure is connected to the Walker Art Center. (See Minnesota—9.) A stuccoed screen around three sides of the building, designed with bold and unorthodox shapes, depicts the excitement of live performances.

Within, the seats are arranged in a 200 degree arc around an open Elizabethan stage, giving spectators a sense of closeness and interaction with the performers. The stage itself is a seven-sided asymmetrical platform measuring thirty-two feet by thirty-five feet and raised three steps above floor level. No seat is more than fifty-two feet from the center of the stage. The charcoal gray walls contrast sharply with the 1,437 bright multihued seats in the auditorium. The theater has such excellent acoustics that the performers can be easily heard throughout the audience.

8) VOYAGEURS NATIONAL PARK

During the eighteenth and early nineteenth centuries when ladies of European society demanded the best North American fur for their clothing, these waters in northern Minnesota rang with the singing of French-Canadian *voyageurs*. Wearing bright red caps and leather boots, these rugged adventurers paddled and portaged in their fragile, birchbark canoes thousands of tons of furs and trade goods yearly over the 3,000-mile waterway extending from Montreal to Lake Athabaska in upper Alberta.

The *voyageurs* are now a romantic legend, but their water highway remains largely as they knew it. Efforts to create a Voyageurs National

During the eighteenth and early nineteenth centuries the waters of northern Minnesota were stroked by the canoe paddles of French voyageurs. Voyageurs National Park preserves these waterways in their natural setting.

Park in the Ontario-Minnesota border wilderness (see **Boundary Waters Canoe Area, Superior National Forest**, Minnesota—2) began in 1891 and finally came to fruition in 1971. Consisting of 139,000 acres of north woods country plus 80,000 acres of water, the park includes large Kabetogama Lake and parts of Rainy and Namekan lakes. Voyageurs is unique in that the waterways themselves will remain the principal means of transportation.

Four times ice sheets edged down from the north grinding the land bare, and each time

Prometheus Strangling the Vulture, by Jacques Lipchitz, is one of the famous pieces of contemporary sculpture in the Walker Art Center. The gallery is noted for its avant-garde exhibitions.

these spectacular forests grew back. During the last century, many thousands of acres of virgin pine forests in this region were stripped clean by loggers, but the land is now covered once again with large second-growth pines, firs, spruce, aspens and birches.

The area provides food and shelter for a wide variety of wildlife. White-tailed deer and black bears are common, as are smaller animals such as minks, otters, bobcats, rabbits and beavers. The park service plans to reintroduce caribou and increase the moose population. It is one of the few places in the country where timber wolves still live. Hawks, golden eagles and a wide variety of songbirds and waterfowl make Voyageurs their home during season. The lake sturgeon, a rare and endangered fish, lives in some of the larger lakes.

9) WALKER ART CENTER

The Walker Art Center in Minneapolis is one of America's oldest art centers. Especially famous today for initiating contemporary exhibitions, the Walker is a descendant of the first art gallery in the Midwest that was open to the public. Built in 1879, that original gallery was a skylighted room, attached to Thomas Barlow Walker's home, furnished with an exhibition of twenty paintings.

By the turn of the century, when his collection numbered around 200 paintings and a thousand other works, Walker began assembling with great thoroughness what proved to be one of the finest collections of jade in the world. To house his acquisitions properly, he commissioned a museum structure which opened as the Walker Gallery in 1927, a short time before his death. In 1940 its name was changed to the Walker Art Center, and the institution has lived up to its name with a variety of activities in the arts.

In the center's permanent collection are some of the landmark paintings and sculptures of the twentieth century. *Blue Horses,* an oil by Franz Marc, is a much reproduced work of *Der Blaue Reiter* (The Blue Rider) movement of 1911-12 in which Marc was a leading force.

Of the older paintings in the collection, one of particular interest is *The Battle Between Carnival and Lent,* a fascinating scene of early seventeenth-century fun and games.

Chief among the contemporary pieces in the Sculpture Court is the large *Reclining Mother and Child* by Henry Moore, while one of the largest major acquisitions is the nine-foot-tall *Cubi IX* by David Smith, the seminal American sculptor who died in 1965. The center also has sculptures by Raymond Duchamp-Villon, Jean Arp and Alberto Giacometti.

Despite the importance of its contemporary collection, the national and international reputation of the Walker Art Center has grown largely from the avant-garde exhibitions it has originated and circulated over the years. Painting constructions by George Ortman, the new art of Brazil, London and Argentina, the slashed canvases of Lucio Fontana, and numerous shows on special themes have fully justified the center's reputation for excellence.

Ohio

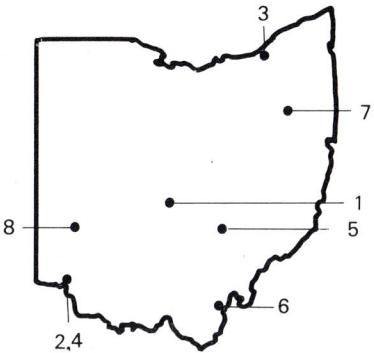

1) CAPITOL, Columbus

The Ohio State House is considered one of the country's outstanding examples of Greek Revival architecture. The building, completed in 1861, twenty-three years after construction was begun, is located in the heart of downtown Columbus. Eight Doric columns, each thirty-six feet high and six feet thick, are located along the main east and west entrances, with four similar columns at each of the north and south entrances. The cupola, which has a shallow conical roof, is 158 feet above ground level.

Double sets of massive bronze doors open onto the four foyers which lead to the rotunda floor. A brightly lighted canvas, bearing the Great Seal of Ohio, looks down from the 120-foot dome. Circling the seal are the names and inaugural dates of the eight Ohioans who served as President of the United States. The floor of the rotunda is inlaid marble.

2) CINCINNATI ZOOLOGICAL GARDENS

The Cincinnati Zoo, begun in 1873 with Andrew Erkenbrecher's bird collection, has developed into one of the world's most outstanding zoological parks. It was one of the first to exhibit animals in barless natural surroundings, allowing visitors to see them moving freely only a few yards away. The zoo possesses the most outstanding feline collection in the United States, including some species seen nowhere else in captivity.

The Cincinnati Zoo's success in the propagation of animals in captivity is recognized throughout the world. Along with the zoo in Basel, Switzerland, Cincinnati holds the record for lowland gorilla births.

Consistent with its "caged free" principle, the Birds of Prey Flight Cage features bald eagles, red-tailed hawks and American black vultures

Located in Canton, Ohio, the site of the first pro football league, the Professional Football Hall of Fame honors the feats of the sport's great heroes. A seven-foot bronze statue of the immortal Jim Thorpe stands at the entrance.

with king and yellow-headed vultures of Latin America and hawks of Africa and India.

3) CLEVELAND MUSEUM OF ART

Located in a Greek-style marble structure overlooking the lovely and colorful Fine Arts Gardens in Wade Park, the Cleveland Museum of Art houses extensive collections representing every culture and period in world history. A British fine arts magazine called it "one of the major museums of the American continent."

To the delight of scholars and casual visitors, the museum's collections have been arranged in groupings and sequences determined by their historic contexts. Outstanding works include the fifth-century bronze *Greek Athlete,* a *Kouros* from the mid-sixth century B.C., the late-Gothic period *Mourners From the Tomb of Phillip the Bold,* and two polychrome sculptures of St. Laurence and St. Steven by Tilman Riemenschneider. Also to be seen is the great Chinese handscroll from the Northern Sung Dynasty, *Streams and Mountains Without End.*

The best of the Western masters of painting are represented. Among their works are Zurburan's *The Holy House of Nazareth,* J.M.W. Turner's *The Burning of the Houses of Parliament* and the best of Picasso's Blue Period.

4) DELTA QUEEN

Paddle-wheel streamers call to mind romantic visions of the Mississippi in the days of Mark Twain. Before the railroad came to prominence, hundreds of steamboats regularly traveled the rivers of the Midwest carrying people and goods and contributing significantly to the nation's westward expansion. Later, showboats and excursion boats brought pleasure to passengers and people living along the rivers.

Today, only a few of these venerable vessels remain. The *Delta Queen,* steaming out of its home port of Cincinnati along the Ohio River from February through November, is the only one making extended excursion trips along the waters of the Mississippi Valley. This great lady has been carefully refurbished, preserving its original character. On board, the atmosphere of an earlier, slower era prevails as the steamboat calls at many historic riverboat cities.

When the *Delta Queen* ventures into "Dixie" it stops at Southern cities associated with the river's heyday, including Paducah, Kentucky, and Cairo, Illinois, as well as Nashville, Memphis, Natchez and New Orleans. Each year in May the *Delta Queen* calls at Louisville, a city where steamboats have been known since Robert Fulton's *Orleans* made its first appearance in 1811.

To the north, the elegant pleasure craft passes through the unsurpassed beauty of the Upper Mississippi River Wildlife and Fish Refuge (see **Mississippi River**, Minnesota—5), where the hand of man has had little effect. It also travels the waters of the Ohio, the Tennessee and the Illinois.

The *Delta Queen* operates under special permission from Congress that exempts it from certain safety standards which the wooden-hulled ship from America's past cannot meet. Thus this last reminder of the nostalgic riverboat era still plies the inland waterways.

5) HOCKING HILLS STATE PARK

Early Indians came to the Hocking Hills area to hunt elk, bison and deer, using the rock shelters for temporary homes. People today come to Hocking Hills State Park in southeastern Ohio when looking for a quiet haven of beauty, for a place to commune with the land. Here, miles of trails follow gorges that are wild, lonely and austere. In the spring or after a heavy rainfall, spectacular waterfalls cascade from the numerous small side valleys entering the deepest gorge in Ohio, Conkle's Hollow.

In most places in the park the rock face has been case hardened, that is, mineral-saturated water has evaporated on the surface of porous rock, causing a cement effect which retards erosion. Where case-hardened rock has been broken, erosion of the sandstone is evident.

One of the principal scenic attractions in Hocking Hills is the massive Rock House with its huge openings separated by large columns of stone letting sunlight into the only true cavern in the area, hollowed by the constant force of water for the last million years. Situated halfway up a 100-foot vertical cliff, Rock House is a natural tunnel with five "windows" overlooking Laurel Run.

The largest overhanging ledge in the area, Ash Cave, received its name from huge piles of ashes, the remnants of countless Indian campfires, found by settlers in the early eighteenth century. Layers of Indian relics—pottery, arrow and spear points, and bones of animals—which date back to 6000 B.C. have been unearthed.

6) OHIO RIVER

The Ohio River, correctly called *la Belle Rivière* (the Beautiful River) by early French explorers, is born from the confluence of the Allegheny and Monongahela rivers at the city of

The Delta Queen *is the only original paddle-wheel steamer still making extended nostalgic trips along the Ohio River. Before railroads, hundreds of steamboats traveled Midwestern rivers carrying goods and people. Later, they were transformed into pleasure showboats.*

Pittsburgh and flows generally southwest until reaching the Mississippi at the old riverboat town of Cairo, Illinois. Part of the route, from Ashland, Kentucky, downstream to Madison, Indiana, has towering, wooded limestone bluffs and is perhaps the most beautiful section of the Ohio. European settlers likened it to the upper part of the Rhine.

Although the Ohio is no longer lined with a continuous forest, there are numerous tree-lined stretches along its banks. Many of the trees and plants found by the first settlers still grow in the valley. Even in the cities, one catches a glimpse of the original valley. In Louisville's seventeen-acre Central Park are magnificent tulip trees which were a part of the Ohio's virgin forest and are older than the city that has grown up around them.

After the Revolution, the Ohio Valley became the Western frontier. Many settlers passed down the wide Ohio heading West. In conjunction with the Mississippi the river became one of the main arteries of commerce in the nineteenth century. Showboats frequented the river in both the nineteenth and twentieth centuries.

For several decades prior to the Civil War, the Ohio was the dividing line between slavery and freedom and much is made of this in Harriet Beecher Stowe's book, *Uncle Tom's Cabin.*

The Ohio Valley has not become one "continued village," but it is one of the most heavily populated and productive regions in America.

Appropriately called La Belle Rivière *("the Beautiful River") by early French explorers, the Ohio winds through some of the loveliest territory in the Midwest. The river was a roadway for pioneers heading west.*

Occupying only about six percent of the conterminous United States, the valley has a labor force of over seven million—ten percent of America's entire civilian labor force—and produces more than ten percent of the nation's gross national product.

The Ohio River played a vital role in this region's remarkable growth. It is navigable for its entire 981-mile course except for the rapids near Louisville, called the Falls of the Ohio, where locks are needed, and is superior to either the Mississippi or the Missouri as a waterway. (See map, p. 292.) Along its banks is some of the best farmland in America as well as rich deposits of coal, petroleum and natural gas.

The Ohio is not always a benign river and the people of its valley have known catastrophic floods. Flood control projects have somewhat lessened the impact of the heavy volume of water introduced into the river in spring.

7) PRO FOOTBALL HALL OF FAME

Professional football's Hall of Fame is located in Canton, the city which saw the founding of the first professional football league, the direct predecessor of the National Football League, as well as many of the feats of the legendary Jim Thorpe, football's first immortal. Thorpe's

On display in the Air Force Museum is the "New Orleans," one of the first two planes to fly around the world.

team, the Canton Bulldogs, was an early NFL member. Featured in the three-building complex are memorabilia from the great teams and players of pro football's past and present.

A seven-foot bronze statue of Thorpe greets fans as they enter the rotunda of the Pro Football Hall of Fame. Priceless mementos are displayed along a ramp circling the fifty-two-foot, football-shaped dome. Something of interest to every fan can be found in the colorful Professional Football Today exhibit, the brightly hued Leagues and Champions Room and the Enshrinees Mementos Room. The Hall of Heroes impressively pays tribute to the Hall of Fame members who have received football's honors.

President William McKinley is buried on Monument Hill, just a short drive through Canton's attractive park land. Canton was the scene of McKinley's front porch campaigns.

8) UNITED STATES AIR FORCE MUSEUM

At the entrance of the United States Air Force Museum at Wright-Patterson Air Force Base near Dayton is a blue panel enscribed with an appropriate introduction: "Since the beginning of time there have been those men who looked to the sky, who envied birds their graceful, soaring flight, who said to themselves, 'If I could but fly....' This is the story of those men, and how they learned to fly, and the remarkable things that have happened since."

The Air Force Museum is the oldest and largest military aviation museum in the world. Since Dayton was the home of the Wright brothers and since their work was crucial to the progress of all aviation, their contribution is especially honored. Featured are a full-scale reproduction of the Wright 1909 Military Flyer, the first military airplane, and such memorabilia as scraps from the original plane flown at Kitty Hawk and a bicycle from the Wright Brothers' shop.

The museum collection of approximately 130 aircraft and missiles includes Gemini series space capsules, the only remaining B-70 aircraft, the airplanes of Presidents Eisenhower and Truman, and exhibits related to the atomic bomb. All of the museum's exhibits are arranged in meaningful chronological sequences, tracing the history of aviation from Kitty Hawk to the present.

Wisconsin

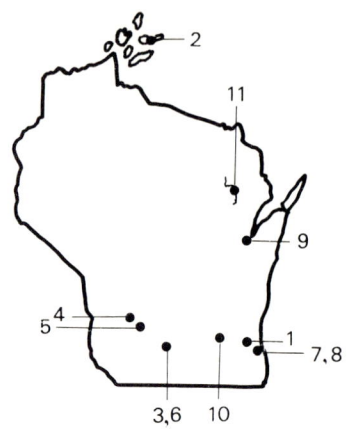

1) ANNUNCIATION GREEK ORTHODOX CHURCH

The last major structure to be designed by the renowned Frank Lloyd Wright, Annunciation Greek Orthodox Church in Wauwatosa, Milwaukee County, was opened in 1961. Its congregation is one of the ten oldest organized Greek Orthodox churches in the United States.

In his plans Wright incorporated elements of the Byzantine style of architecture traditional in Eastern Orthodox churches. Beginning with the Greek cross and its circular components, Wright molded the structure upward and outward into a circle on which the blue-tiled dome is surmounted. The dome rises to a height of 45 feet from the center of the floor and is 104 feet in diameter. Forming a necklace around the beam, just below the dome, are 325 hollow glass spheres. Gold anodized aluminum is used to trim both interior and exterior of the church.

Within the church the floor slopes to the center and the seat arrangement on both upper and lower levels carries out Wright's intention to give the feeling of being cupped in the hands of God. The worshiper feels a participant rather than simply an observer. The traditional Byzantine colors of blue and gold are found outside and inside the dome and in the pews.

2) APOSTLE ISLANDS NATIONAL LAKESHORE

Lake Superior, the largest of the Great Lakes and the one least polluted by man, has many miles of wilderness shoreline, but nowhere else on Superior is there the scenic variety and wealth of historic association that there is in the Apostle Islands region near the western tip of the lake. Throughout the twenty-three islands and nearby Bayfield Peninsula are forests, high lakeside cliffs and wave-sculpted rocky arches, long sandy beaches, marshes, caverns and bays. And yet, despite its primitive, pristine appearance, Wisconsin's Apostle Islands region is rich in history.

The Chippewa Indians entered the region about 500 years ago, and because of harassment from other tribes, they took refuge on the largest of the Apostle Islands, today known as Madeline Island. Here they constructed a great village and remained in comparative peace and safety for 120 years.

In the 1600's a stream of French travelers, traders, explorers and missionaries visited the region. It is believed the French missionaries named the islands, for an old French map labels them the Twelve Apostles. Perhaps because there are almost twice that number of islands the "Twelve" was dropped.

As the fur trade flourished, the French built a fort on Madeline Island in 1693 called La Pointe. It was from here that the great flotillas of forty-foot canoes manned by the legendary *voyageurs* journeyed to Montreal with furs and returned with trade goods and supplies.

As authorized in 1970, the Apostle Islands National Lakeshore includes twenty of the twenty-three islands. Except for Long Island which, until 150 years ago, was part of Chequamegon Point, the islands are the tops of partially submerged sandstone hills of the Bayfield Peninsula's northeasterly extension. They rise above the lake to heights varying from 50 to 480 feet, forming an archipelago about thirty miles long and eighty miles wide, with slightly less than one-fifth of this area in land.

Opposite: The result of centuries of erosion, a pillar of rock juts out of Lake Superior in the Apostle Islands National Lakeshore. Rugged cliffs, stained by lichens and water, have witnessed the passage of Indians, voyageurs and explorers.

A featured wagon in Barnum & Bailey's 1903 circus parade, the ornate Asia wagon is on display in the Circus World Museum in Baraboo, where the circus originated in 1884.

Fortunately, there are few roads either on the mainland or the islands and the water is the lakeshore's main thoroughfare. Madeline Island is the only island with a permanent settlement, and it has historic buildings open to the public.

3) CAPITOL, Madison

Located in the heart of Madison on an isthmus between two lakes, the Capitol is set on a landscaped garden square known as Capitol Park. Streets radiate from the square to all parts of the city, including the nearby campus of the University of Wisconsin.

The building, constructed cruciformly, covers nearly two and a half acres. The architectural style is Roman Renaissance with Corinthian columns on each of the four porticos.

Atop the core is a great white dome, built of granite on a steel frame. On it stands the figure of "Forward," symbol of the state's motto. The work of the celebrated Daniel Chester French, who also did the *Minute Man* statue in Concord, Massachusetts, and the Lincoln Memorial statue in Washington, D.C., the Capitol statue is done in bronze and covered with gold leaf. The distance of 285.9 feet from the esplanade to the top of the statue is, by design, a few inches shorter than that of the national Capitol.

The building was completed in 1917, eleven years after construction began. Durable white Bethel Vermont granite was used on the exterior, and a variety of imported marble was used inside. Granite in contrasting colors was used for the floors, panels and columns.

Within the building, two hundred feet above the large octagonal rotunda, on the ceiling of the dome, is Edwin Howland Blashfield's painting, *Resources of Wisconsin*, nearly thirty-four feet in diameter.

4) CIRCUS WORLD MUSEUM

The circus, that colorful institution of yesteryear, comes to life again in the Circus World Museum in Baraboo. It was here that the renowned Ringling Bros. Circus began in 1884.

The story of the circus is retold not only through fascinating displays and exhibits, but also with live performances and demonstrations—a circus train unloaded using magnificent Percheron horses; a miniature circus parade; an old-fashioned circus under the big

top, patterned after European one-ring circuses and early American dog and pony shows.

Circus World Museum has the largest collection of beautifully preserved circus parade wagons. More than one hundred of these ornately decorated, colorful vehicles reside in the Circus Parade Pavilion. The thirty-three-acre museum also possesses an ear-splitting old American steam calliope. Each summer these wagons, calliope and an assortment of circus performers and animals appear in a full-fledged circus parade in Milwaukee as the main element of the city's Fourth of July celebration, Old Milwaukee Days.

5) DEVILS LAKE STATE PARK

The spectactularly beautiful 4,300-acre Devils Lake State Park, including the high quartzite bluffs which border the lake on two sides, is a product of Wisconsin's last great glacial age. Here, 15,000 years ago, the ancient Wisconsin River had cut a channel through the mountains of the Baraboo Range, but a glacier broke through a gap in the range and dammed up both ends of a section of the river gorge with rocks and gravel pushed in front of the glacier's edge. This forced the river to run elsewhere and created a spring-fed lake with no visible outlet. The gap is still visible today and many rock piles make up the cliffs that were the gorge walls.

From the lake to the top of the sheer bluffs is a breathtaking 500 feet. Considerable variation in temperature because of the difference in elevation enables some 700 species of ferns and flowering plants to thrive.

Effigy Mounds Indians left their mark on the region, building eagle-, bear- and lynx-shaped mounds, and later, Winnebago Indians fished in what they called "Spirit Lake."

Devils Lake was made a state park in 1910, but it had been a major tourist attraction since the 1870's. Nearby are a number of other state parks that protect unique glacial features.

The caliber of these features in Wisconsin has prompted a unique concept in conservation — that Federal, state and local governments join to protect the glacial marks. Thus the **Ice Age National Scientific Reserve** was established in 1971. Composed of nine separate units spread across the state, the reserve is administered by the Wisconsin Department of Natural Resources working in close cooperation with the National Park Service and county governments.

The largest portion is the North Unit of the Kettle Moraine State Forest, about fifty miles north of Milwaukee. Here, the Green Bay and Lake Michigan lobes of the ice sheet crushed together, pushing dirt, rocks and glacial till into large, long heaps called moraines. Similar kinds of moraines, called terminal moraines and marking the farthest southern advance of the ice, can be seen all across the state.

Pines frame Devils Lake in south-central Wisconsin. An ancient glacier plowed through the bluffs, making the pass seen in the distance.

This forty-one-foot-high Haida Indian totem pole guards the entrance to the Milwaukee Public Museum which is known for its outstanding display exhibits.

6) FIRST UNITARIAN SOCIETY CHURCH

Designed by Frank Lloyd Wright, the meeting house of Madison's First Unitarian Society is situated on a lovely four-acre site overlooking Lake Mendota and the University of Wisconsin farmlands. As Wright said, "Here is a church where the whole edifice is in the attitude of prayer."

The basic unit of construction is the triangle, most prominent in the striking prow which forms a forty-foot spire. Extensive use of glass in the two ridges which come together at the prow produces a merging of indoors and outdoors. For worship services movable pews are placed facing a stone pulpit in the prow. The sound canopy and choir loft rise above it. According to Wright, "Instead of excluding the outside prospect which is beautiful, we have allowed it to come in facing the audience to become part of the background for music and preacher."

With its movable pews the auditorium can be used for a variety of functions in combination with or separate from the adjacent and more intimate Hearth Room, the center of the society's social activities.

Frank Lloyd Wright's father helped organize the Madison Unitarian Society in 1879. For many years the noted architect was a member.

7) MILWAUKEE COUNTY ZOO

To wander through the Milwaukee County Zoo is to venture into as accurate and pleasant a reproduction of the animal kingdom as can be imagined. The zoo grounds are amazingly spacious, clean and beautifully landscaped. Its collections are extensive in number and variety.

The zoo is famous for its five continental groupings, displayed in dramatic panoramas. Predators and their prey can be seen together against authentic backdrops. No bars or enclosures are in evidence. Predators are separated from prey by invisible dry moats.

More than 800 birds are housed in the aviary, which maintains a fresh, outdoors atmosphere with lush vegetation and daily rain-soft sprays. The birds are mixed as they are in the wild in four halls: Penguin Hall, Aquatic Hall, Rainforest Hall and Shorebird Hall.

Fitting naturally into the surrounding woodlands, the Primate House, built of multicolored

The Annunciation Greek Orthodox Church was the last major structure designed by Frank Lloyd Wright.

Wisconsin fieldstone, holds these closest relatives of man on view behind clear glass fronts of units containing natural looking props. Two exhibits also have clear glass backs to give both visitor and animal a sense of the outdoors as a backdrop. All the exhibits of animals in the Small Mammal House are also designed in this manner. The zoo's prize primate is the mammoth 610-pound gorilla, Samson, who intrigues visitors with his hypnotic stare and exceedingly solemn performances.

The Milwaukee Children's Zoo on the same grounds provides a marvelous opportunity to view at close range and touch a variety of young animals. A complete miniature farm includes young domestic animals.

8) MILWAUKEE PUBLIC MUSEUM

One can visit the Milwaukee Public Museum dozens of times and never tire of exploring its fascinating exhibits organized by location and period. The museum's outstanding natural history and history collections are displayed in ways that make them uniquely meaningful, providing insights into far-flung cultures and ways of life.

The Milwaukee Museum, founded in 1882, pioneered the concept of "theme presentation" method of display in which men or animals are integrated with their environments in dioramas, realistic to the smallest detail. The idea was developed by Carl E. Akeley, the museum's taxidermist from 1887 to 1895. Two of the largest theme displays in the nation are the Savanna Waterhole/Masai Lion Hunt and the Bamboo Forest/Forest's Edge, both in the new African wing.

The nostalgic Streets of Old Milwaukee exhibit takes the visitor back to the days of gas lights and visits from the ice man. Delightful old silent movies are shown in the exhibit's old-time theater. Nearly all doors, pavement and accoutrements are authentic.

The Crow Indian Bison Hunt, which dramatically greets visitors as they arrive on the second floor, is equipped with sound effects and a piece of bison hide to touch. Details of the Old Delhi Bazaar in India and the Guatemalan marketplace are fascinatingly realistic, creating an aura of foreign romance.

Since 1921 a forty-one-foot-high Haida Indian totem pole from the Queen Charlotte Islands, British Columbia, has guarded the museum entrance. The museum possesses extensive collections of American Indian artifacts.

9) NATIONAL RAILROAD MUSEUM

Instrumental in the growth of the United States, the steam train inspired dreams of adventure and romance for a century. Preserved in an open-air museum in Green Bay are locomotives which recreate the nostalgic era which ended with the coming of the diesel engine in the 1950's. Nearly all of the exhibits can be closely examined and handled by modern-day romantics.

The National Railroad Museum, founded in 1958, is the home for ten locomotives and more than twenty rolling stock. Highlights of the exhibit are the famous Hiawatha, the sleek Mil-

Representative of a unique pre-Civil War style of architecture, Octagon House in Watertown was complete with running water, central hot-air heating, and air conditioning in 1854.

waukee Road observation car, and such unusual features as a snowplow car and a pickle car.

Also exhibited is the immense Big Boy. Reportedly the largest coal-burning locomotive ever made, it could haul a full load through the Rocky Mountains at seventy miles per hour, along with its complement of 25,000 gallons of water and 56,000 pounds of coal. Nearby is the English-built troop train which served as General Eisenhower's staff train in World War II. Attached to it are two of Eisenhower's command cars and Winston Churchill's luxurious Isle of Thanet car. Another immortal is the battle-scarred General Pershing locomotive which carried him into battle during World War I.

The museum's only diesel engine is the stainless-steel Aero from the Rock Island Line. In its coaches, visitors can take a train ride around the grounds, leaving from an old-fashioned depot.

10) OCTAGON HOUSE

Built by lawyer John Richards at 919 Charles Street in Watertown, the Octagon House is a fifty-seven-room mansion. It is not only the best preserved example of this architectural form, but it represents as well the inventiveness of its designer, with its systems of running water, air conditioning and central hot-air heating.

Richards designed and built the house in 1854 with the intention of making it the largest in the State of Wisconsin. The first three floors were to be used for the family, the fourth for the mill workers and the fifth as an observatory.

The floor plans for each of the first four stories are exactly alike. Four large square rooms

This expertly carved ceremonial wolf mask displayed in the Milwaukee Public Museum was handcrafted from cedar by Kwakiutl Indians of the Pacific Northwest.

Famous for its whitewater boating and fine fishing, the Wolf River in northern Wisconsin is one of the most scenic wild streams in the country.

surround a circular, cantilever staircase which extends from the second to the fifth level. The partitioning of these rooms from the octagon base leaves four correspondingly smaller, wedge-shaped spaces. The fifth level consists of an octagonal glass-enclosed cupola designed to provide much of the light for the spiral staircase. The outside walls, surrounded by a colonnaded porch, are thirteen inches thick and constructed in a manner which enabled Richards to improvise an ingenious system of air conditioning and heating.

Succeeding generations of the Richards family occupied the house for eighty-five years before it was donated to the Watertown Historical Society in 1938 with most of the original furnishings intact.

11) WOLF NATIONAL WILD AND SCENIC RIVER

The Wolf River, running through the famed lakes country of northern Wisconsin northwest of Green Bay, is nationally famous for its whitewater boating stretches, its excellent fishing and its spectacular timbered shores of northern hardwoods and conifers. Extending from Keshena north through Menominee County, owned and managed by the Menominee Indians, the Wolf has long been recommended for Federal protection from industrial interests, and with its inclusion in the National Wild and Scenic Rivers System this protection is guaranteed. The system includes unpolluted rivers from all over the country and was established in 1968 to keep them in their original wild and scenic state.

The Wolf remains completely wild with only occasional facilities along its banks. On both sides of the river are tall evergreens and hardwoods, mostly first-growth because the lumbermen never touched this part of the north woods. The Wolf has many interesting scenic spots with names to suit, such as Big Eddy Falls, Spirit Rock, Pine Row, Tea Kettle Rapids, Otter Slide and Shotgun Eddy.

Further west, the St. Croix River and its tributary, the Namekagon, are also included in the wild and scenic rivers system. Vast stretches of water, boiling up at times into white rapids, cut through the dense north woods of Wisconsin and Minnesota. Together with the Wolf, they represent the essence of the beautiful upper Great Lakes country.

Arkansas   Iowa   Kansas   Missouri
Nebraska   North Dakota   Oklahoma
South Dakota   Texas

PLAINS and the PRAIRIES

Spacious and uninterrupted views of sky and planet earth are the inheritance of dwellers on the plains. The impressive views remain, though most of the sea of prairie grasses waving in the incessant wind has been replaced by fields of wheat stealing gold from the sun to ripen and acres of man-high corn.

The far corners of this generally flat, tree-scarce land hold greatest variety. In the western Dakotas are the Black Hills and the Badlands. To the south, west Texas is a veritable desert, while east Texas is lush in vegetation and that part bordering the Gulf of Mexico is tropical. The oldest mountains in the world, the Ozarks, stretch across northern Arkansas, southern Missouri and northeastern Oklahoma. Almost all the major cities, including several oil-rich ones, sit on the perimeter.

Nature reigns solitary on this vast stage. Winter snowstorms and summer heat waves rule the endless reaches. The sky is so huge that sunsets are memorable and often entire self-contained storms can be seen scudding across it.

Thousands of pioneers following the great migration trails to the Southwestern deserts, Pacific Coast valleys and the gold and silver fields have rushed through to the reputedly richer areas, but many stopped here. The directness and bounty of the prairies attracted strong and resilient individuals who feel at one with vastness.

The nation's second longest river, the Missouri, flows from southwestern Montana to join the Mississippi near St. Louis. Here, its silt-laden waters pass through the Great Plains near Newcastle, Nebraska.

Arkansas

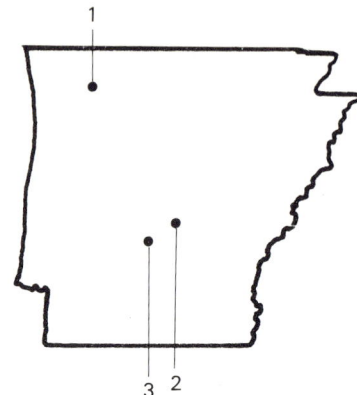

1) BUFFALO NATIONAL RIVER

From high in the mountains of Ozark National Forest of northwest Arkansas trickles a tiny, almost hidden stream that grows and meanders through hill country east of Fayetteville for almost 150 miles until it merges with the larger White River. Clean and free flowing, the Buffalo remains one of our relatively untouched wilderness rivers.

The river winds past hillsides and bluffs sprouting innumerable species of plants and trees. The highest free waterfall between the southern Appalachians and the Rockies is found misting down 200 feet in Hemmed-in-Hollow. Beauty Cave, although quite difficult to reach, offers a collection of gypsum formations outstanding in variety and size.

From before the Civil War until the turn of the century, immigrants homesteaded all the available bottomland, benches, hollows and ridges. When resources were depleted more than fifty years ago, another wave of migration swept the area, and almost everyone left. Now wildflowers again bloom amidst log cabin floors and tender saplings crowd along the timber cutters' decaying tie slides which were constructed along the bluffs.

The Buffalo is the only major stream left undammed in the Arkansas Ozarks. The lower part of the river was protected from development in the 1930's when Buffalo River State Park was established. Twenty years later, action was initiated to preserve the entire stream, and in 1972 Congress authorized 132 miles of the Buffalo as a national river, one of the first of its kind in the United States. The Buffalo differs from rivers in the wild and scenic system in the amount of land scheduled for Federal control, nearly twice as many acres per mile.

2) CAPITOL, Little Rock

The Arkansas Capitol in Little Rock, which resembles the National Capitol in Washington, became the seat of state government in 1911. Standing majestically amid beautifully landscaped grounds, it houses the governor's office, the legislative chambers and other government offices. Until 1901, when construction on the present Capitol began, the site was occupied by the first state penitentiary.

From an architectural point of view, the Arkansas Capitol has been widely recognized as one of the finest in the country. It is constructed of white native stone commonly called Batesville marble and of Indiana limestone. Its interior is of Alabama marble. Six magnificent bronze doors, made by Tiffany of New York, grace the entrance.

In the eerie light of dusk a cabin stands at the edge of the Buffalo River, one of the few remaining untouched wilderness rivers.

3) HOT SPRINGS NATIONAL PARK

A few months before he died, Hernando de Soto, bold Spanish explorer and conquistador, passed through what is now Hot Springs in southwest-central Arkansas in 1541 and possibly bathed in its waters.

Before the arrival of the white man the Indian was reportedly attracted to these hot waters where the "Great Spirit" dwelled. The Springs Mountain in forty-seven springs with an average daily flow of almost a million gallons and an average temperature of 143° F.

There is no certainty about what causes the hot springs. The currently favored theory is that the springs are formed when rainwater sinks into the ground between Sugarloaf and West mountains, then rises along tilted layers of rock to emerge finally through the geological fault at the base of Hot Springs Mountain.

The icicles at Dripping Springs are thought to be caused by rainwater seeping into the ground. Hot Springs is a favorite retreat for many people because of the great therapeutic value of the hot mineral springs.

Dunbar and Hunter Expedition in 1804 mapped the water route from Natchez to the springs and made a chemical analysis of them. Soon after, a permanent settlement developed which by 1820 included an inn and several crude canvas-shack bathhouses. In 1832 Congress set aside the hot springs as a reservation, but without supervision for over forty years.

Established as a national park in 1921, Hot Springs' primary significance is probably that it is this country's most important example of man's centuries-old romance with and affinity for the thermal and mineral waters of the world. The magical liquid minerals boil and bubble up from the west slope at the base of Hot

The heated water is variously attributed to inordinately deep and uncooled rock, chemical reactions near the bottom of the wells, friction from sliding rock masses at profound earth-depths or compression from overlying rock burden and radioactive minerals far beyond the range of the discerning instruments of geologists.

Below Hot Springs Mountain is the gay winter resort city of Hot Springs where horse racing and golfing rival the waters. And in the park itself, one of the nation's oldest national preserves, are five rugged little mountains and oak-hickory-pine forests which consistently bring their own special rewards.

Iowa

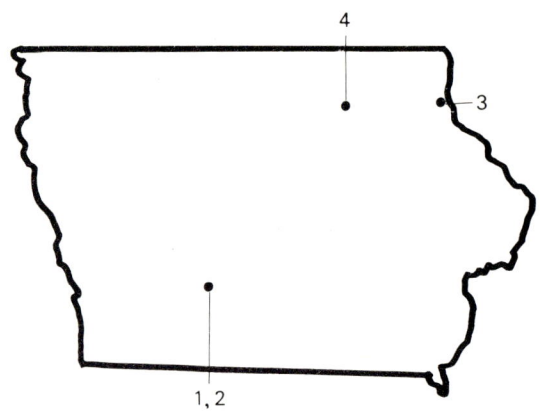

1) CAPITOL, Des Moines

A hilltop overlooking the Iowa countryside provides an ideal site for the Romanesque-style State House in Des Moines. The building, completed in 1884, required extra time and money for construction because the first structure used such cheap materials to stay within the General Assembly's frugal budget that it collapsed during the hard winter of 1871. Materials, mainly stone, for the present building came from Iowa and neighboring states.

The commanding feature of the Capitol is the central towering dome. This was constructed of steel and stone and covered with gold. The dome is surmounted by a lookout lantern reached by long winding stairs and a finial 275 feet above the ground floor. The rotunda beneath the dome is sixty-seven feet in diameter. Four smaller domes of simple design rise from the four corners of the Capitol. The pediment over the front entrance discloses a fine allegorical sculpture.

2) DES MOINES ART CENTER

The Des Moines Art Center, opened to the public in 1948, is housed in a world-renowned building designed by the great Finnish-American architect, Eliel Saarinen. The bequest of James D. Edmundson provided funds for the building and for museum operations "as a gift to the city of Des Moines and to the people of his native state."

Indoors, finding a bronze by Henry Moore and sculptures by Henri Laurens, Jean Arp and Alexander Calder, with paintings by Joan Miró, Ben Nicholson, Oskar Kokoschka, Georges Rouault, Ernst Kirchner, Paul Klee and contemporary Americans, might suggest a purely modern orientation were it not for some works by Auguste Rodin, Jacob van Ruisdael, Francisco de Goya, Gustave Courbet, Camille Pissarro, Claude Monet and numerous nineteenth-century American painters.

Although late in the field, and almost of necessity required to specialize in nineteenth- and twentieth-century art, the center has been fortunate in having funds and receiving gifts that make it possible to relate the present to the historic past by means of older works in the permanent collection as well as through temporary exhibitions.

A notable addition, announced in 1962, is the Impressionist canvas, *Cliffs at Etretat,* by Monet. This 26-by-32½-inch oil, dated 1886, is one of the series painted at Etretat on the English Channel beginning in 1884.

3) EFFIGY MOUNDS NATIONAL MONUMENT

The 1,204-acre Effigy Mounds National Monument in the northeastern part of the state protects 191 known Indian burial mounds. Twenty-nine of these fascinating burial mounds are constructed in the form of bird, snake, wolf, fox and bear effigies, a practice unique to the Upper Mississippi River Valley. Other mounds in the scenic monument area are conical or linear in shape.

A number of the effigy mounds are of immense proportions. The largest, Great Bear Mound, measures 70 feet across the legs and forelegs, 137 feet in length and 3½ feet high.

Several cultures created the conical and linear mounds in the park area. The oldest excavated is from the Red Ocher Culture and dates back 2,500 years. The next culture, the Hopewell, is noted for its pottery and use of material from distant places. A number of mounds have been identified as belonging to the Hopewellian period from 100 B.C. to A.D. 600.

The Effigy Mounds Indians lived in the region from a period overlapping the Hopewellian occupancy until 1300. Though their daily life differed little from the Hopewells, they built their mounds in animal form and did not include permanent offerings with their burials.

The beautiful lands protected in Effigy Mounds National Monument on the Mississippi River escaped the flattening effect of the last glacial age. The area includes open prairie, steep slopes, hardwood forests filling uplands and timbered bottomlands. Along the monument's eastern boundary, the great Mississippi River flows 350 feet below the bluff.

Automat (detail) by Edward Hopper (1882-1967) is one of the fine modern works on display in the Des Moines Art Center.

4) "LITTLE BROWN CHURCH IN THE VALE"

    There's a church in the valley
      by the wildwood.
    No lovelier spot in the dale.

The song, "Little Brown Church in the Vale," was written about the First Congregational Church of Bradford, Iowa, before the church was actually built.

The church was organized in 1855 and the quaint structure erected in 1860-64. Yet it was not the little brown church which inspired William S. Pitts to write his now-famous song, but the beautiful wooded site on Cedar Street which had been donated for the future church structure. Pitts first saw the spot in 1857 when the stagecoach he was taking to visit his future wife stopped briefly in Bradford. Pitts, who knew nothing of the donation, returned to his home in Rock County, Wisconsin, and composed his memorable song, without realizing that his words were to be prophetic.

In 1862, Pitts moved to nearby Fredericksburg and in 1863 he came to teach music at Bradford Academy, naturally surprised and pleased to find that the church had appeared in the meantime and had, in fact, been painted brown. Pitts sang his lovely song for the first time at the church's formal dedication in 1864.

Today the town of Bradford has disappeared, lost because the railroad bypassed it, and the "Little Brown Church in the Vale" stands as a monument to the hardy pioneers who built and maintained it.

Many people come each year to receive the sacrament of baptism and to exchange marriage vows in this picturesque chapel. Religious services have been held continually in the church since 1855.

Kansas

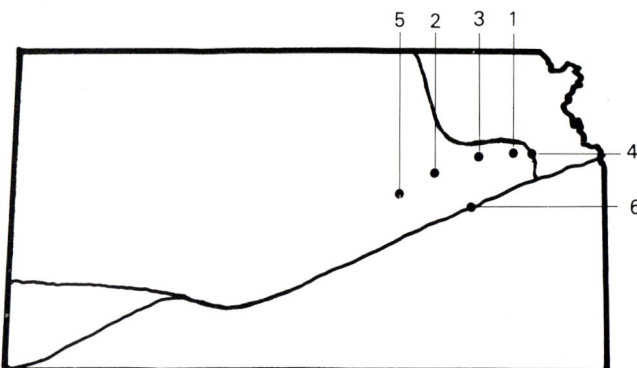

1) CAPITOL, Topeka

The Kansas State House in Topeka, built entirely of native stone in the popular classical style, is 304 feet high with 296 steps leading from the top of the building to the top of the dome. The building, completed in stages during the last half of the nineteenth century, rests on sixteen landscaped acres.

At one time, some state offices had handsome porcelain bathtubs and washstands of pure white marble, built in during the Populist administration, which also added the Georgian marble in the third-floor rotunda. A variety of attractive marbles is used for floors, wainscoting and doors throughout the Capitol building.

The principal features of the Capitol dome's interior are the four large mural paintings near the top. The east panel represents Religion, Knowledge and Temperance; the north panel, Plenty; the west, Peace, and the south, Power.

2) EISENHOWER CENTER

The Eisenhower Center in Abilene, also known as the Dwight D. Eisenhower Library, includes the Eisenhower Museum, the Eisenhower Boyhood Home and the Place of Meditation where the thirty-fourth President is buried.

The Presidential Library preserves papers, books and other materials related to Eisenhower's public life. A simple limestone structure with beautiful marble interior work, the library was dedicated in 1962. Facilities are available for research and exhibits complement the Eisenhower Museum across the street.

Constructed by the Eisenhower Foundation, the unadorned museum was dedicated in 1954 and presented to the nation in 1966. Murals in

Designed in the popular classical style, the Kansas State House in Topeka is built entirely of native stone.

the lobby trace Dwight D. Eisenhower's life from early childhood through his two terms as President of the United States. Exhibits represent all the periods of his lifetime and include memorabilia of other family members.

The adjacent Eisenhower Home was occupied by family members from 1898 until 1946. In this typical Midwestern frame home the six Eisenhower boys were raised. It has been maintained as it was in 1946 when Eisenhower's mother died.

3) KONZA PRAIRIE

In 1835 a U.S. cavalry officer noted that as his mounted unit traversed the undisturbed prairie the grass was so tall that it could be tied in knots across their saddles. Author Willa Cather described the wind-blown prairie as having "so much motion to it; the whole country seemed, somehow, to be running." The cavalry is no longer on the scene; wagon trains that once parted the tall prairie grasses of the Midwest roll no more. And most of the lush, self-perpetuating vegetation of the plains has disappeared with them. Unplowed native grassland is as hard to find today as a covered wagon.

South of Manhattan, Kansas, is a 916-acre tract of pristine prairie that has escaped the farmer's or developer's touch. Indians who lived in the area originally called the region Konza and this name is now the official title of the land owned by the University of Kansas. The area is used for the study of the natural prairie ecosystem and for comparison with manipulated ecosystems. Konza is part of the Ordway Prairie Preserve System, with other parts in Missouri and Minnesota.

Once more than a million square miles of the North American continent's central Mississippi drainage basin were covered with the windswept grasslands which were described in awe by explorers, settlers and cattlemen alike as a "sea of grass." Until well into the nineteenth century prairie grassland was the most abundant habitat type in North America. Within this immense region stretching from Texas to Canada are great variations of climate, rainfall and soil conditions which result in three basic types of prairie, tall-, mixed- and short-grass.

The easternmost of these is the tall-grass prairie, made up of grasses, such as the big bluestem and Indian grass, that grow as high as eight feet. Fires, rather than infertile soil or lack of rain, prevent trees from growing except along rivers or in manipulated areas. The tall-grass prairie extends roughly to the 100th meridian in Kansas and includes the Konza area.

Supporters of proposed prairie national parks say that such a park would be a place where citizens could "see yesterday," and this is true. But there are other, perhaps more urgent reasons. Where the prairie still exists, the

The Konza Prairie is one of the few remaining tracts of unplowed grassland. Before the coming of the pioneers these lush prairie grasses covered more than a million miles of the central Mississippi drainage basin.

supremacy of the grass can be partially attributed to its tenacious root systems. Here the matrix of roots, reaching a depth of five feet or more, holds the soil locked in its grasp. Through the cycle of decay and regrowth the dense mass of root-impregnated soil is continually being fertilized and becoming more loamy. This network of plant life was so thick and firm that many early farmers refused to dull or break their plows (first made of wood, then of cast iron) on it until John Deere's steel plow came into general use on the prairies about 1845. The purpose of the Konza prairie is to study this original prairie system to learn the principles that explain its self-perpetuation. These principles can help our land management practices today.

4) OREGON TRAIL

So many covered wagons moved west along the Oregon Trail that it was known as the great white-topped road (because of the wagon coverings). The 2,000-mile trip from Independence, Missouri, through Kansas and other states northwest to the rich farmlands of the Willamette Valley in Oregon (see map, p. 292) took almost half a year and was grueling. Yet during the 1840's and '50's about 250,000 pioneers walked or rode the Oregon Trail to a new life in the Far West near the Pacific. Most of the travelers came from the Mississippi River area, which less than fifty years earlier had been considered the "West."

The first one hundred miles along the easily traveled flat country of the Platte River in Nebraska were not normally difficult. But after 500 more miles, Fort Laramie in eastern Wyoming was a welcome sight. The fort, now restored and preserved as a national historic site, has been used variously by fur traders, the U.S. Army and the Pony Express.

The trail then turned 300 miles northwest to the challenge of the Rockies, and excess baggage was thrown off. Wagon trains following the turbulent Sweetwater River to the Wind River Range had to traverse a strenuous route. After navigating South Pass, 600 miles of difficult terrain had to be covered, passing through Fort Bridger in western Wyoming and Fort Hall, Idaho, on the Snake River, to Fort Boise in western Idaho. After traveling through Oregon's Blue Mountain Range, the pioneers rafted along the Columbia River to Fort Dalles, Astoria, 1,800 miles from Independence, Missouri, or farther to the Willamette Valley.

Natural "signposts" along the way still earmark the trail. Chimney Rock and Scotts Bluff are landmarks along the North Platte River in western Nebraska. The lofty bluff was used by pioneers as a camping ground. Chimney Rock, a shaft of reddish sandstone, was variously described by diarists as an "inverted funnel" and a "haystack with a pole through its top." Both landmarks are now part of **Scotts Bluff National Monument.**

Turtle-shaped Independence Rock in central Wyoming, where many travelers celebrated the Fourth of July, was a social register. Many of the names etched there are still legible.

South Pass in southwest Wyoming was one of the easiest Rocky Mountain crossings to negotiate. Because of the grassy slopes and gradual inclines, the pioneers who crossed the Continental Divide while moving through the pass were scarcely aware they had done so. When gold was discovered in California in 1848, prospectors followed the Oregon Trail to this point, then branched off the trail southwest through Utah and Nevada to the California gold fields.

Like most other trails, the Oregon had many alternate routes. One of the most famous of these passes a mountain named by Zebulon Pike in east-central Colorado. Hopeful travelers mounted signs on their wagons announcing their destination: "Pikes Peak or Bust."

Almost half of the "Path of Destiny" has been plowed under, paved over or built upon. While studies are being made of the possibility of establishing the entire Oregon Trail as part of a national historic trails system, many areas have already been preserved by county, state or Federal agencies. U.S. Highway 30 and Interstate Highway 80 pass through most of the major stops on the trail.

5) SACRED HEART CATHEDRAL

Salina is in the heart of a great wheat growing belt. Here, immense grain storage tanks hold over 66 million bushels. Since the surrounding Kansas plains are dotted with soaring silos and grain storage tanks, the Sacred Heart Cathedral's grain elevator motif is appropriate.

At the cathedral's 1959 dedication, Bishop Frank A. Thill described the edifice's timeless symbolism: "It is right, therefore, that here in rural Kansas the Angelic Bread of the Eucharist and the spiritual bread of God's holy word should be dispensed in a cathedral that belongs to the contemporary landscape. For the church is indeed God's granary...."

The cathedral's bell tower is patterned after a silo, and nine stone pillars along the east and west walls appear to be lines of grain storage bins. Long, narrow stained-glass windows are placed between the pillars. The entire building

Former President Dwight D. Eisenhower is buried in the Place of Meditation at the Eisenhower Center in Abilene.

is faced with native limestone which has a shell-like quality resembling travertine stone. A crucifix highlights the main entrance and a processional panel of sculpture represents the lay and religious people of the diocese.

6) SANTA FE TRAIL

For a thousand bridgeless miles, the Santa Fe Trail was traced on the prairies from Franklin, Missouri, through Kansas and Oklahoma to Santa Fe, New Mexico (see map, p. 292)—from civilization to sundown.

The first caravan snaked to Santa Fe in 1821. In 1825 the United States government surveyed the trail and within a few years it became very popular. As many as 3,000 wagon trains and 50,000 yoke of oxen a year plodded over the prairies that were "beautiful, unbroken by bush or rock; unsoiled by plow or spade." (See **Konza Prairie**, Kansas—3.)

The trail—sometimes over 400 feet wide—became packed so hard that traces still remain. Ruts can be seen at Arrow Rock, Kansas, upriver from Franklin, where wagons left the ferry and climbed up a grassy swale. A two-mile stretch can be seen west of Dodge City, Kansas, along U.S. Highway 50. Several campsites and springs have been preserved in New Mexico's Clayton Complex, a national historical landmark. Fort Larned, preserved as a national historic site, was the major military outpost in Kansas during the heyday of the trail. A sentinel in New Mexico's Rockies, Rabbit Ears Mountain, still stands out when seen from the Cimarron Cutoff, the main branch of the Santa Fe which sliced through the northwest corner of Oklahoma's panhandle. And Santa Fe's La Fonda Hotel still awaits travelers at trail's end.

The Cimarron Cutoff was dangerous because of the difficulty in finding water along it and the raiding Comanches and Kiowas. Jedediah Smith, perhaps the greatest mountain man of all, was killed here by Indians in 1831 while looking for water. Legendary Kit Carson scouted the area thirty years later.

The Mountain Branch of the trail through southeast Colorado was one hundred miles longer than the Cimarron Cutoff, but was considered safer. A successful trader, Dick Wootton, carved twenty-seven miles of road out of rugged Raton Pass and charged his own toll to everyone except Indians and posses pursuing horse thieves. Near Wootton's territory, at Cimarron, New Mexico, one can still see ruts from the 300-pound wagon wheels lurching toward the West. Wootton later sold his right-of-way to the railroad. It was the railroad, mainly the Atchison, Topeka and Sante Fe in 1880, that siphoned off almost all the trade from the Santa Fe Trail.

When the railroad following the Santa Fe Trail reached the vicinity of Fort Dodge in 1872, a town was established nearby. Almost overnight **Dodge City** became the railhead for the Dodge City Trail which replaced the Chisholm Trail (see Texas—7) to the east as the primary cattle trail from Texas. Today Old Front Street, including the Long Branch Saloon, has been restored as it was in the 1870's and Boot Hill graveyard has been recreated. The Beeson Museum displays relics from the town's early days.

Missouri

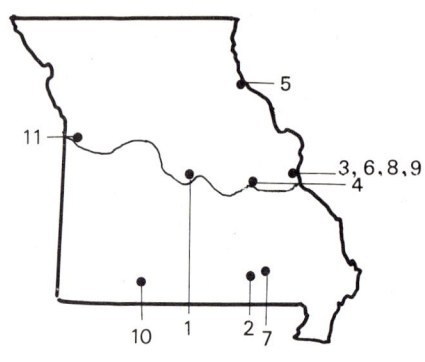

1) CAPITOL, Jefferson City

The magnificent white stone Missouri State Capitol in Jefferson City covers three acres atop the limestone bluffs on the south bank of the Missouri River and overlooks a wide expanse of Cole and Callaway counties.

Occupied in 1918, after more than four years under construction, the Capitol is 238 feet to the top of the dome.

Colossal reclining bronze figures by Robert I. Aitken on either side of the steps leading to the south entrance symbolize Missouri's two great rivers, the Missouri and the Mississippi, while atop is a bronze figure of Ceres, the goddess of agriculture.

Throughout the building are murals and decorative paintings telling the legend and history of Missouri, including the much-discussed murals on the walls of the House lounge by Thomas Hart Benton, famous Missouri artist.

The grand stairway, thirty feet across, is said to be the widest in the world. The front doors are of bronze, each thirteen by eighteen feet— the largest cast since the Roman Empire.

2) ELEVEN POINT NATIONAL WILD AND SCENIC RIVER

The Eleven Point River meanders without hurry or concern through the picturesque Ozark hills of southern Missouri east of Thomasville, its course cut in the shadows of steep bluffs, through forested sloping valleys and low-lying pasturelands. Springs gushing from the rocky cliffs and rushing up from underground reservoirs provide a continuous source of crystal-clear water.

Varying stretches of rapids and clear pools wind beneath shading hardwoods of birch, oak, hickory and sycamore. Intermittently the trees lean far over the river, forming a green canopy, and deep recesses in the surrounding hills contain caves large enough to bring out the spelunker in any visitor, although dangers exist for the visitor untrained in cave exploration.

Foxes, raccoons, beavers, muskrats, turtles and water snakes are common near the waters, as are wild turkeys, great blue herons and bobwhite quail. The Eleven Point is within the Mark Twain National Forest and is primarily a float river. Float camps, trails and primitive campgrounds accessible only by river have been built and more are planned. The Eleven Point is a river where man can forget his machines and contemplate the goodness of the earth.

3) GATEWAY ARCH

Rising majestically to a height of 630 feet, St. Louis' Gateway Arch commemorates the pioneering spirit of those men and women who settled the West after the Louisiana Purchase. Designed by noted architect Eero Saarinen, the arch also stands as a monument to modern man's pioneering technical achievements which have taken him to the frontier of space.

The long, lean lines of the arch are made possible by the strength of its steel combined with the stressed-skin design similar to that used in aircraft construction. Even in a 150 miles-per-hour wind, the sway at its apex would be no more than eighteen inches.

Each leg of Gateway Arch contains a forty-passenger train to transport visitors to the Observation Deck at the top. These trains consist of five-passenger capsules, each mounted like the basket of a ferris wheel. From the top, visitors have a magnificent thirty-mile view to the east and west.

4) LEWIS AND CLARK TRAIL

In 1804 a military expedition set out from St. Louis, Missouri, to find the best route overland to the Pacific Ocean. It returned two years and 8,000 miles later, having reached the Pacific at the mouth of the Columbia River.

The men of Lewis and Clark's group mapped 3,000 miles of wilderness and 1,500 miles of waterways, brought back scientific data of America's newest land, the huge Louisiana

Commemorating the spirit of the pioneers, the magnificent 630-foot-tall Gateway Arch on the bank of the Mississippi frames the night lights of St. Louis.

Purchase, and laid claim to the Pacific Northwest. They traveled through what is now ten states—up the Missouri River to the Bitterroot Mountains in Idaho and Montana, then down the Lochsa, Snake and Columbia rivers to Astoria, Oregon. (See map, p. 292.)

The expedition was financed by Congress which appropriated $2,500 at the request of President Thomas Jefferson. Headed by Meriwether Lewis and William Clark, the group, which numbered about forty, wintered among the Mandan Indians in 1804-05.

Here, a French-Canadian interpreter, Toussaint Charbonneau, and a guide, his wife Sacajawea ("Bird Woman"), a Shoshoni, were hired. Sacajawea has since become almost as well known as Lewis and Clark. The only woman in the group (she carried her newborn son on her back), she showed great courage and scouting ability. Monuments honoring her have been built in Bismarck, North Dakota, and Portland, Oregon.

The group spent their second winter in what is now Oregon, sheltered in a fort named Clatsop after a local Indian tribe. A replica of the fort, now a national memorial, was built in 1955 following Clark's floor plan dimensions.

While the trail as a whole has not received any national designation, many portions of it have been marked for today's travelers.

5) MARK TWAIN HOME

The Mark Twain Home in Hannibal is known throughout the world as the Mississippi River home of Tom Sawyer in the fictional town of St. Petersburg. It was here that Mark Twain (Samuel Langhorne Clemens) was raised and experienced many of the adventures which later produced the tales of Tom Sawyer and Huckleberry Finn.

The two-story frame house was built in 1844 by John Marshall Clemens, Sam's father. George A. Mahan, an avid Mark Twain admirer, purchased it in 1912. Presenting the home intact to the town of Hannibal, and later contributing bronze statues of both Tom Sawyer and Huckleberry Finn, Mahan established the first of many memorials to Twain.

With the interior restored to its nineteenth-century appearance, the house at 206 Hill Street is again the scene where young Sam Clemens administered pain killer to Peter the cat and escaped out of a second-story window to meet Tom Blankenship (later known as Huckleberry Finn) for a round of midnight pranks. Here, also, his mother, his sister Pamela and brother Henry were later transformed into the characters of Aunt Polly, Mary and Sid. The original board fence around the house which Clemens, and later Tom Sawyer, duped neighborhood boys into whitewashing for him is gone, but a duplicate now stands in its place.

Other landmarks in Hannibal which may be noticed in Twain's two memorable works include the Laura Hawkins House, which stands across the street from the Twain home. Clemens' boyhood sweetheart lived here, followed later in Twain's books by Becky Thatcher, who won the heart of Tom Sawyer. Holliday's Hill, known to Twain's adventurous characters as Cardiff Hill, still overlooks the Mississippi River, and Jackson's Island from which the youthful St. Petersburg pirates launched many a dangerous excursion.

Perhaps the most graphic reminder of Twain's boyhood, however, is the cave where Tom Sawyer and Becky Thatcher became lost, fearfully promising themselves to each other forever. For it is here, in the labyrinthine passages two miles south of Hannibal, that tourists retrace their own childhood steps, following the evasive spirit of youth captured by the words of Samuel Langhorne Clemens. (See **Mark Twain House**, Connecticut—3.)

6) NATIONAL MUSEUM OF TRANSPORT

Preserved in the National Museum of Transport in St. Louis are significant memorabilia from the history of transportation and communication. Beginning in 1944 with a mule-drawn streetcar scheduled for scrapping, the museum has grown to include extensive collections which trace mankind's amazing progress in technology and design.

Noteworthy exhibits include a 1931 Greyhound bus which carried its baggage on the roof, a locomotive which towed blocks used in building the Panama Canal, and one of the last of the prestigious and elaborate private railroad cars, furnished as it was in the days when it served the super-rich. Many other fascinating locomotives and railroad cars, as well as automobiles, streetcars, buses, trucks, horse-drawn vehicles and aircraft are displayed. Intriguing pipeline and communication devices may also be examined.

7) OZARK NATIONAL SCENIC RIVERWAYS

This is a place of quiet relaxation and gentle beauty: two swift-flowing Ozark streams that are undammed, unspoiled and unpolluted. Ozark National Scenic Riverways, authorized in 1964, protects the Current River, its tributary, Jacks Fork, and their river banks as they meander through a portion of the Ozark foothills in southeastern Missouri. These were the first rivers in the country to be specifically preserved as part of the National Park System as scenic rivers. This pioneering concept for conservation led to the enactment in 1968 of the National Wild and Scenic Rivers Act. Ozark contains 113 square miles along 140 miles of free-flowing streams. Included within the boundaries are large, natural springs, river-front caves, limestone bluffs and a great variety of flora and fauna.

The Ozarks are among the oldest mountains in the country. Uplifted and then eroded by wind, water and frost, little remains of their once-spectacular heights. Water, turned into carbonic acid as it seeped into the ground ages ago, dissolved the limestone overlaying the basic granite and formed a honeycombed series of underground caverns. Some of the cave roofs have collapsed, causing sinkholes, a striking example of which is the Sunkland along the upper portions of the Current River, a great hollow several hundred feet across and nearly a mile long produced by the successive fall-in of several interconnected underground chambers. In many areas, groundwater drips into the caverns, collects and circulates through the underground conduits and emerges as springs.

The streams themselves are strong and transparent, varying in color from sapphire blue to many shades of green, according to depth and the hour of the day. Quiet waters alternate with chutes or rapids as the streams flow through forests and under rocky bluffs.

8) ST. LOUIS BRIDGE

The St. Louis Bridge, completed in 1874, was the creation of Captain James B. Eads, the first engineer in the American Hall of Fame. Despite the skepticism of the experts of the day, Eads

A light blanket of snow adds charm to this still-operating 1870 corn mill at Alley Spring on the Jacks Fork River, a swift-flowing unspoiled stream in the Ozarks.

succeeded in bridging the treacherous Mississippi, establishing St. Louis as a major railroad crossing and the most important river city.

The Eads Bridge was truly a pioneering achievement. This triple arch bridge was the largest and boldest of the day, its three spans running 582, 520 and 502 feet. It marked the first extensive use of steel in bridge construction and the first use of alloy steel. Since it was necessary to anchor the foundation in the rock beneath the Mississippi bottom, pneumatic caissons had to be used on a large scale for the first time under uncertain conditions. The cantilever construction method was also used for the first time on a major project.

Still standing after a century of use, the bridge is a monument to the ingenuity and persistence of its builder.

Pete Engler's woodcarving shop in Silver Dollar City is typical of the artisans' workshops that demonstrate pioneer crafts to tourists.

9) ST. LOUIS ZOO

Some 3,000 birds, mammals and reptiles constitute the collections of the world-famous St. Louis Zoo. Many of these animals are presented in appropriate family groups and authentic habitat settings, and many are rare and endangered species. The zoo places great emphasis on the preservation of these animals. A new and spectacular one-and-one-half-acre Cheetah Survival Center permits these beautiful but endangered cats to roam freely so as to encourage the propagation of their species.

The Charles H. Talen Children's Zoo on the same grounds features an attractive three-and-one-half-acre park with paths leading through cavelike tunnels and gladelike enclosures.

10) SILVER DOLLAR CITY

Thirteen years ago Mary Herschend and her sons, Jack and Peter, were operators of Marvel Cave, one of America's largest caverns near Branson in the northern Ozark Mountains. They began building Silver Dollar City around the mouth of the cave as an added attraction to tourists, with a tiny restaurant, general store, chapel and post office. One day Peter Engler, a woodcarver, arrived and asked permission to set up shop and work on his carvings there.

hauling freight in the East and South and along the Santa Fe Trail (see Kansas—6), weighed 3,500 pounds and could carry more than six tons. The Silver Dollar City wagons are replicas.

At the dulcimer-maker's shop in one corner of the city, visitors are shown how the instrument's elements—fine walnut, spruce and rosewood—are carved and glued together.

Two thousand acres of Ozark forests surround this quaint hilltop community, which is rooted in the region's early history. A town nearby this site was founded in the 1880's as the mining community of Marmaros. Its residents spoke the pure and authentic Ozark dialect and observed the old hill-country customs. But the town never fully succeeded. Today Silver Dollar City recreates this nostalgic era, when time seemed to pass at a slower, more relaxed pace.

11) TRUMAN LIBRARY AND MUSEUM

The Harry S. Truman Library maintains extensive books, papers and other historical materials related to President Truman. Appropriately, the museum is housed in a crescent-shaped Indiana limestone structure located in Independence, where Truman lived the greater part of his life.

Adjacent is the Truman Museum which contains outstanding exhibits about the nature and history of the American Presidency, especially during the crucial Truman era which saw the dropping of two atomic bombs; the end of World War II; the "Truman Doctrine," aimed at aiding Communist-threatened nations and the subsequent European Recovery Program (or Marshall plan); and the North Atlantic Treaty.

On display are such famous documents as a rough draft of the Truman "Fair Deal" message to Congress and mementos from the 1948 Democratic National Convention, the "Whistle Stop" Campaign and the 1949 Truman inauguration. The table on which the United Nations Charter was signed in San Francisco is also on view, along with the Bibles on which Truman took his oaths as President and books containing signatures of dignitaries in attendance at the Potsdam Conference in Germany at the conclusion of World War II. A reproduction of President Truman's office in the west wing of the White House includes a tape recording explaining its furnishings.

President Truman was born in a modest six-room house in Lamar, south of Independence. His birthplace has been declared a national historic site and has been restored to appear much as it did in 1884 when he was born.

Now many craftsmen specializing in twenty-four different crafts—sixty during the annual fall National Festival of Craftsmen—may be observed at work in Silver Dollar City. Such vanishing arts as soap making, hand weaving, basket weaving and candlemaking are practiced by artisans happy to share their secrets. Oldsters skilled in crafts handed down to them through many generations take time to chat with visitors who have come to see how things were done in the old days.

Wheelwrights and wagon builders labor in the nation's only extant Conestoga wagon works. The Conestoga wagon, which was extensively used during the nineteenth century for

Nebraska

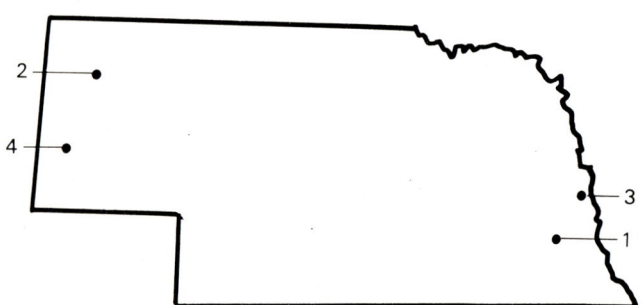

1) CAPITOL, Lincoln

The present Nebraska State Capitol at Lincoln, known as "Tower on the Plains," was rated one of the five best buildings ever constructed in the United States by a 1948 poll of architects. The building, designed by Bertram Goodhue, draws upon elements of architectural styles of ancient Asia, Greece, Egypt, Spain and the American Southwest to produce a structure strikingly modern yet representative of the prairie and the people of the state. The actual construction, begun in 1922, took ten years. More than forty varieties of marble, granite, limestone and slate were used throughout the building. From the two-story base rises the tower, 400 feet high, crowned with Lee Lawrie's thirty-two-foot, eight-ton bronze of *The Sower*.

A particular attraction are the doors to the Senate and House chambers. Plain on the inside but deeply carved on the outside, the "Indian" doors to the Senate represent the "Red Man's Tree of Life." Inlaid tooled leather on the House doors depicts the "White Man's Tree of Life." Both doors are boldly colored in the style of the prairie Indians.

2) FORT ROBINSON

Situated in the Pine Ridge country of strikingly beautiful northwest Nebraska, Fort Robinson played an important role in the "winning of the West." It was built in 1874 by the U.S. Army's Sioux Expedition sent to subdue hostile Indians. The Red Cloud Agency, main camp of over 12,000 Indians and headquarters of a government agent, had already been set up there a year earlier.

It was at Fort Robinson that the venerable Sioux Chief Crazy Horse was killed in 1877, having been betrayed by his own people. In 1879, Dull Knife's Cheyenne Outbreak occurred.

Fort Robinson remained an active military post until 1946. Today the Fort Robinson Museum in the Old Post Headquarters follows military history from the early Indian campaigns through the disappearance of the horse from the U.S. Army. More than thirty buildings survived from the fort's active years. Among these are the restored blacksmith and wheelwright shops, adjutant's office and guardhouse as well as the adobe officers' quarters. The fort is a part of Fort Robinson State Park.

3) JOSLYN ART MUSEUM

Not content with mere acquisition of American and European art to educate the public, the Joslyn Art Museum in Omaha makes a special and unique effort to interpret and explain the fine arts in relation to the historical and utilitarian background of each period.

Scotts Bluff on the North Platte River was a picturesque landmark for pioneers traveling West between 1843 and 1869 on the Oregon Trail (see Kansas—4).

Inside the imposing marble structure built in 1928-31, galleries devoted to the permanent collections offer a rich diet of visual experiences in painting, sculpture and the decorative arts, set in historical context by means of special photographic and dioramic display cases. The museum's famed Venetian masterpiece, Titian's *Man with a Falcon*, is displayed in a case with small sculpture and a view of the Doges' Palace in Venice for background.

The permanent "Life on the Prairie" exhibition illustrates with works of art, many artifacts and photographs the history of 10,000 years in Nebraska, from the aboriginal past through exploration and settlement to the present day. Completely furnished period rooms are included, while artist-explorers of the eighteenth and nineteenth centuries are represented by paintings and prints.

Works by George Catlin, Karl Bodmer, Alfred Jacob Miller and many other artists who accompanied expeditions, or simply set out to make a pictorial record of the new lands and their peoples, have been included, and the paintings by several of the Hudson River School—Albert Beirstadt, Thomas Moran and T. Worthington Whittredge among them—broaden the scope of the exhibit. Displays by contemporary painters and designer-craftsmen complete the story.

4) SCOTTS BLUFF NATIONAL MONUMENT

See **Oregon Trail**, Kansas—4.

North Dakota

1) CAPITOL, Bismarck

The North Dakota State Capitol in Bismarck is a modern nineteen-story structure noted for its simplicity, practicability and usability. The steel-framed "Skyscraper Capitol of the Plains" is faced with Wisconsin black granite base and white Indiana limestone. The main entrance doors are bronze. In the ground-floor lobby and the first-floor Memorial Hall, the walls are covered with Yellowstone travertine and the floor with Tennessee marble. The stairway leading to Memorial Hall has steps and risers of Tennessee marble and walls of Belgium black marble. Memorial Hall is forty feet high; its columns and large window frames are bronze. The interior decor features woods of a variety of colors and sources, including rosewood from Asia and Indian laurel wood, as well as many native American woods.

2) THEODORE ROOSEVELT NATIONAL MEMORIAL PARK

"This country is growing on me more and more," Theodore Roosevelt wrote of the North Dakota badlands. "It has a curious, fantastic beauty of its own." Roosevelt came to love this land of eroded valleys, hills, ridges and gorges in the Little Missouri River basin when he ranched here in the 1880's. It gave him a deep understanding of nature and the importance of conserving it, and Theodore Roosevelt National Memorial Park, the only one of its kind in the country, honors this man who became our twenty-sixth President, by keeping these badlands he knew so well in their natural state.

Although less spectacular than the more famous badlands of South Dakota, this land supports more vegetation and is more colorful. The varying shades of tan and gray of the sand and clay layers mix with the greens of trees and the yellows, reds and purples of wildflowers. Throughout the area are isolated buttes, the tops of which were once the level of the prairies; because of a protecting layer of rock or the hardness of the clay, they have withstood erosion. In the North Unit of the park are great masses of bluish bentonite, a claylike rock which becomes soft when saturated with moisture during rainstorms and slides down the hillsides.

Another curious feature are the lignite coal beds. Millions of years ago the dense vegetation that grew here was deposited in layers, which in time formed large beds of soft, lignite coal. Occasionally the lignite beds catch fire from lightning or other natural causes, burning for years and baking the nearby clay layers into a bricklike substance locally called scoria (although true scoria is the result of volcanic action).

Wildlife has been sharply reduced since Roosevelt's day. Elk, grizzly and black bear and wolf have disappeared from the area, while buffalo, pronghorn antelope and bighorn sheep were "replanted" in the region in recent years. As in the South Dakota badlands, many black-tailed prairie dogs scatter their towns on the flats. Prairie rattlesnakes are sometimes encountered along the roads.

In the South Unit, as well as in the rest of the badlands, are the petrified remains of a large forest. Fossils of snaillike creatures have been discovered here, and occasionally a rock will break open to expose leaf impressions of ancient oaks, maples, magnolias, sassafras and elms.

Theodore Roosevelt National Memorial Park was established in 1947 and contains about 110 square miles of the North Dakota badlands in three units: the South Unit near Medora, the North Unit near Watford City, and the Elkhorn Ranch site midway between the two.

Loved and admired by Theodore Roosevelt, the North Dakota badlands have been preserved in a national memorial park honoring our twenty-sixth President. An abundance of buffalo, pronghorn antelope and bighorn sheep inhabit the area.

Oklahoma

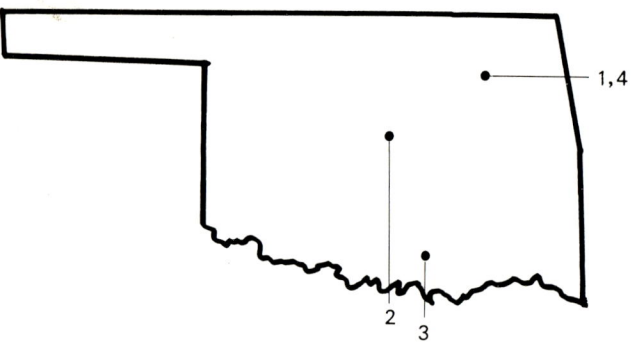

1) BOSTON AVENUE UNITED METHODIST CHURCH

Tulsa's Boston Avenue United Methodist Church, completed in 1929, was the first church in the world to break from traditional styles of church architecture. Contemporary symbolism and original design are used on a grand scale.

The idea of light and uplift predominates at the Boston Avenue Church. The Tower Chapel on the fifteenth floor indicates the primacy of prayer in the life of the church. Seven-pointed stars point up the seven Christian virtues.

The circular dome of the sanctuary implies the infinite, with neither beginning nor end. The pulpit provides the central focus and its open Bible signifies the central importance of the word of God. Two wildflowers indigenous to Oklahoma are found in the windows. The flaming red tritoma proclaims the excitement of Christianity and its profusion of petals symbolizes generosity. The strength of the Christian church is symbolized by the hardy coreopsis which thrives under adverse conditions.

2) CAPITOL, Oklahoma City

As might be expected from the "Oil Capitol of the World," the Oklahoma State Capitol is surrounded by oil derricks and oil has been produced for many years from pools beneath the Capitol grounds.

The design of the building is Gothic, but many features of Greek and Roman architecture are apparent, as well as British influences. Standing guard atop the five-story structure are great statues of lions which seem to protect the building and the state itself. Unlike most capitols, it has no dome, making the lions more dominant.

Construction of the building was begun in 1914 and completed in 1917. Many kinds of stone, primarily white Indiana limestone, were used. The foundation is Oklahoma granite.

3) PLATT NATIONAL PARK

Peaceful Valley of Rippling Waters, the Indians called Platt National Park. The Choctaws and Chickasaws treasured its quiet groves, bubbling mineral springs astride the confluence of the Western plains and the gentle wooded hills to the east.

Platt, our smallest national park at 912 acres, exists because the resident Indians were rigid in conservation and generous toward their fellow Americans. They gave their Peaceful Valley to the United States in 1902 on condition that it be preserved for the benefit of all the people. In 1906 this preserve became a national park.

There are some thirty mineral and freshwater springs in the park, seeping up through three major strata of rock. The lower, or Simpson, group of rock provides the mineral salts for the bromide and sulphur springs with their varied solutions. At the eastern end of the park fresh water courses from Buffalo and Antelope springs, named because herds of these animals came from the prairies to drink.

4) THOMAS GILCREASE INSTITUTE OF AMERICAN HISTORY AND ART

A truly specialized museum is a rarity, and while the scope of the Thomas Gilcrease Institute of American History and Art is certainly broad, the institute has displayed a primary interest in the history and art of the American West, and has collections of the work of artists who recorded the life and spirit of that part of the American scene. The institute also has an excellent library and a large archeological collection containing items from 20,000 years ago.

From the extensive collection of the paintings and writings of George Catlin, who started up the Missouri in 1832 carrying his sketchbook, paint box and easel as part of his traveling gear, to the 1964 acquisition of the complete studio contents—pictures, sketches, models and equipment—of the contemporary painter of the West, William Robinson Leigh, the Gilcrease Institute has assembled notable and informative materials in which art is seen as the incomparable handmaiden of history.

Perhaps the best known of the artists is Frederic Remington (1861-1909), painter, draftsman, sculptor, illustrator, journalist and author of ten books. Of his approximately 3,000 oils, watercolors, drawings and bronzes, nearly all were of Western subjects and one of the largest collections is in the Gilcrease museum.

Portrait of Frank Hamilton Cushing *by Thomas Eakins (1845-1916) pays tribute to the great American ethnologist. This painting is displayed in the Thomas Gilcrease Institute of American History and Art.*

South Dakota

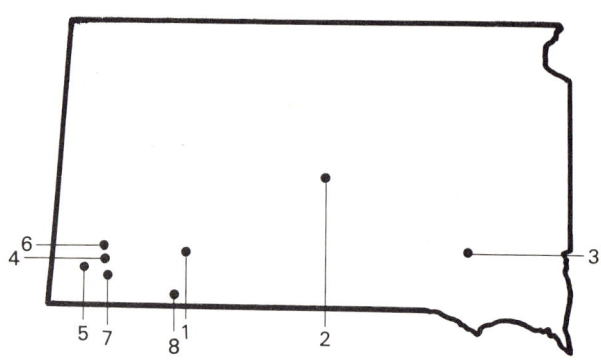

1) BADLANDS NATIONAL MONUMENT

The erosion-scarred landscape of Badlands National Monument has the eerie look of a city that was designed by a mad architect. The land between the Cheyenne and White rivers in southwestern South Dakota is austere and harsh. Sheer cliffs and jagged peaks form skylines of fantastic shapes.

Explorers and pioneers ignored the inhospitable Badlands region until 1846 when an account was published of a fossilized jawbone of a Titanothere found in the Badlands, followed a year later by a report of a fossilized camel described by Dr. Joseph Leidy. Dr. Leidy became an authority on Badlands fossils and by 1869 had inspected fossilized remains of more than 500 ruminating pigs, called Oreodonts, as well as many other now extinct animals that lived twenty-five to forty million years ago.

Early fossil hunters carried away petrified remains by the wagonload. Scientists feared the supply would soon be exhausted, but each new rain still unearths new fossils and geologists now believe that as long as the Badlands remain, erosion will continue to uncover them.

A unique method for preserving and displaying fossils is utilized by the monument's scientists. They carefully brush the soil from around a fossil and cover it with a transparent domelike shield, thus protecting the fossil and allowing it to be viewed in its natural setting.

Regrettably the invasion of settlers, hunters and trappers in the late nineteenth century caused a serious reduction of the once plentiful wildlife populations. Bison, reintroduced to their old haunts in 1963, adapted readily. The original herd of fifty-three tripled in number in just five years.

2) CAPITOL, Pierre

It is most appropriate that the South Dakota State Capitol should stand proudly on a bluff overlooking the storied Missouri River, famed as the highway to the frontier, because the state itself has been so much a part of the history of the frontier. Pierre, the capital city, is located on the site of what had been the capital of the Arikaka Indian nation for 400 years.

The exterior of the present State Capitol, started in 1907 and finished in 1910, is Marquette raindrop sandstone and Indiana Bedford limestone. The surrounding prairie furnished the boulder granite from which the basement was made.

A wide sweep of gleaming white marble steps leads from the rotunda and nearby executive suite to the legislative wings. The staircase, flanked by huge columns of concrete and marble, becomes an auditorium at Christmas and on other special occasions when programs are held in the rotunda. The most impressive view in the Capitol is the dome as seen from the rotunda, with sunlight filtering through stained-glass panels in the circular walls of the dome.

3) CORN PALACE

In 1892, two Mitchell businessmen decided the town needed a special spot for celebrations when the harvest was good. Their corn-covered Corn Palace grew into a Russian-style hall, complete with domes, minarets and kiosks that became a Mitchell landmark. While the original building has been replaced several times, the present Corn Palace at Fifth and Main streets closely follows its theme and now attracts half a million visitors annually.

The bright yellow blossoms of the prickly-pear cactus are a delicate contrast to the rugged landscape of its surroundings in the South Dakota Badlands. Preserved as a national monument, the area is famous for its prehistoric fossil beds.

At each Indian summer the harvest is again celebrated and the larger-than-life frescoes that cover much of the exterior of the building are remade with native grasses and grains. Corn, though, is the prime ingredient of the murals. Red, green, blue and yellow ears of corn—as many as 3,000 bushels—are sliced lengthwise and then arranged in patterns on 230 feet of panels. In the early years the designs were geometric. They have since become educational, patriotic, entertaining or ecological scenes. Since 1948 famous Sioux artist Oscar Howe has annually planned and executed a new overall theme.

The Corn Palace functions as an auditorium, theater and sports stadium year-round.

4) CUSTER STATE PARK

Like a giant mushroom emerging from the soil, shouldering aside anything in its way, a granite dome forced itself into sunlight a billion years ago. The erosive powers of wind and water have sculpted the batholith and the uptilted remnants of what was the covering mantle of sedimentary rock into spires and tunnels in the Black Hills. Abundant mineral crystals and colors of beryls, feldspars, manganese and bentonite from the once horizontal rock run in concentric rings around the ancient dome's center. Forests, interspersed with lakes and streams, now cover much of the area.

North of and adjacent to Wind Cave National Park is Custer State Park, containing the fingerlike projections telling the geological story of the "island in the plains" that is older than the Rockies, Alps or Himalayas. The Cathedral Spires and Needles regions in the northwest section and the bright red Spearfish Formation in the southeast corner of the park attract admiration and wonder the way gold in the area accrued to itself miners in the late nineteenth century.

Formerly a game preserve, Custer was created a state park in 1919. Large herds of bison, elk, deer and antelope now roam the hillsides of this, one of the largest and best known state parks in the country, where Sioux and Cheyenne Indians were once promised a home.

A park ranger views the terrain of Wind Cave National Park in the Black Hills of South Dakota.

5) JEWEL CAVE NATIONAL MONUMENT

Jewel Cave is for the real spelunker—one who dislikes electric lights and wide, established trails. He leaves these things to nearby, almost people-trodden Wind Cave National Park. Located west of Custer State Park, Jewel Cave is still not fully explored.

The entrance of the cave is on the side of a ravine called Hell Canyon. The main passages lead to side galleries and various-sized chambers, the first of which is fine-grained limestone, looking somewhat like Gothic-style architecture. The walls and ceilings of many of the galleries are lined with a thick layer of calcite crystals. Many of them, called dogtooth crystals, are very sharp and sparkle like jewels under a light, thus giving the cave its name. These crystals range in color from light green tints to darker greens and bronze.

"Soda straws," or very thin, hollow stalactites, of up to thirty-eight inches long but only one-quarter inch in diameter, have been found in Jewel Cave, although many of these near the natural entrance were destroyed by early visitors. Flowstone draperies can be found here in rainbow colors—yellows, reds, browns, blues and blacks.

The cave lies beneath a rough terrain of gulches, canyons and ravines. Jewel Cave National Monument includes a virgin stand of ponderosa pine, one of the last remaining such stands in the Black Hills region.

Made part of the National Park System in 1908, about thirty-five miles of Jewel Cave has thus far been explored, already making it one of the most extensive caves known to man.

Built by two Mitchell businessmen in 1892 to celebrate the harvest, the world's only Corn Palace now houses the annual Corn Palace Festival in September and serves as a convention hall.

6) MOUNT RUSHMORE

In the beautiful and rugged Black Hills of South Dakota, the solid granite of 6,000-foot Mount Rushmore is the setting for a uniquely significant man-made American landmark.

One of the most massive sculptures ever completed, the Mount Rushmore National Memorial represents critical phases in this nation's history through the awe-inspiring carvings of four of this country's greatest national leaders. George Washington symbolizes the founding of the nation; Thomas Jefferson, the Declaration of Independence and the Louisiana Purchase; Abraham Lincoln, the preservation of the union and the struggle for equality; and Theodore Roosevelt, the expansion of the country in the twentieth century and the conservation of its natural resources.

The face of each great President is between sixty and seventy feet high and is carved in amazingly minute and perfect detail. Each nose is twenty feet long, each mouth eighteen feet wide and the eyes eleven feet across, carved to the scale of 1:65. Their lifelike expressions project their personalities with uncanny realism.

Work on the memorial began in 1927 under the direction of Gutzon Borglum who also directed the early stages of the Stone Mountain, Georgia, project. (See **Stone Mountain**, Georgia—6.) Actual construction time was six and a half years, but bad weather and lack of funds lengthened the time to fourteen years. Many changes in the original plans were required by the formation and structure of the granite outcroppings. Gutzon died in 1941, before the memorial could be finished. His son,

Lincoln, continued work on the finishing touches until funds were exhausted later that year. Since then no alterations have been made to this gargantuan masterpiece.

7) WIND CAVE NATIONAL PARK

Wind does not usually blow up through the ground but, wandering through the Black Hills in 1881, cowboy Tom Bingham felt an upward draft and stooped in puzzlement, touched with wonder. There he saw a ten-inch natural opening in the limestone rock of the hill—and what could he call it but Wind Cave.

Afterward, explorers got into the cave by digging entrances near the original "blow-hole." Within were the fairyland formations on walls and ceilings, resembling a honeycomb or "boxwork" structure that might have intrigued a Tom Sawyer and Huck Finn into dark and forbidding recesses.

One might first imagine that another aperture higher on the hill would be the air intake. But that is not the case. This strange phenomenon of a breathing hill is believed to be caused by changes in atmospheric pressure. The cave actually completes the cycle of breathing, as it were, by letting in the wind when the outside pressure rises, and by expelling air when the pressure drops.

The weird ornamentation of Wind Cave is unique among famed caverns in that it includes relatively few stalagmites and stalactites. The boxwork was created by a layer of limestone which was sculptured and form-frozen in varied periods of geological uplift and submergence. Then, moisture containing calcium carbonate seeped through and evaporated forming calcite in the cracks. More recently the limestone between the fissures dissolved, leaving calcite fins, some lacelike, some broad enough to resemble the sides of boxes and thus called "boxwork."

The central attraction of Wind Cave National Park, the cavern; is rivaled in naturalistic lure by the wildlife sanctuary surrounding it. Over the park's forty-four square miles of rolling woodlands and plains, graze herds of the historic bison, once slaughtered by callous white men from Pullman car and saddle alike.

Biologically speaking, east meets west in Wind Cave National Park, where ponderosa pine, typical of the Western mountains, grow on the same slopes with Eastern bur oaks. And the animals graze on what is a prime example of mixed-grass prairie, a rich natural blending of medium, tall and short grasses, with a sprinkling of wildflowers which lend dashes of color to the scene.

8) WOUNDED KNEE MASSACRE NATIONAL HISTORIC SITE

The tragic events that occured in 1890 in the valley of Wounded Knee Creek are vividly recalled by the site of the mass grave of Big Foot, Yellow Bird the medicine man, and more than 150 Sioux followers slaughtered by the U.S. Seventh Cavalry, Custer's old regiment.

On December 17, two days after the great Sioux Chief, Sitting Bull, was killed during an attempted arrest under direction of the army, the War Department issued orders for the arrest of Big Foot, leader of a band of Minneconjou Sioux who had taken up the Ghost Dance. Ghost Dance was the name given by white men to the Indian ceremonial dance performed in anticipation of the day the Indians would be free of white men. Because this dance, first performed in 1889, excited the Indians, the War Department feared it would lead to violence and prohibited it. Armed ghost dancers had attempted to prevent Sitting Bull's arrest at the time he was killed.

On hearing of Sitting Bull's death, Big Foot and his band of 350 headed across the badlands toward the Pine Ridge Agency where Chief Red Cloud might protect them. On December 28, they were overtaken by Major Samuel M. Whitside and four troops of the Seventh Cavalry, east of the Pine Ridge Agency.

Weakened from exhaustion, cold and illness, the Indians consented to a military escort, and they camped that night at Wounded Knee, twenty miles east of the agency. During the night, the remainder of the Seventh Cavalry arrived under the command of Colonel James W. Forsyth, bringing the number of soldiers to 500.

The first shot was fired on December 29 as a result of tensions aroused during the soldiers' disarming of the Indians. The Indians were shown no mercy; even women and children were shot as they fled for safety.

When it was over, more than 150 Indians lay dead, including Big Foot and Yellow Bird. Another fifty were injured. Twenty-five soldiers were killed and thirty-nine wounded in the melee. The next day a snowstorm blanketed the area. The bodies of the Indians were buried in a mass grave on New Year's Day.

Located on the Pine Ridge Reservation of the Oglala Sioux, the Wounded Knee Massacre National Historic Site features an interesting museum containing uniforms and rifles used by the Seventh Cavalry and the Indians in the tragedy of Wounded Knee. In addition, the museum possesses collections related to North America and the Old West.

Mount Rushmore National Memorial depicts four of this country's great leaders in one of the most massive sculptures ever completed. The faces of Washington, Jefferson, Theodore Roosevelt and Lincoln are carved into solid granite.

Texas

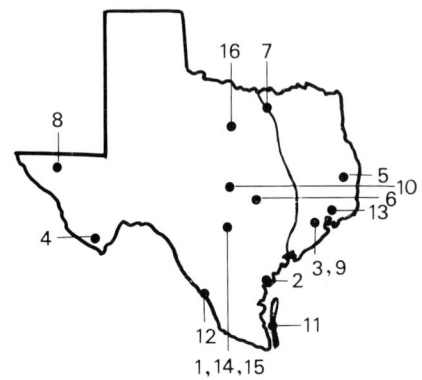

1) ALAMO

Built in 1718 and more properly called the Mission San Antonio de Valero, the Alamo in San Antonio was the site of the most storied battle in the war fought to achieve Texas' independence from Mexico. For two weeks in 1836, a small band of 187 men withstood a siege by General Santa Anna and 6,000 Mexican soldiers. The Alamo was finally overrun on March 6 and all of her defenders were killed, but not until approximately 1,600 Mexicans fell. Though Santa Anna tried to minimize his losses, Mexican Colonel Juan Almente noted, "Another such victory and we are ruined." Among the defenders who gave their lives to the Texas cause were Davy Crockett, Jim Bowie and Colonel William Travis.

Before the battle, the mission, built by Franciscan friars, served as a church, school for Indian converts and refuge for early settlers. In 1793 the era of missions came to an end and civil authorities assumed control. For twelve years after 1801 the former rectory was occupied by Spanish cavalry from Alamo de Parras in Mexico. After they left, the fortress kept the name "Alamo," Spanish for cottonwood.

Today the restored Alamo, under custody of the Daughters of the Republic of Texas since 1905, greets visitors with a plaque near its entrance:

Be Silent, Friend
Here Heroes died
To Blaze a Trail
For Other Men.

Famous defenders of the Alamo who gave their lives in 1836 for Texas' independence from Mexico were Davy Crockett, Jim Bowie and Colonel William Travis. The former mission has been open to the public since 1905.

The world's largest indoor arena, the Houston Astrodome is also the first multipurpose, all-weather combined sports and convention center. Opened in 1965, the 208-foot-high dome will seat 45,000 to 66,000 depending on the event.

2) ARANSAS NATIONAL WILDLIFE REFUGE

It is truly a magnificent creature, this tallest of North American birds. Five feet in height, with a seven-foot wingspan, the whooping crane gives a piping cry that can be heard over a mile away. It is noble and stately in appearance, with its gleaming white plumage, red patch of bare skin on the crown, black wing tips and graceful flight.

Every autumn, the world awaits word of the arrival of the whoopers on the Texas Gulf Coast after a 2,500-mile flight from their summer nesting sites in Canada, for these birds have been on the verge of extinction for many years. It is believed that they have not been really numerous for centuries and there may have been only 1,400 dwelling on the continent at the time the Pilgrims landed. By 1938 only fourteen remained and today there are about fifty. One reason for the modest increase was the establishment in 1937 of the Aransas National Wildlife Refuge at the whoopers' winter grounds on Blackjack Peninsula on the Texas Gulf Coast.

Because whoopers are so sensitive to intruders, especially human, the public is not allowed to enter the birds' wintering grounds in Aransas, but the birds can be usually viewed with binoculars from an observation tower which overlooks a portion of this coastal area.

The marshes, grasslands, brush thickets and woods of Aransas nurture many other species of birds, including the endangered Attwater's prairie chicken. Among the mammals are an abundance of white-tailed deer and an increasing number of javelinas (collared peccaries), the only native piglike animal in the United States.

3) ASTRODOME

A study in superlatives, the 262-acre Houston Astrodome is the largest indoor arena in the world. It is also the first multipurpose, all-weather combined sports and convention center. The dome rises 208 feet, forming a translucent roof for the stadium. Some 4,600 plastic skylights cover the dome which spans 642 feet and is eighteen stories high.

The Astrodome, opened in 1965, was designed to serve a wide variety of functions, including baseball, football, basketball, boxing and conventions. Seating capacity ranges from 45,000 to 66,000, depending on the event.

The list of records set by the Astrodome is seemingly endless. It is the largest clear-span building, the largest air-conditioned stadium, and the first major stadium with a roof. Its electronic scoreboard, measuring 474 feet long and four stories high, is one of the largest in the world. Astro-turf, artificial turf which has now become common on major sports fields, was first installed here. The turf can be removed and put back within a few hours by the use of 79,940 feet of zippers.

4) BIG BEND NATIONAL PARK

The Great River, the Rio Grande, running a fairly straight southeast course while edging the United States and Mexico across the Chihuahuan desert, suddenly bends to its left and cuts to the north past the Chisos Mountains for 107 miles. And before it turns south again it puts a heart-shaped lower boundary on Big Bend National Park. Established in 1944, the park covers a total of 708,221 acres in southwestern Texas.

This is a proud solitary stretch of country, harsh without bitterness, austere without anger and silent with a proud and brooding unfathomable mystery.

The men who knew this area before the days of the park's development were mostly American fugitives and Mexican bandits. Today, however, the men of violence are gone. In the middle of the park, the Chisos Mountains rise up like a string of fortified castles set to hold back the advance of the hordes of sage and cactus on the desert floor.

Flowers begin to bloom in the lowlands in late February but do not reach the mountain heights until May. Spring also brings occasional "northers," sudden storms that bring chill winds and often dust. The mountains are particularly attractive in the summer when temperatures in the desert hover around 100 degrees. Once or twice a year snow comes to the mountains, but usually in the winter the heights are merely brisk while the canyons remain comfortably warm during the day.

The river and mountains have given the park three large canyons. Boquillas ("Little Mouth") is where the river cuts the Sierra del Carmen in two. Upriver in the Santa Elena Canyon the Rio cuts the walls of the Grand Puerta ("Great Door") with a 1,500-foot slash.

The third canyon, Mariscal ("Marshall"), is the most remote, the most difficult to reach, and the most rewarding. Mariscal allows only boatmen to explore its limestone walls and view the fossilized remains of animals who lived in those distant ages of the earth's past.

5) BIG THICKET

Eastern Texas' Big Thicket region has often been described as "the biological crossroads of America." Plant and animal life from the East, West, North and South come together in this unique timberland which originally covered some three million acres. Inroads by man have reduced the size of the Big Thicket to 300,000 acres and the advances of "civilization" are still continuing.

Only in the Big Thicket can flora ranging from pine forests to tidal marshes be found together, provided by nature with necessary soil conditions and nourished by sixty inches of rainfall each year. Eight major plant communities are represented—stream-bottom hardwood, wetland pine savannah, acid bog, prairie, palmetto flats, arid sandland, upland pine savannah, and beech, magnolia and loblolly association.

Forests of oak, pine, magnolia and beech support record-breaking trees of many species, covered with flowering vines and Spanish moss. The forest floors are covered with about thirty types of ferns. Forty species of orchids and four kinds of carnivorous plants have been found.

Many animals whose native grounds have gradually been reduced with the advancement of civilization in other parts of the country still make their homes in the Big Thicket. Alligators, deer, bobcats and snakes share the region with the endangered red-cocked woodpeckers and the ivory-billed woodpeckers, once thought to be extinct. The red wolf, very close to extinction, has been reported here.

Yet this marvelous microcosm of the plant and animal worlds remains without any protection against development. Efforts are currently underway to stop the tragic onslaught which threatens the complete destruction of this ecological wonderland.

6) CAPITOL, Austin

The Texas Capitol, which stands in magnificent splendor in the center of the city of Austin, is a symbol of the history and heritage of the Lone Star State.

The morning sun adds glittering beauty to the shores of Padre Island. The national seashore section of the barrier island is an 80.5-mile expanse of uninterrupted, primitive beach.

Among the largest of the state capitols, it was patterned after the National Capitol. Completed in 1888, it towers 311 feet to the top of the star held aloft by the "Goddess of Liberty." It is constructed of pink Texas granite donated to the state by the owners of Granite Mountain in Burnet County.

The history of the state under the six flags of Spain, France, Mexico, the Republic of Texas, the United States and the Confederacy is depicted in beautiful bright-colored seals inlaid in the terrazzo on the first-floor rotunda. These are flanked on each side by large inlaid names of the battles which were fought to win and maintain Texas' independence from Mexico.

7) CHISHOLM TRAIL

In the twenty years following the Civil War, what was probably the greatest migration of domestic livestock in the world took place regularly on the prairies of Texas and neighboring states. During the era of the open range, a total of about ten million longhorn cattle were driven north to railroad centers, first in Missouri, then Kansas, and finally Wyoming.

Chisholm was the most famous of the cattle trails, and, like the others—Sedalia, Western and Goodnight-Loving—it was not a well-defined path, but many separate and alternate routes. The herds were generally driven (see map, p. 292) from the San Antonio area through

The emblems of each flight in the Apollo manned space program (top) are on display in the Johnson Space Center in Houston. The center is dedicated to the study and exploration of space. Mission control (above) is the control and operations center for all flights.

Austin, Fort Worth, and the Oklahoma Indian Territory to Abilene, Kansas, from where the cattle would be shipped by rail to slaughterhouses in Chicago.

Named after an Indian trader, Jesse Chisholm, who used what became the cattle trail for hauling only supplies, the trail was promoted as the best route for driving cattle by someone who had never done it. A true entrepreneur, Joseph McCoy, an Illinois farmer turned cattle dealer, established himself in 1867 in Abilene, then a town of twelve log cabins, persuaded the Hannibal and St. Joseph Railroad to deal with him, then had handbills distributed through Texas. These handbills advertised the Chisholm as the best way to drive cattle to market—"more prairie, less timber, more small streams and fewer large ones." That same year longhorns began to be corralled into McCoy's newly constructed shipping yards.

McCoy's ploy brought riches to many. About five million longhorns were roaming the prairies and multiplying by a million a year. They were bought at about three dollars a head, herded about 650 miles by half a dozen cowboys during a two- to three-month drive, then sold for tenfold profit.

During the 1880's the trail fell into disuse almost as quickly as it had become popular. No longer could herds averaging 1,000 head graze along the way to the "cow towns." Quarantine laws forbidding such drives became effective and herds of sheep moved in. More importantly, though, farmers crisscrossed the prairies with barbed wire and fenced the open range.

No traces of the actual Chisholm Trail remain today. Many landmarks and historic sites where the cowboys rejuvenated themselves are extant, however. Round Rock, Georgetown and Salado are Texas towns that well remember the lariat-tossing young cowboys. In Oklahoma is Monument Hill, a mesa where herders piled boulders into two hills, then scratched initials and brands into the rocks. In Wichita, Kansas, an attraction called Cow Town has authentically copied the Wichita of the 1870's. Abilene, once thought of as the roughest, toughest, wildest town in the West, is much quieter now, but has recreated in Old Abilene Town a memorial to the pioneers of that day.

8) GUADALUPE MOUNTAINS NATIONAL PARK

In the middle of the Chihuahuan desert of southwestern Texas is an "island in the sky." One-quarter of the Guadalupe Mountain Range dips across the New Mexico border here, only a few miles southwest of Carlsbad Caverns National Park. (See New Mexico—3.) These uplands contain a startling diversity of flora and fauna in an unusual mountain-desert setting, and it was fitting that, in 1966, Congress designated 82,279 acres as a national park.

The most notable feature of the Guadalupes is Y-shaped McKittrick Canyon—a deep cut in the northeastern mountains which embraces a unique, balanced ecosystem. Here, the vegetation ranges from desert scrub to forests of pine, fir and juniper.

Forming a V-shaped wedge pointing south and taking up a large portion of the park is a Permian marine limestone reef. Laid down in shallow coastal waters 280 to 290 million years ago, it is identified as one of the largest exposed fossil reefs in the world. At the point of the "V" is El Capitan, a sheer, thousand-foot cliff visible for over fifty miles. Nearby is the highest point in Texas, 8,751-foot Guadalupe Peak. Just inside the V-shaped highlands, and a part of McKittrick Canyon, is The Bowl, a 670-acre relict forest containing dense stands of ponderosa pine, limber pine and Douglas fir with a thick undergrowth.

9) JOHNSON SPACE CENTER

The hub of the United States manned spaceflight programs, the Lyndon B. Johnson Space Center, was dedicated to the late President from Texas, who had an abiding interest in the frontier of space, shortly after his death in 1973. At the 1,620-acre facility near Houston, astronauts are carefully trained and their spacecrafts designed and tested.

About a hundred different buildings comprise the National Aeronautics and Space Administration (NASA) project, begun in 1962. These range in size and complexity from the nine-story Project Management Building to tiny traffic-control booths at the entrances. A wide variety of scientific and technical disciplines play an important role in each manned spaceflight and are housed in facilities which meet their specific requirements.

Probably the most famous structure is Building 30, Mission Control. Network television has brought people around the world into the busy Mission Operations Control Room during mankind's historic ventures into the last frontier.

Three buildings are open to the public for a fascinating glimpse into the activities of the complex center. Building 1, the Visitor Orientation Center, contains an interesting museum of American space exploration. NASA exhibits include such historic mementos as an early Mer-

cury capsule flown by Gordon Cooper, an Apollo ship similar to the one which carried the first men to the moon, space equipment, and a moon rock display.

In the Mission Simulation and Training Facility, Building 5, astronauts prepare themselves for future missions under realistic conditions. Such facilities as a Skylab Orbital Work-shop spacecraft, an Apollo Telescope Mount and Airlock, and a Multiple Docking Adaptor provide a taste of the difficult and exciting adventures awaiting man in space.

The Flight Acceleration Facility in Building 29 is an immense centrifuge with a fifty-foot arm supporting a three-man gondola. Spun at dizzying speeds, this device simulates the fan-

The Great River, the Rio Grande, bordering the United States and Mexico, cuts a heart-shaped boundary for Big Bend National Park.

tastic gravitational forces to which the astronauts will be subjected as they lift off and reenter the earth's atmosphere.

10) LONGHORN CAVERN STATE PARK

A beautiful, awe-inspiring product of the evolution of the earth, Longhorn Cavern northwest of Austin was at least a million years in the making. A number of caves were begun here when the Texas climate became drier, causing the groundwater level to drop, dissolving the limestone. A labyrinth of passages and huge rooms were gradually carved by underground streams flowing through the caves, and eventually this remote chamber, 130 feet beneath the earth, was completely excavated.

The cavern can be approached through a collapsed sink, or deep depression, in the limestone. Remains of the original roof form a natural bridge over the steps leading to the cave entrance. Within the cavern itself are the magnificent "Hall of Marble," unusual flint formations, clusters of stalactites and stalagmites, and the accent of sparkling calcite crystals.

Longhorn Cavern provided shelter for caveman in prehistoric times. During the Civil War a gunpowder factory was said to have been established in its depths, and later, the notorious Sam Bass supposedly used the cave as a hideout and a place to store his ill-gotten riches.

11) PADRE ISLAND NATIONAL SEASHORE

Along the Texas Gulf Coast is the longest uninterrupted stretch of primitive, warm-weather beach land in the continental United States. For those fascinated by vast expanses of unspoiled shoreline, by a feeling that places where the oceans and land meet have a special message for man, Padre Island will always be memorable.

Over a hundred miles long, Padre Island is a splendid example of a barrier island formed by lateral currents and waves depositing billions of shellfish, the remains of other animals and eroded sediment from mainland Texas. Finally, about five thousand years ago, the island edged above the surface, the winds began building dunes, and vegetation began to establish a tenuous foothold with plants that are resistant to the scouring effect of wind-blown sand. They must grow faster than the sand can pile up around them to survive periods of inundation beneath the shifting surface, and they must resist periodic washing by salt water. The resultant vegetation—including the picturesque, nodding sea oats and the purple-flowered railroad vine (beach morning glory) that stretches its runners for more than twenty-five feet over the sands—are what binds these dunes and protects them against the strong winds and heavy seas of the Gulf, permitting the dunes to grow. In the natural sequence of events, Padre Island will be pushed, during tens of thousands of years, by wind and waves toward the mainland, gradually becoming part of it. Regrettably, by destroying vegetation through overuse, man has speeded up the life cycle of this island.

Padre Island National Seashore, authorized in 1962, includes 80.5 miles of the island. Causeways at both ends provide vehicular access to the narrow island, which ranges in width from a few hundred yards to about three miles.

12) RIO GRANDE RIVER

The "Great River of the North," the 1,800-mile Rio Grande is a mountain stream when it begins in southern Colorado. In northern New Mexico it flows north to south through valleys and canyons like White Rock Canyon with its thousand-foot-high walls. In south-central New Mexico the river bends to the southeast and, after passing the city of El Paso, Texas, becomes the boundary between the United States and Mexico. Here, the broad, shallow river meanders among sandbars, frequently deserting old courses and cutting new ones, until it reaches the Gulf of Mexico. (See map, p. 292.)

Since pre-Columbian days, man has struggled to live along the Rio Grande, using its waters for irrigation. The Rio Grande is a thin ribbon of life running through a desolate and barren land. It is an erratic river that sometimes dries up into a small stream and during other seasons becomes a flooding torrent.

From its headwaters to El Paso, most of the river's water is obtained from melting snow. In contrast to the water-hungry lands of the upper Rio Grande, the towns along the lower river, such as Brownsville, Texas, often suffer from having too much water. The flooding is caused by torrential storms that sweep inland from the Gulf of Mexico.

Although it is one of the longest rivers in America and drains a rather extensive area of 248,000 square miles, the Rio Grande obtains very little runoff water from the desert lands that surround it. The harshness of this region and its impracticability as a waterway have allowed the Rio Grande to remain remarkably well preserved.

At the river's Big Bend some three hundred miles southeast of El Paso is Big Bend National Park. (See Texas—4.) In New Mexico, where the river abounds in rainbow and brown trout, a forty-eight mile stretch of the Rio Grande and four miles of a tributary, the Red River, are protected as part of the National Wild and Scenic Rivers System. Parts of the lower Rio Grande are currently under consideration for inclusion in the system.

13) SAN JACINTO MONUMENT

One of the shortest and most decisive battles in the war to win Texas' independence from Mexico was fought on the San Jacinto Battleground, now protected as a 460-acre state park on the Houston Ship Channel near Houston. On April 21, 1836, General Sam Houston's forces completely routed a larger Mexican army under General Santa Anna in an eighteen-minute battle. To honor the heroes of the Battle of San Jacinto and the many others instrumental in achieving Texan independence, the world's tallest masonry monument, built in 1936-39, rises to a height of 570 feet.

A museum building forms the base of San Jacinto Monument. On its four bronze doors are the six flags which have flown over Texas. The museum chronicles the history of Texas from the old Indian civilization to the present day.

The battleship U.S.S. *Texas* has been moored at the monument since 1948 and open to visitors.

14) SAN JOSÉ MISSION STATE AND NATIONAL HISTORIC SITE

Mission San José y San Miguel de Aguayo was established in 1720 in present-day San Antonio by Franciscan friars and was placed under the jurisdiction of the Missionary College of Guadalupe in Zacatecas, Mexico. An emissary from the college in 1777 described San José as "the Queen of all Missions of New Spain in point of beauty, plan and strength, and is a symbol of the faith, courage and vigor of Franciscan Fathers."

The emissary later described the mission church: "Next to the north side a new church is being built within the walls. It is a beautiful temple with three vaulted naves, fifty varas [one vara equals thirty-three inches] long and ten wide with its transepts. It has a beautiful cupola...." The lovely rose window on the south side of the church, which still holds services, is an excellent example of stone carving.

A number of other buildings on the mission's grounds have been preserved in their original state, including an old grist mill overlooking the

The site of the most decisive battle in Texas' war to win independence from Mexico was fought on April 21, 1836, on the San Jacinto Battleground. A monument was erected to honor the heroes of the battle. The battleship U.S.S. Texas is also located at the site.

mission's fields, the soldiers' barracks and many of the Indian quarters.

With flying stone buttresses and a vaulted roof, the granary, oldest of the mission structures, is an intriguing structure. It was used for a variety of functions ranging from grain storage to a weaving workshop.

15) SPANISH GOVERNOR'S PALACE

The Governor's Palace was established in the mid-eighteenth century at *San Antonio de Bexar,* as it was then called, well after Spanish influence was entrenched in Mexico and further exploration brought the Old World soldiers into the wilderness north of the Rio Grande River. At first, the building served only as a fort, but when Texas was incorporated into the Spanish province of Mexico, San Antonio was chosen as the capital and the fort, of which only the palace survives today, became the residence and headquarters for a long succession of governors.

Facing historic Military Plaza, the palace is constructed largely of stone with a plaster finish and has the long, low silhouette that is typical of Southwestern adobe architecture. The lower windows are reinforced with metal gratings, and massive hand-hewn beams jut through the three-foot-thick walls, supporting a flat gravel roof, also several feet in depth. The grounds are

Opposite: Portrait artist Douglas Chandor designed one of the most beautiful one-man gardens ever built. Flourishing in Texas' extreme climate, White Shadows was fashioned after European and Oriental gardens.

resplendent with gardens and shrubbery. Massive, paneled doors hang in the stone archway of the main entrance and depict, through beautiful, elaborate carvings, Spain's discovery and conquest of Mexico and the Texas territory.

Antique furnishings represent two distinct periods and types. Roughly fashioned benches and tables from the period when the palace was a military outpost exist alongside the handcrafted pieces imported by later governors, which represent some of the finest seventeenth-century Spanish designs. The old palace stands as a symbol of the aspirations and struggles of the Spanish north of the Rio Grande.

16) WHITE SHADOWS

In 1934, the famous portrait artist, Douglas Chandor, married Ina K. Hill, a girl from Weatherford, Texas, and settled down to live in that city. An Englishman by birth, Chandor's now famous portraits include such prominent individuals as Winston Churchill, Andrew Mellon and Eleanor Roosevelt, the only portrait of her from life ever painted.

Chandor loved the sunny, hot land of his new home, but deplored the lack of gardens, and decided to create White Shadows. He designed what was surely one of the most difficult to build and one of the most beautiful one-man gardens in all of gardening history. His basic ideas were drawn from the study of both European and Oriental gardens. Significant aspects from the history of garden design were combined with the unique freshness of Chandor's own artistic spirit.

To grow a garden in the extremes of the Texas climate meant searching out the plants that could withstand not only intense heat, but also the biting cold of Texas winters. Fortunately these happen to include such beauties as azaleas, wisteria, magnolias, Texas roses, crape myrtle and hydrangea. The house, white-painted brick with a tiled roof reflecting the area's Spanish heritage, was nestled into the center of the garden. The total environment was artfully conceived as a whole. With the help of his wife, Chandor built fountains and garden sculptures, walks and seven acres of flower beds. By 1953, when he was taken by sudden death, the plans so carefully drawn in 1936 were almost completed.

Entering White Shadows through white wrought-iron gates, a visitor discovers a land of artful fantasy. Among the attractions is a craggy, rock "mountain" covered with a growth of moss and pines, creeping vines and flaming pink azaleas, which was Chandor's last project and is not yet completed. Its cave and green lagoon still wait for the waterfall that was to have plunged down to the nearby Chinese water gardens.

Ina Chandor, since her husband's death, has devoted her time to keeping up the garden at White Shadows. By charging a modest admission fee she hopes to complete her husband's still unfinished "mountain" and its waterfall.

The rosewood bed in the office-bedroom of the Governor's Palace was imported during Spain's colonial era.

Idaho   Montana   Wyoming

NORTHERN ROCKIES

It is nature at its superlative heights that is compelling here. From the vast plains in eastern Montana across the Continental Divide of the Rocky Mountains to Idaho's mile-deep Hells Canyon on the Snake River, the breathtaking scenery is unforgettable.

Here, the picture-postcard West becomes sensuous reality: monstrous glaciers in Montana's spectacular Glacier National Park; mysterious forest wilderness in Idaho's Sawtooth Mountains; fantastic spraying geysers and gurgling paintpots in Yellowstone National Park; the incredible peaks of Wyoming's Grand Tetons.

Before 1800, Frenchmen came upon Crow and Cheyenne hunting buffalo on the plateau abutting the Rockies to the west where later cowboys closed in on lowing cattle. The Lewis and Clark Expedition found other tribes, the Nez Perce and Flatheads among them, along sparkling streams and in pleasant valleys where now potatoes, sugar beets, hops and many more crops are grown. Trappers were lured by beaver, hunters by abundant game, miners by precious metals and the region slowly became settled, though sparsely. Evidence of pioneer trails, forts and old mines can be seen near the scattered centers of population. Visible, too, are sites where Indians and white men clashed in dispute over territorial rights.

The feeling of openness is manifest. In all seasons, people come from more crowded sections of the country to be in the clearness of "Big Sky Country." Amid the "purple mountain majesties" a heady sense of freedom and optimism prevails. To novelist A. B. Guthrie, Jr., the Rockies are conducive to a "good loneliness."

Autumn colors the landscape surrounding Hendrick Lake in Jackson Hole, Grand Teton National Park, Wyoming. The 13,766-foot Grand Teton peak provides a spectacular backdrop for the flatlands that lead up to the mountains.

Idaho

1) CAPITOL, Boise

Located in the heart of Boise, the Idaho State Capitol commands an impressive view of the capital city.

The original design for the State Capitol, begun in 1906, followed the same classical style of architecture as the national Capitol, but was only for the central section and the dome. Construction took more than six years. Wings were completed in 1920. The height of the building, with the bronze eagle atop the dome, is 208 feet.

Alaskan marble is used on the floors, staircase and interior ornamentation, while the inside walls are of Vermont marble. The rotunda proper has two circular promenades and is supported by columns. The fourth floor features 301 lifelike specimens of birds. On the main floor is a gilded statue of George Washington on horseback, carved from native yellow pine.

2) CLEARWATER NATIONAL WILD AND SCENIC RIVER

The sparkling waters of the Middle Fork of the Clearwater River in northern Idaho and its tributaries, the Selway and Lochsa rivers, are a part of the National Wild and Scenic Rivers System begun to insure "... that certain selected rivers of the Nation ... shall be preserved in free-flowing condition, and that they and their immediate environments shall be protected...." Within the Clearwater, Bitterroot and Nezperce national forests, the streams are under the management of the U.S. Forest Service. Running westward from the Bitterroot Mountains to the town of Kooskia, the rivers are the most accessible of any in the system. The Lewis and Clark Highway parallels the Middle Fork of the Clearwater and the Lochsa rivers, and another road follows the lower Selway River, but the upper Selway is primitive.

The Salmon River winds through Boise, Challis, Payette and Salmon national forests.

Cutting through heavily forested and partly barren mountains, the rivers alternate from swift rapids to smooth, slow-flowing currents, providing variety for the canoeist or rubber-raft floater. Elk, moose and otters may frequently be observed near the Lewis and Clark Highway, and Rocky Mountain goats are a common sight in the Black Canyon area.

3) CRATERS OF THE MOON NATIONAL MONUMENT

A desolate landscape of unyielding blacks, chocolate-to-golden tans and sometimes, rusty-reds, has made another world of an eighty-three-square-mile sector of south-central Idaho. Ebony-colored rock rivers, glinting bluish purple in strong sunlight, are guarded by peculiar open cones, startlingly red inside with side slopes of tawny brown shadings.

Characteristics of this strange land on the northern reaches of the Snake River Lava Plain between the Pioneer and the Lost River mountains bear striking resemblance to the craters and darkened valleys of the moon as viewed through telescopes. Therefore, in 1924, when President Coolidge set aside 53,545 acres of this barren wasteland, it was named Craters of the Moon National Monument.

Volcanic eruptions resulting in extensive lava flows during at least three different time periods encompassing perhaps a million years are responsible for this foreboding wasteland. Although the monument resembles a gigantic, cataclysmic convolution, most of these lava flows and cinder cones rose through what is called the Great Rift—a fissure in the earth's crust that can be traced through the monument—in relatively mild fashion. Cinder cones, both large and small, show that the eruptions occurred along a definite line pattern.

A variety of cinder cones, spatter cones and lava domes are seen in the monument. Cones are formed by lava froth or spray from fire fountains at the time of eruption. Big Cinder Butte is the finest example in the area.

4) SALMON NATIONAL WILD AND SCENIC RIVER

Snaking its way through central Idaho north of Stanley is the Middle Fork of the Salmon River. This mighty stream flows through one of the deepest gorges in North America, called the "Impassable Canyon" by one early explorer. Born at the confluence of the Marsh and Bear Valley creeks, the Middle Fork runs 106 miles northeast to join the main Salmon. Placid, emerald-colored pools alternate with swift cur-

Among the stately evergreens of Kooskia, Idaho, the Middle Fork of the Clearwater winds its blue waters, rippled white from underwater rocks.

rents and dazzling white water. Managed by the forest service, the river lies within Boise, Challis, Payette and Salmon national forests.

5) SUN VALLEY

Immortalized in story and song, Sun Valley is one of the most popular ski areas in the West. It was America's first ski resort. Here, about forty

Reflecting the sunset, the mighty Salmon River, known as the River of No Return, is marked by swift currents swirled with white water which makes passage down its length extremely hazardous.

Opposite: *Spatter cones and lava flows resulting from three different periods of volcanic eruptions comprise the stark landscape of Craters of the Moon National Monument.*

years ago, the idea of a total winter resort with an exciting array of winter sports activities was conceived.

Many miles of beautifully groomed slopes offer challenges to skiers. Sun Valley is 6,000 feet above sea level, with its highest slope just above the timberline at 12,000 feet. Cross-country, alpine, and wilderness skiing are available. Today Sun Valley is a year-round resort with excellent facilities for summer sporting also. Scenery in this world-renowned spot is breathtaking at any season.

Montana

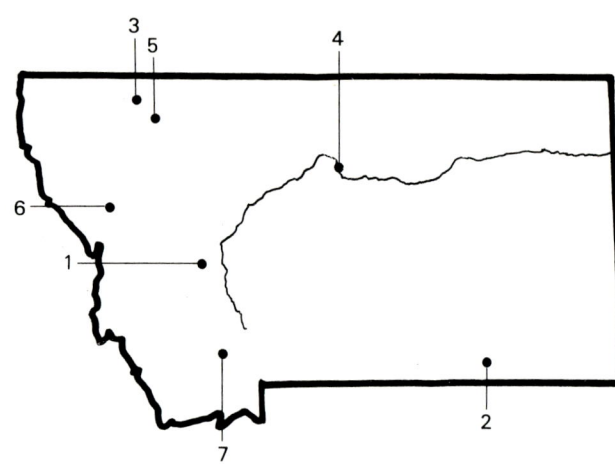

1) CAPITOL, Helena

On a gentle slope, surrounded by ten acres of spacious lawns, native trees and other state buildings, Montana's Capitol in Helena faces out over the beautiful Prickly Pear Valley.

Native Columbus limestone was used in construction of the main section of the Neoclassical Capitol, which was completed in 1902. The two large wings, faced with native granite, were finished in 1912. A statue representing liberty stands atop the Capitol's central copper dome, 165 feet from ground level.

The Capitol's interior, done in French Renaissance style, features flaring staircases, wide corridors and large rooms, as well as many murals and statues. Tennessee marble and tones of deep green, brown and gold decorate the corridors extending east and west from the main floor rotunda. The dome rises to a height of one hundred feet over the rotunda floor and is enhanced by stained-glass windows and fine oil paintings.

2) CUSTER BATTLEFIELD NATIONAL MONUMENT

Here, in the Valley of the Little Big Horn in June 1876, Lieutenant Colonel George A. Custer of the Seventh Cavalry—attempting to round up Sioux and Cheyenne who had left their reservation—and all of the 225 men under his command met their deaths at the hands of several thousand Indians from the Sioux and Cheyenne nations under Chief Sitting Bull. Custer Battlefield National Monument memorializes the site of Custer's famous "last stand," a sad climax to the Indian Wars.

White slabs on Battle Ridge poignantly identify the spots where troopers fell on the uneven prairie landscape. Scattered, alone and in groups, they seem still to be striving for an unobtainable refuge.

A national cemetery was established here in 1879. Soldiers and Indians share the land in death. There are gravestones reading: Coyote, Indian Scout; Bad Heart; Hunts-the-Enemy; and An Indian Child. On Custer Hill a monument commemorates the mass grave of the soldiers killed in the battle. A dramatic panorama of most of the battlefield as well as the valley where the Indian village stood dramatically recalls this American tragedy.

3) GLACIER NATIONAL PARK

Upper St. Mary Lake in Glacier National Park is a sphere of blue—a sapphire of water worn like a jewel, mirroring wisps of cotton clouds and wearing the sharp lines of surrounding mountains as the hands upon the face of a clock. The massive peaks, sheer, sharp walls of stone, are the rulers of this empire of trees and water and wildlife, flower-strewn meadows and living glaciers existing almost side by side in paradoxical enjoyment of their environments.

Here, there are the seekers of this extraordinary beauty, the "Crown of the Continent," which includes more than a thousand miles of trails lacing through nearly 1,600 square miles of wild loveliness. Established in 1910, Glacier was combined with adjacent Waterton Lakes National Park in Canada into Glacial-Waterton International Peace Park in 1932.

The ice-fingers of earth-evolution are not far from the velvety grass spread of hills and valleys sprinkled with summer flowers, one of the four biological life zones found here. Above are the spruce and fir, and surmounting them are subalpine plants, while still farther lie the

The icy fingers of glaciers still stretch through Glacier National Park. Rugged peaks, such as 8,848-foot Mount Grinnell, tower into the clouds high above verdant hills and valleys.

colors—green, white and pastels—which hint at life in the most improbable places. Snowcapped peaks touch the limits of the sky a mile or more above the mirrors of over two hundred lakes.

A million years ago, the valley floors lay beneath great glaciers which relentlessly ground downhill. They gave way years ago to smaller masses of ice, but not before the park's valleys were filled with ice three-fifths of a mile thick. Then the earth became warm again and the ice disappeared, then returned in lesser fury to cover the earth once more.

There is still much evidence of the glaciers here, despite the warming trend. Nearly 300 acres are still covered by Sperry Glacier, about 400 feet deep, a latter-day and comparatively miniscule sample of what shaped this region.

Moose, elk, deer, bears, mountain goats, and smaller animals find Glacier an ideal habitat, as do eagles, woodpeckers and about 210 other species of birds.

It is little wonder Indians chose to live here for about ten thousand years. The Kootenai were displaced by the Blackfeet more than two hundred years ago, and it was possibly their hostility that kept the Lewis and Clark expedition from the region.

The hasty traveler will see a part of the park by driving the Going-to-the-Sun Road, the only road to cross the park. But this is only a hint of what lies beyond.

4) MISSOURI RIVER

The Missouri River physically is not one of our most impressive rivers. The muddy color of this silt-laden river for most of its length (pouring about 250,000 cubic yards of silt into the

Named the "Gates of the Mountains" by Lewis and Clark, the 1,200-foot-deep gorge cut by the Missouri River borders the river for seven miles as it passes through Helena National Forest.

Mississippi each year) further detracts from its appearance.

Only by traversing the entire length of the Missouri and absorbing its cumulative impact, does one become aware of the river's special qualities. The sheer length of the river—the nation's second longest at 2,466 miles—is impressive. (See map, p. 292.) The Missouri is formed by three mountain streams—the Gallatin, Madison and Jefferson rivers—in southwestern Montana at a point called Three Forks, 4,045 feet above sea level. The tumbling river first flows north for 500 miles through a lovely mountainous region. Northeast of Helena, Montana's capital, it has eroded a 1,200-foot gorge named by Lewis and Clark the "Gates of the Mountains," which is surrounded by limestone cliffs and other geologic formations.

The river skirts the northern edge of the scenic Big Belt Mountains and, about 130 miles farther downstream near the Bear Paw Mountains, it swings east. Here, it is truly at home in a wild and rugged area of canyon lands, rock bluffs and fertile bottomlands with numerous groves of cottonwoods along the banks. Eventually the Missouri passes through badlands country—with colored soils and fascinating rock formations—before encountering the low-hilled prairies and becoming the wide, relatively shallow, meandering waterway, dotted with sandbars, that is the river's dominant character as it crosses the Great Plains.

After receiving the waters of the silty Yellowstone and Little Missouri rivers in western North Dakota, the big river flows southeastward through a valley that is generally from a hundred to three hundred feet below the surrounding country due to erosion by the river. In some places the Missouri passes sheer bluffs, while in others, where the valley is several miles wide, the river flows between low, increasingly green-wooded banks. But because these banks are often soft and sandy and easily washed away, the restless Missouri is continually gnawing at its banks. Near today's city of Omaha, Nebraska, the river is joined by a major tributary, the Platte. At the point where the Kansas River enters the Missouri, at Kansas City, the big river swings east across Missouri to merge finally with the Mississippi.

Despite the treacherous nature of the river, hidden from view by the opaque dirt-filled water, the Big Muddy or, as countless lips have muttered along her banks, "that damned river," was, because of its location and tributaries, the major path that enormous numbers of Americans followed in their epic movement to the West. Before the advent of the railroads, steamboats and almost every other type of rivercraft imaginable carried settlers, livestock and supplies down the Missouri.

5) MUSEUM OF THE PLAINS INDIAN

Operated by the Indian Arts and Crafts Board of the U.S. Department of the Interior, the Museum of the Plains Indian and Crafts Center in Browning is dedicated to increasing the understanding of the past and present lives and achievements of the Indian peoples of the region. The museum is located on the Blackfeet Reservation, at the center of modern tribal life.

A wide variety of indigenous art forms is exhibited, providing insight into the cultural heritage of contemporary Indian craftsmen. Included are numerous types of beadwork, porcupine quillwork, featherwork, carvings, skin sewing and hide painting. A library and archives contain early Blackfeet and other Montana Indian agency records.

6) NATIONAL BISON RANGE

At the southern end of the beautiful Flathead Valley, in the shadows of the majestic Mission Mountains in western Montana, is the home of one of the premier herds of American buffalo or bison. This herd in the 18,540-acre National Bison Range varies in size from year to year but is generally between 300 and 500.

The sixty million buffalo that had once roamed North America were nearly completely

White slabs on Battle Ridge mark the places where Custer's men fell in the Battle of the Little Big Horn. A black pennant waves beside Custer's grave.

wiped out by 1883. Largely through the efforts of the American Bison Society, the National Bison Range was established in 1908 to provide a refuge for these magnificent animals, at that time numbering only about twenty in the entire United States.

As with the buffalo, the other large animal herds on this range are maintained at a more or less constant number; 50 to 75 elk (wapiti), 200 to 300 mule deer, the same number of white-tailed deer, 40 to 80 bighorn sheep and 80 to 100 pronghorn antelope. All of these animals, except the bighorns, can be seen at the headquarters exhibition pastures. For those with more time, a nineteen-mile self-guided tour over graveled roads can be taken.

The range is made up of grasslands, steep hills and narrow canyons. In winter, snow piles deep in nearby hills, but the bison range is so located that it is scantily covered. The grasslands are composed largely of Palouse Prairie vegetation, including the grasses the buffalo feed on.

7) VIRGINIA CITY

One day in May 1863, Bill Fairweather discovered gold while panning in Alder Gulch in western Montana. Within a few weeks some 10,000 avaricious miners had arrived and Virginia City was born. The city served as the capital of Montana Territory from the territory's inception in 1864 until 1876.

Life in the region typified the Old West. "Sheriff" Henry Plummer organized the outlaw elements to effectively terrorize Alder Gulch. Within a six-month period over 190 murders were committed. Montana's vigilante movement developed to combat the outlaws. During a two-month campaign, the vigilantes hanged or banished most of the outlaw gang, including ringleader Plummer.

Opposite: *The Museum of the Plains Indian and Crafts Center is devoted to increasing the understanding of the heritage of the region's Indian people.*

Almost completely exterminated by hunters by 1883, the American bison on the 18,540-acre National Bison Range have multiplied to a herd of 300 to 500, varying yearly in size.

Virginia City, unlike other Alder Gulch mining camps, never actually became a ghost town. It remained modestly prosperous throughout the nineteenth and early twentieth centuries. During the Depression Virginia City even experienced a slight regeneration when gold mining, though not highly profitable, appeared better than nothing.

World War II spelled the end of Virginia City's mining industry. With the general exodus many of the old buildings were left vacant and, despite the caring pride of remaining residents, time began to take its toll. A Virginia City Vigilance Club was hampered by lack of funds. Mr. and Mrs. Charles Bovey of Great Falls, long interested in preserving landmarks of the Old West, became involved in saving historic Virginia City for posterity and contributed substantial time and money.

Among the over twenty buildings, now restored to their nineteenth-century appearance, are the state's first newspaper office, where early printing equipment is displayed; a general store, stocked as it was in 1875; an authentically equipped pharmacy of the day; the Bale of Hay Saloon; the Virginia City Opera House; the Wells Fargo Express Office; a blacksmith shop; a dressmaker's shop; and a brewery.

Nearby Nevada City was almost totally destroyed, leaving little evidence on which to base accurate reconstruction. Today, as a result of the Boveys' efforts, the town site has been used for other original Montana Territory structures. Of special interest are the Fort Benton Saddle Shop, the Sun River Jail, a pioneer schoolhouse, a livery stable, miners' cabins, and a home furnished with period pieces.

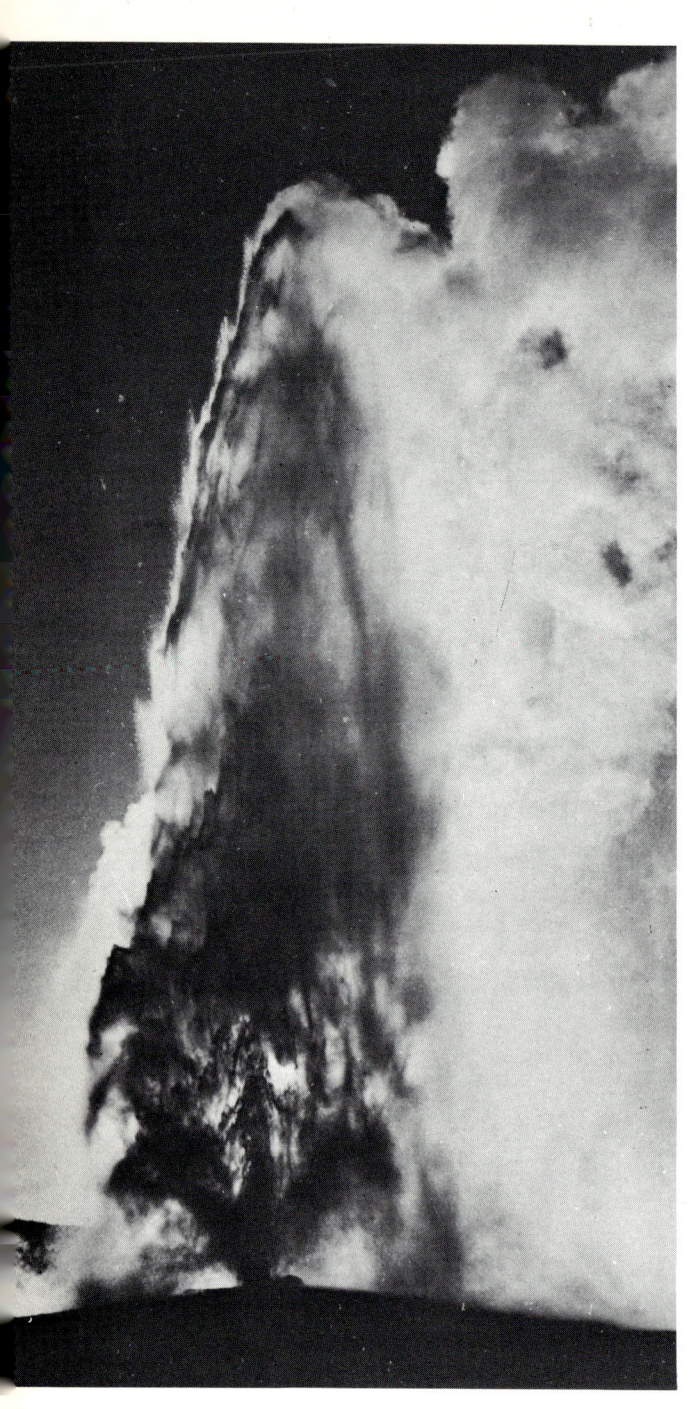

Old Faithful (above), the most popular of the great geysers, and elk roaming their natural habitat (right) are two primary features of Yellowstone park.

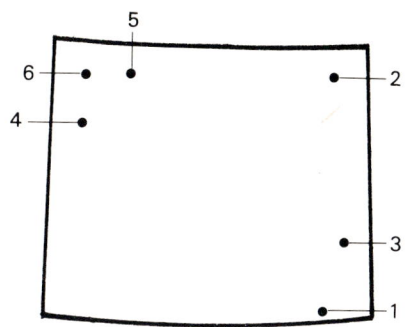

Wyoming

1) CAPITOL, Cheyenne

The Corinthianlike architecture of the Wyoming Capitol in Cheyenne is reminiscent of the National Capitol. Completed in 1890, the building soon became overcrowded, and in 1915 the legislature provided for new east and west wings, completed in 1917. The building is constructed primarily of stone and the dome rises 146 feet above the Capitol grounds.

The rotunda, the primary interior attraction, consists of a circular hall thirty feet in diameter. The distance from the floor to the lantern above the rotunda is fifty-four feet. Cathedral glass reflects a mellow light throughout the interior, which is richly ornamented with plaster and elaborately turned woodwork.

2) DEVILS TOWER NATIONAL MONUMENT

A mighty laccolith resembling a monstrous petrified tree stump thrusts itself 800 feet skyward from a rounded hill above the Belle Fourche River Valley in northeast Wyoming. The massive gray and buff stone has a startling appearance from all sides. It stands alone—a single sentinel visible for more than 100 miles above forest-patched hills and valleys of the surrounding countryside.

A geological prodigy, Devils Tower was created when the volcanic thrust pushed this particular mass of molten materials only to the surface—or perhaps somewhat below the surface—where it cooled. Erosion in the intervening millions of years, possibly during some ancient deluge, gradually eroded away softer formations of surrounding earth and rock, leaving the fluted sides of this gigantic stone standing 865 feet above its base on a hill. It was set aside as Devils Tower National Monument in 1906, the first U. S. national monument to be authorized.

Devils Tower is more than 1,000 feet in diameter at its base. Its top, measuring 200 by 400 feet, is 1,280 feet above the Belle Fourche River and 5,117 feet above sea level. It is the tallest rock formation of its kind in the United States, and geologists continue to study its strange origin and peculiarities.

The Indians were also fascinated by the rock. According to their legends, the fluted sides were made by the claw marks of huge bears attempting to climb the rock.

3) FORT LARAMIE
See **Oregon Trail**, Kansas—4.

4) GRAND TETON NATIONAL PARK

Vast, snow-covered graph lines of gray are etched upon the spring-breath blue of sky, mirroring their mighty heights upon apparently miniscule lakes below; giant shadows are cast across already-dark forests of deep green.

The Tetons of western Wyoming give no hint of their ascension; no foothills lead the viewer's eye to this grandiose essence of all the beauty that the mountains of the West have to offer. For here there is a glassy lake, a stand of conifers and suddenly there are those incredible peaks—the three peaks named the Cathedral Group, comprised of Grand, Middle and South Teton mountains. Called *Les Trois Tetons* ("The Three Breasts") by early French-Canadian trappers, these peaks are a challenge to mountain climbers. The strenuous two-day climb to the 13,766-foot summit of Grand Teton, including the trek across treacherous Teton Glacier, is the supreme achievement.

Through the great valley called Jackson Hole pours the Snake River, a wide and rushing stream flowing clearly across a deep bed of sand and stones where gamefish dart in cool depths and to which adventurous man escapes for a few moments to ply the current in a rubber raft.

Lakes lie among the green like a cool morning's dew on a field of newly mown grain, glistening in the sun between the natural fist of the Tetons on one side and wind-whispered forests of conifers on the other. The largest lake is Jackson Lake, formed by melted glaciers; the most picturesque is Jenny Lake. Here and there

The sun sets with all its splendor over the snow-capped peaks of the Grand Teton mountains reflected in picturesque Jackson Lake.

are sun-splashed meadows, a crown of green wearing the royal jewels of complacent wildflowers, and streams trickling through rich, black humus where the colors of spring blooms push their way through the floor of last autumn's fallen leaves.

The graceful mule deer pick their way down mountain trails in fall, seeking vegetation in the valleys below. High above are a few bighorn sheep, laboring among the rocks finding forage, while thousands of American elk (wapiti) move through the park in herds.

The mountains are hard, crystalline rock, hugging, in part, Cascade Canyon where a trail rims beaver ponds and crosses meadows, skirting great slashes of boulders on hillsides. Jackson Hole is filled with rock and gravel too porous to hold water and is therefore covered with the tenacious sagebrush, common to semidesert regions.

Established in 1929 and covering about 473 square miles, Grand Teton National Park is a spectacular corner of the United States where nature is the great equalizer, enthralling all who reap this majestic scene with their eyes.

5) WHITNEY GALLERY OF WESTERN ART

Just outside Cody, associated with the Buffalo Bill Museum in the Buffalo Bill Historical Center, is the Gertrude Vanderbilt Whitney Gallery of Western Art, which opened in April 1959. Here are collected more than $3 million worth of paintings, drawings and sculpture by artists who first placed on canvas the visual record of the West. Included are pictures once owned by Colonel William F. "Buffalo Bill" Cody, portrayals of that colorful scout, soldier, rancher and showman, the contents of Frederic Remington's New Rochelle studio, and much other documentation of the West.

On the edge of the forty-acre Buffalo Bill Historical Center is the heroic bronze equestrian statue by Gertrude Vanderbilt Whitney of *Buffalo Bill the Scout* reining his mount and peering down as he signals direction with his upraised rifle. The attractive, modern museum building, looking out past the statue to the mountains, provides a fine contemporary setting for the artistic heritage of the West.

The Whitney Gallery, while stating that it is a gallery of documentary art and realistic pictorial records of the historic past, nonetheless is also a first-rate art museum because of the quality of its exhibits. Included are seventy-two paintings by George Catlin, made during his explorations up the Missouri River in 1832.

6) YELLOWSTONE NATIONAL PARK

It is like the creation of the very devil himself: Angry forces of the underworld locked in combat beneath the earth with the sounds and visible fury of their struggle seeping through fissures to enthrall the curious above ground who come to see what the monumental forces of fire and ice have spawned.

This is Yellowstone National Park in the northwest corner of Wyoming (and narrow strips of Idaho and Montana), where nearly all that nature has to offer has been concentrated in a spectacular display unmatched anywhere on earth. Boiling springs, steam vents, mudpots spewing mud and, as a climax, the great geysers hurtling tons of water hundreds of feet skyward—these dot the otherwise pastoral land to make a strangely beautiful if not sometimes forbidding world.

A few scars of the violent volcanism which created Yellowstone's strange landscape remain, as do a handful of open wounds which could never quite heal because of the cancerous fury far beneath. The heat of these prehistoric volcanoes remains, much like a storage battery to provide power for the sights which greet the visitor today.

One of the best known of nature's wonders, Old Faithful geyser is aptly named, for it is prompt, appearing about once an hour, day and night, hurling 15,000 gallons of hot water in a single, magnificent unleashing of force.

Old Faithful has 200 cousins at Yellowstone, among them the Riverside, Grotto, Castle and Beehive geysers, all sustained in the same way. Cold water from the long winter's melted snows finds its way through the hard volcanic rock around the geysers. Thousands of feet below the surface it is heated by hot rocks and also by gases and natural steam escaping from still deeper molten rock. Soon the cool water begins to boil, building pressure as steam forms, forcing the water higher into the geyser column. Then as the pressure is relaxed, huge quantities of steam are formed within the underground chambers, forcing the column of water to the

Independence Rock on the Oregon Trail (see Kansas—4) was the site of many pioneers' Fourth of July celebrations as they headed West toward a new life. Many of the names scratched in the rock by the early travelers are still legible.

An office in restored Fort Laramie as it might have appeared to travelers on the Oregon Trail when they stopped to rest at the fort.

surface in a pulsating, continuous finger of dancing liquid, pirouetting on the surface for four or five minutes. Suddenly the mad ballet ends, the crown of vapor floats skyward and the water recedes as the steam energy dissipates.

The rest of Yellowstone is not quite so forbidding, but has a rugged loveliness all its own: A cliff of obsidian, or black volcanic glass, overlooks columns of lava rock; fossil forests exist in silence not too far from craggy mountains caressed with the green of conifers; a multitude of wildlife, one of the greatest concentrations in the nation, roams fearlessly through great forests of pine; roaring waterfalls plummet into a yellow rock canyon, the sun forming a rainbow above its splashing waters.

High above much of the park is Yellowstone Lake, a body of water stretching twenty miles in one direction, fourteen in the other. Its mirrorlike surface can be broken into giant whitecaps within minutes as storms blow in from the snowcapped mountains beyond, or great bolts of lightning are discharged between the surface and the sky.

Even after 1872, when it became the world's first national park, it was not a safe place for tourists. While some Indians possibly lived in fear of the geysers, others raided hunters, trappers and explorers. But there is now peace and ultimate grandeur in Yellowstone, a legacy left by nature and 2,221,771 acres of exquisite beauty preserved for all the heirs of tomorrow.

Arizona   Colorado   New Mexico   Utah

SOUTHERN ROCKIES

Although historian Walter Prescott Webb had a different meaning in mind when he dubbed the West a "perpetual mirage," much of the Southern Rockies does seem a head-shaking illusion. The wonders are endless: broad mesas, deep gorges, soaring peaks, painted deserts, tiers of multicolored cliffs and eroded shapes.

In the waterless warm air, colors are sun-drenched and aromatic—umber, ocher, sienna and buff. But the whole of the area is not desertlike; mountain heights offer cool forests and even year-round snow.

Almost a century before the English settled on the Atlantic Coast, the Spanish were here, exploring Indian pueblos constructed three centuries earlier. Spanish influence remains, particularly in New Mexico. Gold, silver and copper brought prospectors at the same time wars were being fought between Indians and whites. A religious migration unparalleled in our history occurred as the Mormons filled Utah around the Great Salt Lake. Nineteenth-century geologist John Wesley Powell explored the area, particularly the awesome Grand Canyon of the Colorado River, and introduced it to the rest of the United States.

Water supplies are controlled by huge dams (admired throughout the world) that enable large areas to be cultivated. Much, however, is untouched. The quality of eternity in this semiarid wonderland draws visitors. Novelist Mary Austin has aptly described it: "This is the sense of the desert hills, that there is room enough and time enough."

The ever-changing colors and shadows of the magnificent Colorado River Gorge, cut throughout two billion years of history. The Colorado, life-blood of America's semiarid Southwest, flows wild and nearly untamable for much of its 1,450 miles.

Arizona

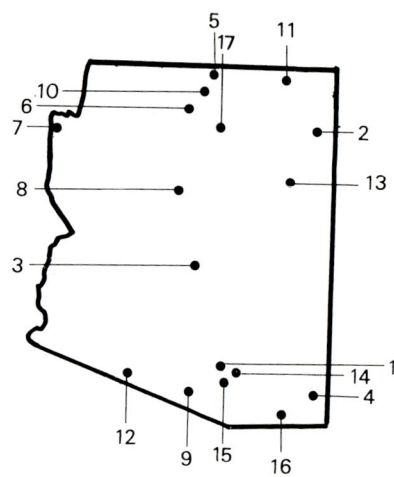

The tall limestone walls of Canyon de Chelly sheltered Indians of the Anasazi (Navajo for "ancient ones") culture for nearly 1,000 years. In their Pueblo stage, they built large cliff houses.

1) ARIZONA-SONORA DESERT MUSEUM

Set in the ruggedly beautiful Tucson Mountain Park west of Tucson is a remarkable "living" museum of natural history. The Arizona-Sonora Desert Museum, opened in 1952, presents the animal species indigenous to the great Sonoran Desert of Arizona and the Mexican State of Sonora.

Ranging in size from insects to rodents, most of the residents of the small animal room are displayed in "living dioramas." The collections of desert snakes and lizards are especially extensive. Among the larger animals presented throughout the museum are mountain lions, coyotes and wildcats.

A close-up look at the subterranean homes of such desert animals as the kit fox, ringtail (a member of the raccoon family) and rattlesnake is available in a fascinating underground tunnel exhibit. A bat cave complete with stalactites and a colony of fruit-eating bats is tremendously intriguing.

The museum also offers an aviary, a prairie dog town, a typical canyon habitat, and a number of nature trails through botanical gardens.

2) CANYON DE CHELLY NATIONAL MONUMENT

These steep-walled, red limestone canyons are breathtakingly beautiful, ranging from 30 to 1,000 feet. Indians found shelter here for nearly 1,000 years, from 350 to 1300, and ruins of several hundred of their villages are preserved within Canyon de Chelly National Monument. Pictographs on the sheer walls date from the earliest Indian occupancy.

Canyon de Chelly runs twenty-six miles and the connecting Canyon del Muerto is thirty-five miles long. The monument, established in 1930,

Rising 710 feet above bedrock, Glen Canyon Dam, the second largest in the United States, backs up the Colorado River to form Lake Powell, a popular recreation area.

covers approximately 130 square miles of what is now Navajo land. Over 300 Navajo use the canyon floors each summer for peach orchards, farming and grazing.

Several stages of the Anasazi (Navajo for "ancient ones") culture have been identified in the monument. Beginning in A.D. 350, basketweavers produced exquisite baskets and built intriguing sunken pithouses. Eventually, by A.D. 700, the Anasazi had evolved into the Pueblo stage. They constructed the rectangular stone masonry "apartment houses," one against another as communal dwellings. Most of the large cliff houses in the monument were built between 1100 and 1300.

A prolonged drought struck the area in the thirteenth century, driving the Pueblo people to other parts of the Southwest by 1300. After their departure, the Hopi Indians of Arizona, related to the Pueblo, occupied Canyon de Chelly sporadically. About 1700 the aggressive Navajo began to move into the region. Their hogans—circular houses of logs and poles—dot the canyon floor.

Among the major ruins in the monument is the White House in Canyon de Chelly, occupied from 1060 to 1275 and named for a long wall in the upper part of the ruin which is covered with white plaster.

3) CAPITOL, Phoenix

Completed in 1900, the Arizona State Capitol in Phoenix served Arizona during its late territorial days and its move to statehood in 1912.

The original building, now the east wing of the State House, has a dome forty-four feet in diameter, above which stands the winged "Victory Lady," sixteen feet in height and nearly ninety-three feet above ground.

The most striking interior architectural feature of the east wing is a central light shaft, twenty-two feet in diameter, which reaches to the dome. On each floor a railing encircles the great shaft and defines the inside border of a commodious rotunda. The four-story structure is constructed almost entirely of Arizona granite and other materials.

The second section of the Capitol, which now forms the connecting bar between the east and west wings, was erected in 1918. The west wing, known officially as the Department of Justice Building, was completed in 1939. The Senate and House of Representatives wings, completed in 1960, are constructed of tufa stone, Ozark marble, Roman travertine marble and polished rainbow granite. The conforming lines of classical architecture and landscaping enhance the setting of modest, Southwestern atmosphere.

4) CHIRICAHUA NATIONAL MONUMENT

Grotesquely eroded spires, pinnacles, towers and massive battlements guard the canyons and shaded glens of the Chiricahua Mountains in the southeast corner of Arizona. In this fascinating wonderland of rocks, Cochise and Geronimo, famous Chiricahua Apache warrior leaders, fought against overwhelming odds to hold their Indian ancestral lands against settlement by outsiders. Geronimo was fighting for more than forty years in Mexico and the United States until he voluntarily surrendered in 1886.

The battle of the forces of nature forming these magnificent bulwarks against the arid grasslands below began millions of years ago, and continues changing the many faces of this ancient upheaval. Rising steeply from the dry sparseness of southwestern New Mexico and northern Mexico into the corner of Arizona, this mountain range presents a verdant, forested island in a sea of grass. In 1924, after a bloody earlier period of American settlement, some seventeen square miles of the most spectacular sector was set aside as Chiricahua National Monument.

Mighty geological forces created the basic structures of these peculiar pinnacles and delicately balanced rocks during intermittent volcanic eruptions at least twenty-five million years ago. As the rock weathered, soil formed and collected. Plants gained a foothold, then spread and began accumulating more soil. This activity caused the development of ecological niches and communities of varying altitudinal requirements that are a fascinating part of the monument today. Botanists estimate that there is a greater range of plant life here than in any area of like size in the country. For example, more than 500 plant species are found in the monument. Biologists learned, too, that the isolation meant that some forms of both plants and animals are distinctly different from anywhere else.

5) GLEN CANYON DAM AND NATIONAL RECREATION AREA

Harnessing the restless waters of the great Colorado River, Glen Canyon Dam and beautiful man-made Lake Powell are part of the extensive Colorado River Storage Project. Built between 1956 and 1964, the Glen Canyon Dam is the second largest in the United States. It contains almost five million cubic yards of concrete, rises 710 feet above bedrock, 583 above the original river channel and is 1,560 feet across at its crest. On the rim of Glen Canyon above the dam is the Carl Hayden Visitor Center which includes displays explaining the bridge's construction and the structure of Glen Canyon Bridge, as well as examining Lake Powell and its environs.

Near the monolithic Glen Canyon Dam, the narrow red Navajo sandstone walls are steep and high. The sandstone is actually solidified sand dunes, possibly 150 million years old. Most of Lake Powell's nearly 2,000 miles of shoreline are noted for their picturesque sandstone formations and enchanting fjordlike side canyons. Environmentalists, however, have long been against the dam and its lake, pointing out that many of the now-drowned canyons were irreplaceable in their beauty. Famous Rainbow Bridge (see **Rainbow Bridge National Monument**, Utah — 12) is still threatened by Lake Powell's rising waters and may already be damaged.

6) GRAND CANYON NATIONAL PARK

The wind blows gently down this vast wound in the earth, rippling the surface of its creative force, the Colorado River, and carrying occasional small puffs of red dust from the awesome walls. The breeze wanes and the eerie silence fans out in four directions, held captive within the impenetrable fortress nature spent nine million years to create.

"Whoever stands upon the Grand Canyon beholds a spectacle unrivaled on this earth," wrote one observer. The nine-mile-wide sloping and vertical desert has an unforgettable and wonderful grandeur that Theodore Roosevelt further defined as a "great loneliness."

The spectacular depths and contours of the Grand Canyon are inspiring to any who view it. Cut by the Colorado River, the ancient walls reveal the earth's history to the beginning of life and beyond.

The Grand Canyon is true to its name, yet a mere, momentary glance from either the North or South rims prods the beholder's mind, searching for a word more expressive than "Grand." The majestic, water-wrought stone sculpture in northern Arizona is 217 miles long, averages a mile deep and spreads nine miles across in a panorama of pastels, each a page in the book of the canyon's continuing evolution.

In places where the bottom can be reached, the long hike or ride on muleback gradually unfolds in a geological layer cake—gray limestone walls formed when a long-forgotten sea shimmered in the prehistoric sunlight; green shale holding primitive fossils; pastel layer upon pastel layer, until finally millions of years have been passed in a drop of three-fifths of a mile. In the Inner Gorge are sheer walls growing

Built by James "Rawhide Jimmy" Douglas in 1916 after striking a rich vein of ore in the Little Daisy Mine, the old Douglas Mansion in Jerome is now a mining museum.

progressively darker as they plunge toward the rushing Colorado River, walls so ancient they were formed before life on the earth, their fossilless bulk existing in the dark centuries when creation was building its foundation.

The river is still building the Grand Canyon, widening it and deepening it an unmeasurable, infinitesimal fraction of an inch each year. Until completion of the Glen Canyon Dam in 1964 (see **Glen Canyon Dam**, Arizona — 5), the pulsating red torrent of water carried half a million tons of soil downstream each day, each abrasive bit gently, imperceptibly wearing away at the captive walls, loosening other particles in the interminable process of erosion. Today it carries approximately one-sixth as much sediment.

Hardy Indians wrested a livelihood from the forbidding land, but each day must have been a supreme effort. Evidence of primitive hunters 3,000 and more years old has been discovered.

The hunters sought more fertile lands, and in their place came the basketmakers, followed by the Pueblo tribe and its intricate culture. They lived in the area for about 600 years and their villages are among the more than 500 Indian sites found within the 1,050-square-mile park.

The Navajo and Hopi live to the east of the park while the dwindling Havasupai dwell in a small area in the western section of Grand Canyon.

7) HOOVER DAM AND LAKE MEAD NATIONAL RECREATION AREA

Hoover Dam (called Boulder Dam until 1947) is an engineering marvel. Selected by the American Society of Civil Engineers as one of this country's Seven Modern Civil Engineering Wonders, the dam project on the Colorado River in the Black Canyon between Arizona and Nevada has controlled the mighty river, turning its power to a variety of constructive uses since it began storing water in 1935.

At 726 feet above bedrock, it is the highest concrete dam in the Western Hemisphere. Measuring 660 feet thick at its base and 45 feet thick at its crest, Hoover Dam stretches 1,244 feet across the canyon.

Hydroelectric power generated by the dam serves public and private customers throughout much of the Southwest. The dam controls floods and stores water for irrigating three-quarters of a million acres in the United States and nearly half a million acres in Mexico. Water is supplied for industrial and municipal uses in a number of major Pacific Southwest cities.

The monumental dam can be viewed from both sides of Black Canyon and the canyon can be crossed on the dam's crest. Elevators descend 528 feet into the dam to the power plant. At the west end of the dam is an exhibit building featuring a model of a generating unit and a topographical model of the Colorado River Basin.

Man-made Lake Mead, the dam's reservoir, has become an extremely popular recreation area, offering fishing, swimming, boating and skiing the year around. The clear waters of Lake Mead extend 110 miles upstream to the lower end of Grand Canyon, with 550 miles of attractive shoreline. The lake's volume is equivalent to two years' flow of the Colorado River.

8) JEROME

Jerome is now a small picturesque artists' colony, perched precariously on a 2,000-foot mountainside above the floor of the Verde Valley in central Arizona. At one time, however, this town, where 1,500 vertical feet and a thirty-degree grade separate the upper level houses from those in the gulch, supported 15,000 people as a booming copper-mining town.

From the staking of the first claim in 1876 until the United Verde Branch mines of the Phelps Dodge Corporation stopped production in 1953, Jerome suffered with the extreme fluctuations in copper prices and with the monumental difficulties involved in the remote mining operations. Yet in just seventy-two years

Jerome mines had produced some $800 million worth of copper.

As a "ghost town," Jerome is a marvelous museum detailing a rich and robust period of the American past. Traveling its switchback streets as they wind their way up Cleopatra Mountain, the day in 1882 when the United Verde Copper Company was formed seems little more than yesterday.

By the late 1800's Jerome was overflowing with people and faced with all the problems inherent in being a boom town. Between 1897 and 1899 Jerome burned three times, yet the town continued to flourish and was incorporated in 1899 as Arizona's fifth largest city. The town even revived after the devastating blows of the Great Depression, until its veins of copper were eventually exhausted. Only the empty buildings, such as the Little Daisy Hotel, and abandoned mines remain to tell the story. The Jerome Museum contains interesting memorabilia, and the museum in the old Douglas Mansion in the Jerome State Historic Park features exhibits tracing the history of mining in the region from prehistoric times to the present. There is also a self-guided tour of an old mine.

9) KITT PEAK NATIONAL OBSERVATORY

On Kitt Peak in the Quinlan Mountains of the northern Sonora Desert are the facilities of the Kitt Peak National Observatory, established in 1958 as this nation's first national astronomical observatory. The site is ironically appropriate because this mountaintop on the edge of the Papago Reservation was known in Indian legend as the favorite dwelling place of *Ee-Ee-Toy,* the Papago god whose main residence was "at the center of the universe" on the 6,875-foot Baboquivari Peak twelve miles south.

Kitt Peak is one of the advanced centers for ground-based optical astronomy. Among the outstanding facilities are the Mayall Four-Meter Telescope which allows the study of the observable limit of the world of outer space; the McMath Solar Vacuum Telescope, the largest designed for observation of the sun; and a highly versatile and productive eighty-four-inch reflecting telescope which in 1970 obtained a spectrum from what was then the most distant astronomical object, a quasar almost ten billion light-years from Earth.

10) MARBLE CANYON NATIONAL MONUMENT

Located adjacent to even more spectacular Grand Canyon, Marble Canyon was the last major Colorado River canyon to be Federally protected. The fifty-two-mile stretch was proclaimed a national monument in 1969.

This chasm has remained so wild that Major John Wesley Powell would immediately recognize it as the place that he named Marble Canyon in 1896. The only way to see the canyon is to ride the rafts through its dangerous rapids. It is an unforgettable experience. Some of the rapids are more than seventy-five feet wide with a consequent violent churning of water.

In the early part of this century two brothers, Emery and Ellsworth Kolb, described their journey through Marble Canyon:

The wonderful marble walls now rose from the water's edge to a height of eight or nine hundred feet, the surface of its light blue-gray rock being stained to a dark red, or a light red as the case might be, by the iron from the sandstone walls above. There were a thousand feet of these sandstone layers, red in all its varying hues, capped by the four-hundred-foot cross-bedded sandstone wall, breaking sheer, ranging in tone from

(continued on p. 220)

The "White Dove of the Desert," Mission San Xavier del Bac is possibly the finest example of Spanish mission architecture in America.

Overleaf: Brilliant fingers of lightning twist around the illuminated observatory on Kitt Peak.

a soft buff to a golden yellow, with a bloom, or glow, as though illuminated from within.

The rock walls support little vegetation, only a few varieties of yucca and cactus, and it comes as a shock to the river runner to come across Vasey's Paradise, an oasis in a canyon of emptiness. Beautiful streams gush from holes in the rock walls, which are in turn covered with maidenhair fern, vines and watercress. In front of this green background are willow trees, their leaves flapping in the breeze.

11) MONUMENT VALLEY

A favorite filming location of movie producers, spectacular Monument Valley is a land of brilliantly colored spires, buttes and arches, some as high as 1,000 feet above the valley floor. The rocks in this section of the vast Navajo Indian Reservation in northeast Arizona and southeast Utah are formed by the constant wearing action of the elements.

Named the "Place Where the Rocks Stand Up" by the first Navajos in the area almost 1,000 years ago, Monument Valley appeals to those with an appreciation of altitude and distance. Famous landmarks, such as Agathla Peak, the Three Sisters spires and the Totem Pole group, are now part of a 96,000-acre tribal park, which includes a visitor center with a glassed-in observatory.

12) ORGAN PIPE CACTUS NATIONAL MONUMENT

In 1853 under the terms of the Gadsden Purchase, the United States bought from Mexico a large tract of land at the southern extremity of the Arizona Territory and so acquired a portion of desert unlike that of any in the country. The Sonoran Desert ranges from northern Baja California through the Mexican State of Sonora into southern Arizona. Although most of this desert is in Mexico, Organ Pipe Cactus National Monument preserves a representative portion of 516 square miles of stark mountains, sweeping bajadas (outwash plains), rocky canyons, flats, dry washes and distinctive plants and animals.

The area is the merging point of three different kinds of desert vegetation—the drought-ridden California Microphyll (small-leaved) Desert, the upland Arizona Succulent Desert and the tall-cactus Gulf Coast Desert of the Gulf of California.

The most common plant is cactus. There are over thirty species here, and outstanding among these is the organ-pipe cactus (*Lemaireocereus thurberi*), found nowhere else in the United States. The second largest cactus in the country, it may produce over thirty unbranched stems up to twenty feet tall from one plant, bearing close resemblance to a church organ. This curious plant dominates the landscape on the lower slopes of mountains and ridges of the bajadas.

Cactus is not the only type of vegetation in the monument. If winter rains have been sufficient, spring may bring an array of desert colors from the spectacular blooms of the cacti and the wide variety of desert flowers.

The large variety of vegetation supports an equal variety of wildlife, including coyotes, ringtails, bobcats, cottontails, jackrabbits, foxes, mule deer and an occasional mountain lion.

Established in 1937, Organ Pipe Cactus National Monument has two loop roads of twenty and fifty miles to take visitors along the base of Mount Ajo, at 4,800 feet the highest point in the monument. No visa is needed to cross the border to Sonora; however, a visa is necessary to go farther south into the interior.

13) PETRIFIED FOREST NATIONAL PARK

Fossilized contours of an era claimed by the mists of time, and a vast horizon of alternately mingling, emerging reds, blues, browns and yellows—this is the Petrified Forest and Painted Desert area of east-central Arizona. The "forest" of stone tree logs and trunks, coupled with the sweep of the desert's rainbowlike proscenium, constitutes a national park paradise of over 94,000 acres which can be driven over, on the thirty-four miles of roads.

The stone forest emerges from a prehistoric period called the Triassic, over 180 million years ago, when pinelike trees grew beside streams which flowed through a seaside desert. The trees probably died of natural causes.

Then the wondrous process of petrification took place along with patient sculpturing by nature. After the trees fell, they were buried by stream-carried mud and silt containing volcanic ash. In successive ages mile-thick deposits of similar material accumulated above the logs, mountain building lifted the logs far above sea level and, comparatively recently, the logs and multicolored layers of the Painted Desert were exposed by erosion. During the time the trees were buried, silica-laden waters percolated into the air and pore spaces of the logs, filling these openings with multicolored quartz.

The unique wonder of the Painted Desert, especially for the tourist, is the titillating kaleidoscopic effect of the changing colors. After rainfall, and following the shift of cloud

Sand dunes ripple across the flat land of Monument Valley, a favorite filming location of movie producers because of the brilliant colors and magnificent formations.

shadows, the most stunning and varied suddenness of color combinations takes place.

In addition to the natural wonders preserved within the park, there are also about 300 archeological sites, spanning the period from about 300 to 1400. The Anasazi and other Indian cultures left clear marks in this area, especially at Puerco Indian Ruin, which had 150 rooms when occupied 600 years ago.

In the 1880's serious threats to the petrified wood through commercial exploitation and sheer vandalism aroused strong public protest and adroit Government action. In 1906 President Theodore Roosevelt created Petrified Forest National Monument, which became Petrified Forest National Park in 1962.

14) SAGUARO NATIONAL MONUMENT

The saguaro is the epitome of the North American desert. Because it has been silhouetted against a lavender sunset in travel folders and pictured in old cowboy movies, the saguaro has become famous all over the world as a landmark of the American Southwest. Actually, this cactus is the epitome of only one of the four North American deserts—the Sonoran Desert. But the saguaro—the name (pronounced sa-WAH-ro) believed to be a Spanish corruption of an Indian word—is in trouble. This fragile, slow-growing giant is slowly disappearing from some areas of the desert scene in the Southwest.

One place where these unusual plants are now protected from extensive grazing and civilization is Saguaro National Monument. Consisting of two sections on either side of Tucson, the Rincon and Tucson Mountain sections, the monument preserves the unique environment of the Arizona Upland or Succulent Desert, a subdivision of the Sonoran Desert.

The largest cactus in the United States, the saguaro's stem is composed of a skeleton of twelve to thirty slender vertical ribs that support a mass of spongy tissue covered with a thick green skin that is waxy to retard evaporation and pleated to permit expansion for water storage. It may live up to two hundred years and, at maturity, weigh six or seven tons when taking on water through its widespread root system during summer rains.

As the apartment building of the desert, the saguaro provides living space for several species of birds. The Gila woodpecker, elf owl, gilded flicker, sparrow hawk, purple martin and flycatcher nest inside the stems, while larger birds such as the red-tailed hawk and great horned owl live among the branches.

15) SAN XAVIER DEL BAC MISSION

Located in the Santa Cruz Valley southwest of Tucson on the Papago Indian Reservation is the "White Dove of the Desert." Mission San Xavier del Bac is possibly the finest example of Spanish mission architecture in America. The mission, completed about 1783, rises majestically from the desert floor, a brilliant white edifice set against the brown tones of the surrounding hills and the violet shades of the mountains in the distance. An imposing dome, slender soaring towers, rounded parapets and graceful spires distinguish its design and sketch a hauntingly beautiful pattern against the deep blue sky. Flying buttresses with scroll-like curves provide a harmonious transition from the ornately carved facade above the main entrance to the simple, straight lines of the dome and towers. One tower has been left uncompleted.

Within, exquisite murals decorate the walls. The apse contains unique and fanciful statuary, including a fantastic crouching lion. The retable behind the altar is composed of burned brick covered with gilded and painted ornamentation in plaster which, although deeply faded by time, still presents a tableau of arabesques and color making it the focal point of the church.

The foundation for the first mission was laid near the present site before 1700 by Jesuit Father Kino. Father Kino established a number of outstanding Spanish missions throughout the Southwest. This is the only one still actively ministering to the Indians.

16) TOMBSTONE NATIONAL HISTORIC SITE

Begun as a mining camp in 1877, Tombstone became a boom town as word of the rich silver strike spread. The name of the town derives from the warning from early prospectors that, instead of finding a silver strike, newcomers would find their "tombstones." Nevertheless, by 1881 it had a population of 12,000.

Although active mining lasted only seven years, Tombstone played an exciting role in the development of the Old West and truly proved to be "the town too tough to die." Here, the infamous gun battle at the O.K. Corral was fought between the Clantons, on the one hand, and the Earps and Doc Holliday on the other, climaxing a turbulent lawless era. Much of the atmosphere of the 1880's has been preserved in old Tombstone.

In 1880 John P. Clum founded what is now Arizona's oldest continually published newspaper, *The Epitaph*, with the statement, "Every Tombstone needs an epitaph." St. Paul's Episcopal Church is the oldest Protestant church in Arizona still standing. Schieffelin Hall was early Tombstone's cultural and civic center. One of the largest adobe structures in the West, it has been restored.

The Bird Cage Theater remains very much as it was when it was built in 1881. Original furnishings and fixtures have been preserved, including fourteen private box seats suspended from the ceiling to provide Tombstone's leading citizens with exclusive seating. The heyday of this combination theater and dance hall, which inspired the song "Only a Bird in a Gilded Cage," does not seem so far away.

At the O.K. Corral the Earp-Clanton gunfight of October 26, 1881, is recreated with life-size representations of the participants. Boot Hill Cemetery is the last resting place of some 180 desperados, many of them notorious. Tombstone's courthouse has been made a state historic monument and houses a museum with interesting mementos of early Tombstone life.

Around the old business district modern Tombstone is supporting a growing population attracted by its moderate, healthful climate. The beautiful Dragoon Mountains which once sheltered the Apache warrior, Cochise, provide a dramatic backdrop.

17) WUPATKI AND SUNSET CRATER NATIONAL MONUMENTS

Wupatki National Monument, covering 35,693 acres north of Flagstaff, contains about 800 Indian ruins. Many are in remarkably good condition, providing intriguing insights into the Indians who made this region a unique "melting pot of cultures."

From about the seventh century the Sinagua (Spanish for "without water") Indians cultivated the land in this area without irrigation. In 1065, they were startled by a volcanic eruption in their fields. A small earthquake caused a minor break in the earth's crust, and steam and gasses hissed from the hole. As the vent grew, ashes and cinders were tossed skyward. Heavier particles and cooling lava built up a cone around the hole, today called Sunset Crater; the

Expanded from a small pueblo to the largest in the region, Wupatki (Hopi for "Tall House") contained more than 100 rooms. The national monument contains nearly 800 Indian ruins in good condition which provide insights into the Indian cultures that prevailed in the area.

ashes spread over several hundred square miles, effectively preserving some Indian pithouses.

This porous layer of volcanic ashes created an excellent mulch which trapped moisture in the soil, making it very fertile farmland. Neighboring peoples arrived as stories of the region spread. Anasazi dry farmers from northeastern Arizona, Hohokam irrigation farmers from the south, Mogollons who grew corn on mountain slopes from the east, and Patayan lowland farmers from the valley of the Colorado River mingled here during the 1100's, living together and exchanging life-styles.

However, a drought beginning in 1215, as well as continuous use of the soil, began to take their toll. By 1225, all the Indians had deserted the area, but their villages remain.

Wupatki, the Hopi word meaning "Tall House," contains more than 100 rooms. From a small pueblo, it was gradually expanded until it was the largest in the region. Most of the impressive ruin has been excavated.

Near Citadel Ruin, more than 100 ruins have been found within a square mile area. The Citadel itself was a fifty-room apartment house, probably two stories high. Wukoki Ruin has also been preserved with most of its three stories still in their original state.

Sunset Crater, eighteen miles from Wupatki National Monument, derives its name from the reddish mineral-stained cinders around its rim. Protected as Sunset Crater National Monument, spatter cones and other traces of volcanic activity seem barely cool.

Colorado

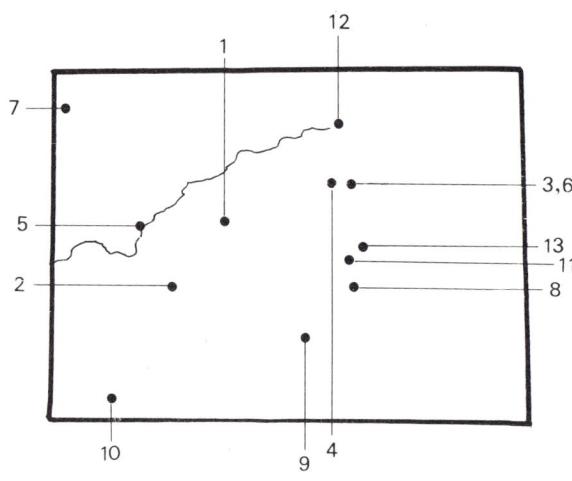

Sheer walls of crystalline-textured granite plummet 2,000 feet in the Black Canyon of the Gunnison River as the river cuts its way from high in the Rocky Mountains to the Colorado River.

1) ASPEN SKI AREA

The world famous resort community of Aspen was founded in the late 1800's as a silver mining town. By 1892 Aspen boasted three banks, ten churches, three schools, a large hospital, six newspapers, the opulent Wheeler Opera House, the Hotel Jerome, an outstanding courthouse and a population of nearly 12,000 people. Unexpectedly, the Silver Panic of 1893 nearly turned the thriving community into a ghost town.

In the 1930's Aspen was a small, sleepy cowtown with striking scenery, its skiing potential unrealized until William Fiske and the Thomas Fortune Ryan family became interested in its resort possibilities. The biggest impetus to development came in World War II when the 10th Mountain Division was training at nearby Camp Hale. The men who had skied all over the world found perfect skiing conditions at Aspen, and its fame began spreading. By 1947 the Hotel Jerome and the Wheeler Opera House were carefully restored and the ski trails more extensively developed.

Today many noted world figures come to Aspen regularly. Some maintain residences in the charming, revitalized Rocky Mountain community, taking advantage of its four mountains, thirty-one lifts and 300 miles of beautifully groomed trails.

2) BLACK CANYON OF THE GUNNISON NATIONAL MONUMENT

From the rim, this gigantic slash in the mountains of southwestern Colorado appears like the jagged jaws of some natural cataclysm. The Gunnison River has carved forbidding rock walls that rise almost perpendicular for more than 2,000 feet above the river's surface as it slices its way from high in the Rocky Mountains to its confluence with the Colorado River.

Functionally designed for the spectator, the galleries of the seven-story Denver Art Museum were planned so that each could be well covered in forty-five minutes. The museum is noted for its North American Indian art and textile collections.

A mist frequently hangs over the river, and the sun, even in summer, strikes the bottom of the dark, tortuous gorge for only a few minutes each day. Here and there, the towering walls have zig-zag patterns of white where molten rock has pushed its way into the formations. Huge, angular slabs of rock lying in the river attest to the continual collapse of the walls.

A feeling of wilderness and uncontrolled power pervades this cleft between the Uncompahgre and West Elk mountains. Fifty miles in total length, the canyon's most spectacular section is within Black Canyon of the Gunnison National Monument, created in 1933.

The monument sector of the river has walls as close as 1,300 feet and as wide as 3,300 feet at the rim. The narrowest point in the gorge bottom is about forty feet. The erosive force necessary to channel this deep path through solid rock formations can be partially conceived in hearing the roar from the depths. Occasionally sounds of rock slides add to the din.

The rock in the walls is mostly crystalline-textured granite in which feldspar, quartz and mica form an intricate tracery. The various formations are stained black and streaked by the elements, thus the name Black Canyon.

Eight miles of scenic drives, plus hiking trails and numerous overlooks on both rims, provide ample opportunity to view this panorama. Access to the 13,176-acre monument is sometimes limited by heavy snowfalls in winter.

3) CAPITOL, Denver

Colorado's State Capitol is located in Denver, the "mile-high city" with an elevation of 5,280 feet. With its great, gold-covered dome—42 feet in diameter and rising 272 feet above the ground—the Corinthian edifice stands on a ten-acre site. The cornerstone was laid on July 4, 1890, and the building was first occupied in 1895. Seventeen years were required to actually complete the structure, which contains 160 beautifully appointed rooms. The granite, sandstone, onyx and marble are native.

The floor plan is designed in the form of a Greek cross. Each face of the structure is dominated by a high Corinthian portico. Broad corridors, paved with white marble, extend from

each of the four entrances to the grand staircase in the rotunda. Immediately above, a circular well pierces the structure to the tower beneath the dome, where the inside and outside observation galleries are located. In the dome, sixteen circular stained-glass windows bear the portraits of outstanding Colorado pioneers.

4) CENTRAL CITY

Established in 1859 when John Gregory discovered gold in a gulch nearby, Central City quickly became a city of over 40,000 people, the "metropolitan" center for the surrounding territory. Central City prospered in that volatile

The striking hues of another sunrise touch the walls of the Grand Canyon that has been carefully carved by the Colorado River.

Today much of the atmosphere has been restored. The Opera House, built in 1878, once attracted such outstanding performers as Sarah Bernhardt, Otis Skinner and Edwin Booth. Once again the theater, decorated with lovely murals and crystal chandeliers, presents the great artists of the day.

Teller House, a hotel dating from 1872, has been restored to its former glory. On the floor of the Teller House Bar is the "Face on the Barroom Floor," inspired by Hugh D'Arcy's ballad.

The Colorado Narrow Gauge Railway carries passengers on a delightful trip up the mountain as far as Packard Gulch.

5) COLORADO RIVER

The mighty Colorado River, the life-blood of America's semiarid Southwest, has created some of the world's most magnificent scenery. From its birthplace in the Colorado Rockies, the river flows for about 1,450 miles, draining about 250,000 square miles, before finally emptying into the Gulf of California. For over 1,000 of these miles, the river is imprisoned by the great walls of nineteen canyons. The cliffs are so formidable and the river such a wild torrent of white foam and raging, brown water that, for more than 325 years after their discovery, the canyons of the Colorado and the river itself had areas that were unexplored and unmapped.

Today we know that after leaving Colorado the river flows southwestward into eastern Utah, where it is joined by the Green River. In northern Arizona it merges with the Little Colorado, and after swinging through the Grand Canyon (see **Grand Canyon National Park**, Arizona—6) it flows south. Just north of the Mexican border, it is joined by Arizona's Williams and Gila rivers and then flows for ninety miles through Mexico before reaching the Gulf of California. (See map, p. 292.)

The great tear that the Colorado has created in the earth's crust reveals more than two billion years of history. Its colorful walls have "great unconformities" that tell of whole mountain ranges being totally worn away to leave a difference of 500 million years between the ages of two rock layers. Contained in each succession of strata is a record of evolving life that begins with evidences of one-celled plants during the late Precambrian. Hidden within canyon caves are the ruins of buildings, the last remnants of

era when fortunes were made and lost overnight in the "richest square mile on earth."

Everything was to be found in this town perched precariously on a rocky hillside. While smartly dressed people attended the opera, prospectors, adventurers and women of the night patronized saloons and dance halls.

Traveling sand dunes provide a backdrop for cottonwood trees in the Great Sand Dunes.

ancient civilizations. Because of the great difference in elevation between the canyons' rims and the river, desert-dwelling reptiles, like the chuckwalla lizard, and evergreens, such as the blue spruce, that only grow at high altitudes are found at a single latitude. For geologists, zoologists, botanists and archeologists, the Colorado River country contains unique insights and invaluable information.

The Colorado is well known for its murderous rapids where the boiling water's deafening roar drowns out the sounds of life. Many of the perils that the early explorers of the Colorado faced have been greatly reduced by modern equipment and professional boatmen, who know the hazards of each rapid. Boating down the Colorado is a thrilling adventure for those who like the outdoors and do not mind getting wet.

Although some of its rapids are still the most powerful and dangerous in the world, modern technology has changed the Colorado River. In the 1930's Hoover Dam was built south of the Grand Canyon and the onrushing water of the lower Colorado backed up to form Lake Mead. (See **Hoover Dam**, Arizona—7.) In 1963 the upper Colorado was flooded back into Glen Canyon for over 180 miles, creating Lake Powell.

There is a point beyond which man-made controls are undesirable. If the Colorado is overly tamed, a unique and beautiful ecosystem that took hundreds of thousands of years to evolve will perish. It is not known how the plants and animals that are adapted to the river's seasonal changes will be affected by the artificial water levels that are now imposed by the dams.

Over 200 consecutive miles of the Colorado River's canyons are presumably safe from all man-made changes by virtue of their being national parks or monuments. The Colorado is still a great and powerful river. But for it to remain so, we must heed Theodore Roosevelt's words:

Leave it as it is. You cannot improve on it. The ages have been at work on it, and man can only mar it.

6) DENVER ART MUSEUM

Housed in a modern building in downtown Denver's Civic Center, the Denver Art Museum contains some 20,000 pieces representing nearly every major cultural period in world history. Of special interest are the North American Indian art and the textile collections.

In the striking museum structure, completed in 1971, the entire collection can be simultaneously exhibited. Designed with the comfort and convenience of art viewers in mind, the museum is uniquely functional. The seven-story building is composed of twin cubes placed like a squared figure eight, meeting at the main entrance facade with a utility core. Elevators in the core allow the individual galleries which are stacked in the towers to be reached quickly and directly. Each gallery is planned so that it can be covered well in forty-five minutes, the attention span of the average visitor.

The exterior of the museum is covered with one million gray glass pyramidal-faceted units which sparkle as they reflect varying lights and shadows, creating an ever-changing facade. The wall surface is broken into twenty-eight vertical panels of varying sizes. Flat glass sections in the same warm color provide relief on the main wall, at the edges of walls and around the window openings.

7) DINOSAUR NATIONAL MONUMENT

Straddling the Colorado-Utah border just south of Wyoming is an ancient burial ground containing the world's largest known deposits of petrified skeletons of dinosaurs. Here also are deep canyons cut by swift-flowing rivers, and sculptured land contours carved by centuries of erosion.

Dinosaur National Monument is not all fossil beds, but these remnants of past ages are remarkable in their extent and number. Mostly found in a sandstone ledge in the southwestern corner of the monument, the bones were first discovered in 1909 by Earl Douglass of the Carnegie Museum. From then until 1922 the museum unearthed tons of fossils of ancient animals, from the Nannosaurus, which was about the size of a chicken, to the huge Apatosaurus (Brontosaurus), with a length of seventy feet and a weight of thirty-five tons. Paleontologists thought all discoveries had been made, but others were found, and reliefing work continues even today. Visitors to the unusual Dinosaur Quarry Visitor Center, which is built directly on the quarry face, can see a working archeological project in progress as workmen use jackhammers, chisels and ice picks to cut away the rock and expose more fossils.

The canyons within the monument are impressive. The Green River has cut deep gorges through the eastern flank of the Uinta Mountains. The Gates of Lodore on the north has long been known for its magnificent narrow canyon with colorful deep red walls over 2,000 feet high. The Yampa River, a Green tributary, also has been active in cutting canyons. Near the junction of these rivers is Steamboat Rock, a massive, thin, elongated piece of rock over 1,000 feet high.

This greatest of the world's fossil finds may have named the monument, but the rivers, scenic canyons and eroded mountains are equally worthy of preservation.

8) FLORISSANT FOSSIL BEDS

In a gentle valley of the Colorado Rockies, fifteen miles west of Pikes Peak, wildflowers provide a brilliantly colored mantle for sedimentary layers preserving one of the largest deposits of insect and plant fossils in North America. These rich fossil beds have yielded specimens representing more than 1,000 species of the plant and animal life of a bygone era.

Scientists studying the formations believe that for many prehistoric centuries the Florissant area experienced periodic volcanic erup-

A branch of a species of dwarf cypress left fine details in volcanic ash now preserved with many other fossils in the Florissant Fossil Beds.

tions. These eruptions dropped layer upon layer of volcanic ash which carried birds, leaves and twigs with it to the bottom of an ancient lake in the valley below. Further ash-falls and mud flows covered and preserved the debris.

In recent years, scientists have gained much information by excavating portions of that prehistoric valley. The various digs have yielded whole petrified tree trunks, often ancient sequoias up to ten feet in diameter, and trunks of trees similar to modern-day elm, along with bark and leaves of oak, walnut, pine, beech, willow and maple. Almost all the fossil butterflies of the New World have come from this site in the Rocky Mountains.

Florissant Fossil Beds National Monument covers about 6,000 acres and was added to the National Park System in 1969.

9) GREAT SAND DUNES NATIONAL MONUMENT

In sharp contrast with the snowcapped peaks of the mountains nearly surrounding them, the dunes of Great Sand Dunes National Monument stand at the edge of a grasslands valley in southern Colorado, 1,000 miles from the nearest ocean or sea. The highest inland dunes in the country, they rise over 600 feet from the San Luis Valley floor and are shifted, sorted, piled and repiled by winds.

Three conditions are generally necessary for the formation of sand dunes—sand, wind and a natural trap. Here streams fed by melted snow carried sand, silt and gravel into this basin for thousands of years. Most of these streams dropped their loads of material and sank into the valley floor.

The floor itself had little vegetation, and there was not much to hold the sand in place. Once in the valley the sand and silt were exposed to prevailing southwesterly winds which blew and bounced the sand grains toward the Sangre de Cristo Mountains on the east and northeast of the valley. On reaching the abrupt mountain barrier, the wind swept over and upward through the mountain passes with a subsequent loss in velocity. The sand was then too heavy to be swept through the passes and was dropped at the foot, caught in the curvature of the range. The sand gradually piled up and these dunes were born, stretching ten miles along the base of the mountains.

Today the ceaseless southwesterly winds sometimes change direction and reshape the dunes. The ridges of the dunes are shifted until they seem to lean over backwards until the winds change once again and restore the ridges to their previous shape.

A lack of water and the moving grains of sand prevent any plants from gaining a foothold, except in depressions where small patches of grass, a species of low pea plant or sunflowers find conditions suitable to their growth and stabilize the sands.

10) MESA VERDE NATIONAL PARK

Mesa Verde National Park, consisting of 52,074 acres in southwestern Colorado, commemorates and preserves the memory of a fascinating Indian culture. For 800 years enterprising Anasazi Indians (see **Canyon de Chelly National Monument**, Arizona—2) lived on these mesa tops and in many of the canyons which slice through them. They were an agricultural people who, in this inhospitable climate, gradually evolved sophisticated farming techniques, as well as great skill in masonry. Yet, by the time of Coronado's ruthless and romanticized quest for the "Seven Cities of Cibola" in 1540, these cliff-dwelling people had disappeared into archeological history. The reason for their mass migration, beginning about 1276, remains a mystery to this day.

News of the cliff dwellings spread rapidly after they were rediscovered in the 1880's. Though they had lain undisturbed for centuries, careless tourists and curio seekers soon caused serious damage to the ruins. In 1906 efforts to protect the ancient dwellings attained fruition and Mesa Verde National Park was established.

So successful has been the excavation and repair of the early damage to these precipitous Indian mansions that Cliff Palace, Balcony House and Spruce Tree House are now considered to be the best examples of cliff dwellings to be found in the continental United States. These citadels of man, built like the eagle's aerie in inaccessibility to enemy attack from below, are an everlasting tribute to how primitive man mastered the craft of masonry.

In the Mesa Verde museum are restored fragile artifacts of cookery, agriculture, jewelry and pottery which tell the history of the vanished cliff-dwelling civilization in graphic detail.

11) PIKES PEAK

See **Oregon Trail**, Kansas—4.

12) ROCKY MOUNTAIN NATIONAL PARK

High over the mile-high city of Denver, fifty miles to the northwest, is the "roof of America." The 400 or more square miles of craggy heights which were designated as Rocky Mountain National Park in 1906 contain 107 named peaks over 11,000 feet in skyward reach.

What has been aptly called an alpine tundra is predominantly a terrain of few trees. Beyond the treeline ranges one-third of the park area, with rolling, grassy slopes softening the panoramic onslaught of granite cliffs and spires.

In the two brief months of the highland summer the park is a land of enchantment, the atmosphere heady with the fragrance of tiny alpine wildflowers. In other seasons it is often bleak and desolate, windswept, with gales of Arctic intensity swirling the snows into multiple hollows and crevices amid great peaks.

Far to the east, the leveling edges of the Great Plains give one a literal sense of the immensity and variety of our continent. To the north, south and west, the skyline is broken by the serrated crests of other mountain ranges.

This is obviously the prime attraction for visitors: the view, as it were, from the top of our land. Unparalleled in its accessibility because of the Trail Ridge Road, which winds through these uplands, tourists find themselves positioned, without need for the skill and strain of mountain climbing, at an elevation of 12,183 feet. And the view from the summit of 14,256-foot Long's Peak, accessible from two foot trails, is extraordinarily beautiful.

But visitors also find meadows resplendent with wildflowers, forests of spruce, pine and fir, and a variety of wild creatures in their natural habitat—elk, deer, bears, coyotes, bighorn sheep and beavers among them.

The contemporary Cadet Chapel is the focal point of the campus of the United States Air Force Academy. Three separate houses of worship— Protestant (shown here) Catholic and Jewish—are within the unique building.

13) UNITED STATES AIR FORCE ACADEMY

Located on a beautiful 18,000-acre campus at the foot of the Rampart Range of the Rocky Mountains near Colorado Springs, the United States Air Force Academy is the youngest of the four service schools. Creation of the Academy was authorized by Congress in 1954 to prepare young men for professional careers in the U.S. Air Force. The first Academy class entered in July 1955 at interim facilities on Lowry Air Force Base, Denver. The present facilities were completed in August 1958. Today, the Academy's student body includes more than 4,000 students.

From the academic campus, sweeping vistas of Cathedral Rock to the north, the Rampart Range to the west and the Black Forest to the east provide an inspiring backdrop for the Academy. Buildings on the campus—all designed by the noted architectural firm, Skidmore, Owings and Merrill—are functionally beautiful. Their contemporary designs featuring white marble, glass, aluminum and steel blend perfectly with the striking setting.

Completed in 1963, the Air Force Academy Cadet Chapel is the architectural focal point of the campus. Within one uniquely inspirational and harmonious building, three houses of worship—Protestant, Catholic and Jewish—have been designed to meet the cadets' spiritual needs. In the Protestant Chapel multihued shafts of light come through the lovely stained-glass windows placed between the aluminum tetrahedrons which come together ninety-nine feet above the terrazzo floor. The inspiring chapel seats 900 and has a 100-seat choir loft.

Our Lady of the Skies Catholic Chapel is located beneath the Protestant Chapel on the terrace level. The chapel is built primarily of pre-cast concrete beams and columns. On the side walls amber glass panels are accented with hand-faceted stained-glass windows. The soft multicolored light is reflected in the nave by the dove-gray ceiling and white terrazzo floors.

Entered separately but also on the terrace level is the unusual and beautiful 100-seat Jewish Chapel. Circular in shape, the Jewish Chapel is enclosed in cyprus stanchions separated by translucent pebble glass. In the foyer purple-violet glass panels are alternated with green and blue accent windows.

New Mexico

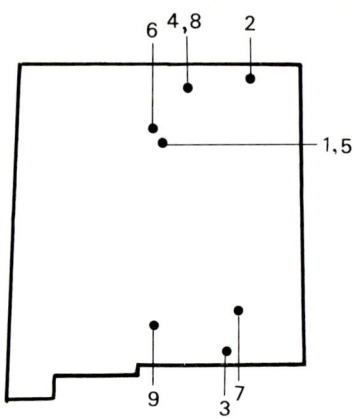

1) CAPITOL, Santa Fe

One of the nation's newest capitol buildings, being completed in 1966, the New Mexico State Capitol at Santa Fe also has one of the most unusual styles. Its circular design is an adaptation of the Pueblo Indian kiva and incorporates the Zia Pueblo sun symbol, which also appears in the state flag. The Capitol's facade is in modified New Mexico Territorial style.

The main floor of the Capitol is given over to the legislative chambers, spaced as segments of a circle. The rotunda rising from this floor is twenty-five feet in diameter and sixty feet high, faced with marble quarried on the Laguna Indian Reservation and highlighted by the state seal cast in its terrazzo floor.

2) CAPULIN MOUNTAIN NATIONAL MONUMENT

A mantle of green trees and grass softens the violence which built this cone-shaped mountain of cinders and ashes. The reds, rusty-browns and blacks of the 1,000-foot-high crater come from material thrown from inside the earth in volcanic eruptions many centuries ago. Although vegetation has partially stabilized the slopes, continuing rock slides in some places show this crater to be young in the stream of geologic time. It is one of the largest, most symmetrical cinder cones in the United States.

Capulin Mountain National Monument, 775 acres of recent geological history, was established in 1916. Rising from a relatively level plain in northeastern New Mexico, it had already become a conspicuous landmark as early as the nineteenth century.

An abundance of stabilizing vegetation enhances Capulin's quiet beauty with patches of ponderosa and pinyon pine, Rocky Mountain juniper and mountain mahogany.

3) CARLSBAD CAVERNS NATIONAL PARK

Plunging to a known depth of 1,100 feet, the Carlsbad Caverns were hollowed by sweeping groundwater in limestone beds laid down by ancient seas. Prior to the explorations of a cowboy named James Larkin in 1901, this now famous landmark of southeastern New Mexico had been known only to a handful of ranchers, when the austere desert lands of the Guadalupe Mountains were settled just after the Civil War. But like most of our great national wonders, the existence of the caverns was known to the Indians of the region and their forebears for many centuries prior to the incursions of the white man. Cooking pits and colored clay paintings or pictographs attest to historic and prehistoric habitation in the sheltering vaulted arch of the caverns' entrance.

For many years the awesome depths were known simply as the Bat Cave, from which hordes of the insect-eating mammals came wheeling and fluttering each summer day at sunset. The bats still arrive en masse in spring.

The breathtaking height of the ceiling, the vastness of the many-acred floor areas and the variety of exquisite forms on cavern roofs, walls and floors show Carlsbad to be one of the largest and most intriguing of American caverns. Some of the primary features include the Big Room with fourteen acres of floor space, the large Temple of the Sun formation, and the Totem Pole, a forty-foot stalagmite. Due to the indefatigable efforts of its early explorers, Carlsbad Caverns was established as a national monument in 1923 and a national park in 1930, covering 46,753 acres.

4) KIT CARSON HOME AND MUSEUM

When Kit Carson bought this twelve-room adobe house in Taos for his Spanish bride in

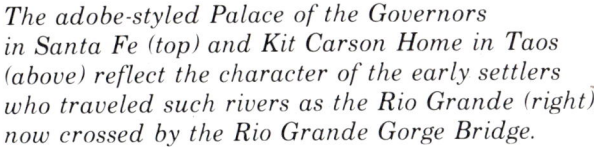

The adobe-styled Palace of the Governors in Santa Fe (top) and Kit Carson Home in Taos (above) reflect the character of the early settlers who traveled such rivers as the Rio Grande (right), now crossed by the Rio Grande Gorge Bridge.

1843, his reputation as a frontiersman and guide for John C. Frémont's Western expeditions was already well established. This house remained Carson's permanent residence until he died twenty-five years later.

Constructed in 1825, the single-story house is designed in stockade fashion around a central patio or garden. Peculiar in its original construction were the different levels of each of the rooms, caused by raising the walls first and then packing the dirt floors to the easiest accessible level in each room. Until a saw mill was available in the 1860's the dirt floors were retained throughout the house. The exterior walls of the building were constructed from adobe brick, reaching a thickness of thirty inches.

Today, three of the rooms have been restored, using many of the original furnishings. Other rooms contain collections of articles which provide a commentary on the different periods of Carson's life, as well as other aspects of the rich Indian and Spanish past. Adjacent to the Kit Carson Memorial State Park, the house opened in 1952 and remains as a monument to a frontiersman who sought peace through justice.

5) PALACE OF THE GOVERNORS

The 350-year-old low, long-walled, adobe-styled Palace of the Governors marked the original settlement of Santa Fe when it became the capital of the Province of New Mexico in the Viceroyalty of New Spain in 1610. Probably completed the same year, the palace is the oldest surviving public building within the continental United States, having housed a total of six different governments.

Through the centuries the palace was modified a number of times, reflecting its changing occupants. The flavor of history can still be sensed here.

In 1900, after 290 years as the seat of various governments, another building was designated as the capitol for the territorial government. Nine years later the Palace of the Governors was redesignated as the Museum of New Mexico. The museum exhibits various historical material from New Mexico's Indian, Spanish and early American periods.

6) RANCHO DE LAS GOLONDRINAS

"The Ranch of the Swallows" is a truly living museum of more than two centuries of Spanish culture in the American Southwest. Architecture, religion, agriculture, crafts—all are displayed in an authentic, active context. Located fifteen miles south of Santa Fe, it was a day's horseback ride on the *Camino Real* ("Royal Road") that ran between New Spain's northern frontier capital and Mexico City, and thus was frequently used as an overnight stop. The region is known as Ciénega because of its marshland, another appealing fact for travelers moving through this semiarid country.

Diego Manuel Baca died in the Ciénega in 1727 and his descendants have lived there ever since. The ranch, first mentioned in records of 1776, was for many years the Baca family estate. In 1971 its remaining 200 acres were turned over to the Colonial New Mexico Historical Foundation.

Today the ranch contains: a *descanso*, a resting place for religious processions; four mills of different types in which flour is still ground; *hornos*, Hispanic dome-shaped outdoor ovens in which bread is actually baked; a burro-powered sorghum grinder; a blacksmith and a wheelwright shop; and an early hacienda-type dwelling with enclosed *placita* and low doorways so constructed as to put entering strangers at a momentary disadvantage in case their intentions were other than benign. All interior furnishings at the ranch are originals or carefully made replicas.

Beyond a *morada* (a meetinghouse of the Penitentes, a lay Catholic movement that flourished in the nineteenth century) are buildings from a mountain village, including a *torreón*, or "tower," from which villagers could scan the surrounding hills for approaching strangers, especially Apaches.

7) ROSWELL MUSEUM AND ART CENTER

There is something admirable about a museum that is wise enough and not afraid to collect and show the works of artists who live in its own environs. The Roswell Museum's Southwestern Collection is devoted to artists who are natives or who have worked in the American Southwest, and presents paintings, sculpture, drawings, prints and crafts by contemporaries, including Henriette Wyeth and Peter Hurd. Among the other represented artists are John Marin, Marsden Hartley and Georgia O'Keeffe; of the many, some are fugitives from Manhattan who found inspiration in the Southwest and created part of its cultural heritage.

Perhaps the real surprise, coming as it were from a New Mexican source, is the Witter Bynner Chinese Collection, a 1953 gift of the distinguished New Mexican poet. Over 200 examples of Chinese painting and work in jade and bronze, collected during his years in China, are rotated in a special gallery.

While honoring its artists, the Roswell Museum and Art Center honors the pioneer rocket scientist, Robert Hutchings Goddard, who in 1926 successfully tested the first liquid fuel rocket. Often called the "Father of Modern Rocketry," he carried on his theoretical and experimental work from 1930-41 near Roswell. The Goddard Wing, completed in 1959, features actual engines, fuel pumps and early rocket models. An exact reproduction of Goddard's shop at Mescalero Ranch, even to the 1931 calendar, was dedicated in 1969.

Hollowed by seeping groundwater in the limestone beds of ancient seas, the Queen's Chamber is only one of the fascinating features of Carlsbad Caverns.

8) TAOS PUEBLO

Unlike many other Indian pueblos, Taos Pueblo near the city of Taos is not a ruin, but a busy, thriving community. Some 1,400 people live in the two five-story, flat-topped, adobe "apartment buildings" which have sheltered the Taos Indians since pre-Columbian times. Set against a backdrop of New Mexico's highest mountains, the soaring Sangre de Cristo Range, Taos Pueblo provides a fleeting glimpse into an intriguing civilization of the past.

The highest pueblo structure in the Southwest and the northernmost still occupied, it has changed little since Spanish explorers first saw it in 1540. At that time, as now, the Indians farmed the surrounding fields.

The traditional *cacique* (priest) and the clan groupings are still extremely important in the life of the pueblo. The Indians observe their ancestral religious ceremonials with traditional dances and songs. Many ceremonials are open to the public but manners consistent with their deeply religious nature are expected.

9) WHITE SANDS NATIONAL MONUMENT

White Sands National Monument, established in 1933, preserves the most spectacular part of the world's largest gypsum dune field—great rolling hills of dazzling white sand that provide a severe environment for the animals and plants which have managed to survive in it. The monument is set in the Tularosa Basin of southern New Mexico that extends for over 100 miles between mountains and highlands, the remnants of a plateau.

These mountains contain massive layers of gypsum rock that seasonal rains and melting snows have been eroding for centuries. Dissolved gypsum is eventually carried to Lake Lucero, the lowest part of the basin at the southern end, where the warm sun and dry winds evaporate the lake, leaving it a gypsum-crystal encrusted marsh much of the year. Gypsum also lies beneath the basin floor, evidence that it was once part of the high plateau around it. Capillary action draws the gypsum-laden underground water to the surface which, after evaporation, leaves extensive alkali flats north of the lake. Persistent scouring winds from the southwest disintegrate the crystals in the lake bed and the alkali flats into brilliant white grains of sand, pile them into dunes up to fifty feet high and push the dunes across the landscape as new ones are constantly formed.

Yet life survives, including over 100 species of hardy plants—purple sand verbena, rice grass, pickleweed, yucca and cottonwood trees among them. Animals, however, are few, primarily coyotes, porcupines, gophers and a species of mice that have evolved protective white coloration.

Utah

1) ARCHES NATIONAL PARK

The Colorado Plateau contains the most colorful, varied, sculptured land on the face of the earth, and Arches is one of its masterpieces. In this 137-square-mile national park in southeastern Utah, sedimentary rock, formed in lakes and floods before the memory of man, has been shaped gloriously by the carving tools of wind-blown sand, frost and moisture. The result is a superb display of eroded formations that together form a collection of stone arches, windows, spires and pinnacles unequalled in this country.

Established in 1929 as a national monument, the size of Arches doubled in 1969. Three years later Congress declared the area a national park. Inside the park are eighty-eight natural arches carved from Entrada sandstone, layered above the hues of Navajo and Carmel sandstone formations.

These huge sandstone masterpieces, formed near the confluence of the Green and Colorado rivers, are surrounded by picturesque canyons, tall, snow-capped mountains in the distance, and an azure desert sky floating above the red, yellow, buff and brown layers of time-worn rock. Elemental forces have produced beautiful land forms in a surprising number of ways. Giant monoliths tower above all else. Balanced rocks teeter unbraced on fragile pedestals and daring arches connect the cliffsides.

Perhaps the most fascinating of these arches is Landscape Arch. Thought to be the longest natural span in the world, it is 291 feet across and towers to a height of 120 feet, with the smallest point in the arch now eroded to less

Double Arch is one of the eroded rock formations in Arches National Park that was carved by the forces of the elements.

than six feet in diameter. Other splendid natural arches in all stages of erosion may be seen in the park with rock strata standing out in bold colors.

The shifting angles of sunlight through the day cause captivating changes in the appearance of some of the monoliths as light and shadows play across the texture of the rock faces. Erosion still causes a constant change in the cliff walls and sandstone facings. Occasional rockfalls occur when a formation splits under the forces of freezing, thawing and gravity, adding variety to the valley floor's appearance.

Lovely lakes and aspen glades in the northern portions of the La Sal Mountains outside the park provide contrast with the red rocks of the valley. On the stark escarpments in the park, stunted Utah juniper and pinyon-pine forest communities produce larger vegetation.

2) BEEHIVE HOUSE

The Beehive House was aptly named. From the time the Mormon leader Brigham Young built the elaborate, pillared, Greek Revival mansion in 1854, it swarmed with family and followers. If the Mormons, more accurately known as Latter-Day Saints, had had their way, Utah would have been called Deseret which, in their own language, means a honeybee, the Mormon symbol of industry. Instead, they settled for a beehive-shaped gilded finial crowning the square cupola atop their leader's house in Salt Lake City as a symbol of their persistent belief that if they wanted to build up the Kingdom of God or establish Zion upon the earth they would have to work.

The handsome three-story house at 75 East South Temple Street has deep porches and balconies, and tall pillars echo, in many ways, the mansions of Young's native Vermont. The Beehive House served as his office, as well as a dwelling for one family or another.

The Mormons decided in 1959 to restore the structure. Using old manuscripts describing the house in Brigham Young's time and old photographs, the Beehive House has been made to look as it did when he lived in it, except for the 1888 additions made by his son.

Once more the stuccoed adobe brick is accented with forest-green shutters and immaculate white trim. Additions and false ceilings have been ripped away and the furniture, although including many Victorian pieces gathered from old houses in Utah, also includes some of the original pieces used by Young.

3) BRYCE CANYON NATIONAL PARK

Bryce Canyon is a unique and elementally beautiful example of the fact that there can be creation in destruction. Stretching for about thirty miles along the eastern edge of 8,000-foot Paunsaugunt Plateau are the famous Pink Cliffs, one of the finest of Utah's eroded landscapes. Primordial forms (sometimes called "castles" and "temples") have been constructed by the relentless forces of water rushing down the slopes of the plateau. Variations in the weather and the erosion resistance of the rock layers account for the unusually interesting forms in the canyon. Systems of cracks and joints have created such phenomena as the Natural Bridge and the Queen's Garden. The varying intensities of red are the result of the iron content of the rock. The Paria River and other streams are still nibbling away at the layers of rock at the rate of two feet every century.

The history of Bryce Canyon began long before the Paiute Indians gave Paunsaugunt ("home of the beaver") Plateau its name and called the area "red rocks standing like men in a bowl-shaped canyon." It was sixty million years ago that inland lakes and seas in this area started to lay down deposits of silt, sand and lime in beds as much as 2,000 feet thick. The deposition of the Bryce strata ended about twenty-five million years ago and the lands of southern Utah began to rise slowly. During this gradual elevation, produced by pressure within the earth, beds of rock were broken into blocks many miles in width and length. Some blocks were raised more than others, producing seven plateaus.

Today 36,010-acre Bryce Canyon National Park, established in 1928, is enhanced by stately ponderosa pines, ancient weather-beaten bristlecone pines, spruce, fir, junipers and many wildflowers. These in turn give a setting for the colorful birds, deer, fox and other wildlife.

4) CANYONLANDS NATIONAL PARK

This is a land where rock is master. It is everywhere in every form and shape imaginable, as if other objects had somehow been changed into it. The names of these fantastic rocks are as imaginative as the shapes themselves—Washerwoman Arch, Six-Shooter Peak, Silver Stairs, Spanish Bottom, Candlestick Spire, Dead Horse Point, Peekaboo Arch, Paul Bunyan's Potty.

Established in 1964, southeastern Utah's Canyonlands National Park includes 337,258 acres of a seemingly endless variety of desert landscapes, from mesas to spires and cliffs.

Beehive House was named by its owner-builder, Brigham Young, for the honeybee, the Mormon symbol of industry. A beehive-shaped gilded finial stands atop the home.

The center of Canyonlands is where the Green and the Colorado rivers come together. And all around the confluence of these streams, the land is laced with tangles of small gorges down which, after a sudden cloudburst, a raging torrent will smash its violent way for an hour and then leave a dry and soon-dusty creek bed for perhaps another year, or even longer. Since the beginning of time this cut and slash of water has eaten away the land into a complex mass of sand, sagebrush and sandstone.

The southeast section of the park, known as The Needles, is perhaps the most exciting part. Here, the sandstone has been broken, eroded and pushed about into a jumble of pillars thrust up, arches thrown out, and valleys stamped down into wildly unusual shapes, such as Angel Arch, resembling an angel leaning on his harp, and Druid Arch, named after England's mysterious Druid ruin, Stonehenge.

The Grabens (from the German word for "ditch") are places where the land seems to have dropped down an elevator shaft, leaving behind them immense flat-bottomed valleys of stone bordered by vertical walls. Such is the immensity of the surrounding distance, that what are deep faults in the earth's crust seem much smaller than they are.

Long departed Indians, or their predecessors, have left their mark on Canyonlands. Storehouses of grain, with the corn still in them and dried iron-hard by a thousand summers, are still standing almost as they were left. Palm prints of prehistoric men are still visible on the walls of some caves. And at Newspaper Rock (outside Canyonlands' boundaries at Utah's Indian Creek State Park) the visitor can see the pictographs that someone scratched there on the "desert varnish" of the cliff.

5) CAPITOL, Salt Lake City

Situated on a "bench," or natural terrace, of the Wasatch Range foothills 300 feet above the valley floor, the Utah State Capitol can be seen from almost every approach to Salt Lake City. Although the site was granted by the city to the Territorial Government in 1888, actual construction did not begin until several years after Utah finally won statehood in 1896. The Capitol

The steep, nearly impassable cliffs of Capitol Reef have been expertly colored by nature's chemicals.

is a mainly Corinthian-style structure of Utah granite. Utah copper covers the 285-foot dome atop the four-story building, completed in 1915.

Inside, a 3,200-pound brass chandelier is suspended by a ninety-five-foot chain from the center of the dome, 165 feet above the rotunda floor. A skyscape with huge seagulls is painted on the dome ceiling. The gull is referred to as Utah's "sacred bird" because a large flight of them once devoured vast numbers of crickets which endangered the settlers' crops.

6) CAPITOL REEF NATIONAL PARK

The violent upthrust of multicolored barrier cliffs stretching 100 miles across the south-central Utah desert looks like a huge ocean wave suspended between the Fremont River and its two tributaries. These interruptions in the striking shale and sandstone escarpments resemble the clustered buildings of a city—hence the appellation Capitol Reef given to this area by the famous explorer John C. Frémont, who viewed the area from Thousand Lake Mountain in 1854.

This magnificent escarpment is the western face of a folding of the earth's crust that occurred in some ancient upheaval. Major John Wesley Powell, a geologist who first explored this region in 1869, called this upthrust the Waterpocket Fold. Capitol Reef National Park preserves 250,000 acres of the most picturesque parts of this geological museum. Here, the term "paintbrush of nature" takes on special meaning with vermilion-hued shale layers and walls of glowing pink and white mixing with splatters of orange and ocher. The brilliance deepens to "a land of horizontal rainbows" as day wears on.

The surging and folding of the earth's surface caused the eastern segment of the fold to top the western side and erosion has exposed the stratified crust formation. Cliffs range from 1,000 to 2,000 feet high, making an almost impassable barrier to crossing the desert from west to east. At the base of the cliffs natural cisterns called potholes catch and retain the only fresh water to be found for many miles across the desert. These water catchments caused Powell to call it the Waterpocket Fold.

Isolated and desolate, this part of the mile-high land of southern Utah was first set aside as a national monument in 1937. In 1969 it was extended by more than 200,000 acres to preserve the most spectacular parts of the

Waterpocket Fold. It was designated a national park in 1972.

7) CEDAR BREAKS NATIONAL MONUMENT

A gigantic natural amphitheater, carved from multihued stone, slopes steeply westward from two-mile-high Markagunt Plateau in southwestern Utah. This is a spectacular example of the deterioration of limestone formations uptilted by ancient shiftings of the earth's crust. The gently rolling rim of this grotesquely eroded area is covered by a verdant growth of trees interspersed with lush meadows which display mountain wildflowers soon after the retreat of melting snow. Color, both from various metallic mixes in the limestone and from the lush plant growth, is probably the dominant characteristic of this dramatic area.

Early Mormon settlers called the area "breaks" or "badlands." That early name became Cedar Breaks because settlers mistakenly identified the mountain juniper of the area as cedar. About ten square miles of the area was established as Cedar Breaks National Monument in 1933. From the rim of the plateau at 10,300 to 10,400 feet above sea level, the amphitheater drops half a mile to its lowest point.

Bold rock shapes and cliffs carved from stone layers 2,000 feet thick are revealed from outlook points along the rim. Sidewalls are furrowed, corroded and broken into massive ridges that seem to radiate from the center like spokes of a wheel. This geological display of color starts at the top with white or orange limestone ranging downward through rose and coral tints. Yellows, lavenders and even purples and chocolate hues are seen in many sections of the prodigious natural bowl. The Indians called it "circle of painted cliffs."

Even the brilliant coloring, however, is surpassed by the grotesque sculpturing of wind and water. Formations of columns, pinnacles, standing walls, gateways and terraces suggest structures ranging from cathedrals to tombstones.

During summer, mountain wildflowers compete with the rock colors as the monument's major attraction. The lush vegetation supports a wide variety of wildlife, including chipmunks, deer, porcupines, badgers and many birds.

8) DINOSAUR NATIONAL MONUMENT

See Colorado—7.

Massive rock formations have been sculpted in Canyonlands National Park by the Colorado River and the slash and cut of violent cloudbursts.

Within Temple Square in Salt Lake City are the historic Mormon Tabernacle, completed in 1867, and the towering Mormon Temple, begun by pioneers in 1853.

9) GLEN CANYON NATIONAL RECREATION AREA

See Arizona—5.

10) MONUMENT VALLEY

See Arizona—11.

11) NATURAL BRIDGES NATIONAL MONUMENT

Southern Utah is renowned throughout the world for its fantastic landscape of brilliantly colored cliffs, tortuous box canyons, sandstone arches, pinnacles, towers and natural bridges. Three of the most impressive bridges are the principal features of Natural Bridges National Monument, established in 1908. These bridges were formed by meandering rivers, gouging canyons and then wearing away the canyon walls of the inside parts of sharp bends. As the waters flowed through the holes, they expanded to form bridges. Although similar in looks, arches differ in that they were not formed by river erosion, but wind, rain and frost erosion.

In White Canyon, the Sipapu Bridge stretches 268 feet across at a height of 220 feet and is the largest and most graceful. The symmetrical arch suggested to those who named it the *Sipapu*, a hole through which Hopi Indians believe their ancestors emerged from a lower, dark world into the present one.

Kachina Bridge, at the junction of White and Armstrong canyons, reaches 210 feet above the stream bed and 206 feet between the cliffs; it is the bulkiest bridge, though still in its youth geologically as flood waters continue to enlarge the opening. On one of the abutments are numerous pictographs, some of which resemble Hopi masked dancers or *kachinas*, thus explaining the name.

The last and smallest bridge, Owachomo in Armstrong Canyon, is also the thinnest (nine feet thick) and the oldest of the three, no longer being eroded by stream waters. Named for the large rounded rock mesa near one end (*owachomo* means "rock mound" in the Hopi language), its life expectancy is less; perhaps the fatal crack may already have started.

A cliff dwelling of about twenty rooms, whose occupants were early Anasazi Indians, can be seen along the trail between the Sipapu and Kachina bridges.

12) RAINBOW BRIDGE NATIONAL MONUMENT

Navaho Indians called it *nonnezoshi*, meaning "rainbow-turned-to-stone." Today it is known as Rainbow Bridge, but no matter what name is used, it remains the same—a soaring massive pink arch between two cliffs in southeastern Utah. The bridge was proclaimed a national monument in 1910.

The dimensions of the bridge are staggering. It is the largest, most spectacular natural bridge in the world—278 feet long, nearly the length of a football field. At a height of 309 feet, the National Capitol would fit underneath. It is 42 feet thick, more than the height of a three-story building, and 33 feet wide, enough to accommodate a two-lane highway.

Unlike most natural bridges, which are straightened and flat at the top, Rainbow Bridge is a true symmetrical arch. It was formed by a stream, Bridge Creek, which meandered through canyons in Utah's red "slick-rock" country. One of the sharp bends was nearly a complete circle and ages of slow erosion wore away the thin piece of canyon wall separating the two sections of stream until the water broke through and gradually enlarged the opening to its present size.

The bridge is composed of salmon-pink Navaho sandstone, with dark stains caused by iron oxide and hematite. During rainstorms hematite in the sandstone is washed down the sides of the arch and deposited by evaporation, leaving streaks of reds and browns.

13) TEMPLE SQUARE

Salt Lake City centers around a ten-acre block called Temple Square. Surrounded by a high wall, the quiet and peaceful square in the middle of the bustling city is also the center of the Church of Jesus Christ of the Latter-Day Saints (Mormons). Mormon pioneers led by Brigham Young came to Salt Lake Valley in 1847 to escape the persecution which had befallen them in earlier settlements. Before any buildings had been erected, Young selected the site between two forks of a mountain stream, saying, "Here will be the temple of our God."

Within Temple Square are the historic Mormon Tabernacle, completed in 1867, and the Mormon Temple begun by the pioneers in 1853

and finally finished in 1893. The Tabernacle, home of the world-famous Mormon Tabernacle Choir, is a massive edifice surmounted by a great oval roof which is supported only by huge wooden arches spanning the width of the building. The building, seating 8,000 people, is well known for its remarkable acoustics.

The spired Temple, the square's most commanding structure, some forty years in construction, is used only for special church ceremonies. Its six central towers rise 212 feet. A gold-leaf-covered figure of an angel with a trumpet stands on the capstone of the tallest tower. Since the Temple's dedication as the House of the Lord, only Mormons have been permitted to enter the hallowed building.

14) TIMPANOGOS CAVE NATIONAL MONUMENT

While hunting cougars in the American Fork Canyon of the Wasatch Mountains of Utah in 1887, Martin Hansen came across an entrance to a small cave high up on the slopes of 12,000-foot-high Mount Timpanogos. The cave contained many colorful dripstone formations, but, for the next thirty-four years, it was only locally known. In 1921 two other caves were discovered close by, both larger and more spectacular than the first. The following year Timpanogos Cave was proclaimed a national monument.

Much of the interior is covered by pink and white translucent crystals which glow and sparkle in the slightest light. Larger formations are composed of myriads of smaller features— feathery boas, braided wreaths and needlelike stalactites. Pools of water reflect the sheafs of pink- and brown-striped draperies suspended from dark niches and pendants hanging from the ceiling, while pedestals rise above the cave floor. The walls are encrusted with glistening aragonite crystals and bedecked with tangled masses of root-shaped stone called helictites. Varying amounts of iron, combined with other mineral impurities, tint the odd shapes with hues of lemon yellow, red, brown, green, blue and lavender.

The names themselves describe the major formations—The Giant's Comb, Father Time's Jewel Box, Coral Gardens, Hidden Lake, Chocolate Falls, Chimes Chamber, Cavern of Sleep and the Great Heart of Timpanogos, a huge bulbous stalactite.

The canyon has abundant plant and wildlife typical of the central Rockies. A hike up the top of snowcapped Mount Timpanogos leads to a spectacular view of the Great Basin and Great Salt Lake below, with no visible evidence of the fantasy world that exists inside the mountain.

15) ZION NATIONAL PARK

"Canyonland in color." That is 147,035-acre Zion National Park in southwestern Utah which Mormon pioneers, in 1858, called a place of "peace and comfort."

The park's sheer-wall formations are unique among the world's geological phenomena. Over 150 million years of natural processes formed this colorful canyon. Here, visitors can actually follow the path of the large three-toed dinosaur and discern its huge footprints in hard sandstone rock layers.

These primeval wonders excited the imagination and determination of dedicated Mormon pioneers in 1847. Within a decade the Mormons had settled around the Virgin River and named the region, appropriately, Zion, "the heavenly city of God."

Greenery tumbles richly about the banks of the Virgin, contrasting with the majestic red of Navajo sandstone precipices and the intense blue of the skies overhead. Along the effervescent North Fork of the Virgin River is the Watchman, 6,555 feet high and glowing like a vast reddish-brown jewel in the glints and starts of a remorseless sun. The panorama continues up Zion Canyon, a distance of eight miles, to the Temple of Sinawava. To the left, in succession, are the reverently named heights: the Towers of the Virgin, the Altar of Sacrifice, the Beehives, Sentinel Peak, the Three Patriarchs and Majestic Mountain; to the right, East Temple, Mount Spry, the Twin Brothers, Mountain of the Sun, Red Arch Mountain and the Great White Throne.

Beyond the Great White Throne, the river twists to the west at The Organ, behind which Angels Landing rises 1,500 feet above the canyon bed. To the west is Cathedral Mountain with Observation Point and The Pulpit, soaring to the right and left. Numerous trails lead to the canyon rims and a road follows the Virgin River through the canyon.

Such is Zion, the bequest of forgotten, prehistoric seas. "A great reservoir," as Donald Culross Peattie once wrote, "of the serene order of nature."

Opposite: *Appropriately named by the Mormons who settled around the Virgin River, the sheer pink walls of Zion National Park suggest peace and comfort to visitors.*

Alaska   Oregon   Washington

PACIFIC NORTHWEST and ALASKA

In 1578 Englishman Sir Francis Drake was searching for the fabled Northwest Passage, a direct route from Europe to rich India. He touched the coast of Washington and Oregon, lands whose splendid diversity became known only when more regular incursions began two centuries later by trappers, traders, and, eventually, settlement by immigrants who used the overland migration routes.

The Pacific Ocean pounds on a coastline that is alternately rockbound, silvery beached or wooded, and often misty with fog. A verdant coastal forest crowned by Douglas fir stretches inland, cut through by many enchanting waterways, particularly the powerful Columbia River. Parallel to the ocean, about two-thirds of the distance to the states' western borders, rises the stunning, snow-capped Cascade Range, a control factor in rainfall distribution: abundant to the west, meager to the east. East of the Cascades, foothills forested by Ponderosa pine gradually flatten out into the Columbia Basin.

Whatever is said of Washington and Oregon (or any other state), it is true to an even greater degree of Alaska. Largest of all states, it has the greatest natural resources, recreation opportunities, geographical distinctions and temperature extremes.

Geographically misunderstood, its usual image—miles of frozen tundra over which the aurora borealis nightly dances—exists in reality only in the north and east. The south and west are hospitable and temperatures match those of pleasant Seattle, Washington, and Portland, Oregon.

This land of the midnight sun has been the country's last frontier. Many Alaskans have known within their lifetimes the building of a new life in a new country, and are eager to share their memories with any who appreciate the land.

Summer greens soften the harsh contours of narrow Oneonta Creek Gorge in Oregon's Mount Hood National Forest. After cutting through the canyon the little creek feeds into the Columbia River.

The sun sets over the ice-covered peaks of Glacier Bay (above). The verdant primeval forests (right) heavy with moss at the southeastern end of the monument are a striking contrast to the glaciers.

Alaska

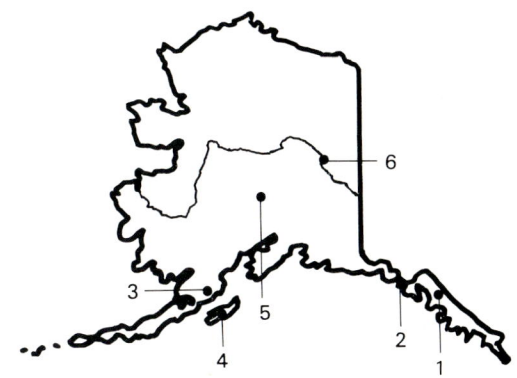

1) CAPITOL, Juneau

Located on Fourth Street between Main and Seward streets in Juneau, the present Alaska State Capitol was originally the Federal and Territorial Building, but was ceded to the state by the 1958 Alaska Statehood Act. Alaska was admitted to the Union on January 3, 1959.

Completion of the building in 1931 climaxed twenty years of effort by the citizens of the territory. Frills were at a minimum. As Alaska's delegate to Congress, Judge James Wickersham, said at the dedication, "... more attention is given to serviceable space and ease of access and use by a busy people..."

The building is of brick-faced reinforced concrete, with Indiana limestone used for the lower facade. The four columns of the portico, as well as the building's interior trim, are of light and dark native Tokeen marble.

The world's largest carnivores, Kodiak bears stand ten to thirteen feet high on their hind legs and may grow to 1,200 pounds. Despite their size, they are quick and agile.

2) GLACIER BAY NATIONAL MONUMENT

Usually nature moves so slowly that its effects are not noticeable during the lifetime of a man. But not at Glacier Bay National Monument, established in 1925 and located along Alaska's southeast coast in the midst of towering mountains, perpetually clad in snow. Here, over twenty tremendous glaciers, hundreds and even thousands of feet thick, move down the mountainsides, carving new valleys in the slopes, pushed by the great weight of the snow and ice constantly accumulating on their tops. Ocean-born storms feed these rivers of ice so consistently that many of them flow all the way to the waters of the bay, where they end in magnificent ice cliffs. Great chunks of ice continually break away from the glacier cliff faces as their support of ice melts or crumbles. When these blocks, some over 200 feet high, crash into the bay, they cause huge waves. The larger ones fill the tidal inlets with thousands of floating icebergs, many of which could swamp a boat.

All stages of glacial action can be seen here, from active, moving ice masses to the slowly dying, stagnant ones. Muir Glacier, one of the most active on the entire Alaskan coast and named for famous naturalist-writer John Muir who visited the bay in 1879, has a sheer face rising over 200 feet from the water and is nearly two miles wide. Most of the fingerlike inlets of Glacier Bay terminate at similar cliffs.

The bay, about seventy miles long and between three to ten miles wide, lies between paralleling mountain ranges, the St. Elias and the Fairweather, higher than any in the continental United States. It is dotted with islands large and small; some, like the Beardslee Islands at the southern entrance of the bay, are low and densely wooded, and others, such as the Marble Islands just to the north, are steep and mostly treeless, serving as rookeries for thou-

sands of seabirds. The majority of the islands in the mid and upper bay are solid rock, worn and scarred by the ice sheets.

Seals, sea lions, whales and porpoises may frequently be seen in the bay, and various waterfowl inhabit the inlets and islands. In the heavily wooded shores of the bay, and in the mountains are minks, martens, wolves, bears and other animals.

3) KATMAI NATIONAL MONUMENT

This is the Last Wilderness. Although other states may have patches of wilderness, only Alaska's is so primeval and untamed that you could wander for weeks without seeing another human being. It is the kind of wilderness that even people who know they will never see it are deeply satisfied that it still exists. Katmai National Monument, established in 1918 and one of the largest units of the National Park System, protects over 4,200 square miles of this wilderness on the east coast of the peninsula leading to the Aleutian chain.

Katmai contains three distinct geographic sections. To the east is the seacoast on Shelikof Strait, a coastline of unsurpassed beauty, including a series of deep fjords nearly surrounded by cliffs rising abruptly 1,000 or more feet above the blue waters. The great gray whale sometimes hunts in the offshore waters.

Inland from the coast is the Aleutian Mountain Range, forming the backbone of Katmai. These snow-capped peaks, as high as 7,600 feet, are continually being carved by glaciers and some of them are active volcanoes.

In the western portion of Katmai is a huge mixture of grasslands, green forests and large, deep blue lakes. Large mammals, especially Alaskan brown bears, wolves, moose, lynx and red foxes, are plentiful.

This area's spectacular wilderness was first widely noticed when Novarupta Volcano erupted in 1912. It was one of the largest eruptions in earth's history and caused the top of nearby Mount Katmai to collapse with a tremendous roar. For many decades afterward, steam and gasses escaped through innumerable small holes and cracks in a nearby valley, called Valley of the Ten Thousand Smokes.

4) KODIAK NATIONAL WILDLIFE REFUGE

Kodiak Island, the largest island in the Gulf of Alaska, contains the 2,780-square-mile area of Kodiak National Wildlife Refuge, established in 1941. Unlike many other refuges, Kodiak has remained unchanged over the centuries.

The island is wild and mountainous, with snowy peaks reaching 4,000 feet above sea level. It is lush with vegetation in some areas while barren in others. Sitka spruce forests dominate the mountains of the northern part of Kodiak, while grassy slopes and Arctic tundra are characteristic of the southern portion.

Numerous clear streams carry the water from the high alpine lakes to the long, fjordlike bays of the Pacific Coast. Often misty and dismal with low clouds surrounding the peaks, the island averages 105 inches of precipitation annually, and winters, unlike most of Alaska, are mild with temperatures seldom below zero.

The variety of wildlife is extraordinary, and particularily impressive are the almost 200 pairs of bald eagles, the national emblem. But Kodiak Island is best known as the primary habitat of the Kodiak or Alaskan brown bear, the largest carnivore on earth. The refuge protects over 2,400 of these tremendous animals.

5) MOUNT MCKINLEY NATIONAL PARK

The Alaska Range in central Alaska rises in a succession of brilliant ridges, peaks and cornices—each magnificent in its own right, but nearly lost in the greater picture. Higher they rise, leading the eye to the massive upsurge that is *The Mountain*. A full three vertical miles above the living tundra soars its peak.

Nothing lives on Mount McKinley, but the mountain lives. Avalanches leap from its walls. Seracs crash; glaciers rumble and grind. Clouds swirl about its flanks, and a snow plume is torn by the wind from its uppermost crests. In the evening, the glare of the eternal ice softens, glows with the color of fireweed, then pales to ivory against the darkened sky.

It is fortunate that one of the earliest explorers of the area was a naturalist and conservationist. Charles Sheldon, hunting specimens for the National Museum, roamed the country for three years and felt its impact. Recognizing the intrinsic value of the landscape and its wildlife, he conceived the idea of making the area a national park while camping there in the summer of 1906. His vigorous efforts to create a refuge for the swarming wildlife, brought about the establishment of Mount McKinley National Park just eleven years later. Today it is the only park service area which harbors the white Dall sheep and the barren-grounds caribou, and its 3,030 square miles embrace more untouched wilderness than any other national park.

Relatively little has changed since Sheldon fought to make this area a park. A single grav-

Smoke drifts from the top of Martin Volcano, one of a chain of active volcanoes—Trident, Mageik and Martin—that are located just west of Mount Katmai in the Aleutian Mountain Range.

eled road winds its leisurely way eighty-six miles into the park, climbing from the deep green spruce of the taiga to the sweeping tapestry of the alpine tundra. You may see from the road the same wild peaks and teeming wildlife that thrilled the first visitors. Over the tundra range groups of caribou, the bulls in late summer bearing brilliant white capes and towering, blood-red antlers. Moose, looking shiny black at a little distance, feed knee-deep in ponds or browse in willow thickets. The deceptively lethargic-looking grizzly keeps his head down, gobbling berries, roots and grasses. If you are very lucky, you may even see a wolf. When you have seen the eyes of a wolf, you have seen the quintessence of wildness.

6) YUKON RIVER

Because of its aridity and the protective mountains surrounding it, the Yukon Basin, unlike most of the northern half of the world, was not blanketed with ice and the river's path became a corridor that led the first Americans into the New World. Investigation has shown that the Yukon was the first river in the Americas to be seen by man; yet it was the last major river of America to be discovered by the white man.

The Yukon, about 1,800 miles in length, is one of the longest rivers in North America and runs through this country's last great wilderness. The headwaters in the southwestern part of Canada's Yukon Territory are formed by the Pelly River, which flows northwestward out of the Canadian Rockies, and by the lake-fed Lewes River, which flows northwestward out of the Coast Range. The rivers join at Selkirk, Yukon Territory, and enter Alaska after a few hundred miles.

The upper river is fast-moving and filled with rapids. After entering Alaska, however, it broadens out and meanders across the swampy flats of central Alaska. At some points, where there are shoals and islands, the river is from ten to thirty miles wide. At Fort Yukon on the Arctic Circle the river bends to the southwest and flows into the Bering Sea near Norton Sound. (See map, p. 292.)

The lower river flows through an almost treeless tundra. Here are found Arctic hares, foxes that grow thick white coats in winter and lemmings, the most abundant mammal of the tundra. About 150 miles from the delta begins the transitional territory between the tundra and the northern coniferous, or boreal, forests. Like a great artery that breaks down into myriad capillaries, the Yukon empties into the sea through many mouths that are spread over some seventy-five miles. This is a swampy, boggy region that is filled with ponds and flooded low ground.

The Yukon is a powerful river that could be a major source of power for a growing Alaska. It enters the state from Canada at an average of 138,000 cubic feet per second. Some 1,260 miles later, this flow has increased to an estimated 216,000 cubic feet per second as the river empties into the Bering Sea. This mean flow drops off sharply during the winter months because most of the water that it drains from some 330,000 square miles comes from melting snow and glaciers. To overcome this seasonal fluctuation, there have been recommendations to dam and back up the Yukon to form a great lake. But any development of the Yukon must be carefully weighed against its impact on the wilderness environment.

The "midnight sun" reflects against the mighty Yukon River, the last major river in America to be discovered by the white man.

Oregon

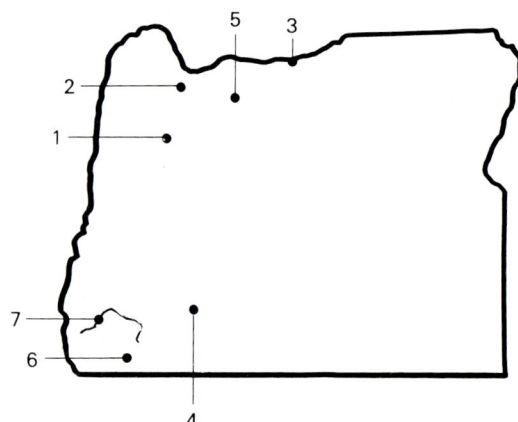

1) CAPITOL, Salem

The beautiful Oregon State Capitol in Salem, built of white Vermont marble, is simple in design. It looks northward, with other state buildings on each side, over a lovely landscaped mall toward the Cascade Mountains. Marble is also used extensively on the interior.

Atop the tower of the statehouse, 128 feet high, is the gilded eight-and-one-half-ton, forty-two-foot-high statue of the *Pioneer* by Ulric Ellerhusen, one of the West's greatest sculptors, which can be seen for miles. Other Ellerhusen decorations over the various entrances depict figures symbolic of Oregon's economy and history. Ellerhusen also created the bronze of the state seal which is set in the center of the rotunda floor.

Among the rotunda decorations is a sunburst with stars overhead, representing Oregon and the other states at the time of Oregon's entry into the union in 1859. Four murals on the rotunda walls show scenes from Oregon's history. Another four, on its industry, flank the stairs to the Senate and House.

2) CENTRAL LUTHERAN CHURCH

Portland's Central Lutheran Church is an aesthetic modern conception of the Gothic stone cathedral. Noted church architect Pietro Belluschi described his design as being on "a more human scale ... so as to produce the kind of atmosphere most conducive to worship."

Laminated wood arches closely follow the straight wall line, then curve suddenly to meet the roof, producing a nearly rectangular shape and muting the traditional Gothic pointed arch while emphasizing the vertical lines.

The delicate latticework of the bell tower rises above the flat roof and adds to the simple beauty of the wooden Gothic translation. The main entrance harmonizes with the tower and walls with a graceful wooden canopy.

Attention within the church is directed towards a chancel area which curves in a half circle wider than the nave and taller than the nave roof. Light enters through amber glass panes in a clerestory and the offset sides of the chancel shell, creating a focused brilliance centering on the altar.

3) COLUMBIA RIVER

See Washington—2.

4) CRATER LAKE NATIONAL PARK

A quarrel between two mighty Indian gods created Crater Lake—so went the lore of the local Indians who told us that the earth collapsed to a depth of almost 2,000 feet, forming the circular lake's basin, because of a raging struggle between "chief of the world above" and "chief of the world below."

The myth, not quite as old as the actual geological earth movement of 7,000 years ago, which carved out the second deepest lake in the Western Hemisphere, tells us that the underworld deity retreated below just as the chief of the upper regions let fall a mountain top on any possible exit to the surface.

Wizard Island, situated in the center of Crater Lake, is actually a volcano within a volcano. The second deepest lake in the Western Hemisphere was formed when the volcanic cone of Mount Mazama collapsed nearly 7,000 years ago.

Yet science more factually hypothesizes that predecessors of the Indian myth-makers may have seen the collapse of volcanic Mount Mazama thousands of years ago and built their myth, like most myths, on a residue of fact.

Crater Lake, astride the Cascade Range in southern Oregon, has since gathered to itself the snows and rains of centuries, tinged gradually into the vast and stunning royal blue of its present setting.

It is said that the lake has only two seasons: an eight-month, snow-shrouded winter and an Edenlike two-month summer. But there is a brief snow-melting spring, and a haunting, chill-touched momentary fall. Yet, in all seasons, there endures the onslaught of arboreal beauty with hemlock, fir and pine clothing the pumiced slopes in varied shades of green, dappling the warm tones of summer and richly dotting winter's wide, white mantle.

Mount Scott, highest point in the park at 8,926 feet, commands the eastern side of the lake and overlooks blue waters twenty square miles in area. Multicolored canyonlike walls 500 to 2,000 feet high surround the lake, their heights majestic with conifers and bleak with sporadic barren surfaces.

William Gladstone Steel is outstanding among the lake's many admirers. He came, for the first of many visits, to the brink on August 15, 1885. A six-day sojourn lengthened into a lifetime rendezvous. Leader of the seventeen-year campaign to protect the lake, he achieved his goal when, in 1902, President Theodore Roosevelt signed a bill establishing Crater Lake National Park.

5) MOUNT HOOD

Englishman William Broughton must not have believed his eyes that day in October 1792. Sailing a short distance up the Columbia River, he sighted a single magnificent snowcapped peak jutting up from the surrounding hills still a hundred miles further inland. He named it Mount Hood after his friend, British Admiral Lord Samuel Hood.

Mount Hood is the most famous of the many individual peaks running the length of the Cascade Range from Mount Rainier (see Washington—4) south to Mount Shasta (see California—17). The 11,245-foot mountain is an ancient but not yet fully extinct volcano, and fumaroles still steam near its summit. Indians believed it was the dwelling place of a god, and modern visitors can still sense the awe that these early Americans must have felt. The highest point in Oregon, it can be seen thrusting skyward as it is approached from any direction. From its top, accessible only to hikers and climbers, Mount Hood's companions, Mount Adams and Mount St. Helens, can be seen to the north across the Columbia River, and to the east a patchwork of orchards stretch to the horizon.

The mountain is the dominant feature of Mount Hood National Forest, an area of over one million acres rich in wildlife and scenic wonders. Conifer forests march up the peak to timberline at about 6,000 feet, where the alpine tundra begins. The deep snows of winter do not have a chance to melt completely in the brief summer at this height, yet many tiny plants still manage to survive here.

A few clear lakes, the most picturesque being Lost Lake, surround the mountain, and small streams scurry toward the Columbia River at the mountain's northern base. The river cuts through the Cascades here, forming the Columbia River Gorge, its mountainous sides lined with spectacular waterfalls like 620-foot Multnomah Falls and tributary canyons like narrow Oneonta Gorge.

6) OREGON CAVES NATIONAL MONUMENT

Oregon Caves National Monument, established in 1909, is on the slopes of Mount Elijah, a peak of almost 6,400 feet in the Siskiyou Mountains of southwestern Oregon. Although long called Oregon Caves, it is in fact a single marble cavern consisting of an intricate complex of corridors. The main entrance is the northernmost and lowest point in the cave at an elevation of 4,000 feet. The chambers in the southern regions of the cave are at considerably higher levels.

The myriad of shapes found in the cavern have caused many of the galleries to bear highly descriptive names. Passageway of the Whale is a fine example of an enlarged crevice. The Wigwam Room has a formation called Chief Rain-in-the-Face. In the Banana Grove and Potato Patch is flowstone drapery that resembles bunches of bananas. Niagara Falls provides an example of cascading flowstone. One chamber, reminiscent of an undersea cave and thus known as Neptune's Grotto, has a vertical shaft, called a domepit or chimney, formed by water flowing from a sinkhole above, down to the water table. The Ghost Chamber, measuring 40 feet high, 50 feet wide and over 300 feet in length, is the largest known room in the cave. Paradise Lost, with its five great cones in a line

The towering, snow-clad heights of Mount Hood are reflected in the mirrorlike surface of Lost Lake. The tallest point in Oregon at 11,245 feet, the mountain stands in the center of the scenic Mount Hood Wilderness, an area of clear mountain lakes and deep conifer forests.

and three formations of flowstone drapery extending from floor to ceiling, is frequently called the most beautiful room in the cave.

7) ROGUE NATIONAL WILD AND SCENIC RIVER

Although it starts in the high Cascades of southern Oregon, the Rogue River does not complete its course until it cuts through the coastal range to the Pacific Ocean. Here, it varies from quiet smoothness to rushing, gurgling rapids, swirling over boulders and racing through narrow rock canyons. The Rogue River area from just west of Grant's Pass to eleven miles short of its ocean mouth was included as part of the original National Wild and Scenic River System in 1968.

Douglas fir is the dominant tree, and in some places along the river unbroken stands of fir reach several miles to the ridgetops. Side streams are lined with such flowering plants as azalea, rhododendron, Pacific dogwood and Oregon grape.

Deer, elk and bears are the most commonly seen large mammals. A large variety of birds make the river area their home, and salmon and steelhead trout use the Rogue as a "fish highway" to travel upstream and spawn.

Besides floating down the waters, an excellent way to see this primeval wilderness is to hike the moderately graded Rogue River Trail, which follows the river from Grave Creek to Ilahe, a distance of forty miles.

Washington

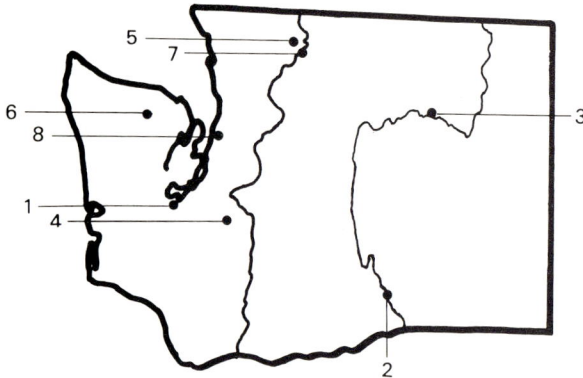

1) CAPITOL, Olympia

Standing on a trim green knoll amid the complex of state buildings, the imposing structure known as the Washington State Legislative Building looks out over the city of Olympia.

From the dome of the Legislative Building, Mount Rainier, Mount Baker, Mount Saint Helens and Mount Adams can be seen on a clear day. The snow-capped Olympic Mountains are visible from the lower portico. Rising 287 feet from the base, the dome is encircled by Corinthian-capped columns more than twenty feet high and is topped by a lantern thirty-one feet in diameter and forty-seven feet high. Modified Roman-Doric architecture and Wilkeson sandstone give strength and charm to the building. Doric columns enclose the building. The main entrance colonnade consists of eight Corinthian columns, each more than thirty feet high.

The rotunda is located in the center of the building, covered with an inner dome rising 185 feet above the floor level. Suspended from this dome is a bronze chandelier, beautifully carved between the open fretwork, twenty-five feet in length and weighing five tons.

2) COLUMBIA RIVER

Once thought to be the mythical River of the West whose headwaters would be just on the other side of the Continental Divide from the headwaters of the Missouri, the Columbia River is a powerful stream of water. It annually empties into the Pacific more than twice the volume of the Nile.

The birthplace of the Columbia is glacial-fed Lake Columbia on the western slopes of the Canadian Rockies in British Columbia. From there it flows northwestward for 180 miles through rugged, forested country where waters from snow and ice fields feed it before it turns southward to Washington. Here, the Columbia swings westward and then southward again along the Big Bend. Just below the point where it is joined by the Snake River, the Columbia makes a final turn westward. The John Day, Deschutes and Willamette rivers flow into it before it reaches the sea after a 1,214-mile journey. (See map, p. 292.)

Although overshadowed by the Mississippi in the number of acres drained, the Columbia is the most powerful river in the United States and, perhaps, the world. The rivers of America possess a total potential energy of 150 million horsepower. The Columbia accounts for one-third of this total or 50 million horsepower. It is the function of dams to transform this potential energy into real energy and provide water for transportation and irrigation.

Lewis and Clark's expedition was the first to explore the Columbia, reaching its mouth in 1805 and building a stockade, which they named Fort Clatsop after the Indian tribe living in the area. (See **Lewis and Clark Trail**, Missouri—4.) South of the river's estuary, it was the first American settlement west of the Continental Divide. Lewis and Clark had successfully followed the Columbia's system for over 4,000 miles to the Pacific; and even though it was not the vital link of a transcontinental waterway that President Jefferson had envisioned, the American claim to the Columbia River had been affirmed.

3) GRAND COULEE DAM

Grand Coulee Dam, begun in 1933 and finished in 1942, is one of the largest concrete dams in the world, measuring 550 feet high, 500 feet wide at the base, with a length of 4,173 feet. The Grand Coulee, sitting on a granite remnant of an old mountain, is a gravity dam, depending primarily on its tremendous weight to hold it in place. This monumental structure harnesses the Columbia River to irrigate the po-

The white, feathery caps of early summer beargrass are abundant on the slopes of 14,410-foot Mount Rainier. The soaring heights, once the site of spectacular volcanic activity, were not conquered until 1870.

tentially fertile but dry Columbia Basin lands and produces well over its rated capacity of 1,974,000 kilowatts of hydroelectric power. When the third giant powerhouse now under construction is completed, the Grand Coulee Dam will be the greatest producer of hydroelectricity in the world. The dam also controls flood waters, provides water for irrigation, and improves downstream navigational conditions.

Behind the dam a scenic reservoir, Franklin D. Roosevelt Lake, stretches 151 miles nearly to the Canadian border. Formed to supplement power production during the Columbia's low winter flow, its clear waters and attractive shoreline have become a recreational area.

4) MOUNT RAINIER NATIONAL PARK

Rainier stands like a silent sentinel over the Cascade Range, a color covering of blue and green and tones of gray, clad in the white cap of cold and age, a garment which belies its fiery parentage.

The mountain soars above the Cascade Mountains of west-central Washington, rising 14,410 feet above sea level, its size so ponderous it covers a quarter of the national park's almost 380 square miles.

Deep green stands of trees, alpine lakes, the diamond-tipped rush of icy water crashing over smooth boulders, delicate flowers hidden in shady glens, sprawling wildflower meadows—all are subdued by the spectacle of ice, laced like a child's finger painting across the faces of Mount Rainier. It has the greatest expanse of glaciers—about forty in number—found in the United States outside of Alaska.

Rainier, part of that once-spectacular circle of volcanic activity which rings the Pacific from the Americas to Asia, still retains reminders of its origins. At the summit are three peaks; Columbia Crest to the east is the highest, then two smaller but obvious volcanic craters. The summit craters on Columbia Crest retain small vents which whisper steam into the thin air, melting the snow which lies about.

For all its beauty, Rainier must have been a forbidding scene to the Indians, since none of the dozen nations that visited the region is

The Gap of the Columbia River provides a gateway for the most powerful river in the United States, producing one-third of the nation's rivers' total horsepower.

believed to have established permanent settlements. The mountain, an object of worship to some, was a hunting ground for others.

Captain George Vancouver of the Royal Navy is thought to be the first white man to see the mountain in 1792, while on a journey of exploration for the British government. He named it after his friend, Rear Admiral Rainier. The peak stood unconquered for years. The first attempt in 1857 failed, and it was not until 1870 that a climbing party reached the summit. Mount Rainier National Park was established in 1899.

Clouds and fog often obscure the mountain. There is, however, usually warm, clear weather from about July 1 to mid-September. In many years, Indian summer weather continues well into October, when autumn colors bring out still another kind of quality possessed by this magnificent mountain and surrounding land.

5) NORTH CASCADES NATIONAL PARK

Sometimes called the American Alps, the peaks, valleys and lakes of the Cascades, sculpted by huge glaciers, are considered by many outdoorsmen to be the most scenic mountain wilderness in the conterminous U.S.

The Cascade Range stretches from British Columbia to northern California, but the North Cascades in Washington contain more spectacular scenery than any other section.

The high mountains intercept some of the wettest prevailing Pacific Ocean winds. Their heavy precipitation has produced a region of hanging glaciers, ice-falls, ice caps, hanging valleys, waterfalls and alpine lakes nestled in glacial cirques. There are about 318 glaciers, most of which are stable or slightly retreating, and numerous snowfields within North Cascades National Park, established in 1968 and including the north and south units of the park and Ross Lake and Lake Chelan national recreation areas—over 1,000 square miles of mountain wilderness. The park also includes Mount Shuksan, possibly the most photogenic peak in America.

Over 130 alpine lakes dot the landscape and innumerable streams and creeks rush down the mountainsides, forming graceful waterfalls. Lake Chelan near Stehekin occupies a glacial trough exceeding 8,500 feet in depth, one of the deepest gorges on the continent. Fifty-five miles long and one to two miles wide, it has all the features of a Norwegian fjord.

Rain and an average of 516 inches of snow fall on the west side of the Cascades annually for a total of 110 inches of precipitation. On the drier, eastern slopes, however, the precipitation averages only thirty-four inches. The Cascade Range is thus responsible for the semiarid plains of eastern Washington.

Naturally there is extreme variation in plant communities between the moisture-laden west side and the dry east slopes. From western rain forests, the vegetation changes to subalpine conifers, verdant meadows and alpine tundra, and then to eastern pine forests and sunny, dry shrublands. All communities support a wide variety of wildlife.

Supreme Court Justice William O. Douglas, who has hiked this region for a long lifetime, has written, "The wilderness of the North Cascades is a national resource of the future, not merely a local commodity, and we need it all, as a nation." This park of towering, craggy ice mountains, flashing streams and waterfalls, blue alpine lakes, forested valleys, colorful flowers and abundant wildlife is one of the crowning gems of the National Park System.

6) OLYMPIC NATIONAL PARK

At Olympic National Park, in northwestern Washington, the civilization of man defers almost totally to the realm of the tree. Amid these 1,400 square miles of mountain and coastal wilderness, the tropic-like luxuriance of rain forests vies in beauty and splendor with the majestic eminence of an immense conifer empire on primeval coasts and on the flanks of soaring peaks.

Such is man's deferment to the almost preternatural infinitude of green—the hushed, eternal realm of the Sitka spruce, Western hemlock, Douglas fir and red cedar, among others—that park trail crews often cut narrow, wandering foot trails through the wilderness. In the forest depths abounds the natural civilization of wildlife and wildflowers—the animals, birds and both familiar and exotic blooms—which flourish in protective privacy.

Pacific Ocean tides break, ebb and flow against the park's western shoreline. Eastward, Puget Sound and Hood Canal form the added gift of isolation, separating, with saltwater barriers, the Olympic peninsula from the mainland of Washington.

Impressions of the rain forest are overwhelming. As one man said, "When one is inside the forest and the sun comes out, it is like being inside a giant emerald." Here, giant cone-bearing trees rise to nearly three hundred feet above the forest floor. Red alders and black cottonwoods edge the stream banks where cutthroat, rainbow and brook trout thrive and steelhead seek the secluded streams in winter.

The disappearance of the great rain forests, which once covered a coastal area from northern California to southern Alaska, highlights the preciousness of this magnificent "remnant" in Olympic National Park, established in 1938. It is almost as if a splendid tropical jungle lies at the foot of the more typically Northwestern snow-covered peaks which pierce the clouds at elevations of 3,000 to 8,000 feet. Majestic Mount Olympus, at 7,965 feet, dominates the uplands where more than sixty glaciers grow and recede, and these twenty-five square miles of ice hone down the mountain in the slow, eternal movement of time.

7) PACIFIC CREST NATIONAL SCENIC TRAIL

Eventually the Pacific Crest National Scenic Trail will extend from the Canadian border through the rugged mountains of Washington, Oregon and California to the Mexican border, covering 2,400 miles mainly along the crests of two major mountain ranges. The wilderness route extends through twenty-three national forests, seven national parks and a number of state parks and other managed areas. (See map, p. 292.)

The trail was begun in the early 1930's with the establishment of the Oregon Skyline Trail along the Cascades. In 1935 the Cascade Crest Trail was established in Washington. Other sections, among them the John Muir Trail, were being developed simultaneously in the Sierra Nevada Range of California. Since 1968 when the National Scenic Trails System Act went into effect, these individual trails have been components of Pacific Crest Trail, the first trail established under the act.

In Washington the trail follows the crest of the Cascade Range for 450 miles from Canada to the Columbia River. Portions of the trail were used by Indians and the early pioneers who first penetrated this wild land in the last century.

At the Columbia River near Bonneville Dam the Oregon section begins. Ascending from the Columbia River Gorge it cuts some 400 miles across the state along the ridges of the Cascades at altitudes from 4,000 to 7,100 feet.

The California segment begins in the southern Cascades and traverses some of the most impressive landscapes in the country at heights ranging up to 13,200 feet in the Sierra Nevadas. It terminates at the Mexican border. More than 500 miles of the proposed 1,600 miles of California trails have been completed and more are underway.

8) SPACE NEEDLE

Soaring 600 feet above the Seattle Center, a seventy-four-acre cultural and recreational park, the graceful Space Needle was the symbol of the 1962 Seattle World's Fair. The dramatic structure is shaped like a sheaf with three pairs of slender steel "legs" and a triangular core. Tapered above the waist, the steel legs flare out at the 500-foot level to support the top part.

A 300-seat glass-enclosed restaurant at the top imperceptibly revolves 360 degrees each hour, and diners can view the beautiful snowcapped Cascades, majestic Mount Rainier, lovely Puget Sound and the Olympic Mountains, and metropolitan Seattle.

Above the restaurant is an observation deck surmounted by a fifty-foot stainless steel beacon. The gas-lit beacon lights every fifteen minutes in a succession of colors.

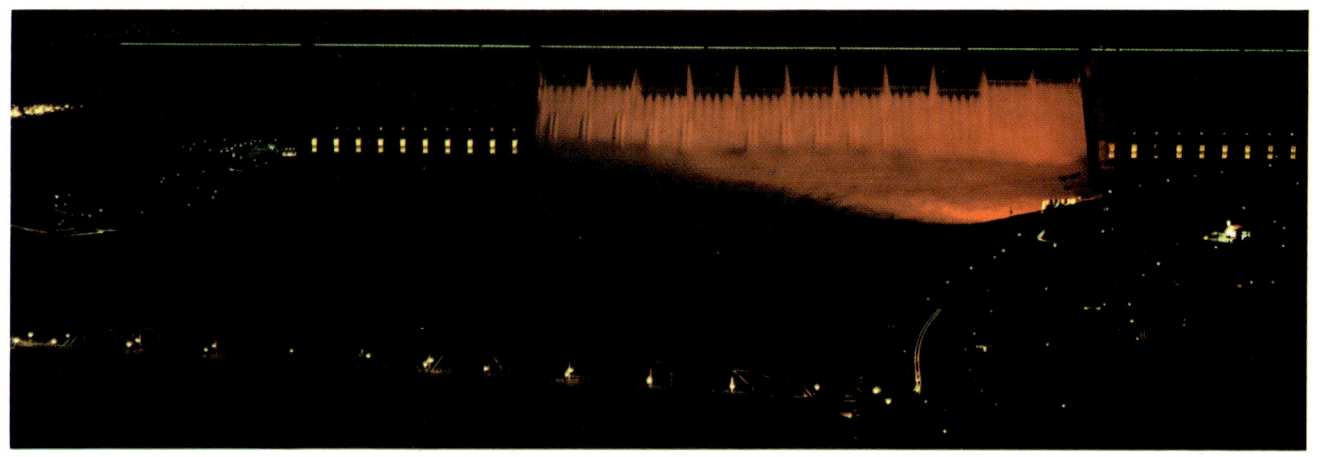

Spotlights illuminate the monumental Grand Coulee Dam (above). Built on a granite remnant of an old mountain, it harnesses the Columbia River for hydroelectricity. Mount Shuksan (below) in the North Cascades is one of the most photogenic peaks in the United States.

California   Hawaii
Nevada

CALIFORNIA, NEVADA and HAWAII

"Bring me men to match my mountains," proclaims an inscription on California's capitol building. There are more than matchless mountains here: forests of tremendous sequoias and redwoods, the impressive Cascade and Sierra Nevada mountains a few hours' ride from desert chaparral; a fruit and vegetable cornucopia to the south in Imperial Valley; cities incomparable in their vivacity. The inhabitants are convinced that they live in El Dorado, the earthly Utopia for which seventeenth-century Spaniards were searching the Pacific Coast from Mexico. The search led to the establishment of the many handsome missions and gradually to permanent settlement.

Nevada, settled by gold and silver miners, ranchers and farmers, is incredibly beautiful. Its chain after chain of north-south mountain ranges, a feature of the Great Basin (part of the Great American Desert), colorfully lead across the state to the High Sierras along the western border. The inviting Lake Mead Recreation Area is found in the south, and in the east, many exciting caves.

It is a myth that Nevada is barren. The creosote bush, sagebrush, sugar pine and juniper grow here in the warm, dry air, along with twenty-eight species of cacti, as well as wild peach, blue lupine, wild rose and red Indian paintbrush. Wildlife includes the great desert bighorn, the roadrunner, Gambel's quail, pinyon jay and an occasional cougar. Even in the supposedly sterile alkaline desert, salt bush, seep weed and iodine bush are not difficult to find.

More than 2,000 miles west of the Pacific Coast, two centuries ago, Englishman Captain Cook stumbled upon a beautiful archipelago. Now called Hawaii, these islands are an alluring tropical haven. Black lava beaches are fringed by coconut palms. Lush vegetation and brilliant blue water are washed daily in sparkling sunshine. Sky-scraping volcanoes still erupt. The strikingly cosmopolitan islands retain many traditions of the native *kamaainas* ("children of the soil") including the often-heard word of greeting, friendship and parting, *aloha.*

Opposite: *Cloud's Rest Peak rises majestically over the Merced River in Yosemite. Hundreds of miles of hiking trails wind through shaded valleys and open meadows, past giant sequoias and plunging waterfalls, and up rugged cliffs and mountainsides.*

California

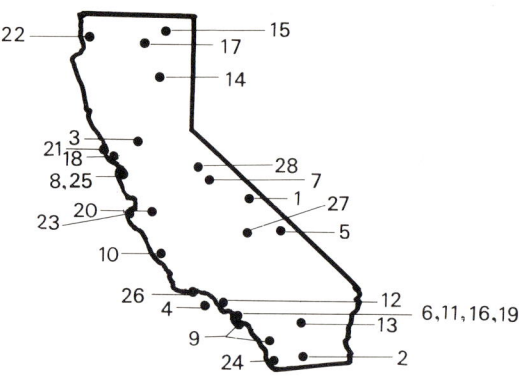

1) ANCIENT BRISTLECONE PINE FOREST

On the rocky slopes of the White Mountains east of Bishop, part of Inyo National Forest, is a venerable stand of twisted, weathered trees called *Pinus aristata*, bristlecone pines.

Seventeen of the trees, preserved driftwood-like on the 28,000 acres, are known to be more than 4,000 years old, far older than the more majestic sequoia redwoods. The bristlecones are short and squat, most no more than twenty-five feet high. These trees have grown slowly, sometimes less than an inch in one hundred years. Yet the cones from some of the oldest trees still produce fertile seeds.

In the otherwise barren, windswept region of the high peaks, these trees have been carved by the elements—fire, wind, sand and ice particles. Most of the trees' branches, winding around each other, may actually be dead. Bristlecones cling so fiercely to life that part of it will die so that the little minerals found here can sustain the living tissue.

Schulman Grove at 10,100 feet is the area where the oldest trees are found. A half-mile foot path from Schulman Grove leads to Pine Alpha, one of the very oldest at 4,300 years. This bristlecone measures four feet across with only a ten-inch strip of bark, and while only ten percent of its circumference has living tissue, it produces fertile seeds. Nearby is Methuselah, the oldest known living thing—4,600 years old.

2) ANZA-BORREGO DESERT STATE PARK

The Colorado Desert once presented a final barrier in the journey of Butterfield Overland Mail coaches along the southern postal route (initiated in 1858, it ran from Missouri to San Francisco via El Paso, Texas) to *Pueblo de Los Angeles*. Today this arid region south of Palm Springs lies within easy reach of the population centers of southern California and provides a

The mighty granite mountains of Kings Canyon National Park.

The stark contours of Zabriskie Point were formed by an ancient lake. The hopes and lives of many travelers and sourdough prospectors have been destroyed beneath the scorching sun of Death Valley.

pleasant retreat for many. Anza-Borrego Desert State Park, the nation's largest true state park, preserves some 488,087 acres of beautiful and varied desert landscape.

Here are clear skies and unspoiled vistas ranging from rugged 8,000-foot mountains and hot eroded badlands to pockets of tropical vegetation and valleys permeated with the colors of desert wildflowers in winter and spring. A sparse and delicate cover of plant life supports a surprising number of animals, among them the desert bighorn sheep.

Water is the key to the fluctuating and fragile charms of Anza-Borrego. Rainfall varies drastically from season to season and area to area within the park. The spiny-stemmed ocotillo cactus is a reliable rain gauge. When rain has recently fallen, the ocotillo sprouts green leaves. At other times as the moisture dries up in the following days, it sheds its leaves so as to keep from perspiring. At times an area of ocotillos can vary colors from green in the foreground, then brown, then green again on the horizon. Bright red flowers explode from its stems each spring.

3) CAPITOL, Sacramento

Set in a forty-acre park, magnificent with its wide stretches of green lawn and numerous native and exotic plants, the State Capitol is one of the most beautiful and substantial capitols in the United States.

The original structure, completed in 1874, is of Roman-Corinthian design, four stories in height and surmounted by a great dome of copper-covered wooden sheathing. At the apex of the dome is a "lantern" cupola with a small domed roof supported by twelve columns. The crowning ornament of the roof, which is covered with gold leaf, is a thirty-inch ball made of cop-

Space Sculpture *by Norbert Kricke stands in front of the Ahmanson Gallery which houses the fine permanent collection of the Los Angeles County Museum of Art.*

per and plated with gold coins, 237 feet above the ground.

In the center of the rotunda, and facing the main or west entrance of the building, is a statue of Columbus making his last appeal to Queen Isabella of Spain. The walls are decorated with murals depicting historically significant periods of the state.

4) CHANNEL ISLANDS NATIONAL MONUMENT

A brilliant expanse of treelike sunflowers on the springtime meadows and hills of Santa Barbara Island, thirty-eight miles west of San Pedro, serves as a golden beacon to ships at sea. This gleam is from the largest known stands of giant coreopsis in the world. Forty miles northwest, three tiny islets comprise Anacapa Island, a chain tipped on the eastern point by Arch Rock, a forty-foot-high wave sculpture, and isolated as a preserve where thousands of seabirds, rare seals and other marine creatures nest and breed. The barking of the sea lions and the occasional earth-shaking bellow of an angered northern elephant seal bull blend with the cry of gulls and crashing waves.

These two islands are part of the Channel Islands chain which stretches from due west of San Diego northward to Point Conception and carries the archeological threads of prehistory for early man, plants and wildlife. Santa Barbara and Anacapa, like the other six Channel Islands, are mountaintops which were surrounded by ocean after the western parts of the ancient Santa Monica Mountains were submerged about a half-million years ago. Almost completely girded by startling cliffs, some rising vertically more than 500 feet, these two islands, comprising almost 18,000 acres, were set aside as a national monument in 1938.

The islands have been called an "evolution factory" because disassociation from the mainland for upwards of half a million years has allowed subtle changes to occur in generations of both plants and animals. Taxonomists have described distinctive characteristics and recognize new species and subspecies known only to the islands.

5) DEATH VALLEY NATIONAL MONUMENT

Heat waves shimmer in the scorching sun as it beats down upon the flats and crags of this barren valley situated between severe mountain ridges rising from a distant desert. It is a heartless master, this valley, unchanged by the softening touch of time.

Indians who once dwelled in nearby mountains and attempted to harvest a little food from the sparse vegetation called the valley *tomesha,* meaning "red earth," because it yielded a fire-colored clay that warriors used to produce warpaint for their bodies. Sourdough mountain men claimed the Indian word meant "ground afire." But the name that finally attached itself unshakeably to this harsh valley is Death Valley.

The name is inappropriate, for this is a land of light, color and considerable beauty. Each shift of light, shadow or perspective casts a different spell because of the infinite variations of color, form and texture.

The old sourdough prospectors are gone. But the wry, sometimes grim, humor with which they named the ghost towns and other features that remain in the valley recalls the period when an ore strike would stampede thousands to raw frontier areas in a single day. Only the memory and a little rubble remains of such places as Panamint City and Greenwater.

But the prospectors' burros, now wild and abundant, have added to the animal life of the area. These hardy scruffy-looking creatures roam the mountains and flats, surviving and increasing on the sparse grass and bushes, searching out their own water.

Few of the men who loved and fought the elements in Death Valley became wealthy. But Walter Scott, later known as Death Valley Scotty, was able to combine his love for the valley and a comfortable living in his last thirty years. In 1924, Scott and another wealthy friend built a huge Moorish castle at about the 3,000-foot level in Grapevine Canyon. This monstrous spoof, patterned after European castles, had eighteen fireplaces and a 185-foot swimming pool. The place Scott called his "shack" remains as a monument to his eccentricities.

Seeing Scotty's castle perched halfway up a stark canyon is no more surprising than the sight of wildflowers blooming in the desert after an early spring rain. Golden primroses shine like newly minted coins. Some bright cactus flowers blossom for several days, while others burst into bloom, lose their petals, and drop their seeds in a single day. Because of the unique abilities of desert flowers to adapt, they bloom and seed only when conditions of moisture and temperature are correct. Sometimes, they bloom only at intervals of several years. As late as 1920, many believed Death Valley sustained no life, yet there are actually some 600 species of plants in the nearly 3,000 square miles of Death Valley National Monument. The plants grow from sea level and below near Badwater, at 282 feet below sea level the lowest point in the Western Hemisphere, to the sides of the 11,000-foot Telescope Peak in the Panamint Range.

6) DESCANSO GARDENS

In its English translation *descanso* means "where I rest." No truer name could be given to this picturesque garden set in a natural bowl among the verdant San Rafael Hills in Los Angeles County. Once the site of an unproductive nineteenth-century mining camp, the long abandoned, overgrown property was discovered in the early 1930's by Manchester Boddy, a wealthy Los Angeles publisher. Impressed by the potential beauty of the land, he spent many years constructing these exquisite gardens. The gardens were opened to the public in 1951 when the property was purchased from Boddy by the County of Los Angeles for $1.4 million.

Of the gardens' 165 acres, thirty are devoted to the shade-loving plants such as camellias, azaleas and rhododendron. In these acres, the hot California sun is filtered through the leafy latticework of ancient California oaks to create the green translucence of forest shade.

The History of the Rose Garden, unique in the annals of American gardening, has some 350 types of historic blooms in chronological order from pre-Christian times to the present. It includes examples of such important varieties as *Rosa damascena,* the Damask rose. With its beautiful carmine-red blooms, it is known as the rose of romance and poetry, and is thought to be a native of Syria imported into France and England by the Crusaders. Nearby is the Garden of

Opposite: *Impressive Mount Shasta, an extinct volcano, overlooks the white waters of the Sacramento River. The haunting mountain of snow-driven blizzards and steaming sulfur springs was once revered by the Indians as the sacred dwelling place of the Great Spirit.*

Modern Roses containing the finest All-American Rose selections.

7) DEVILS POSTPILE NATIONAL MONUMENT

The tremendous gray-brown mass of columnar stones, rising vertically from among the lush forests and brilliant wildflower meadows of the high Sierra Nevada between Yosemite and Kings Canyon national parks, resembles a pipe organ from some legendary age of giants. On a talus slope at the foot of this perpendicular facing are fragmented sections of polygonal columns strewn in a jumbled mass as though the giant, tiring of his prodigious toy, had smashed parts of it in a fit of anger.

Here, 7,600 feet above sea level, this convoluted mass is the remnant of a million-year-old volcanic eruption. Dominating the surrounding forests and meadows, the entire formation is approximately 900 feet long and as much as 200 feet high. The columns are from forty to sixty feet tall.

This geological oddity, one of the most remarkable of its kind in North America, is formed of dark, basaltic lava flows, and is included in a one-by-three-mile area set aside in 1911 as Devils Postpile National Monument.

Volcanic eruptions higher in the Sierra Nevada, to the east of the monument, caused the original flow more than 900,000 years ago. As the mass cooled, the lava cracked (something like drying mud) into forms with three to seven sides. These forms extend from the surface downward into the mass, and seen in cross section, they resemble columns.

8) GOLDEN GATE BRIDGE

San Francisco's Golden Gate, the mile-wide strait which forms the entrance to the city's magnificent harbor, takes its name from the panorama to be seen from ships leaving the port in the evening, sailing out towards the setting sun. The Golden Gate Bridge presents an inspiring gateway to this busy port. When completed in 1937, it boasted the longest single span in the world. The span of New York's Verrazano-Narrows Bridge (see **Bridges of New York City, New York—2**) now exceeds its 4,200 feet by sixty feet. Its total length is 8,981 feet. Reaching skyward 746 feet, the inspiring bridge towers are still the world's highest.

Construction of the Golden Gate Bridge offered a number of challenges. Not only is the water of San Francisco Bay and its entrance deep, but the foundation had to be anchored in bedrock to make it earthquake-proof. Bridge traffic is carried across the water at the awesome height of 265 feet, which allows the passage of the largest ocean-going vessels.

9) HALE OBSERVATORIES

The Mount Wilson Observatory north of Pasadena and the Palomar Observatory northeast of Escondido were both developed by noted astronomer George Ellery Hale. Some of the finest equipment for studying the far reaches of the Universe are located on these peaks.

Mount Wilson in the San Gabriel Mountain Range rises 5,713 feet. Its location offered accessibility and an unusually large number of cloudless days. The first telescope was installed on its summit in 1904. What is today the second largest reflecting telescope was installed in 1917. This one-hundred-inch telescope remained the world's most powerful for thirty years and permitted the first glimpse of millions of other galaxies moving away from us at incredible speeds.

The large Mount Wilson telescope proved the need for a still larger instrument. Since the populous Los Angeles area would interfere with a clear view of the sky from Mount Wilson, the monolithic fifteen-mile-long and five-mile-wide Palomar Mountain was given the honor. Palomar Observatory, at an elevation of 5,600 feet, is accommodated on a relatively wide expanse of level ground. Five domes are incorporated into the observatory structure, the largest of which houses the immense 200-inch telescope put into use in 1947.

10) HEARST-SAN SIMEON STATE HISTORIC PARK

High atop the 1,600-foot mountain that William Randolph Hearst called *La Cuesta Encantada* ("The Enchanted Hill"), the Hearst-San Simeon State Historic Park overlooks San Simeon and the Pacific Ocean. The magnificent 123 acres of gardens, terraces, pools and palatial guest houses against the backdrop of the

Once the final barrier to stagecoaches traveling the southern route of the Butterfield Overland Mail, the Anza-Borrego Desert is now the nation's largest true state park.

Santa Lucia Mountains form a perfect setting for the huge, 137-foot-high Hispano-Moorish mansion known as La Casa Grande.

Begun in 1919 and first occupied in 1925, La Casa Grande has one hundred rooms of exquisite furniture and antiques, Gothic and Renaissance tapestries, lovely wood carvings, immense French and Italian mantels, great carved ceilings, fine silver, Persian rugs, Roman mosaics and beautiful statuary, all in rooms specifically designed to frame them.

Hearst transformed this rocky promontory into a veritable wonderland. When the publishing magnate died in 1951 he still did not consider the home complete. Water for the gardens among the majestic native oaks had to be piped from natural springs five miles away, and the barren hilltop soil had to be replaced with rich topsoil, often specially mixed to meet the needs of exotic flora.

11) HUNTINGTON BOTANICAL GARDENS

In 1892 Henry E. Huntington, one of the nation's wealthiest businessmen, first saw the spectacular view from the San Marino Ranch—to the north across the majestic Sierra Madre Range to Mount Wilson and Mount Lowe, and on clear days, the lofty summit of Mount San Antonio; and to the south, rolling acres of sun-soaked orchards and the blue haze of the Whittier Hills. He was so taken with the site that ten years later he bought it for his California home. In 1904 he hired a young horticulturist, William Hertrich, to develop and landscape the 200-acre estate. Today few places in the United States contain as much of the rare and beautiful as Huntington Botanical Gardens in San Marino, near Pasadena.

The Desert Garden covers ten acres and is the largest assemblage of mature specimens of cactus and other succulents in the world. Many of the plants were brought here full grown from Mexico, Africa and South America.

Adjoining it is the beautiful Palm Garden with 200 specimens from all over the world, and nearby, the colorful and dramatic Lily Ponds. Past the ponds one enters an entirely different world of carefully arranged gardens whose spacious green lawns and pathways are shaded by tall trees. The scene is dominated by the coolly elegant white facades of the library and the Huntington Art Gallery (which includes Thomas Gainsborough's *The Blue Boy*).

12) JEAN PAUL GETTY MUSEUM

The J. Paul Getty Museum in Malibu was begun in 1954 as an extension of the home of Getty, one of the world's wealthiest men. In 1974 the collections were moved to an enlarged building on a ten-acre site adjacent to the Getty residence. This unique museum is a faithful reproduction of the ancient Villa dei Papyri, a large Roman seaside villa at Herculaneum near Pompeii. The villa housed a wealthy patrician family from the first century B.C. until it was buried by the eruption of Mount Vesuvius in A.D. 79. The lovely villa gardens have also been carefully reconstructed.

The museum contains three major groupings—Western European paintings, Greek and Roman antiquities, and French decorative arts. The Western European paintings include an extensive Italian Renaissance and Netherlandish Baroque collection, fourteenth-century Italian paintings and a number of noted French works by such artists as Georges de la Tour and François Boucher.

The Greek and Roman antiquities collection specializes in exquisite sculpture. Featured are the Landsdowne *Herakles*, the Cardinal Mazarin *Venus* and an Amazon head from the Temple of Hera in Argos. Other outstanding additions to the museum's impressive holdings are a collection of fourth-century stela and Greek-Roman portraiture.

Peace on Earth by Jacques Lipchitz is featured in front of the Dorothy Chandler Pavilion at the Los Angeles Center for the Performing Arts.

Featured in the Decorative Arts collection is French furniture from the late seventeenth and early eighteenth centuries, along with silver, ceramics, tapestries and Oriental carpets.

13) JOSHUA TREE NATIONAL MONUMENT

These trees that grow up, down and out in every possible direction are called Joshua trees, said to have been named by the Mormons who saw the crooked, asymmetrical branches as a symbol pointing to the promised land they were seeking, just as the Biblical Joshua pointed the way into the promised land of the Israelites.

In spite of its prickly appearance, the Joshua tree is not a cactus, but a kind of yucca *(Yucca brevifolia)*, a member of the greatly varied lily family, and is one of the most spectacular plants of the Southwestern deserts. Growing mostly in southern California, Joshua trees may attain heights of forty feet and during March and April bear creamy white blossoms in clusters eight to fourteen inches long at the ends of the branches.

One of the best stands of Joshua trees in the world is the focus of 558,184-acre Joshua Tree National Monument, established in 1936, one hundred miles east of Los Angeles. Located on the border of the California Mojave and Colorado deserts, the monument is rich in species of cacti and other desert plant life.

Joshua Tree National Monument has many oases that contrast sharply with the surrounding desert. The largest, Lost Palms near the southern boundary, contains more than one hundred native California fan palms.

The outstanding scenic point in the monument is Salton View at 5,185 feet. Here in one sweep is an impressive panorama of deserts, valleys and mountains.

14) LASSEN VOLCANIC NATIONAL PARK

Lassen Peak, once called San José by Spanish explorers, is the largest inactive plug dome volcano in the world. Located in northeastern California, it was once considered the only active volcano in the United States, having erupted as recently as 1915.

The 10,457-foot peak was the habitat and wonderment of four tribes of Indians long before Spaniard Luis Arguillo discovered it in 1821. This once fierce, lava-spewing mountain in the southern Cascade Range served as a territorial monument, dividing the regions of the Atsugewi, Maidu, Yana and Yahi, who foraged in its vicinity and lived in harmony around its slopes. The Indians must have known the fearsome majesty of volcanic heights now called Cinder Cone, Devils Kitchen and Bumpass Hell, sixteen acres of boiling sulfur springs which

Opposite: The 3,500-year-old General Sherman tree in Sequoia National Park is the largest living thing on earth. The giant sequoia towers 272 feet above the ground and has a base circumference of 101 feet.

may indicate that Lassen is really dormant rather than extinct.

Now, as then, coniferous forests, flower-blanketed mountain meadows, sun-glinting and tree-shadowy lakes and streams characterize the 165 square miles of Lassen Volcanic National Park, established in 1916.

15) LAVA BEDS NATIONAL MONUMENT

From a distance the land looks fairly level, dotted in places with symmetrical cinder cones and craters. But closer examination reveals that the "level" blackness is extremely rough, jagged and rocky, for this is where the earth vented its anger thousands of years ago. Established in 1925, 46,239-acre Lava Beds National Monument near the California-Oregon border is unique among volcanic areas because no large volcano existed here; all the formations were caused by many small holes in the earth's crust.

About 300 lava tubes, formed when the outside of a lava river cooled faster and hardened before the interior, have been found in the monument, and many more are believed to exist. Many of the cave roofs have collapsed in places to form serpentlike natural trenches 20 to 100 feet deep and 50 to 250 feet wide, with narrow bridges occasionally arching over them.

As the lava flow in the crusty tubes diminished, the cooling lava splashed against the ceilings, creating lava stalactites. Some of them were also formed when hot gases remelted pieces of the shell. Rivulets of lava on the walls of the tubes hardened into ribs.

Many of the caves are quite large and contain unusual formations. Catacombs Cave in the southern part of the monument is so named because of the niches in the walls, which resemble the Christian burial caves of ancient Rome.

About seventeen smooth black cinder cones rise from 100 to over 500 feet above the lava beds. Many small spatter cones can be seen on the beds, and some of them form deep holes resembling chimneys from the earth's hot core.

16) LOS ANGELES COUNTY MUSEUM OF ART

A beautifully functional three-structure complex in Hancock Park, completed in 1965, houses the Los Angeles County Museum of Art. The pavilionlike buildings rise on a central plaza set in a reflecting pool.

Permanent exhibits spanning the entire history of visual arts, enriching special exhibitions and a variety of concert and lecture programs attract visitors to this unique cultural center. All facets are easily accessible from the attractive plaza. The Ahmanson Gallery houses the superior permanent collection in galleries around a four-story atrium. Special displays are presented in the Frances and Armand Hammer Wing. Among the rare treasures in the museum are a gilded statuette of the Egyptian god Osiris, dating from 1500 B.C., and Rembrandt's luminous portrait of *Maarten Looten*.

The museum's distinguished history dates to 1913 and the inception of the Los Angeles County Museum of History, Science and Art. In 1961 the Art Division, having accumulated outstanding and comprehensive collections, became officially independent.

17) MOUNT SHASTA

An extinct volcano at the southern end of the Cascade Range in northern California, Mount Shasta was once regarded by Indians as the dwelling place of the Great Spirit. They called it *Weohow*, "the Stone House," and accounted the place so sacred, and the power of the mountain so terrifying, that they would not climb its slopes above timberline.

Hot springs and ice coexist on the 14,162-foot peak in Mount Shasta National Forest. While the two volcanoes, Shasta proper and younger Shastina, are considered extinct and five glaciers guard the peaks, boiling sulfur springs near the crest defy the frigid atmosphere.

John Muir, founder of the Sierra Club, spent a brutal night bivouacked near the crest of the mountain. Snow and ice driven by blizzard

(continued on p. 278)

Overleaf: San Francisco's famous fog rolls in around the Golden Gate Bridge, the gateway to the magnificent harbor. The bridge towers are the world's highest at 746 feet, and it is also the second longest single span at a length of 8,981 feet.

winds battered one side of his body, while the other side was burned by wind-whipped steam from the sulfur springs.

As stories of the mountain spread, its strange history and peculiar isolation from its neighbors began to exert an almost magnetic influence. When they arrived, many people believed, as had the Indians before them, that they had truly found a dwelling place of the Great Spirit.

From its low, wooded slopes where early settlers first cut tamarack and fir, up past the dwarf whitebark pine at timberline, to the thin ribbon of steam that rises from the high hot springs, it is a place to haunt the imagination.

18) MUIR WOODS NATIONAL MONUMENT

From the hillsides of San Francisco you can see it, touching the sky twenty miles to the north. This is Mount Tamalpais, the Fujiyama of the Golden Gate, and in a valley at its foot is Muir Woods, a virgin stand of coast redwoods.

To walk through a virgin forest is an experience in itself. Great varieties of plants do not clutter up the ground here; this is a forest that knows where it is going and has weeded out those plants which do not fit in with its natural scheme. Tall, stately redwoods stretch over 200 feet above the soft, spongy forest floor, covered with redwood needles and cones, green ferns and rainbow-colored mushrooms of all shapes and sizes. The growth is so thick that only single shafts of sunlight can reach through and brighten the forest floor.

Many years ago, this relatively small forest was threatened by commercial timber cutting and to save it, Congressman William Kent of Marin County and his wife purchased just over 500 acres of the woods outright and donated it to the Federal Government on condition that it be designated a national monument in honor of John Muir (1838-1914), the famed writer, naturalist and conservationist who roamed the Western wilderness for many years. Theodore Roosevelt proclaimed the woods a national monument in 1908.

Muir Woods is noted for its redwood peculiarities of burls and albino shoots. Burls are large, lumpy growths on the sides of the trees. They are not caused by disease but rather by some kind of genetic disorder. Rare albino shoots are caused by the lack of chlorophyll, the chemical responsible for a plant's green color.

19) MUSIC CENTER FOR THE PERFORMING ARTS

A magnificent cultural center contained in three architecturally beautiful and artistically functional theaters, the Music Center of Los Angeles County has presented the best in the performing arts. The buildings are situated about the striking Mall Plaza at the Civic Center, surrounding the reflecting fountain and evergreen trees. A dramatic bronze sculpture by Jacques Lipchitz, who is renowned for his achievements in Cubism, was dedicated in 1969, and prayerfully faces the Dorothy Chandler Pavilion as "a symbol of peace to the peoples of the world."

The 3,250-seat Chandler Pavilion was opened in 1964. The grand facility effectively serves such diverse art forms as symphony concerts, opera, musical comedy and dance. Amazing flexibility in acoustics, staging and lighting are achieved in this large theater. Ninety percent of the audience is within 105 feet of the stage.

Opened in 1967 were the 750-seat Mark Taper Forum and the 2,100-seat Ahmanson Theater. Chamber music, drama and other performances are given in the circular Mark Taper Forum which rises out of the center of a 175-square-foot reflecting pool. Musical comedy, drama and symphonies are presented in unusual intimacy on the bowed stage of the Ahmanson Theater.

20) PINNACLES NATIONAL MONUMENT

The shaded path called the Moses Spring Trail that skirts Bear Gulch is invitingly cool on a hot May afternoon. A soft breeze rustles the tree leaves slightly and twitterings of warblers and wrens are heard overhead. Suddenly, as the trail goes under a broad, overhanging rock face, a loud screech echoes from across the small gulch. Near the treetops is a large hawk, repeatedly swooping down on a boulder, as if protecting her nest from some unknown predator. The bushes near the boulder move and you are soon gazing at the prince of the wilderness, the rare cougar.

In 14,498-acre Pinnacles National Monument, as in many of the wilderness areas in the West, the cougar is present but rarely seen.

The monument, established in 1908, is a prime example of the type of habitat the cougar loves. Arid, rocky and rough, the Pinnacles region is located in the Gabilan Range a short distance east of the Monterey and Big Sur peninsulas. It was named for the spectacular spires, columns and jagged peaks, many over 1,000 feet high, which are found throughout the monument. Formed when water eroded the volcanic-laid rock many centuries ago, they con-

The rough sandstone walls and intriguing Moorish towers make the San Carlos Borromeo del Rio Carmelo Mission the romantic jewel of the California missions.

trast sharply with the smooth contours of the surrounding area.

Mantling these rugged slopes is a dense, brushy plant cover called chaparral. The stiff-branched, leathery-leaved shrubs have many of the characteristics of desert plants and often grow quite large, thus chaparral is sometimes called a pygmy forest. The chaparral at Pinnacles is considered the best of the entire National Park System.

21) POINT REYES NATIONAL SEASHORE

Wind, waves and fog are the three elements which dominate the coast of the Point Reyes peninsula north of San Francisco. The gusts, picking up force across thousands of miles of the Pacific Ocean, constantly lash this point of land jutting from the California shore. The winds push the water into powerful waves which batter the coast with spectacular force, creating tall, craggy palisades and smooth, sandy beaches. The monstrous breakers, whose wind-swept spray sometimes reaches a height of one hundred feet, are usually covered with a sheet of fog stretching up to fifty miles out to sea.

Inland on the peninsula both the terrain and the climate are different from the shore's. Sand dunes and rolling grassy hills enclose quiet lagoons, esteros and saltwater marshes; sharp ridges covered with evergreen forests surround freshwater lakes. The strong winds on the coast have become gentle breezes here, and due to the lack of fog, the temperatures are much higher.

Point Reyes' only contact with the mainland is directly over the San Andreas Fault between Bolinas Bay on the south and Tomales Bay on the north. The fault is responsible not only for the long, thin bays, but also for the striking Inverness Ridge which parallels the fault on the peninsula. For the last eighty million years the peninsula has been moving slowly north along this fault, with an average rate of movement of about two inches a year.

Because of this gradual movement, the rocks on the peninsula west of the fault are totally different in age and variety from those opposite, east of the fault on the mainland. Point Reyes is thus an isolated geological unit, and conservationists call it an "island in time."

Within 64,546-acre Point Reyes National Seashore, established in 1962, is Drakes Bay, the probable landing place of Sir Francis Drake in 1579.

22) REDWOOD NATIONAL PARK

Along the coast of northern California stand some of the oldest living things on earth. In this redwood country there are groves of giant trees which were growing during the Golden Age of ancient Greece.

In order to save as many of these groves as possible for posterity, conservationists in 1918

formed the Save-the-Redwoods League and began a campaign for a national park in northern California. Exactly fifty years later, in 1968—after a series of stormy battles—their goal was finally realized. Embracing 57,000 acres of redwoods, bluffs and beaches, Redwood National Park also includes thirty continuous miles of beautiful California coastline. Within the boundaries are three state parks—Jedediah Smith Redwoods, Del Norte Coast Redwoods and Prairie Creek Redwoods—created earlier through the efforts of the Redwoods League.

Once growing the entire length of the Pacific Coast from Oregon to the Big Sur peninsula, coast redwoods are now confined to relatively small areas, and some of these last groves are being logged as these words are written. There are also private landholdings within the park itself which will be logged unless they are added to the park.

The coast redwood's scientific name is *Sequoia sempervirens*. Sequoia comes from the Cherokee Indian, Sequoyah, who invented an Indian alphabet and taught his people to read and write; *sempervirens* means evergreen. Its close relative, the Sierra redwood *(Sequoia gigantea)*, found in the Sierra Nevada Mountains, is larger in girth and much older, but *sempervirens* is taller.

Notable individual features of the park include the tall trees area along Redwood creek where the world's tallest tree, 368 feet high, grows. Wildlife is plentiful; one of the last surviving Californian herds of Roosevelt elk can be seen in the open meadows or along the coast.

23) SAN CARLOS BORROMEO DEL RIO CARMELO MISSION

The rough-hewn beauty of San Carlos Borromeo del Rio Carmelo makes her the romantic jewel of the California chain of missions. Set in the lovely Carmel area of the Monterey Peninsula, this mission was Father Junipero Serra's favorite and his headquarters for the entire California chain of twenty-one missions stretching 700 miles, from San Diego to Sonoma, along *El Camino Real*, California's first road.

Only the second mission to be founded, in 1771, the present stone edifice was not dedicated until 1797, thirteen years after Father Serra's death. He is buried beneath the church.

This is a solidly built church, designed by a master craftsman and fashioned by devoted Indian pupils. Rough sandstone walls and intriguing unequal Moorish towers are highlighted by the striking star window "that seems to have been blown out of shape in some wintery wind, and all its lines hardened again in the sunshine of the long, long summer."

The mission was secularized in 1834 and for many years was left in neglect. Complete restoration was begun in the 1930's. Extensive research has been done into physical and written church records, resulting in an extremely authentic restoration.

24) SAN DIEGO ZOO

One of the largest zoos in the world, the one-hundred-acre San Diego Zoo maintains vast collections of wild animals including 5,000 specimens of 1,400 species. Among the extremely rare and vanishing species represented in attractive, natural settings are the beautiful okapi, a close relative of the giraffe, from the dense Congo rain forest; Przewalski's horse, the prototype of today's domesticated animals; the giant Galapagos tortoise; pigmy chimps; Indian rhinoceros; golden-shouldered parakeets and proboscis monkeys. The zoo possesses one of the largest free-flight birdcages, 90 feet wide, 80 feet high and 170 feet long.

The San Diego Wild Animal Park, thirty miles north of the city, was opened in 1972. On a 1,800-acre preserve, some 1,000 animals roam in large herds in environments very similar to their native lands. Sections containing animals found in regions of northern, southern and eastern Africa, the Asian swamps, the Asian highlands and the Australian plains are separated by concealed barriers.

A fifteen-acre Nairobi Village complex provides a dramatic introduction to the park. The world's largest walk-through aviary houses 300 birds, mainly from eastern Africa.

25) SAN FRANCISCO-OAKLAND BAY BRIDGE

The immense San Francisco-Oakland Bay Bridge stretches across the deep waters of San Francisco Bay connecting that city with Oakland and other East Bay communities. It was opened in 1936 at a cost of $77 million, the largest bridge project until 1956.

Spanning four and one-half miles of navigable water with a total length of eight and one-

Opposite: *The blooms of golden poppies beneath many-branched Joshua trees add brilliant spring color to the desert.*

quarter miles, this structure is really a number of bridges. Between San Francisco and Yerba Buena Island, two suspension bridges with main spans of 2,310 feet share a central anchorage and form the only double suspension bridge in the world. A double-deck tunnel through part of the island joins this section with another, less impressive bridge connecting Oakland.

26) SANTA BÁRBARA MISSION

Known as the "Queen of the Missions," Mission Santa Bárbara sits regally above the beautiful city to which it gave its name. The Santa Ynez Mountains are a fitting backdrop for the graceful and revered church.

This historic mission was founded in 1786 and was at first housed in humble structures. The present stone edifice, an adaptation of a Greek temple design, was dedicated in 1820 and the second of the twin towers, rising to eighty-seven feet, was completed in 1833. Splayed Moorish windows adorn the mission walls.

Mission Santa Bárbara was greatly damaged by a severe earthquake in 1925, with most harm done to the lovely towers and facade. The church walls and roofs were reinforced, as were the mission living quarters, and the interior was entirely restored. New and colorful reredos and new altars were based on the originals.

In front of the mission are a fine Moorish fountain dating from 1808 and a long trough in which Indian women once washed clothes.

27) SEQUOIA AND KINGS CANYON NATIONAL PARKS

The tree is king here, peering down over a majestic domain of gray granite mountains, deep forests and valleys making a harsh but welcoming slash in the landscape. It stands, holding silent court over a seemingly untouched panorama, beginning beyond one horizon and going past the other.

This tree, the sequoia, is the largest living thing in the world, gently elbowing aside white firs and sugar pines, its cinnamon-red bark and pointed needles unchanged from the time when frightening creatures rumbled the earth with their ponderous tread. Their relatives, the coast redwoods, are not as large but are taller. (See **Redwood National Park**, California—22.)

One can count nearly 4,000 years since some of them were born, and science believes none have died simply because of old age. They usually find their life-giving roots exposed by slow erosion, perhaps nature's way to return organic material to the soil. Then they topple and die with a crash, to lie fallen beside other warriors fighting the long battle against time in Sequoia and Kings Canyon national parks, which protect a total of over 1,300 square miles of the southern Sierra Nevada.

Save for the efforts of a few, these mighty trees might have disappeared to the logger. Sequoia National Park was established in 1890 to preserve the giant trees, and adjacent Kings Canyon National Park was established in 1940.

The most famous of the trees is in Sequoia park's Grant Forest, the General Sherman tree, 3,500 years old and the largest of all living things on earth. This tree towers more than 272 feet above the ground and measures more than 35 feet across the base. Because it is hard to imagine such a tree, perhaps this helps: The trunk alone weighs approximately 1,450 tons and has 50,010 cubic feet of wood, enough to build about forty homes. The General Grant Tree nearby in Kings Canyon is only five feet shorter and contains only a bit less wood.

Smaller than the sequoias, but with much value of their own, are the flora and fauna of the parks. The floor of the forest is covered with dogwood, colorful lupines and the red-flowered snow plant. Bears, deer, bighorn sheep, bobcats and smaller animals roam at will.

Beyond the Giant Forest, named by that great naturalist, John Muir, is the Sierra Nevada's high country, a vast, tilted block in the earth where snowcapped peaks—crowned by 14,495-foot Mount Whitney, the highest mountain in the conterminous United States—rise to more than 14,000 feet to cast giant shadows on glacial valleys and lake basins.

28) YOSEMITE NATIONAL PARK

The dawn sun lies poised over Yosemite National Park, then the murmuring thunder of Bridalveil Creek seems to bring forth the hushed melody of the early morning wind blowing through spires of the groves of sequoias and evergreens in this area of nearly 1,200 square miles in the High Sierra.

Congress saw its great beauty in 1864, and granted it to the State of California. In 1890 the national park was created around this Yosemite Grant. It dictated the concept which has since served as the basis for all national parks.

It was fitting that this splendid region be such a first. There are hundreds of miles of trails leading from the valley through the coolness and fragrance of deep woods, across the sun-splashed meadows to high mountain lakes teeming with fish growing fat and ferocious in their chill depths.

Spring blossoms delicately frame Yosemite Falls, one of many large waterfalls in Yosemite Park, as it cascades 2,425 feet to the valley below.

But let us start at the valley, seven square miles of cragginess that becomes beautiful at once to the beholder. Mountainsides and cliffs overhang the canyon where the Merced River threads. A few miles later, the roadway widens to a flower-flecked meadow, dominated by El Capitan, a flawless granite monolith rising more than 3,600 feet toward the sky. Nearly as imposing are the Cathedral Spires, Sentinel Rock and the Three Brothers, named for the sons of Chief Tenaya whose land this once was.

Water shaped Yosemite, and still is slowly wearing away the rock as it must, seeking the lower levels and carrying with it bits of stone and vegetable matter, endlessly creating. The Upper Yosemite Fall drops 1,430 feet, and the Lower Yosemite Fall a bit less than a fourth of that. Water cascades with a roar over the top of the cliffs for a total drop of 2,425 feet.

Not all is the sound and fury of nature. There is solitude in Yosemite to be found in her stands of sequoias, one, the Grizzly Giant, believed to have been born from seed more than 3,000 years ago. This magnificent tree is 209 feet tall and more than 34 feet in diameter across the base. Growing silently, contributing to its grandeur, are the park's incense-filled forests of pine, fir, cedar and oak, providing habitat for band-tailed pigeons, pygmy owls, chipmunks and squirrels.

Deer and bear pause to feed here, then move on to the high country, a land of lakes and meadows, capped by high peaks casting great dark shadows on the rainbow of wildflowers below. Tuolumne Meadows at 8,600 feet is the largest subalpine meadow in the High Sierra. Though it can be best enjoyed on foot, there are auto roads leading to jewellike Tenaya Lake and Tioga Pass, between granite boulders polished to a shine by glaciers and past high domes of the same stone. Another road leads from the valley thirty miles to Glacier Point, giving a panoramic view of the High Sierra and Yosemite Valley 3,300 feet below.

Deep-colored cacti and other succulents are artistically arranged in the Plantation Garden on the "Garden Island" of Kauai. Because of the tropical environment, cacti develop rich shades of green in comparison to similar duller-colored plants on the mainland.

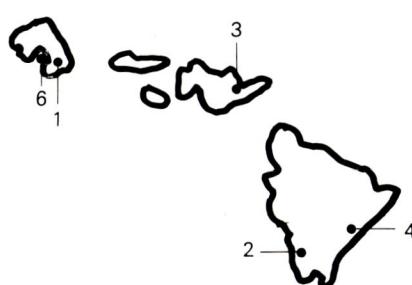

Hawaii

1) CAPITOL, Honolulu

One of the initial acts of the legislature after Hawaii achieved statehood in 1959 was to appropriate funds for the design of a new Capitol to be erected opposite Iolani Palace, the old Capitol and the only royal residence in the United States. The Palace was designated a national historic site in 1962.

The new Capitol, dedicated in 1969, is highly functional in design and manifests symbolism of both the cultural and the natural aspects of Hawaii. From a distance, it suggests an ancient Hawaiian house. At close range, it appears to rise out of a lovely moat—symbolic of the Pacific Ocean—on tall columns which resemble royal Hawaiian palm trees. The exterior walls of the legislative chambers slope upward in the manner of a volcanic cone. The impression of the volcano, so characteristic of the origin and geology of Hawaii, is further enhanced by the upward view from the lobby. Here, one can look up at the sky through the huge conical opening, which exposes the lobby to the natural elements of Hawaii's tropical climate.

2) CITY OF REFUGE NATIONAL HISTORICAL PARK

More properly called the Place of Refuge at Honaunau, the City of Refuge is located on the big island of Hawaii on a six-acre ancient lava shelf which dips into the ocean. Forming roughly a square, the area is bounded by the Pacific on the north, south and west and by the ten-foot-high Great Wall, built about 1550, on the east. The true beginnings of the City of Refuge are lost in antiquity.

Until approximately 1819, defeated warriors, noncombatants in a war, and those who had broken a Kapu, a firm system of rules, could find refuge and protection if they could reach Honaunau ahead of their pursuers. Such refuges were established by ruling kings and watched over by the priests of an adjoining temple, whose gods protected the refuge. The refuge at Honaunau was historically the most important and the only one to have survived to modern times.

Besides the Great Wall, park visitors today may view the ruins of three temples and the restored royal mausoleum, which once housed the bones of relatives and ancestors of King Kainehameha the Great, who unified the islands into a single kingdom about 1800.

3) HALEAKALA NATIONAL PARK

To Polynesians, Haleakala means "House of the Sun," and it was once that, belching forth angry torrents of fire and lava, making night as day, until it subsided in placid surrender to time, leaving as a heritage one of the showplaces of the National Park System so that all might understand the forces of geological evolution. Located on Maui Island, the park, established in 1916, covers 27,283 acres.

On a clear day—and there are many in the Pacific—the summit affords a spectacular view of the neighboring islands of Hawaii, Lanai, Molokai and occasionally Oahu. Turn the eyes a bit downward, and unfolding beyond the crater's rim is a vast hole in the earth, gouged by water erosion, leaving acres of symmetrical cinder cones painted with primeval colors huddled inside the great formations of cliffs whose tops are hidden in the moist clouds, lending even more vastness to the gigantic, dormant Haleakala Crater seven and a half miles long and two and a half miles wide.

Haleakala's history is shrouded in the still-growing science of geology, yet many scientists agree that this "House of the Sun" was once more than 11,000 feet high, a summit about 1,000 feet greater than the one we now see. She once slowed her volcanic eruptions, and water came to carve two deep valleys on opposite sides of the mountain which eventually met. Then, the fury of the subterranean eruptions began anew and lava flows cascaded into the valleys atop one another after their first outpourings reached the sea. The level of the valleys seen today is the height of the cooled, molten rock, save for a bit of topsoil created by time alone.

Haleakala is quiet now, for no eruptions have occurred here for centuries. But there is the appeal of something new, raw, a just-formed land, and in geological terms it is that. Lava is sterile stuff, for nothing can survive its heat. Generations of plant life have rained down upon the cooled rock until, in places here and there, a plant has been able to gain a foothold. That is fortunate, for they will flourish, then die, deepening the topsoil by a fraction of a millimeter so that other plants might follow eventually. Life grows slowly at Haleakala National Park, for this is still a new land.

4) HAWAII VOLCANOES NATIONAL PARK

Here is a link with the past; geological history in the making as the Hawaiian Islands continue to emerge from the sea as they first did five to ten million years ago. Hawaii Island, largest of the chain, is the site of Mauna Loa, a 13,680-foot summit where Hawaii Volcanoes National Park, established in 1916, begins, stretching southeast to the seacoast and covering 220,345 acres, a place of contrasts where umbrella-shaped palms and dense jungles of ferns lie near gaunt mountains and beside lava deserts.

From the eleven-mile Crater Rim Drive around the summit caldera of Kilauea Volcano, Kilauea Crater, the visitor can see the destruction wrought by the forces of nature—cones of cinder, bluffs alive with steam and recent flows of lava. One of the most impressive sections is the "devastated area," which was denuded of vegetation during the 1959 eruption of Kilauea Iki. The ancient Hawaiians made a deity of Pele, the goddess of volcanoes, whom they believed lived in Halemaumau, Kilauea's most active vent. It was her wrath, they said, which caused the eruptions, destroying villages and tilled lands.

From the summit caldera, the visitor passes along the Chain of Craters, part of the east rift of the volcano where the road winds past deep craters in which eruptions have recently taken place. In March 1965, a fissure on the side of Makaopuhi Crater poured forth a lake of lava almost 300 feet deep. During the 1959 eruption of Kilauea Iki, lava spewed more than 1,900 feet high, filling a crater with molten lava to a depth of about 400 feet. Until recently, the most spectacular of all volcanoes here was Mauna Loa, but it has not erupted since 1950.

From Makaopuhi Crater near the end of the chain, the road passes along the southeast coast, past ancient villages and sites of religious temples. The mighty mountains of fire must

Ferocious temple images guarded the City of Refuge on the Big Island of Hawaii and were a welcome sight to defeated warriors or lawbreakers who sought sanctuary with the temple priests.

have prompted these peoples to great religious fervor. At Wahaula Heiau near the eastern edge of the park is one of the island's best-known places of worship where it is reputed that one of the last human sacrifices was performed under the old religion.

5) PLANTATION GARDEN (MOIR'S)

Along the southern shore of the "Garden Island" of Kauai, near Poipu, is Plantation Garden, formerly Moir's Gardens, one of the most beautiful places in this most scenic part of the world. In 1968 the Moirs retired and leased the estate to Plantation Gardens, Inc. Hawaiian *tutus* (grandmothers) conduct the tours and have a wealth of legends and stories to tell about Kauai and Moir's estate.

Much of the area is devoted to fine collections of cacti and other succulents. There are hardy desert plants, set among different levels of lichen-covered volcanic rock, and colorful water lilies in the cascading pools. One of the most interesting of the cacti is the *Cereus*, which often reaches heights of thirty feet. All of the cacti in this tropical environment develop rich shades of green as compared to the dull color of many similar plants found on the mainland.

In addition to the many kinds of cacti, Plantation Garden has the largest collection of "wonder healing" African aloes in the world. These colorful plants are especially desirable for

Exotic blossoms that bloom with an intensity of color rarely seen on the mainland abound in countless varieties in the paradise which is the Hawaiian Islands.

garden decoration since their candle-shaped spikes bloom all winter. From the time of the early Greeks they have been grown for the healing properties of the liquid in their thick leaves. At Plantation Garden the brilliant red, yellow and orange of blooming aloes contrast beautifully with the darker red of volcanic rock and the greens of surrounding succulents.

Adjacent to the cactus and succulent garden is a tropical garden, built around a series of inviting water-lily pools. The exquisite bloom of the many orchids blends with the color of birds-of-paradise, anthuriums, bromeliads, ferns, palm trees and the fragrant frangipani.

6) U.S.S. ARIZONA MEMORIAL

On Sunday morning, December 7, 1941, "a day that will live in infamy," 2,341 Americans lost their lives in the Japanese attack on Pearl Harbor, including more than 1,100 of the officers and men of the battleship U.S.S. *Arizona*. Within one minute of the onset of the attack the *Arizona* was shattered and in flames. There were only 289 survivors and more than 1,000 still remain trapped inside the ship, which quickly settled to the bottom. The small part of the still-commissioned ship that remains above the water continues to fly the American flag as a symbol of national survival.

The U.S.S. *Arizona* Memorial, dedicated in 1962, now spans the sunken hull. The 184-foot enclosed bridge touches no part of the ship. According to the memorial architect, the structure which "sags in the center but stands strong and vigorous at the ends, expresses initial defeat and ultimate victory." Included in the memorial are a museum housing mementos of the ship, an assembly room and a shrine room where the names of those lost on the *Arizona* are engraved on a large marble wall.

Monumental Hoover Dam (see Arizona-7) backs up the Colorado River in the Black Canyon between Arizona and Nevada to form Lake Mead. As well as controlling floods and storing water for irrigation, the dam provides hydroelectric power for much of the Southwest.

Nevada

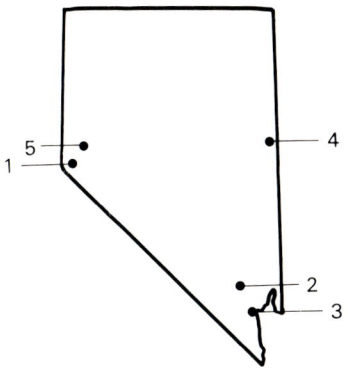

1) CAPITOL, Carson City

The cornerstone of the Nevada State Capitol in Carson City was laid in 1870. Construction moved rapidly, and that same year the Capitol building was ready for the fourth session of the State Legislature.

Despite speedy construction, Nevada had a handsome and imposing building—a two-story structure in the form of a Grecian cross featuring Corinthian, Ionic and Doric styles. The interior was both lavish and lasting. Windowpanes of twenty-six-ounce French crystal, double-arched sashes, vaulted columns and chandeliers hanging from ornate, scrolled centerpieces were just some of the touches. Alaska marble was shipped to California in twenty-ton blocks where it was cut, polished and forwarded to Carson City to be inlaid into the wainscoting, arches and floors of the building.

Since those frontier days, the Statehouse has been expanded. The first addition came in 1905 when a state library, octagonal in shape, was built as an annex to the east side.

2) DESERT NATIONAL WILDLIFE RANGE

The people trying their luck at the gaming tables in Las Vegas are probably little aware that less than ten miles north is a spectacular, vast desert wilderness used primarily for the preservation of one of nature's most intriguing animals, the desert bighorn sheep. This stocky animal's magnificent curling horns had made him one of the West's prize game animals, and his numbers had diminished significantly.

The Desert National Wildlife Range, established in 1936 and containing over a million and a half acres, is one of four ranges whose objective is to protect these sheep in their natural environment. Once numbering about 300, the sheep in the range have now increased to 1,000 head through the management programs of the U.S. Fish and Wildlife Service.

The refuge has a number of mountain ranges, notably the Sheep Range whose highest crest, Hayford Peak, is 9,912 feet high. Vegetation varies with elevation, with saltbrush, creosote bush and mesquite in the lower valleys; yucca on the flats; and forests of juniper, pinyon pine, mountain mahogany, ponderosa pine and fir in the mountains. Some bristlecone and limber pines are found at higher elevations.

The range is also the habitat of a number of other animals, such as mule deer, coyotes, bobcats, foxes, ground squirrels and kangaroo rats.

Because this area is maintained to preserve the habitat of these animals, roads and trails on the range are limited. The best way to see the country and the bighorn is to hike or ride horseback along mountain ridges, up canyons, over dry lakes and through drifting sands.

3) HOOVER DAM AND LAKE MEAD NATIONAL RECREATION AREA

See Arizona—7.

4) LEHMAN CAVES NATIONAL MONUMENT

Lehman Caves National Monument is in the foothills on the eastern slope of towering Wheeler Peak (13,063 feet), the highest point in Nevada.

This quartzite peak was originally sandstone and its eastern slopes are covered with layers of limestone. The heat from a granite intrusion changed some of the limestone to its metamorphic state, marble. Lehman Caves was formed from this marble.

Wherever one goes in these caverns he will see in the myriad of unusual formations shapes resembling animals, tom-toms and figurines, even a "cypress swamp." These outlines of shapes, color-splashed ceilings and enveloping shadows stimulate the imagination as only treasure caves such as Lehman can do.

Virginia City appears a sleepy Western town, but in its heyday "the Queen of the Comstock" was the West's liveliest and most prosperous mining metropolis.

5) VIRGINIA CITY

"The Queen of the Comstock," Virginia City was the West's mining metropolis in its heyday. One of the richest deposits of gold and silver, the Comstock Lode, was discovered here in 1859. By the 1870's the town had a population of 30,000 with four banks, six churches, 110 saloons and the only elevator between San Francisco and Chicago. Great mansions, churches, opera houses, hotels and stores of all kinds were built by people who could afford the best of everything. Here also was Nevada's first newspaper, the *Territorial Enterprise*, which employed both Mark Twain and Western author Bret Harte.

A great fire destroyed nearly three-quarters of the city in 1875, but it was rebuilt bigger and better than ever. Its citizens were at the height of their prosperity. Another lode, the "Big Bonanza," had been discovered in 1873 and the source of their wealth was seemingly endless.

By the turn of the century, however, Virginia City's days of glory were in the past. The ore produced by the mines was no longer so rich and much of the money had been siphoned off by the growing city of San Francisco.

Yet Virginia City never really died. A campaign based on the slogan, "Save Virginia City—She Saved the Union," has supported the restoration of the historic community to its 1870 appearance. The slogan is based on the contribution of Virginia City's silver to bolster the credit and buying power of the Union Army during the Civil War.

Nearly all of Virginia City's business buildings and many of its residences date from the era of the "Big Bonanza." Once again the boardwalks of Virginia City lead past picturesque saloons and interesting shops. Old churches and cemeteries recreate the grand Victorian age of Western wealth and splendor.

The Castle, built in 1868 and furnished with valuable period pieces, reflects the opulence of the mining days, as do other restored and unrestored mansions. Among the beautiful churches is St. Mary's in the Mountains, a Gothic structure dating from 1876. Piper's Opera House once attracted such stars as Sarah Bernhardt and Edwin Booth. Consolidated Virginia Mine was one of twenty-three or more mines along the Comstock Lode.

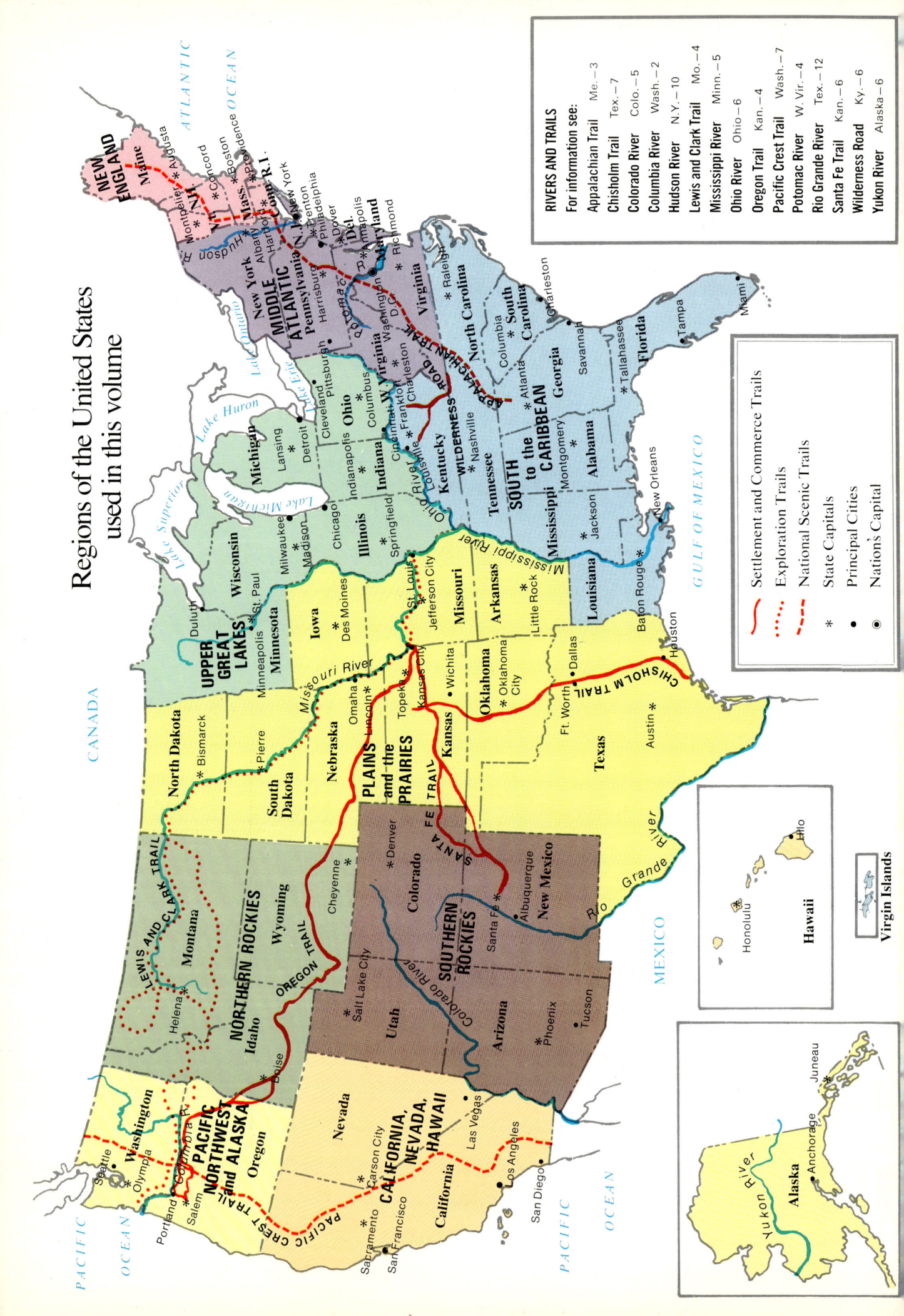

Lost Arrow, a rocky pinnacle on the north wall of Yosemite Valley, gives climbers a dramatic view of cabins below. (See Yosemite National Park, California—28.)

INDEX

INDEX

Italic numbers refer to illustrations; **bold** numbers refer to major information

Abbreviations: N.C.—National Cemetery; N.F.—National Forest; N.H.P.—National Historical Park; N.H.S.—National Historic Site; N.L.—National Lakeshore; N.M.—National Monument; N.Mem.—National Memorial; N.Mem.P.—National Memorial Park; N.M.P.—National Military Park; N.P.—National Park; N.R.A.—National Recreation Area; N.S.R.—National Scenic Riverways; N.W.R.—National Wildlife Refuge; N.W.Range—National Wildlife Range; S.F.—State Forest; S.P.—State Park.

Adams, John, 24, 44, 65
  Old House, **18**, *19*
Alamo, *180*, **180**
Allen, Ethan, 32, 54
Ancient Bristlecone Pine Forest, **266**
Antiques
  Colonial Williamsburg, 69
  1850 House, New Orleans, 94
  Essex Institute, **20**
  Henry Ford Museum, **125**
  Museum of the Confederacy, 13
  Museum of History and Technology, 42
Architecture
  Annunciation Greek Orthodox Church, **142**, *148*
  Auditorium Theatre, *116*, **116**
  Boston Avenue United Methodist Church, **172**
  Columbus, **121-122**
  First Christian Church, **120**
  First Unitarian Society Church, **147**
  Gateway Arch, **162**
  Mission San Xavier del Bac, **222**
  Monticello, **73**
  North Christian Church, **122**, *123*
  Old Ship Church, **24**, *24*
  Sacred Heart Cathedral, **160-161**
  St. John the Baptist, Abbey and University Church of, **130**
Art (see also Museums)
  Art Institute of Chicago, *114*, **114-115**
  Biltmore House, **99**
  Boehm Gallery, **80**
  Cloisters, The, **53**
  Corcoran Gallery of Art, **38**
  Des Moines Art Center, **156**, *157*
  Freer Gallery of Art, 42
  National Collection of Fine Arts, 42
  National Gallery of Art, **42**, *43*
  National Portrait Gallery, 42
  Thomas Gilcrease Institute of American History and Art, **172**, *173*
  Walker Art Center, 134, *136*, **136**
  Whitney Gallery of Western Art, **206-207**
  Yale University Art Gallery, **13**
Astrodome, *181*, **181-182**
Authors' Homes
  Emily Dickinson House, **19-20**
  Ralph Waldo Emerson (Old Manse), **23**
  Nathaniel Hawthorne (Old Manse), **23**
  Washington Irving (Sunnyside), **57**
  Henry Wadsworth Longfellow House, **22**, *21-22*
  Henry David Thoreau retreat (Walden Pond), **26**
  Mark Twain Home, **163-164**
  Mark Twain House, **10**, *12*
  Thomas Wolfe House, **101**

Battlefields (see individual wars and Indians, North American)
Beehive House, **238**, *239*
Big Thicket, **182**
Boone, Daniel, 91, 93
Borglum, Gutzon, 90, 177
Boscobel, **56-57**
Boundary Waters Canoe Area, **130**
Bridges
  Brooklyn, **50**
  Chesapeake Bay Bridge-Tunnel, **67-68**
  Covered
    Cornish-Windsor, **27**, *29*, *28*
    Parke County, Indiana, 123
    Philippi, **76**
    Shelburne, 33
  George Washington, **50-51**
  Golden Gate, **276**
  Mackinac, **125**, *127*
  St. Louis (Eads), **164-165**
  San Francisco-Oakland Bay, **281-282**
  Verrazano-Narrows, *51*, **51-52**, 270
Brumidi, Constantino, 44
Buffalo (bison), 170, *171*, 172, 174, 175, 178, 201, 202, *203*

Calhoun, John C., 102
  house, **104-105**
Camino Real, El (California), 281
Camino Real, El (New Mexico), 234
Carson, Kit, 161
  Home, **232**, *234*, *233*
Catlin, George, 169, 172, 208
Caves
  Beauty, 154
  Carlsbad Caverns N.P., **232**, *235*

Jewel Cave N.M., **176**
Lava Beds N.M., **275**
Lehman Caves N.M., **289**
Longhorn Cavern S.P., **187**
Mammoth Cave N.P., **92**
Old Cave, Hannibal, 164
Oregon Caves N.M., **256-257**
Ozark N.S.R., 164
Timpanogos Cave N.M., **244**
Wind Cave N.P., **178**
Cedar Hill, 39
Champlain, Samuel de, 14, 33
Charleston Historic District, **102-103**
Chimney Rock, 160
Church, Frederick Edwin, house (Olana), **56**, *56*
Churches (see also Missions)
  Air Force Academy Chapel, **231**, *231*
  Annunciation Greek Orthodox, **142**, *148*
  Boston Avenue United Methodist, **172**
  Central Lutheran, **254**
  Central Moravian Church and Old Moravian Chapel, **63**
  Christ (Alexandria), **68**
  Christ (Philadelphia), **63-64**
  Episcopal (Jamestown), 72
  First Christian, **120**
  First Church of Christ, **10**
  First Scots Presbyterian, 102
  First Unitarian Society, **147**
  French Huguenot, 102
  "Little Brown Church in the Vale" (First Congregational), **157**
  North Christian, **122**, *123*
  Old North, 10, **24**, *23-24*
  Old Ship, **24**, *24*
  Roofless, *122*, *123*
  Sacred Heart Cathedral, **160-161**
  St. Augustine Cathedral, **84**
  St. John the Baptist, Abbey and University Church of, **130**
  St. John the Divine, Cathedral of, **52**
  St. Louis Cathedral, 94
  St. Mary's in the Mountains, **290**
  St. Michael's Episcopal, 102
  St. Patrick's Cathedral, **61**
  St. Paul's Episcopal, **222**
  Trinity, **62**
Churchill Downs Racetrack, *91*, **91-92**
Circus
  Circus World Museum, *144*, **144**, 146
  Ringling Museums, **86-87**
City Parks
  Central Park, *51*, **52-53**
  Jackson Square, 94
Civil War
  Alabama Capitol, 81
  Appomattox Court House N.H.P., **66**
  Chickamauga & Chattanooga N.M.P., *106*, 108
  Cumberland Gap N.H.P., **93**
  Fort Massachusetts, 85
  Fort Sumter N.M., **105**
  Gettysburg N.M.P., *63*, **64**
  Harpers Ferry N.H.P., *75*, **76**
  Museum of the Confederacy, **74**
  Philippi Covered Bridge, 76
  Shenandoah N.P., **74**
  Shiloh N.M.P., **97**
  Vicksburg N.M.P., **97**
Clemens, Samuel L. (see Twain, Mark)
Constitution (document)
  Independence Hall, **64**, *64*
  Christ Church, **64**
Corn Palace, **174-175**, *177*
Crafts
  Acadian House Museum, 95
  Colonial Williamsburg, **68-69**
  Greenfield Village and Henry Ford Museum, **124-125**
  Jamestown, 72
  Museum of the Plains Indian and Crafts Center, **201**
  Mystic Seaport, **12**
  Old Sturbridge Village, **24**
  Rancho de las Golondrinas, El, **234**
  Shelburne Museum, **32-33**
  Silver Dollar City, *166*, **166-167**
Custer, George, 178, 198

Dams
  Bonneville, 262
  Boulder (see Hoover below)
  Glen Canyon, *213*, **214**, 228
  Grand Coulee, **258**, **260**, *263*
  Hoover, **216**, 228, *288*
Davis, Jefferson, 67, 79, 81, 90, 96

Deserts
  Anza-Borrego Desert S.P., **266-267**, *272*
  Arizona-Sonora Desert Museum, **212**
  Death Valley N.M., *267*, **269**
  Desert N.W.Range, **289**
  Joshua Tree N.M., **273**, *280*
  Organ Pipe Cactus N.M., **220**
  Painted Desert, **220**
  Saguaro N.M., **221-222**
  Sonoran Desert, 212, 220, 221
Douglas Mansion, 217
Douglass, Frederick, 39

Edison, Thomas, 124
Eisenhower, Dwight D., 140, 149
  Center, **158-159**, *161*
Emerson, Ralph Waldo, 26, 33
  house (Old Manse), **23**
Empire State Building, **52**, *53*

Folk Art
  Hancock Shaker Village, **20-21**
  Old Sturbridge Village, **24**
  Winterthur Museum, **36-37**
Forts
  Alamo, *180*, **180**
  Clatsop N.Mem., 163, 258
  Laramie N.H.S., 160, *209*
  Larned N.H.S., 161
  Massachusetts, 85
  Michilimackinac, **124**, *125*
  Robinson, 168
  Sumter N.M., **105**
  Ticonderoga, 54
Fossil Sites
  Badlands N.M., 174
  Dinosaur N.M., **229**
  Florissant Fossil Beds N.M., **229**, *229*
  Theodore Roosevelt N.Mem.P., 170
Foster, Stephen, house (My Old Kentucky Home), 92
Franklin, Benjamin, 64
Frémont, John C., 233, 240
French, Daniel Chester, *9*, **38**, 41, 131, 144
French Quarter, New Orleans, **94**, *95*
Fulton, Robert, 56, 62, 138

Gardens
  Bellingrath, **80**, *80*
  Biltmore, **99**
  Busch, *83*, **83-84**
  Cypress (Charleston), **104**
  Cypress (Florida), *82*, **84**
  Descanso, **269-270**
  Huntington Botanical, **272**
  Magnolia-on-the-Ashley, *79*, **104**
  Middleton Place, **104**
  Plantation, *284*, **286-287**
  Rock City, 108
  White Shadows, **190**, *191*
  Winterthur Museum, 36, 37
Gateway Arch, **162**, *163*
Geological History, Ancient
  Black Canyon of the Gunnison N.M., **224**, *224*, 225
  Colorado River, *211*, 227, 228
  Grand Canyon N.P., **214**, **215**, *215*, 216, **226-7**
  Marble Canyon N.M., 217
  Petrified Forest N.P., **220**
Golf
  Augusta National Golf Club, 88
Grant, Ulysses S., 66, 97
  house, **119-120**, *120*

Hale, Nathan, 10
  house, *12*, **12-13**
Halls of Fame
  Baseball, **58**, **60**
  Basketball, **23**
  Ice Hockey, **132**
  Pro Football, *137*, **140**
Hearst, William Randolph, mansion (San Simeon), **270-271**
Hyde Park, **55**, *56*

Independence Hall, 64, *64*
Independence Rock, 160, *208*
Indians, North American
  Custer Battlefield N.M., **198**, *201*
  Denver Art Museum, 228

294

Milwaukee Public Museum, 148
Monument Valley, **220**
Museum of the American Indian, **59-60**
Museum of the Plains Indian and Crafts Center, 201, *202*
Wounded Knee N.H.S., **178**
Indians, Pre-Columbian
    Anazazi, 213, 221, 223, 230, 242
    Cahokia Mounds S.P., **116-17**
    Canyon de Chelly N.M., *212*, **213**
    Canyonlands N.P., **239**
    Devils Lake S.P., **146**
    Effigy Mounds N.M., 146, **156**
    Etowah Mounds Archeological Area, **88-89**, *90*
    Grand Canyon N.P., 216
    Hocking Hills S.P., **138**
    Mesa Verde N.P., **230**
    Museum of the American Indian, 60
    Petrified Forest N.P., 220
    Wupatki N.M., 223, *223*
Indian Pueblos
    Canyon de Chelly N.M., **212-213**, *212*
    Mesa Verde N.P., **230**
    Taos, **235**
Indian Tribes, North American
    Apache, 214, 234
    Cheyenne, 168, 175, 198
    Chippewa, 127, 129, 142
    Crow, 148
    Haida, 148
    Havasupai, 216
    Hopi, 213, 216, 223, 242
    Museum of the American Indian, 59
    Navajo, 213, 216, 220, 242
    Papago, 217, 222
    Sioux, 168, 175, 178, 198
    Winnebago, 146
Irving, Washington, 52, 56
    house (Sunnyside), 57
Islands (see also National Seashores)
    Apostle Islands N.L., **142**
    Buck Island Reef N.M., *109*, **109-110**, *111*
    Channel Islands N.M. (Santa Barbara and Anacapa), **268-269**
    Ellis, 62
    Isle Royale N.P., **125-127**, *126*
    Kodiak, 250
    Manitou Islands, 129
    Mount Desert Island, 14, *14-15*
    Virgin Islands N.P., *110*, **110-111**

Jackson, Andrew, house (Hermitage), **108**
Jamestown, **72**
Jefferson, Thomas, 44, 47, 65, 67, 163, 177
    house (Monticello), *35*, **73**
    Memorial, *4-5*, **40-41**
    Virginia Capitol, *66*, 67
Jones, John Paul, House, *27*, **29**

Kennedy, John F., 18, 38, 45
    grave, 66
Kentucky Derby, *91*, 91, 92,

Lee, Robert E., 64, 66, 67, 68, 76, 90
    home (Shirley), *69*, **72**
    house (Custis-Lee Mansion), 67
Lighthouses
    Cape Cod Light, 18, *20*
    Pemaquid, **17**
    Split Rock Lighthouse S.P., *133*, **134**
Lincoln, Abraham, 64, 105, 124, 177
    Home, **114**, *115*
    Lincoln Birthplace N.H.S., **114**
    Lincoln Boyhood N.Mem., **114**
    Memorial, **38**, **41-42**
    New Salem S.P., **114**, *117*
Longfellow, Henry Wadsworth, 95, 127, 129
    house, **21-22**, *22*

Marble House, **30**, *31*
Marquette, Father Jacques, 128, 129
Missions
    San Antonio de Valero (Alamo), **180**
    Santa Bárbara, **282**
    San Carlos Borromeo del Rio Carmelo, *279*, **281**
    San José Mission N.H.S., **188-189**
    San Xavier del Bac, **217**, *222*
Monroe, James, 44, 47
Monument Valley, **220**, *221*
Mormons, 238, 241, **242**, 244
Morven Mansion, *48-49*, **49**
Mount Rushmore N.Mem., **177**, *179*
Mountain Peaks
    Adams, 256, 258
    El Capitan (Texas), 185
    Grand Teton, *193*, 205
    Guadalupe Peak, 185
    Hood, **256**, *257*
    Katahdin, *16*
    Katmai, 250
    Kitt Peak, 216
    Lassen Peak, 273
    Long's Peak, 230
    Lookout Mountain, *106*, 108
    Mansfield, 33
    Mauna Loa, 286
    McKinley, **250**

Pikes Peak, 160
Rainier, 258, *259*, **260**, 262
Saint Helens, 256, 258
Shasta, **271**, **275**, **278**
Shuksan, 261, *263*
Stone Mountain, 90
Washington, **29**
Whitney, 282
Mountain Ranges
    Adirondacks, 55, 58
    Appalachian, 16, 74, 76, 92, 100
    Black Hills, 175, 176, *176*, 177, 178
    Blue Ridge, 16, 74, 76
    Cascade, 254, 256, 257, 260, **261-262**, 273, 275
    Grand Teton, *193*, **205**, *206*
    Great Smoky, 16, **98**, 100
    Guadalupe, **185**, 232
    Olympic, **262**
    Ozark, 154, 162, 164, 166
    Porcupine, **128**
    Rocky, 160, 161, 224, 230, 244
    Sangre de Cristo, 229, 235
    Sierra Nevada, 262, 270, 282
    White (California), 266
    White (New Hampshire), **29**
Muir, John, 275, 278, 282
Museums (see also Art)
    Acadian House Museum, 95
    American Museum of Atomic Energy, **107**
    American Museum of Immigration, 62
    American Museum of Natural History, **50**
    Antique Auto and Music Museum, 90
    Arizona-Sonora Desert Museum, **212**
    Buffalo Bill Historical Center, 206
    Circus World Museum, **144**, *146*, *145*
    Cleveland Museum of Art, **138**
    Denver Art Museum, *225*, **228-229**
    Essex Institute, **20**
    Field Museum of Natural History, **118**
    Franklin Institute, **64**
    Harry S. Truman Museum, 167
    Henry Ford Museum, **125**, *128*
    Jean Paul Getty Museum, **272-273**
    Jerome Museums, 216
    Joslyn Art Museum, **168-169**
    Kentucky Derby Museum, 92
    Los Angeles County Museum of Art, **268**, **275**
    Louisiana State Museum, 94
    Milwaukee Public Museum, *147*, **148**, *150*
    Metropolitan Museum of Art, **58-59**
    Museum of African Art, **39**, *39*
    Museum of the American Indian, **59-60**
    Museum of the Confederacy, **71**, 74
    Museum of Fine Arts (Boston), **22-23**
    Museum of Modern Art, **59**
    Museum of New Mexico, **234**
    Museum of the Plains Indian and Crafts Center, **201**, *202*
    Museum of Science and Industry, **119**
    National Museum of Transport, **164**
    National Railroad Museum, **148-149**
    New Orleans Jazz Museum, **94**
    Philadelphia Museum of Art, **65**
    Ringling Museums, **86-87**
    Roswell Museum and Arts Center, **234**
    Shedd Aquarium, *118*, **119**
    Smithsonian Institution, **38**, **42**, *42*
    U.S. Air Force Museum, **140**, *140*
    Winterthur Museum, **36-37**
    Wounded Knee N.H.S. Museum, 178
Museum Villages (see also Western Towns, Old and Restored; and Western Ranches)
    Colonial Williamsburg, *68*, **68-69**
    Greenfield Village, **124-125**
    Hancock Shaker Village, **20-21**, *21*
    Jamestown, **72**
    Mystic Seaport, *9*, **12**
    New Harmony, **122-23**
    New Salem S.P., **114**
    Old Sturbridge Village, **24**, *25*, *26*
    Plimoth Plantation, 25
    Shelburne Museum, **32-33**, *33*
    Silver Dollar City, *166*, **166-167**
    Yorktown, 72, 73
Music
    Antique Auto and Music Museum, 90
    New Orleans Jazz Museum, 94
    Preservation Hall, 94

National Cemeteries
    Arlington, **66-67**
    Custer Battlefield, 198, *201*
    Vicksburg, 97
National Forests
    Inyo, 266
    Mark Twain, 162
    Monongahela, 77
    Mount Hood, *246*, **256**, *257*
    Mount Shasta, **271**, 278
    Ozark, 154
    Superior, **130**
National Historical Monuments and Parks
    Appomattox Court House N.H.P., **66**
    Canyon de Chelly N.M., 212, **212-213**
    City of Refuge N.H.P., **285**, *286*
    Colonial N.H.P., **72**
    Custer Battlefield N.M., **198**, *201*
    Cumberland Gap N.H.P., **93**
    Effigy Mounds N.M., **156**
    Fort Sumter N.M., **105**
    Harpers Ferry N.H.P., *75*, **76**

    Independence N.H.P., *64*, **64-65**
    Minute Man N.H.P., *9*, **22**
    National Capital Parks, *4-5*, **39-42**
    Scotts Bluff N.M., 160, *169*
    Statue of Liberty N.M., *62*, **62**
    Wupatki N.M., **222-223**, *223*
National Lakeshores
    Apostle Islands, **142**, *143*
    Indiana Dunes, *121*, **122**, 129
    Pictured Rocks, **127-128**
    Sleeping Bear Dunes, *129*, **129**
National Nature Monuments
    Badlands, **174**, *175*
    Biscayne, **82-83**
    Black Canyon of the Gunnison, *224*, **224-225**
    Buck Island Reef, *109*, **109-110**, *111*
    Capulin Mountain, **232**
    Cedar Breaks, **241**
    Channel Islands, *1*, **268-269**
    Chiracahua, **214**
    Craters of the Moon, **195**, *197*
    Death Valley, *267*, **269**
    Devils Postpile, **270**
    Devils Tower, **205**
    Dinosaur, **229**
    Florissant Fossil Beds, *229*, **229**
    Glacier Bay, *248*, **249-250**
    Great Sand Dunes, *228*, **229-230**
    Jewel Cave, **176**
    Joshua Tree, **273**, *280*
    Katmai, **250**, *251*
    Lava Beds, **275**
    Lehman Caves, **289**
    Marble Canyon, **217**, **220**
    Muir Woods, **278**
    Natural Bridges, **242**
    Oregon Caves, **256-257**
    Organ Pipe Cactus, **220**
    Pinnacles, **278-279**
    Rainbow Bridge, *2-3*, **242**
    Saguaro, **221-222**
    Sunset Crater, **223**
    Timpanogos Cave, **244**
    White Sands, **235**
National Parks
    Acadia, **14-15**
    Arches, **236**, **237**, *237*
    Big Bend, **182**, *186-7*
    Blue Ridge Parkway, **74**
    Bryce Canyon, **238**
    Canyonlands, **238**, *241*
    Capitol Reef, *240*, **240**
    Carlsbad Caverns, **232**, *235*
    Crater Lake, **254-255**, *255*
    Everglades, **84-85**
    Glacier, **198-199**, *199*
    Grand Canyon, *172*, **214-216**, *215*, *226*
    Grand Teton, *193*, **205-206**, *207*
    Great Smoky Mountains, 16, *98*, **100-101**
    Guadalupe Mountains, **185**
    Haleakala, **285-286**
    Hawaii Volcanoes, **286**
    Hot Springs, **155**, *155*
    Ice Age National Scientific Reserve, 146, *146*
    Isle Royale, **125-127**, *126*
    Kings Canyon, **266**, **282**
    Lassen Volcanic, **273**, **275**
    Mammoth Cave, **92**
    Mesa Verde, **230**
    Mount McKinley, **250-251**
    Mount Rainier, *259*, **260-261**
    National Capital Parks, *4-5*, **39-42**
    North Cascades, **261-262**, *263*
    Olympic, **262**
    Petrified Forest, **220**
    Platt, **173**
    Redwood, **279**, *281*
    Rocky Mountain, **230**
    Sequoia, **274**, **282**
    Shenandoah, 16, *73*, **74**
    Theodore Roosevelt N.Mem.P., **170**, *171*
    Virgin Islands, *110*, **110-111**
    Voyageurs, **134-135**, *135*
    Wind Cave, 176, *176*, 178
    Yellowstone, **204**, **208-209**
    Yosemite, *265*, **282-283**, *283*, *293*
    Zion, **244**, *245*
National Recreation Areas
    Glen Canyon, *213*, **214**
    Lake Chelan, 261
    Lake Mead, **216**, **288**
    Ross Lake, 261
National Seashores
    Assateague Island, **46-47**, *47*
    Cape Cod, **18-19**, *20*
    Cape Hatteras, **99-100**, *100*
    Cape Lookout, **99-100**
    Fire Island, *53*, **53-54**
    Gulf Islands, **85-86**
    Padre Island, *183*, **187-188**
    Point Reyes, **279**
National Wildlife Refuges
    Aransas, **181**
    Chincoteague, 46
    Delta, 134
    Desert N.W.Range, **289**
    Great Dismal Swamp, **69-70**
    Kodiak, **249**, 250
    Loxahatchee, *85*, **86**
    Mark Twain, 132
    Monomoy, 18
    Moosehorn, **17**

National Bison Range, **201-202**, *203*
Okefenokee, *89*, **89**
Pea Island, 100
Upper Mississippi Wildlife and Fish Refuge, **132**
Natural History (see also Zoos)
    American Museum of Natural History, **50**
    Field Museum of Natural History, **119**
    Milwaukee Public Museum, **148**
    Museum of Natural History, 42
    Shedd Aquarium, **119**
Niagara Falls, *59*, **60**

Octagon House, *149*, **149-150**
Olana, *56*, **56**
Old Exchange Building, Charleston, 102
Old Faithful geyser, *204*, **208**
Old Manse, 23
"Oldest House," St. Augustine, **86**, *87*
Olmsted, Frederick Law, 43, 53, 99

Palace of the Governors, *233*, **234**
Penn, William, 49, 63
Pictographs and Petroglyphs
    Canyon de Chelly N.M., 212
    Canyonlands N.P., 239
    Carlsbad Caverns N.P., 232
    Natural Bridges N.M., 242
    Petrified Forest N.P., 220
Planetariums and Observatories
    Franklin Institute, **64**
    Hale Observatories (Mt. Wilson and Palomar), **270**
    Kitt Peak National Observatory, **216**, *218-219*
Plymouth, **25**
Powell, John Wesley, 217, 240
Prairie
    Joslyn Art Museum, 168-169
    Konza, *159*, **159-160**
    National Bison Range, 201, 202
    Theodore Roosevelt N.Mem.P., 170

Railroads, Old and Scenic
    Colorado Narrow Gauge, 227
    Stone Mountain Scenic, 90
Remington, Frederic, 72, 206
Revere, Paul, 19, **23**, *23*, 24
    house, **24-25**
Revolutionary War
    John Adams' "Old House," 18, *19*
    Colonial Williamsburg, *68*, 68, 69
    Fort Ticonderoga, **54**
    Nathan Hale House, 12-13
    Independence N.H.P., **64-65**
    John Paul Jones House, **27**, 29
    Henry Wadsworth Longfellow House, **21-22**
    Minute Man N.H.P., *9*, **22**
    Morven Mansion, **48-49**, 49
    Old North Church, **23**, *23-24*
    Paul Revere House, 24-25
    Valley Forge S.P., **65**, *65*
    Yorktown Battlefield, **72-73**
Rivers
    Buffalo National River, **154**, *154*
    Colorado, *211*, 214, 216, 217, 224, **227-228**, 239, 292
    Columbia, 160, 162, 256, **258**, *260-261*, 263, 292
    Green, 227, 229, 239
    Hudson, **54**, *54-56*, 292
    Little Missouri, 170, 201
    Mississippi, 94, 96, 97, *112-113*, **131**, **132**, **134**, 138, 139, 156, 160, 162, 163, *163*, 292
    Missouri, 132, *152-153*, 162, 163, 174, **199-201**, *200*, 292
    National Wild and Scenic
        Allagash, **15-16**
        Clearwater, Middle Fork of the, **194-195**, *195*
        Eleven Point, **162**
        Rio Grande, **188**, *233*
        Rogue, **257**
        Saint Croix-Namekagon, 150
        Salmon, Middle Fork of the, **194**, *195*, **196**
        Wolf, **150**, *151*
    Niagara, **59**, 60
    Ohio, 134, **138-140**, *139*, *141*, 292
    Ozark N.S.R., **164**, *165*
    Platte, 160, *169*, 201
    Potomac, *4-5*, **76**, *77*, 292
    Rio Grande, 182, *186-187*, **188**, 292
    Shenandoah, 76
    Snake, 160, 163, 195, 205, 258
    Yukon, **251-252**, *252-253*, 292
Roosevelt, Franklin D., home (Hyde Park), **55**, 56
Roosevelt, Theodore, 44, *177*, 214, 228, 256, 278
    home (Sagamore Hill), *60*, **60-61**
    N.Mem.P., **170**, *171*

Saarinen, Eero, 121, 122, *123*, 162
Saarinen, Eliel, 120, 156
Sacajawea, 163
Sagamore Hill, *60*, **60-61**
San Jacinto Monument, **188**
San Simeon (See Hearst)
Sault Ste. Marie, **129**

Science and Technology (see also Planetariums and Observatories, Space Flights, Transportation)
    American Museum of Atomic Energy, **107**
    Franklin Institute, **64**
    Henry Ford Museum, **125**
    Museum of History and Technology, **42**, *42*
    Museum of Science and Industry, **119**
    Oak Ridge National Laboratory, 107
    U.S. Air Force Museum, **140**, *140*
Sculpture, Outdoor
    Mount Rushmore N.Mem., **177**, *179*
    Stone Mountain, 90
Ships
    Delta Queen, **138**, *139*
    Mayflower II, **25**
    S.S. *Ticonderoga*, 33
    Susan Constant, Godspeed and *Discovery*, 72
    U.S.S. *Arizona*, **287**
    U.S.S. *Constellation*, **47**
    U.S.S. *Constitution*, **25-26**, *26*
    U.S.S. *Ranger*, 29
    U.S.S. *Texas*, **188**, *189*
Sitting Bull, Chief, 178, 198
Ski Areas
    Aspen, **224**
    Lake Placid, **58**
    Stowe, 33
    Sun Valley, **195-196**
Skidmore, Owings and Merrill, 231
Southern Mansions
    Berkeley, **70-71**
    Biltmore House, **99**
    The Briars, 96
    Carter's Grove, 69
    Cherokee, **96**
    Custis-Lee Mansion, 67
    D'Evereux, **96**, *97*
    Edmondston-Alston House, 102
    Fort Hill, *103*, **104-105**
    Haywood-Washington House, **102**
    The Hermitage, *108*, **108**
    Isaiah Davenport House, **88**, 90
    Juliette Gordon Low House, **90**
    Monticello, **35**, *73*
    Mount Vernon, *70*, **73-74**
    "My Old Kentucky Home", **92**
    Nathaniel Russell House, **103**, *105*
    Owen-Thomas House, **89-90**
    Shadows-on-the-Teche, *95*, **95**
    Shirley, **69**, *72*
    Stanton Hall, **96-97**
    Tryon Palace, *101*, **101**
    Westover, **71-72**
Space Needle, **262**
Space Flights
    Lyndon B. Johnson Space Center (Manned Spacecraft Center), *184*, **185-187**
    Museum of Science and Industry, 119
    National Air and Space Museum, 42
    Roswell Museum and Arts Center, 234
    U.S. Air Force Museum, 140
Spanish Governors Palace, **189-190**, *190*
State Parks and Forests
    Anza-Borrego Desert S.P., **266-267**, *272*
    Baxter S.P., 15, **16**
    Cahokia Mounds S.P., **116-117**
    Custer S.P., **175**
    Devils Lake S.P., **146**, *146*
    Fort Robinson S.P., **168**
    Hocking Hills S.P., **138**
    Itasca S.P., *131*, **132**
    Kettle Moraine S.F., **146**
    Longhorn Cavern S.P., **187**
    Longfellow-Evangeline S.P., **95**
    New Salem S.P., **114**, *117*
    Niagara Frontier S.P., **60**
    Porcupine Mountains S.P., **128**
    San Jacinto Battleground S.P., **188**, *189*
    San Jose Mission S.P., **188-189**
    Split Rock Lighthouse S.P., *133*, **134**
    Stephen Foster S.P., **89**
    Turkey Run S.P., *122*, **123**
    Valley Forge S.P., **65**, *65*
Steuben, Baron von, 65, 72
Stock Exchange, New York, **60**
Stowe, Harriet Beecher, 10, 139
Sunnyside, **57**

Swamps
    Big Thicket, **182**
    Dismal, **69-70**
    Everglades N.P., **84-85**
    Loxahatchee N.W.R., **86**
    Okefenokee N.W.R., **89**

Temples and Synagogues
    Baha'i Temple, **116**
    Beth Elohim Reform Temple, 102
    Mormon Tabernacle, **242**, *243*
    Mormon Temple, **242**, *243*
    Touro Synagogue, **30-31**
Texan War for Independence
    Alamo, **180**, *180*
    San Jacinto Battleground, S.P., **188**, *189*

Theaters and Opera Houses
    Auditorium Theatre, *116*, **116**
    Avery Fisher Hall (Philharmonic Hall), 58
    Bird Cage Theater, 222
    Dock Street Theater, 103
    Goodman Theater, 115
    John F. Kennedy Center for the Performing Arts, **38**
    Juilliard School of Music, 58
    Lincoln Center for the Performing Arts, **57**, *58*
    Metropolitan Opera House, 58
    Music Center for the Performing Arts, **273**, *278*
    Tyrone Guthrie Theater, *132*, **134**
Trails and Roads (see also Camino Real, El)
    Appalachian, **16**, 292
    Cascade Crest, 262
    Chisholm, **183**, *185*, 292
    Dodge City, 161
    John Muir, 262
    Lewis and Clark, **162-163**, 200, 258, 292
    Oregon, **160**, *208-209*, 292
    Oregon Skyline, 262
    Pacific Crest, **262**, 292
    Santa Fe, 161, 167, 292
    Wilderness Road, **92-93**, 292
Transportation (see also Railroads)
    Antique Auto and Music Museum, 90
    Henry Ford Museum, **125**
    National Museum of Transport, **164**
    National Railroad Museum, **148-149**
Truman, Harry S., 45, 140
    Library and Museum, **167**
    birthplace, 167
Twain, Mark, 134, 138, 290
    House, **10**, *12*, *13*
    Home, **163-164**

United Nations Headquarters, *61*, **62**
United States Air Force Academy, **231**, *231*
United States Capitol, *40-41*, **43-44**

Van Cortlandt Manor, **57**
Vanderbilt houses, **30**, *31*, 99
Volcanoes or Volcanic Eruptions
    Capulin Mountain N.M., **232**
    Crater Lake N.P., **255**, 256
    Craters of the Moon N.M., **195**, *197*
    Devils Postpile N.M., **270**
    Devils Tower N.M., **205**
    Haleakala N.P., **285-286**
    Hawaii Volcanoes N.P., **286**
    Katmai N.M., **250**, *251*
    Lassen Volcanic N.P., **273**, *275*
    Lava Beds N.M., **275**
    Mount Rainier N.P., **260**
    Sunset Crater N.M., **223**
    Yellowstone N.P., 208, 209
Voyageurs, 130, **134**, 142

War of 1812
    U.S.S. *Constellation*, 47
    U.S.S. *Constitution*, 25, *26*
Washington, George, 22, 41, 44, 47, 65, 68, 69, 70, 72, 177
    house (Mount Vernon), *70*, **73-74**
    Monument, *4-5*, **39-40**
Western Ranches
    Rancho de las Golondrinas, **234**
Western Towns, Old and Restored
    Central City, **226-227**
    Cowtown, Wichita, 185
    Dodge City, 161
    Jerome, *216*, **216-217**
    Nevada City, 203
    Old Abilene Town, 185
    Tombstone N.H.S., **222**
    Virginia City, Montana, **202**
    Virginia City, Nevada, **290**, *290-291*
White House, *4-5*, **44-45**, *45*
Wilson, Woodrow, home, **74**
World War I
    Arlington N.C., **66**
    National Railroad Museum, 149
World War II
    Arlington N.C., 66
    Eisenhower Center, **158**, *159*
    Harry S. Truman Library and Museum, 167
    National Railroad Museum, 149
    U.S.S. *Arizona* Memorial, **287**
    U.S.S. *Texas*, 188
Wright, Frank Lloyd, 116, 142, 147, *148*
Wright, Wilbur and Orville, 99, 124, 140

Young, Brigham, 238, 242

Zoos
    Brookfield, **116**
    Cincinnati Zoological Gardens, **137-138**
    Milwaukee County, **147-148**
    National Zoological Park, 42
    Saint Louis, **166**
    San Diego, 281
    San Diego Wild Animal Park, 281